AUM

THE SANSKAR VIDHI

(The Procedure of Sacraments)

of

Swami Dayanand Saraswati

English Translation

by

Acharya Vaidyanath Shastri

Publisher :

Sarvadeshik Arya Pratinidhi Sabha

3/5 Dayanand Bhawan, Ramlila Ground,

New Delhi-110002 (India)

Publisher by :

Sarvadeshik Arya Pratinidhi Sabha

3/5 Dayanand Bhawan, Ramlila Ground,

New Delhi-110002 (India)

Phones : 011 - 3274771, 3260985

Fax : 011 - 3270507

E-mail : vedicgod@nda.vsnl.net.in

saps@tatanova.com

Website : http://www.whereisgod.com

http://www.sarvadeshik.org

Reprint May 2002

Price Rs. [illegible]

Printed at :

Prince Offset Printers

1510, Pataudi House,

Dayga Ganj, New Delhi-2

Phones : 3280126, 3277153

PUBLISHER'S NOTE
(First Edition)

It gives me great pleasure to present English version of 'Sanskar Vidhi (code of Aryan rituals and sacraments) of Swami Dayanand Saraswati, the illustrious founder of the Arya Samaj (Vedic Church) before the general public. It is to meet an overdue necessity and to fill up a gap which was actually felt when I was abroad on *prachar* mission, that this version has been brought out.

This book formed a very important item of the publications that were designed to be undertaken on the sacred occasion of Arya Samaj foundation centenary.

My thanks are due to Shri Acharya Vaidyanath Shastri who needs no introduction. At Sabha's request specially that of mine, he took up the work and carried out the way.

I hope that this will enjoy greatest possible popularity.

O.P. TYAGI
Ex. M.P.
Secretary

Sarvadeshik Arya Pratinidhi Sabha,
3/5, Maharshi Dayanand Bhawan,
Ramlila Ground, New Delhi.

Publisher's Note
(Second Edition)

For us it is a matter of great pleasure that we are presenting the Second Edition of Sanskar Vidhi (the procedure of sacraments) by Great Swami Dayanand Saraswati who galvanized a new spirit and enthusiasm among the scholars and the people towards the study of the Vedas and practice of Vedic sacraments rituals and Yajnas. This english translation proved to be a gift for the english-knowing people in country and abroad. We are not required here to express any word regarding the antecedents of the author of the translation as his performance of tremendous task itself fulfil that need.

The work is ready and very soon go to the hands of the readers. We express here own sense appreciation for the work done by Shri Ramesh Chandra Shastri, the Karyalaya Sachiva and Shri Rambhul Sharma Accountant of the Sabha and the printer Jan Shakti Mudran Yantralaya, Shahadra, Delhi who took great interest in reading the proof, designing get up and printing the book.

Ramgopal Shawlwale
President
Sarvadeshik Arya Pratinidhi
Sabha, New Delhi-110002

Dated 1st January 1985

CONTENTS

It was a great, important and equally difficult task which was not done upto this time. The requirements, pressing needs and requests were made from all the corners of the Aryan world that "Sanskarvidhi" should be appropriately translated into English. I, without desiring any credit due to the tremendous work, have to say that I took this undertaking and completed to my satisfaction. Without having any air of self aggrandizement, I can say that I translated this book in true letter and spirit of the great teacher, Swami Dayananda Saraswati and the translation is completely and unscruplously faithful.

My thanks are due to my friends, who asked me to take up the venture as well as the Publisher and Printers and other colleagues for their unstinted cooperation.

ACHARYA VAIDYANATH SHASTRI

BARODA
7th January, 1976

॥ ओ३म् ॥

नमो नमः सर्वविधात्रे जगदीश्वराय ।

अथ संस्कार विधिं वक्ष्यामः

ओं सह नाववतु । सह नौ भुनक्तु । सह वीर्य्यं करवावहै । तेजस्वि नावधीतमस्तु । मा विद्विषावहै । ओं शान्तिः शान्तिः शान्तिः ॥

तैत्तिरीय आरण्यके। अष्ठमप्रपाठके । प्रथमानुवाके ॥

सर्वात्मा सच्चिदानन्दो विश्वादिर्विश्वकृद्विभुः ।
भूयात्तमां सहायो नस्सर्वेशो न्यायकृच्छुचिः ॥ १ ॥

गर्भाद्या मृत्युपर्य्यन्ताः संस्काराः षोडशैव हि ।
वक्ष्यन्ते तं नमस्कृत्यानन्तविद्यं परेश्वरम् ॥ २ ॥

वेदादिशास्त्रासिद्धान्तमाध्याय परमादरात् ।
आर्यैतिह्यं पुरस्कृत्य शरीरात्मविशुद्धये ॥ ३ ॥

संस्कारैस्संस्कृतं यद्यन्मेध्यमत्र तदुत्तमम् ।
असंस्कृतं तु यल्लोके तदमेध्यं प्रकीर्त्यते ॥ ४ ॥

अतः संस्कारकरणे क्रियतामुद्यमो बुधैः ।
शिक्षयौषधिभिर्नित्यं सर्वथा सुखवर्द्धनः ॥ ५ ॥

कृतानीह विधानानि ग्रन्थग्रन्थनतत्परैः ।
वेदविज्ञानविरहैः स्वार्थिभिः परिमोहितैः ॥ ६ ॥

प्रमाणैस्तान्यनादृत्य क्रियते वेदमानतः ।
जनानां सुखबोधाय संस्कारविधिरुत्तमः ॥ ७ ॥

बहुभिः सज्जनैस्सम्यङ् मानवप्रियकारकैः ।
प्रवृत्तो ग्रन्थकरणे क्रमशोऽहं नियोजितः ॥ ८ ॥

दयाया आनन्दो विलसति परो ब्रह्मविदितः ।
सरस्वत्यस्याग्रे निवसति मुदा सत्यनिलया ।
इयं ख्यातिर्यस्य प्रततसुगुणा हीशशरणाऽस्त्येनेनायं
ग्रन्थो रचित इति बोद्धव्यमनघाः ॥ ९ ॥

चक्षू रामांकचन्द्रेऽब्दे कार्तिकस्यान्तिमे दले ।
अमायां शनिवारेऽयं ग्रन्थारम्भः कृतो मया ॥ १० ॥

विन्दुवेदांकचन्द्रेऽब्दे शुचौ मासेऽसिते दले ।
त्रयोदश्यां रवौ वारे पुनः संस्करणं कृतम् ॥ ११ ॥

All humble obeisance to Om who is the creator of all and the master of the universe.

Now here to begin with we will describe the procedure of sacraments.

Let us both, the teacher and taught preserve the standard of education together, let us eat to-gether, let us resort to endeavour and exertion together, let whatever we have learnt be sound and fruitful.

Taitiriya Aranyka, VIII-1

May God Who is the spirit of all, who is Existent, conscious and All-bliss, who is the creator of the universe, who is the first cause of the universe, who is All-pervading, who is the master of all, who is holy by nature and who is the dispenser of justic, be our helpful guide (in this undertaking).

The sixteen sacraments beginning with impregnation and ending with death will be described by us after paying our homage to Him who is the paramount Lord and Possessor of infinite knowledge.

(These sacraments will be described by us for the purification of the body and the soul by giving full consideration to the principles of the scriptures of which the first is the Veda, with due respect and keeping the history of the Aryas before our mind.[3]

Whatever is purified and refind through the sacramental process in this world is pure and excellent and whatever is not thus purified and refined is described impure in this world.[4]

Therefore, auspicious endeavour should be made in performing the sacraments, by the learned men through instruction and herbacious plants always altogether.[5]

In this subject various procedures of conducting sacramental ceremonies have been laid down by the persons engaging themselves in compiling the books, who are bereft of the knowledge of the Veda and have selfish motives and are totally confused.[6]

Refuting them with proofs, authorities and reasons this excellent book of sacramental procedures in being written by me according to the dicta and dictates of the Veda for the easy perspicuity of the people.[7]

On having been persuaded from time to time by many gentlemen devoted to the good of the people. I took up the work of writing this book.[8]

O pious persons! let it be known to you that this book (*the sanskarvidhi*) is written by this author in whose name the word '*Anand*' which is found in Brahman, the Supreme Being occurs after the word '*Daya*' the word '*Sarasvati*' who resides in truth gets its place thereafter i. e. after Anand, and thus whose conspecuity is Dayanand Sarasvati, which disseminate virtues and the only home of which is God.[9]

This book I began to write in the middle of the month *Kartika* on Saturday, the day of *Amavasya* in the year 1932 (Vikram).[10]

The amended edition of this book was prepared again on Sunday, the day of Trayodashi of dark half of the month *Ashadha* in the year 1940 (Vikram).[11]

In the beginning of all the *Sanskaras* one learned of sensible man should chant the following Mantras with the meaning thereof and thus take to the eulogium, glorification, prayer and meditation on God with concentrated mind and others present should heare attentively and consider over them seriously.

Invocation Prayer and Communion

१. विश्वानि देव सवितर्दुरितानिपरासुव ।

यद्भद्रन्तन्न आसुव ॥

(१) यजु० अ० ३० मं० ३

O All-creating, Almighty, Pure-natured God Thou art the giver of all pleasures, please keep far from us all evils, bad habits and pains and make us attain whatever be beneficial to us,

२. हिरण्यगर्भः समवर्त्तताग्रे भूतस्य जातः पतिरेक आसीत् ।

स दाधार पृथिवीं द्यामुतेमां कस्मै देवाय हविषा विधेम ॥

(२) यजु० अ० १३ मं० ४

The Divine Power who is refulgent by nature and who possesses all the luminous worlds within Himself and existed before the creation of this world and from the very eternity is the only one conspicuous and animate Lord of all the created objects. He is sustaining this earth and the Sun etc. to that All-blissful Divinity we offer our humble worship with attainable yogic concentration and devotion.

३. य आत्मदा बलदा यस्य विश्व उपासते प्रशिषं यस्य देवाः ।

यस्यच्छायाऽमृतं यस्य मृत्युः कस्मै देवाय हविषा विधेम ॥

(३) यजु० अ० २५ मं० १३

He who is giver of spiritual impiration and physical, spiritual and social vigour. He who is worshipped by all, whose governance and order is carried out by all luminouse bodies and enlightened, whose shelter (*grace*) is immortality whose disfavour and disobedience is the cause of pains like death etc., to that All-blissful Divinity who is the giver of all knowledge we offer our humble worship with conscience and spirit and be ready to obey His commandments.

४. यः प्राणतो निमिषतो महित्वैक इद्राजा जगतो बभूव ।

य ईशे अस्य द्विपदश्चतुष्पदः कस्मै देवाय हविषा विधेम ॥

(४) यजु० अ० २३ मंत्र ३

He who by His sublimity is the sole ruler of the living and non-living beings existing in this world, He who governs the bipeds and quadrupeds; to that All-blissful Divinity we offer our humble homage dedicating to Him all that belongs to us in obeying His command.

५. येन द्यौरुग्रा पृथिवीं च दृढा येन स्वः स्तभितं येन नाकः ।
यो अन्तरिक्षे रजसो विमानः कस्मै देवाय हविषा विधेम ॥

(५) यजु० अ० ३३ मं० ६

He by whom the resplendent Sun and the earth have been made firm, who has held under His possession the pleasure and the bliss of salvation, who has measured, created and gave motion to all the worlds in the unbounded space moving in the manner as birds fly in it, to that All-blissful Divinity we offer our worship with our full devotion.

६. प्रजापते न त्वदेतान्यन्यो विश्वा जातानि परिता बभूव ।
यत्कामास्ते जुहुमस्तन्नो अस्तु वयं स्याम पतयो रयोणाम् ॥

(६) ऋक्-१०-१२१-१०

O *Prajapati* (Lord of the entire creatures) there is no other entity besides Thee who can maintain command over and surpass all these created animate and inanimate objects, i. e. Thou art Paramount. Aspirant of whatsoever we offer our wiorship to Thee please grant them, we may by Thy grace be possessors of all kinds of wealths and high possessions.

७. स नो बन्धुर्जनिता स विधाता धामानि वेद भुवनानि विश्वा ।
यत्र देवाअमृतमानशानास्तृतीये धामन्नध्यैरयन्त ॥

(७) यजु० अ० ३२ मं० १०

He is giver of all prosperity to us like brother, He is our procreator and He fulfils all of our aspirations, He knows all the worlds, all the names, localities and created objects of this universe, it is in Him where the men of wisdom obtaining salvation move freely after having been free from worldly pleasures and pains in the third stage of their divine life. He is our preceptor, teacher, ruler and administrator of justice. We with all offer our worship to Him.

८. अग्ने नय सुपथा राये अस्मान् विश्वानि देव वयुनानि विद्वान् ।
युयोध्यस्मज्जुहुराणमेनो भूयिष्ठान्ते नम उक्तिं विधेम ॥

(८) यजु० अ० ४० मं० १६

O Self-refulgent Divinity Thou art All-knowledge and illuminator of all the universe. Please lead us on the path of virtue for the acquirement of physical and spiritual wealth inclusive of science, Kingdom etc, Thou knowest all the procedures of works and wisdom underlying therein and please grant all this to us leading us on the path of righteousness. Please keep us immune from sinful acts which transgress nature and its law. We may remain ever-engaged in uttering Thy praises in various ways.

It is the end of the performance of invocation, prayer and communion.

———

Recitation of Benedictory Hymns

१. अग्निमीडे पुरोहितं यज्ञस्य देवमृत्विजम् ।
होतारं रत्नधातमम् ॥

ऋक् १-१-१

I describe the attributes of Self-refulgent Divinity who is upholder of universe from very eternity the illuminator of all activities and the sole object of adoration in all seasons, the most Bounteous and the great possessor of shining wealth.

२. स नः पितेव सूनवे ऽग्ने सूपायनोभव ।
सचस्वा नः स्वस्तये ।

ऋक् १-१-९

That Thou O Self-refulgent Divinity ! be easily accessible to us and be with us ever for our well-being just like a father to his son.

३. स्वस्ति नो मिमीतामश्विना भगः स्वस्ति देव्यदितिरनर्वणः ।
स्वस्ति पूषा असुरो दधातु नः स्वस्ति द्यावापृथिवी सुचेतुना ॥

ऋ० ५-५१-११

O Great Lord ! May the teacher and preacher by Thy grace be engaged to do our good; may the science of electricity be for our prosperity when we are deperived of other means of conveyance, may the cloud with its protective power bestow prosperity upon us, may the heaven and earth being the source of all sciences be for our prosperity.

४. स्वस्तये वायुनुपब्रवामहै सोमं स्वस्ति भुवनस्ययस्पतिः।
बृहस्पतिं सर्वगणं स्वस्तये आदित्यासो भवन्तुनः॥

ऋ० ५-५१-१२

O Ye Lord, May we by Thy grace propagate the knowledge of air for our prosperity. may we spread for our prosperity the knowledge regarding moon which gives protection to word by its operation, may we preach for our well-being the knowledge of the Lord of speach with His other co-operating forces, may twelve months of the year be for our prosperity.

५. विश्वे देवा नो अद्या स्वस्तये वैश्वानरो वसुरग्निः स्वस्तये।
देवा अवन्त्वृभव स्वस्तये स्वस्ति नो रुद्रः पात्वंहसः।

ऋ०५-५१-१३

O ye Divine spirit ! may all the physical forces and men of wisdom be for our prosperity at present, may the all-pervading universal fire serving multifarious purposes be for our prosperity, may the various forces operating in the world give us protections, may the vital heat operate its activities in pleasant way to secure our prosperity.

६. स्वस्ति मित्रावरुणा स्वस्ति पथ्ये रेवति।
स्वस्ति न इन्द्रश्चाग्निश्च स्वस्ति नो अदिते कृधि॥

ऋ० ५-५१-१४

O Indivisible Divine Power ! please give me all prosperity may the forces of worldly integration and disintegration be, for our prosperity, may the all-powerful air and electricity be for our benefit, and may there be pleasure for us in the way of prosperous life.

७. स्वस्ति पन्थामनुचरेम सूर्याचन्द्रमसाविव।
पुनर्ददताघ्नता जानता संगमेमहि॥

ऋ० ५-५१-१५

May we adopt and traverse the path of prosperity like the sun and moon and may we be accompanied by munificent, constructive and prudent persons.

८. ये देवानां यज्ञिया यज्ञियानां मनोर्यजत्रा अमृता ऋतज्ञाः ।
ते नो रासन्तामुरुगायमद्य यूयं पात स्वस्तिभिः सदा नः ।।
ऋ० ७-३५-१५

Those who are specially skilled in performance of *Yajna* among the expert possessing the dexterity of performing *Yajnas* who have extraordinary mental development, who have attained immortality in their present life, who know the law and uniformity of nature, impart to us now the knowledge aspiring to high eminence. Those experienced persons be engaged always to protect us by means of pleasure and prosperity.

९. येभ्यो माता मधुमत्पिन्वते पयः पीयूषं द्यौरदितिरद्रिबर्हाः ।
उक्थशुष्मान् वृषभरान्त्स्वप्नसस्तां आदित्यां अनुमदा स्वस्तये ।।
ऋ० १०-६३-३

O Lord! Please make us have amongst us for our prosperity those strong, righteous and conscientious learned persons for whose sake the earth produces sweet juices (milk, fruit juices etc.) and unbounded atmosphere overwhelmed with cloud produces rain.

१०. नृचक्षसो अनिमिषन्तो अर्हणा बृहद्देवासो अमृतत्वमानशुः ।
ज्योतीरथा अहिमाया अनागसो दिवो वर्ष्माणं वसते स्वस्तये ।।
ऋ० १०-६३-४

The learned who know the nature and habit of men, who are diligent and admirable, who have attained the high sense of immortality in their life. who are endowed with enlightenment, who have insuremountable knowledge, who are sinless and attain the state of sublime spiritual light be for our prosperity.

११. सम्राजो ये सुवृधो यज्ञमाययुरपरिह्वृता दधिरे दिवि क्षयम् ।
तां आ विवास नमसा सुवृक्तिभिर्महो आदित्यां अदितिं स्वस्तये ।।
ऋ० १०-६३-५

For our prosperity we keep in our conscience the Imperial Lord of the universe with right invocations and serve with water and food those highly learned persons who possess spiritual light, are mature in their thought, attend our yajnas and who reside in Divine Light uninterruptedly.

१२. को वः स्तोमं राधति यं जुजोषथ विश्वे, देवासो मनुषो यतिष्ठन ।
को वोऽध्वरं तुविजाता अरं करद्यो नः पर्षदत्यंहः स्वस्तये ॥
ऋ०१०-६३-६

Enquire the devotees :–

O ye learned persons ! always have in your mind that who among you accomplishes the hymn of invocation which all of you use in the *yajnas* and prayers. (No one but Almighty God makes this hymn). O ye sharpsighted thoughtful persons ! who among all of you in whatever numbers you are, accomplishes that (*adhvaram*)inviolable performance inspiring Veda, the knowledge which removes evils from us to attain spiritual happiness.

१३. येभ्यो होत्रां प्रथमामायेजे मनुः समिद्धाग्निर्मनसा सप्तहोतृभिः ।
त आदित्या अभयं शर्म यच्छत सुगा नः कर्त्त सुपथा स्वस्तये ॥
ऋ० १०-६३-७

For whose well-being the thoughtful performer of *yajna* performs important *yajna* employing his mind and seven senses, may those learned persons make easy, and good path leading to our prosperity and give us the pleasure free from fear.

१४. य ईशिरे भुवनस्य प्रचेतसो विश्वस्य स्थातुर्जगतश्च मन्तवः ।
ते नः कृतादकृतादेनसस्पर्यद्या देवासः पिपृता स्वस्तये ॥
ऋ० १०-६३-८

Those learned persons who are fully conversant with the animate and inanimate world, who are held in esteem now for our prosperity remove us from the sin of which we have any intentions and of which there is possibility in future.

१५. भरेष्विन्द्रं सुहवं हवामहेंऽहोमुचं सुकृतं दैव्यं जनम् ।
अग्निं मित्रं वरुणं सातये भगं द्यावा पृथिवी मरुतः स्वस्तये ॥
ऋ० १०-६-३९

In our *yajnas* we invoke the Indra, the Almighty Lord whom all worships are due. who is free from sin, who is supranatural person and is the embodiment of right and good activities. For the attainment of wealth and prosperity we get our hold upon fire, vital air, water, light, heaven and earth and various gases.

१६. सुत्रामाणं पृथिवीं द्यामनेहसं सुशर्माणमदितिं सुप्रणीतिम् ।
दैवीं नावं स्वरित्रामनागसमस्रवन्तीमा रुहेमा स्वस्तये ।।
ऋ० १०-६३ १०

O ye Dlvine Lord ! By thy grace may we board ourselves on the ship equipped with the means of safety,having vast accommodation, free from all defects, enjoyable, unbreakable, skilfully constructed, furnishned with light, provided with necessary machines, strong in structure and sailed by electricity, for our prosperity.

१७. विश्वे यजत्रा अधिवोचतोतये त्रायध्वं नो दुरेवाया अभिह्रुतः ।
सत्यया वो देवहूत्या हुवेम शृण्वतोदेवा अवसे स्वस्तये ।।
ऋ० १०-६३-११

O ye learned persons deserving our obeisancel preach us for our safety and save us from the painful indigence. O ye learned ones assiduous to our request ! We call you among us with true courtesy for our sefety and benefit.

१८. अपामीवामप विश्वामनाहुतिमपारातिं दुर्विदत्रामघायतः ।
आरे देवा द्वेषो अस्मद्युयोतनोरुणः शर्म यच्छता स्वस्तये ।।
ऋ० १०-६३-१२

O learned person ! Please keep away from us all kinds of diseases, remove all sorts of unrighteousness, throw away covetousness, make the sinners get rid of the tendencies of committing sin send away from us the men affected with the tendency of aversion and animousity and shower your blessings upon us for our benefit.

१६. अरिष्टः समर्त्तो विश्व एधते प्र प्रजाभिर्जायते धर्मणस्परि ।
यमादित्यासो नयथा सुनीतिभिरति विश्वानि दुरिता स्वस्तये ।।
ऋ० १०-६३-१३

O learned persons ! that person whom you lead on the right path by your fair ways of life removing all his short-comings flourishes with children in this world to attain prosperity adhering to principles of righteousness.

२०. यं देवासोऽवथ वाजसातौ यं शूरसाता मरुतो हिते धने ।
प्रातर्यावाणं रथमिन्द्र सानसिमरिष्यन्तमा रुहेमा स्वस्तये ॥

ऋ० १०-६३-१४

O persons of science ! We, for our well-being mount upon that mechanical, conveyance, which you preserve for acquiring wealth and after having in possession such amassed wealth you utilize the same in the battle, and which is furnished with electrical artifices and is defectless and conductible for long duration.

२१. स्वस्ति नः पथ्यासु धन्वसु स्वस्त्यप्सु वृजने स्वर्वति ।
स्वस्ति नः पुत्रकृथेषु योनिषु स्वस्ति राये मरुतो दधातन ॥

ऋ० १०-६३-१५

O learned men, secure us our good in thoroughfare secure us our good in space, secure us our good in water, secure us our good in the well equipped army, give protection to children in the womb, and bless us to attain all sorts of wealth.

२२. स्वस्तिरिद्धिः प्रपथे श्रेष्ठा रेक्णस्वत्यभि या वाममेति ।
सानो अमासो अरणेनिपातु स्वावेशा भवतु देवगोपाः ॥

ऋ० १०-६३-१६

That this earth which is convenient for giving path to the persons treading on it, wnich is grand and full of wealth, which extends place for our righteous performances, may be soucer of of protection, may this our abiding home and forest, and may this sustained by physical forces, provide us good dwelling places.

२३. इषे त्वोर्ज्जे त्वावायवस्थ देवो वःसविता प्रार्पयतु श्रेष्ठतमाय कर्मण
आप्यायध्वमघ्न्या इन्द्राय भागं प्रजावतीरनमीवा अयक्ष्मा मा वस्तेन
ईशत माघशंसो ध्रुवा अस्मिन् गोपतौ स्यात बह्वीर्यजमानस्य पशून्
पाहि ॥

यजु: १-१

O Lord Divine ! We pray thee for the attainment of grains and knowledge. We pray thee to secuore physical and spiritual strength. O ye souls ! be active like wind, may All-creating God employ you to perform the *yajna* which is the most excellent act. By this *yajna*, O ye men ! increase you share of excellence; to serve the purpose of *yajna* possess the Cows which are prohibited to be killed and which be progenitive, unaffected of diseases and free from the germs of tubercculosis; thieves and scoundries do not govern you; the Person protecting cows may possess a large number of strong cows; O merciful Lord protect the animals of rhe performer of the *yajnas*.

२४. ग्रानो भद्राः क्रतवो यन्तु विश्वतोऽदब्धासो ग्रपरीतास उद्भिदः ।
देवा नो यथा सदमिद्वृधे ग्रसन्न प्रायुवोरक्षितारो दिवे दिवे ॥
यजुः २५-१४

O God ! may benevolent activities always accompany us. may the learned who are unyielding to pressure from any side, who are excellent and guarding pillar against calamity, work for our progress in our parliament in such a way as they could prove them industrious guardians of ours day by day.

२५. देवानां भद्रा सुमतिर्ऋजूयतां देवानां रातिरभि नो निवर्त्तताम् ।
देवानां सख्यमुपसेदिमा वयं देवा न ग्रायुः प्रतिरन्तु जीवसे ॥
यजुः २५-१५

May we attain the auspicious noble counsel of the enlightened persons, may the bounty of enlightened persons descend on us; may we gain the friendship of enlightened persons and may the enlightened persons help us to live long by supplying us with all the necessary means of life.

२६. तमीशानं जगतस्तस्थुषस्पतिं धियं जिन्वमवसे हूमहे वयम् ।
पूषा नो यथा वेदसामसद्वृधे रक्षिता पायुरदब्धः स्वस्तये ॥
यजु। २५-१

For our protection we adore Him who is the master of the world that moves and that moves not, He is the inspirer of our intellect, just as He is our sustainer so as He being protector of our physical and spiritual wealth and guardian to save us from calamities, be our saviour for our progress and prosperity.

२७. स्वस्ति न इन्द्रो वृद्धश्रवाः स्वस्ति नः पूषा विश्ववेदाः ।
स्वस्ति नस्तार्क्ष्यो अरिष्टनेमिः स्वस्ति नो बृहस्पतिर्दधातु ॥
यजुः २५-१९

May the almighty lord commendable by all be for our prosperity, May the All-sustaining Omniscient Lord be for our prosperity, May the All-impelling merciful Divine be for our prosperity, may the master of speech and physical forces vouchsafe us prosperity.

२८. भद्रं कर्णेभिः शृणुयाम देवाः भद्रं पश्येमाक्षभिर्यजत्राः ।
स्थिरैरंगैस्तुष्टुवांसस्तनूभिर्व्यशेमहि देवहितं यदायुः
यजुः २५-२१

O ye associable enlightened persons ! may we hear with our ears whatever is good, may we see with our eyes whatever is good, ever praying with our firm limbs may we attain such a state of life through our bodies which will be helpful to serve the cause of the enlightened persons.

२९. अग्न आ याहि वीतये गृणानो हव्यदातये ।
निहोता सत्सि बर्हिषि ॥ सामं० छन्दः प्रपा १-१

O Agni (self-refulgent God) ! being praised by us make Thyself manifest within us for the sake of illuminating our soul with thy radiance and conferring on us such objects which are offered and accepted. O ye accepter of our devotion ! please remain ever present in the recess of our heart.

३०. त्वमग्ने यज्ञानां होता विश्वेषां हितः ।
देवेभिर्मानुषे जने ॥ सा० छ० प्रपा० १-२

O Self-refulgent God ! Thou art the inspirer of the knowledge of all *yajanas* and Thou art present in the heart of men with thy extraordinary qualities.

२१. ये त्रिषप्ताः परि यन्ति विश्वा रूपाणि बिभ्रतः ।
वाचस्पतिर्बला तेषां तन्वो अद्य दधातु मे ॥

अथर्व० १-१-१

May the Lord of speech give strength now in our bodies which are the result of the three times seven elements (*maha bhutas* 10 limbs of sense and action,5 Vital airs and *antahkarna*) that assuming all the worldly formes mingle and unmingle in their turn.

———

Hymns of Auspiciousness and peace

१. शन्न इन्द्राग्नी भवतामवोभिः शन्न इन्द्रा वरुणा रातहव्या ।
शमिन्द्रा सोमा सुविताय शं योः शन्न इन्द्रापूषणा वाजसातो ॥

ऋ०-७-३५-१

May the electricity and fire with their constructive operations be auspicious for us, may electricity and water extending their advantages to us be auspicious for us, may the electricity and herbaceous plants be auspicious for us in the attainment of excellence and happiness, may the electricity and air be beneficial to us in battle.

२. शन्नो भगः शमु नः शंसो अस्तु शन्नः पुरन्धिः शमु सन्तु रायः ।
शन्नः सत्यस्य सुयमस्य शंसः शन्नो अर्यमा पुरुजातो अस्तु ॥

ऋ० ७-३५-२

May our fortune be auspicious to us, may our discipline be gladdening to us, may our extensive wisdom and all our riches be the source of happiness to us, may our well-regulated and truthfull life be blessings to us and may the administrator of justice chosen by many be just to us.

३. शन्नो धाता शमु धर्त्ता नो अस्तु शन्न उरूची भवतु स्वधाभिः ।
शं रोदसी वृहती शन्नौ अद्रिः शन्नो देवानां सुहवानि सन्तु ॥

ऋ० ७-३५-३

May the thing sustaining us be auspicious for us, may the things supporting us be auspicious for us, may the earth be auspicious for us with grains and other products, may the vast earth and heaven be auspicious for us, may clouds be for our happiness and may the sermons of learned persons be for our prosperity.

४. शन्नो अग्निर्ज्योतिरनीको अस्तु शन्नो मित्रावरुणावश्विना शम् ।
शन्नः सुकृतां सुकृतानि सन्तु शन्न इषिरो अभिवातु वातः ॥

ऋ० ७-३५-४

May the fire which is effulgent and powerfull consuming agent, be auspicious for us, may the hydrogen and oxygen gases be beneficial to us, may night and day be for our happiness, may the good acts performed by righteous and conscientious persons be to serve our benefit, and may the blowing wind be auspicious for us.

५. शन्नो द्यावापृथिवी पूर्वहूतौ शमन्तरिक्षं दृशये नो अस्तु ।
शं न ओषधीर्वनिनो भवन्तु शं नो रजसस्पतिरस्तु जिष्णुः ।

ऋ० ७-३५-५

May the electricity and earth serve our benefit in our graceful attainments, may the space between heaven and earth helping visibility be auspicious for us, may the medicinal plants and the trees of forest be wholesome for us, may the victorious administrator of the land be the source of our happiness.

६. शन्न इन्द्रो वसुभिर्देवो अस्तु शमादित्येभिर्वरुणः सुशंसः ।
शन्नो रुद्रो रुद्रेभिर्जलाषः शं नस्त्वष्टाग्नाभिरिह शृणोतु ॥

ऋ० ७-३५-६

May the brilliant sun with earth,moon etc. be auspicious for us, may the laudable water with the twelve months of the year be auspicious for us, may the Peaceful Lord of the universe punishing evil-doers with all His administrative powers be favourable to us, may the persons of wisdom by their instructive speeches give peaceful audience to us.

७. शं नः सोमो भवतु ब्रह्म शं नः शं नो ग्रावाणः शमु सन्तु यज्ञाः ॥
शं नः स्वरूणां मितयो भवन्तु शं नः प्रस्वः शम्वस्तु वेदिः ॥

ऋ० ७-३५-७

May the moon be auspicious for us, may the grain and other eatable things be for our happiness, may the clouds be auspicious for us, may the *yajnas* and other excellent acts including scientific achievements be for our favourable end may the measurement of the pillars of our *yajnashala* be useful for us in attaining mathematical knowledge, may the herbs used in *yajnas* be useful for us in removing diseases and may the altar (Vedih) of the *yajna* be for our Intellectual and physical benefit.

८. शं नः सूर्य उरुचक्षा उदेतु शं नश्चतस्त्रः प्रदिशो भवन्तु ।
शं नः पर्वता ध्रुवयो भवन्तु शं नः सिन्धवः शमु सन्त्वापः ॥
ऋ० ७-३५-८

May the luminous sun rise up for our weal, may the four directions be auspicious for us, may the firmly rooted mountains be the source of happiness to us and may the rivers and waters be pleasing to us.

९. शं नो अदितिर्भवन्तु व्रतेभिः शंनोभवन्तु मरुतः स्वर्काः ।
शं नो विष्णुः शमु पूषा नो अस्तु शं नो भवित्रं शम्वस्तु वायुः ॥
ऋ० ७-३५-९

May the educated mothers by their good acts make us prosperous, may the men of noble intentions shower their blessings upon us, may the Omnipresent Divinity give us peace and prosperity, may the invigorating continenial power strengthens our physical, mental and spiritual happiness, may our destiny lead us for happiness and may the air be auspicious for us.

१०. शंनो देवः सविता त्रायमाणः शं नो भवन्तूषसो विभातीः ॥
शं नः पर्जन्योः भवतु प्रजाभ्यः शं नः क्षेत्रस्य पतिरस्तु शम्भुः ॥
ऋ० ७-३५-१०

May the All-creating Divinity protecting us make us blessed may the lustrous dawns bring happiness to us; may the rainy clouds bring prosperity to us and all creatures and may the peasant be the source of our prosperity.

११. शं नो देवा विश्वदेवा भवन्तु शं सरस्वती सह धीभिरस्तु ।
शमभिषाचः शमुरातिषाचः शं नो दिव्याः पार्थिवाः शन्नो अप्याः ॥
ऋ० ७-३५-११

May all the physical elements be auspicious for us, may the holy words of the Vedic speech with their pure knowledge be the source of universal peace and happiness. May the generous ones and who have taken the vow of serving all living being be the promoters of general welfare and may all the heavenly objects together with the product of earth and water be helpful to our prosperity.

१२. शं नः सत्यस्य पतयो भवन्तु शं नो अर्वन्तः शमु सन्तु गावः ।
शं न ऋभवः सुकृतः सुहस्ताः शं नो भवन्तु पितरो हवेषु ॥

ऋ० ७-३५-१२

May the custodians of truth be auspicious for us, may the horses be for our pleasant service, may the cows give us pleasure, may the righteous dexter wise persons lead us to happiness and may the parents guide us to acquisition of happiness.

१३. शं नो अज एकपाद्देवो अस्तु शं नोऽहिर्बुध्न्यः शं समुद्रः ।
शं नो अपां नपात्पेरुरस्तु शं नः पृश्निर्भवतु देवगोपाः ॥

ऋ० ७-३५-१३

May Infinite Unbegotten Divinity bless us with His beatitude may cloud moving in the atmosphere be for our well being, may ocean be for our benefit, may our boats in the water pleasantly sail us to our destination and may the vast space as residence of the celestial bodies be auspicious for us.

१४. इन्द्रनेविश्वस्य राजति । शं नो अस्तु द्विपदे शं चतुष्पदे ॥

यजु० ३६-८

Indra, God of Supreme Power illumines the entire universe, may there be happiness for our bipeds and happiness for our quadrupeds.

१५. शन्नो वातः पवतां शन्नस्तपतु सूर्यः ।
शन्नः कनिक्रदद्देवः पर्जन्यो अभिवर्षतु ॥

यजु ३६-८

May the winds blow pleasantly for us, may the sun warm the atmosphere pleasantly, may the roaring cloud rain pleasantly for us.

१६. अहानि शं भवन्तु नः शं रात्रीः प्रतिधीयताम् ।
शं न इन्द्राग्नी भवतामवोभिः शं न इन्द्रावरुणा रातहव्या ।
शं न इन्द्रापूषणा वाजसातौ शमिन्द्रासोमा सुविताय शंयोः ॥

यजु० ३६-११

May our days bring us pleasure, may our nights be auspicious for us, may ths electricity and fire with their constructive powers be auspicious for us, may the sun and moon extending their physical utility be for our well-being, may the atmospheric air and earth be beneficial to us in attaining grains and orher eatable products, may our spirit and mind work in co-operation for attaining happiness.

१७. शन्नो देवीरभिष्टये ग्रापो भवन्तु पीतये ।
शंयोरभिश्रवन्तु नः ॥

यजु० ३६-१२

May the All-pervading Divinity be the source of pleasure to us, and for the sake of satisfying our mental cravings may He be blissful and may He rain down happiness on us all around.

१८. ग्रो३म् ! द्यौः शान्तिरन्तरिक्षं शान्तिः पृथिवी शान्तिरापः शन्तिरोषधय शान्तिः । वनस्पतयः शान्तिर्विश्वे देवाः शान्तिर्ब्रह्म शान्तिः सर्वंशान्तिः शान्तिरेव शान्तिः सा मा शान्तिरेधि ॥

यजु० ३६-१७

May there be peace in heaven, may there be peace in atmospheric region, may peace reign on the earth, may the waters be soothing and may the medicinal plants be conducive to health, may the plants be the source of peace to all, may all the men of science bring peace to us. may the science conructively spread peace throughout, may all othere objects give us peace and may peace even be peace to all and may that peace come to us.

१९. तच्चक्षुर्देवहितं पुरस्ताच्छुक्रमुच्चरत् । पश्येम शरदः शतं जीवेम शरदः शतं श्रणुयाम शरदः शत प्रब्रवाम शरदः शतमदीनाः स्याम शरदः शतः भूयश्च शरदः शतात् ॥

यजु ३६-२४

The Supreme Being is All-vision, Pure and Genuine. He is benevolent to enlightened persons. He exists from eternity to eternity, by His grace a hundred autumns may we see, a hundred autumns may we live, a hundred autumns may we hear, a hundred autumns may we remain able to speak, and a hundred autumns may we enjoy unfettered liberty. In case we live longer than this we enjoy all those blessings likewise.

२०. यज्जाग्रतो दूरमुदैति दैवं तदुसुप्तस्य तथैवैति। दूरंगमं ज्योतिषां
ज्योतिरेकं तन्मे मनः शिवसंकल्पमस्तु ॥

यजु० ३४-१

That celestial entity which goeth far when man is in awakening phase and wanders similarly which he is in slumbering phase and that which travels for and wide is the only one light of all lights; may that mind of mine be possessed of auspicious intentions.

२३. येन कर्माण्यपसो मनीषिणो यज्ञे कृण्वन्ति विदथेषु धीराः।
यदपूर्वं यक्षमन्तः प्रजानां तन्मे मनः शिवसंकल्पमस्तु ॥

यजु० ३४-२

Through whose agency the patient wise men perform their works or sacrifices and that which is mysterious seated in the inmost recess of all creatures, may that mind of mine be possessed of auspicious intentions.

२२. यत्प्रज्ञानमुतचेतो धृतिश्च यज्ज्योतिरन्तरमृतं प्रजासु।
यस्मान्न ऋते किञ्चन कर्म क्रियते तन्मे मनः शिवसंकल्पमस्तु ॥

यजु० ३४-३

That which is endowed with the faculties of cognition, recollection and retention and that which is the immortal light placed with in the self of all creatures and that without whose agency no work can be accomplished, may that mind of mine be possessed of auspicious intention.

२३. येनेदं भूतं भुवनं भविष्यत् परिगृहीतममृतेन सर्वम्।
येन यज्ञस्तायते सप्तहोता तन्मे मनः शिवसंकल्पमस्तु ॥

यजु० ३४-४

That immortal substance by which all this world which was is and will be, is full comprehended and under whose authority the *yajna* presided over by seven *hotars* is extended; may that mind of mine be possessed of auspicious intentions.

२४. यस्मिन्नृचः साम यजूँषि यस्मिन् प्रतिष्ठिता रथनाभाविवाराः ।
यस्मिंश्चित्तँ सर्वमोतं प्रजानां तन्मे मनः शिवसंकल्पमस्तु ॥
यजु० ३४-३

Wherein, the Rg. the Saman the Yajuh and wherein the Atharva Vedas are placed together like spokes in the navel of the chariot weel and wherein the congitive faculty of all the creatures is interwoven:may that mind of mine be possessed of auspicious intentions.

२५ सुषारथिरश्वानिव यन्मनुष्यान्नेनीयतेऽभीशुभिर्वाजिन इव ।
हृत्प्रतिष्ठं यदजिरं जविष्ठं तन्मे मनः शिवसंकल्पमस्तु ॥
यजु० ३४-६

As the skilful charioteer drives the horses with the reins the mind controls mankind; This mind remains within the heart, it is most swift agile; may that mind of minc be possessed of auspicious intentions.

२६ स नः पवस्व शं गवे शं जनाय शमर्वते
शं राजन्नोषधीभ्यः ॥
साम उत्त० १-१

O ye Imperial Ruler ! Thou art manifest Lord of the universe. Please be kind upon us for our cows, be gracious for our men, benevolent for our horses, and for the sake of medicinal plants please shower blessing upon us.

२७ अभयं नः करत्यन्तरिक्षमभयं द्यावापृथिवी उभे इमे ।
अभयं पश्चादभयं पुरस्तादुत्तरादधरादभयं नो अस्तु ॥
अथर्व १९-१५-५

May the atmosphere give us peace and safety and may both these heaven and the earth be secure for us, may we be free from west and east and may there be no fear for us from north and south.

अभयं मित्रादभयममित्रादभयं ज्ञातादभयं पुरो यः ।
अभयं नक्तमभयं दिवा नः सर्वा आशा मम मित्रं भवन्तु ॥

अथर्व १९-१५-६

May we be fearless of our friends and even of those who are unfriendly to us, may we never fall in dread of those whom we know and even of those whom we do not know. may we remain free from any apprehensiven by night and in the day time and may all the quarters be friendly to us.

———o———

Here Begins the Common Procedure Chapter

The performances given below should be performed in all the *Sanskaras*. But wherever there will be any special act to do or not to do, will be indicated. Whatever more should be done and whatever should not be done whould be directed at its proper places.

The place of yajna. The place of yajna should be neat, clean and pure. It should be pure in ground and air and its vicinity should be pure. This should be free from any kind of disturbance and perturbation.

Yajnashala. This is also called *yajnamandap*. This should be utmost 16 hands square (8 yards square and atleast 8 hands square (4 yards square). If anywhere the soil of the ground is dirty then in the case of *yajnashala* two hands (one yard) deep and in the case of *Vedi* to the proportion of the depth of it, the ground should be dug out, the dirty soil removed and the dug filled with the pure and clean soil. If the *yajnashāla* is made of 16 hands square there should be 20 pillars and if eight hands square then the pillars should be 12 in number. There should be a shed of roof on the pillars over the whole area.

The height of the roof of *yajnashala* should surely be 10 hands and there be four doors or entrances in four sides of it. There should be flags fixed on all cornors and decoration of it with leaves etc. This *yajnashala* should be cleaned with brush every day. It should be made neat and clean by anointing with Cow dung and pure water. This should also be decorated with lines and drawings of saffron, *Circuma Longa* and powder of wheat or rice, It is obligatory to all the men that they should pray Divinity through the performance of *yajna* for the well-being of the men who are their own as well as men who are not their own. For this purpose they offer the oblation of sweet-smelling or fragrant plants. grains; herbs, cereal preparations etc. As has been written hereafter in their context, in the *Vedi* of yajna.

N. B. Here in the above and in other similar context hand is equal to half yard or 18 inches and *Angula* is equal to half inch.

The Dimension of *yajnakunda*. If one lac oblations are to be dropped therein the *yajnakunda* should be of four hands square. It should be four hands deep but in the bottom it should be one fourth of the upper surface, e. i. one hand squate In this manner the length, breadth, depth etc. of the *Kunda* should be according to the numbers of the oblations to be dropped. If more oblations are desired to be offered the space of the *Kunda* should be increascd by adding to hands square, that is, in offering two lacs of oblations the *Kuna* should be proportionately 6 hands square. The bottom should be one fourth of the upper surface,

If only fifty thousand oblations are to be offered there should be one hand decrease that is the *Kund* should be only three hands square and to the same standard deep . If only 25 thousand oblations are to be offered the *Knnda* should be two hands square and to the same extent deep. But the bottom should be half hand. Upto ten thousand oblations the same should be area etc. of the K*unda* that is it should be two hand square to the same extent deep with bottom of half hand. If the oblations to be offered are upto five thousands the *Kunda* should be 1½hands Square and to the same extent deep but bottom should be of 8½ *Angulas*.

This above described dimensions of the *Kunda* is only for particular oblations of *ghee*. If the oblations of M*ohanbhogha* or *Khira* are 2500 and of ghee 2500 in addition thereto, the *Kunda* should be two hands spuare and 2 hands deep with the bottom of half hand. If only one thousand oblations of *ghee* are to be offered the *Kunda* should not be less then 1¼ hand squar and 1¼ hand deep, The bottom should be one fourth of the upper surface. In all these *Kundas* there should be three *Mekhalas* .of fifteen inches each five inch high. These three *Mekhalas* s h o u l d be constructed from the ground floor of the *Yajnashala* not of the *Kunda*, raised upward. The first of three Mekhalas should be 5 inches high and five inches wide. The same should be the scale of the second and the third Mekhalas.

The wood-fuel prescribed for the *yajna*

Palasha पलाश (Butra Frondosa), *Shami* (Mimosa Suma), पीपल (Ficus Religiosa) बड़ (Banyan), *gular* (Ficus glomerata) *Amb* [Amra] आम (Mango tree) Bilva (Aegle Marmelos) are the woods prescribed as the wood-fuel of the yajna. The wood-fuel sticks should be kept after cutting them into piece in proportion to the area of the *Yajna Vedi.* These wood fuels should not be eaten by worms, produced in dirty land and spoiled with dirty things. These should be examined thorough and should be arranged squarly in the middle of the *Kunda*.

The four kinds of articles for the HOMA, the oblation.

(The first of good fragrance) *Kasturi* (Musk), *Keshar* (Rotileria Tinctoria). *Agar* (Aquilaria Agellocha). *Tagar* (Tebernamutan Caronaria), *Shveta Chandan* (White sandal wood or powder) *ilayachi* (Feronia Elephantum) *Jayphala* (Nutmeg) and *Javitri* (Mace) etc. (The second strengthening) *Ghee*, Milk, Fruit, Herbacious roots, cereal, rice, wheat and *Urada* (Phaseolus Radiatus). (The third sweet) Sugar, honey, date, vine etc. The fourth herbacious plants) *Somalata ie Giloya* (Cocculus cordifolius) etc, herbs.

Sthalipaka **the Cereal preparation.**

Cooked rice, ingredient of rice and *Urada*, the Phaseolus Radiatus, *Khira*, the rice cooked in milk and sugar, *laddoo* (Small round sweetmeat prepared in *ghee* with powder of *munga* and sugar), *Mohanabhoga*—a kind of sweetmeat prepared with flour of grain and *ghee* and sugar, should be prepared according to the method described as under. The authority of scripture.

ओ३म् । देवस्त्वा सविता पुनात्वच्छिद्रेण पवित्रेण वसोः सूर्यस्य रश्मिभिः ॥

गो० गृ० प्र० १ खण्ड ७ सूत्र २४

The purport of this *Mantra* is that things to be prepared for the oblation should be entirely cleaned, These should be carefully examined, sifted and sieved. The *Paka* should be made after mixing them in appropriate proportion. For example if *Mohanbhoga* is to be prepared in one seer of ghee; one *Ratti* of musk; one *Mashas* of Rotilerio; Tinctoria; two *Mashas* of Nutmeg; two *Masha* of mace. one seer of sugar be mixed in the preparation. In the same manner sweet rice, *Khir* (Rice cooking in milk and sugar, *Khichari* (rice cooking with the mixture of *Urad or Munga* without salt) *Modak* (round small balls prepared in *ghee* and with the powder of grain) should be prepared for the sake of *Homa*.

The Method of preparing *charu*, the cerial preparation by cooking—

ओम् अग्नये त्वा जुष्टं निर्वपामि ।

आश्व० गृ० अ० १ कं० १० सू० ६

That is, the four *Muthis* (the quantity which a clenched hand may contain in it, i e, about two or three *tolas* hardly) of rice etc. for each of the oblation according to the numbers of the oblations totally offered, should be taken and by pronouncing the Mantra

अग्नये त्वा जुष्टं प्रोक्षामि

आ० गृ० अ० १ कं० १०-सू० ७

and washing and cleaning with the water the same should be put in caldron and be cooked. When this is to be taken in another pot for the sake of *homa*, it should be taken away from the caldron and be kept entirely safe and molten *ghee* should be poured on it.

———

YAJNAPATRA, the pots of *Yajna*

Especially the *Yajnapatra* should be of silver, gold or wood, They should be as follows:

यज्ञपात्र

विशेषकर चांदी, सोना अथवा काष्ठ के पात्र होने चाहिए, निम्नलिखित प्रमाणे: —

अथ पात्रलक्षणान्युच्यन्ते—बाहुमात्र्यः पणिमात्रपुष्करा:, षडङ्गुलखाता-स्त्वग्बिला हंसमुखप्रसेका:, मूलदन्डास्चतस्रः स्रुचो भवन्ति। तत्र पालाशी जुहू:, आश्वत्थ्युपभृत् वैकङ्कती ध्रुवा, अग्निहोत्रहवणी च।

अरत्निमात्रः खादिरः स्रुव:, अङ्गुष्ठपर्वमात्रपुष्करः। तथाविधो द्वितीयो वैकङ्कतः स्रुवः।

वारणं बाहुमात्रं मकराकारमग्निहोत्रहवणीनिधानार्थं कूर्चम्।

अरत्निमात्रं खादिरं खड्गाकृति वज्रम्

वारणान्यहोमसंयुक्तानि। तत्रोलूखलं नाभिमात्रम्, मुसलं शिरोमात्रम् अथवा मुसलोलूखले वार्क्ष्ये सारदारुमये शुभे इच्छाप्रमाणे भवतः। तथा—

खादिरं मुसलं कार्यं पालाशः स्यादुलूखल।

यद्वोभौ वारणौ कार्यौ तदभावेऽन्यवृक्षजौ।

शूर्पं वैणवमेव वा, ऐषीकं नलमयं वाऽचर्मबद्धम्

प्रादेशमात्री वारणी शम्या।

कृष्णाजिनमखण्डम्।

दृषदुपले अश्ममये। वारणीं २४ हस्तमात्रीं, २२ अरत्निमात्रीं, खातमध्यां मध्यसंगृहीतामिडापात्रीम्॥

अरत्निमात्राणि ब्रह्मयजमानहोतृपत्न्यासनानि।

मुञ्जमयं त्रिवृतं व्याममात्रं योक्त्रम्।

प्रादेशदीर्घे अष्टाङ्गुलायते षडङ्गुलखातमण्डलमध्ये पुरोडाशपात्र्यो।

प्रादेशमात्रं द्व्यङ्गुलपरीणाहं तीक्ष्णाग्रं श्रृतावदानम्।

आदर्शाकारे चतुरस्रे वा प्राशित्रहरणे। तयोरेकमीषत्खातमध्यम्।

षडङ्गुलकङ्कतिकाकारमुभयतः खातं षडवत्तम्।

द्वादशाङ्गुलमर्द्धचन्द्राकारमष्टाङ्गुलोत्सेधमन्तर्द्धानकटम्।

उपवेशोऽरत्निमात्रः ।

मुञ्जमयी रज्जुः ।

खादिरान् द्वादशाङ्गुलदीर्घा चतुरङ्गुलमस्तकान् तीक्ष्णाग्रान् शङ्कून् ।

यजमानपूर्णपात्रं पत्नीपूर्णपात्रं च द्वादशाङ्गुलदीर्घं चतुरङ्गुलविस्तारं चतुरङ्गुलखातम् ।

तथा प्रणीतापात्रञ्च ।

आज्यस्थाली द्वादशाङ्गुलविस्तृता प्रादेशोच्चा ।

तथैव चरुस्थाली ।

अन्वाहार्यपात्रं पुरुषचतुष्टयाहारपाकपर्याप्तम् ।

समिदिध्मार्थं पलाशशाखामयम् ।

कौशं बर्हिः ।

ऋत्विग्वरणार्थं कुण्डलाङ्गुलीयकवासांसि ।

पत्नीयजमानपरिधानार्थं क्षौमवासासश्चतुष्टयम् ।

अग्न्याधेयदक्षिणार्थं चतुर्विंशतिपक्षे एकोनपञ्चाशद् गावः, द्वादशपक्षे पञ्चविंशतिः, षट्पक्षे त्रयोदश, सर्वेषु पक्षेषु आदित्येष्टौ धेनुः । वरार्थं चतस्रो गावः ॥

सामान्यप्रकरणम्

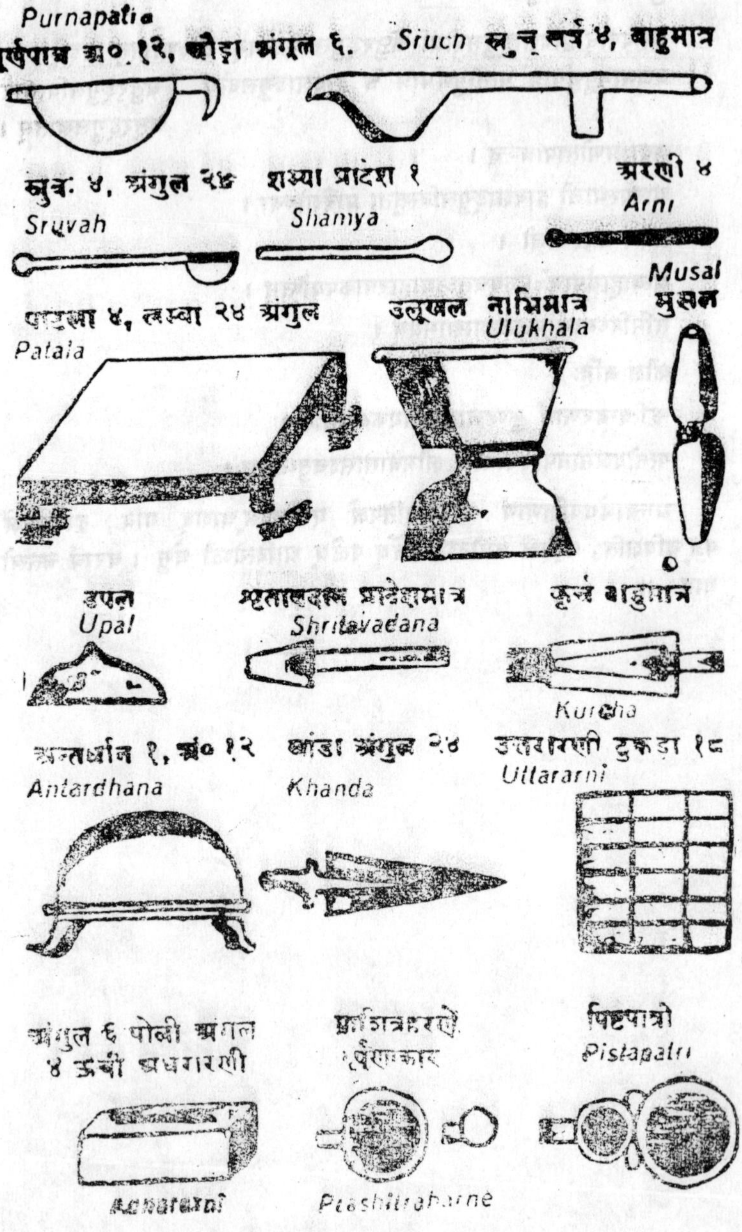
Purnapatra
पूर्णपात्र अं०. १२, चौड़ा अंगुल ६.
Sruch स्रुच लम्बे ४, बाहुमात्र
स्रुव: ४, अंगुल २४
शम्या प्रादेश १
अरणी ४
Arni
Sruvah
Shamya
Musal
पटला ४, लम्बा २४ अंगुल
उलूखल नाभिमात्र
मुसल
Ulukhala
Patala
उपल
Upal
शृतावदान प्रादेशमात्र
Shritavadana
कूर्च बाहुमात्र
Kurcha
अन्तर्धान १, अं० १२
खांडा अंगुल २४
उत्तरारणी टुकड़ा १८
Antardhana
Khanda
Uttararni
अंगुल ६ पोली अंगुल
४ ऊंची अधरारणी
प्राशित्रहरणे
दर्पणाकार
पिष्टपात्री
Pistapatri
Adharani
Prashitraharne

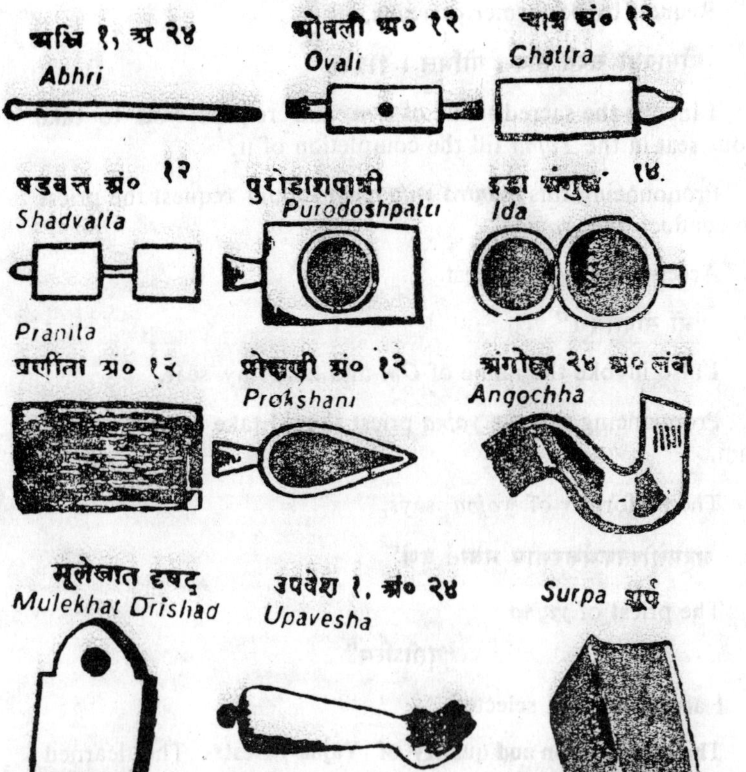

समिध पलाश की १८ हस्त [मा] अ. प्रथम परिधि ३ पलाश की बाहुमात्र. सामिधेनी समित प्रादेशमात्र, सम्मीलना मेर ५, शाटी १, दृषदुपल १, दीर्घ अंगुल १२ पृ० १५, अपल अं० ६, नेतु व्याम हाथ ४ त्रिवृत्तृण वा गोवाल का ॥

SELECTION AND APPOINTMENT OF YAJNA PRIESTS

Request by performer of *yajna*,

ओमावसो सदने सीद । गोभिल । १।६।५

I invoke the sacred name of *Om* and request you to take your seat in the *Yajna* till the completion of it.

Pronouncing this *mantra yajamana* should request the priest to conduct the *yajna*.

Acceptance by the priest.

"ओं सीदामि ।"

I also invoke the name of *Om* and take my seat.

Pronouncing this the *yajna* priest should take seat fixed for him.

The performer of *yajna* says.

अहमद्योक्तकर्मकरणाय भवन्तं वृणे'

The priest of *yajna*.

"वृतोऽस्मि"

I accept myself selected.

The qualification and quality of Yajna-Priests- The learned who are well accomplished, righteous, continent, skilled in conducting and performing the acts required, uncovetous, benevo lent, free from bad habits, of good family, of good characteristics, the follower of vedic cult and creed and the master of *Vedas* should be selected and appointed as the priests of *Yajna* and the number should be one or two or three or four as be required.

If the priest is one his designation be *Purohita*, if there be two they should be designated as *Ritvik* and *Purohita*, if there are three they be described as *Ritvik*, *Purohita* and *Adhyaksha* and if there are 4 priests they be given the titles of *Hotar*, *Adhvaryu*, *Udgatar* and *Brahman*. The seats of these four priests should be arranged on the four sides of the *Yajnavedi* in the manner that the *hotar* be in the west keeping his face towards east, Adhvaryu sit in the north keeping his face towards south, the *Udgatar* be on his seat in the east keeping his face towards west and *Brahman* should take his seat in the south keeping his face towards north. *Yajmana* the performer of *Yajna* etc. take his seat in the west keeping his face towards east or take his seat in the south and keep his face towards north. These priests should be seated with due respect and they should take their respective seats delightfully and none should do any other thing or talk except the performance which is present and which they are entrusted with.

SIPPING OF WATER

All those who are sitting to perform yajna should sip water thrice from their respective water-pots with these *Mantras* i.e. one sipping by one *mantra*, and the *mantras* are as follows:

ओम् अमृतोपस्तरणमसि स्वाहा ॥१॥

ओम् अमृतापिधानमसि स्वाहा ॥२॥

ओम् सत्यं यशः श्रीर्मयि श्रीः श्रयताम् स्वाहा ॥३॥

आश्व० गृ० अ० १।कं० २४।सूत्र १२, २७, २२

This water is the means of protection from blow, whatever is uttered herein is right.

This water is the means of protection from above, whatever is uttered herein is right.

May the truth, the fame and the weal be always with me, whatever is uttered herein is right.

TOUCHING BODILY PARTS

Afterwards the performers of *yajna* touch the parts of the body with water by the following *mantras*

ओं वाङ्म आस्येऽस्तु- by this mouth
ओं नसोर्मे प्राणोऽस्तु- by this both the nostrils
ओं अक्ष्णोर्मे चक्षुरस्तु- by this both the eyes
ओं कर्णयोर्मे श्रोत्रमस्तु- by this both the ears
ओं बाह्वोर्मे बलमस्तु- by this both the arms
ओं ऊर्वोर्मे ओजोऽस्तु- by this both the thighs
ओं अरिष्टानि मेऽङ्गानि-by this taking the water in the
तनूस्तन्वा मे सह सन्तु-right hand *Marjana* should
पार० गृ० कां १।कं० ३ सू० २५ be done

O God, Let speech reside in my mouth.
O God, Let breath reside in my nose.
O God, Let vision reside in my eyes.
O God, Let hearing reside in my ears.
O God, Let strength strengthen my arms.
O God, Let there be power in my thighs.
O God, Let my body and its parts be healthy.

ARRANGEMENT OF WOOD–FUEL

This arrangement of wood-pieces should be done in the *Vedi*, the altar.

PUTTING FIRE IN THE VEDI

Then:–

ओं भूर्भुवः स्वः ।
गो० गृ० १-१-११

The all–protecting Divinity is existent, conscious and all-bliss.

Pronouncing this above cited *mantra* bringing fire from the house of *Brahmana*, *Kshatriya*, or *Vaishya*, performer or the priest of *yajna* should light a lamp of *ghee* and lighting a piece of camphor from this lamp he should place it in a dish and drop small pieces of wood therein and raising the dish by his both hands,(in the case of its being hot he should hold it by means of doubled-fork) should place the fire in the centre of the *vedi* after pronouncing the following hymn :

ओं भूर्भुवः स्वर्द्यौरिव भूम्ना पृथिवीव वरिम्णा,

तस्यास्ते पृथिवि देवयजनि पृष्ठेऽग्निमन्नादमन्नाद्यायादधे ॥ यजु० ३-५

I,for obtaining grains as well as other edible products of the earth, place on the back of the earth whereon the *Yajnas* are performed by the righteous learned persons this fire which consumes all that is offered to it as oblations, which is luminous as the Sun in heaven and as grand as the earth with its grandeur and which is residing in three localities; the earth, the atmosphere and the heavenly region.

FANNING THE FIRE

Putting the fire in the middle of the *Vedi* with the Mantra ओं भूर्भुवः स्वर्द्यौरिव० arranging the piece of wood-fuel and a small bit of camphor on it and pronouncing the following hymn the performer of yajna should fan the fire:

ओं उद्बुध्यस्वाग्ने प्रति जागृहि त्वमिष्टापूर्ते

सं सृजेथामयं च ।

अस्मिन्त्सधस्थे अध्युत्तरस्मिन् विश्वेदेवा यजमानश्च सीदत ॥ यजुः १५-४४

May this fire rise and boom, may this fire and *yajamana*, the performer of *yajna* accomplish the desired performances like *yajna* etc and the other works of public utility. May the learned persons and the performer of *yajna* encircling north side take their seats on the *Vedi*

ADDITION OF WOOD-FUEL TO THE FIRE OF *Vedi*

When fire begins to make its way in the wood-pieces arranged in the *Vedi* the performer of *yajna* dip three sticks of sandal wood or *palash* as mentioned above, each of four inches in length and taking one of them at each turn add to the fire pronouncing the hymn assigned for it. The hymns assigned for the purpose are as follows:

ओम् अयन्त इध्म आत्मा जातवेदस्तेनेध्यस्व वर्धस्व
चेद्ध वर्धय चास्मान् प्रजया, पशुभिर्ब्रह्मवर्चसेनान्ना-
द्येन समेधय स्वाहा ॥ इदमग्नये जातवेदसे इदन्नमम ॥१॥

आश्व० गृ० १।१०।१२

This woodful is the power of endurance to fire which is present in all the created objects, by this it may be lighted and may increase its strenght and in the same manner be it source of our progress blessed with offspring animals, knowledge, radiance, physical spiritual, and edible things like grains etc. Whatever is uttered herein is right. This offered oblation is meant for *jatavedas agni only*, it is not for me. With this hymn first woodfuel be added to.

ओं समिधाग्निं दुवस्यत घृतैर्बोधयतातिथिम् ।
आस्मिन् हव्या जुहोतन स्वाहा ॥
इदमग्नये इदन्नमम ॥२॥ यजुः ३-१

With this hymn and;—

सुसमिद्धाय शोचिषे घृतं तीव्रं जुहोतन ।
अग्नये जातवेदसे स्वाहा ॥
इदमग्नये जातवेदसे इदन्न मम ॥३॥

यजुः ३-२

With this hymn i. e, with both of the hymns
(समिधाग्निम्०) and (सुसमिद्धाय०)

The second wood-fuel be added to.

O performer and conductor of *yajna* (the *yajmana* and ***Ritvik***, the priests) feed the permanently preserved fire with fuel, enkindle it with *ghee* and offer *havis* in it. Whatever is uttered herein is right. This offered oblation is meant for *jatavedesagni* only, it is not for me.

O ye performers of *yajnas* and conducting priests! offer purified molten *ghee* in the well-burnt enkindled fire which is present in all the wordly objects, Whatever is uttered herein is right. This offered oblation is meant for *jatavedas* only, it is not for me.

ओं तन्त्वा समद्भिरंगिरो घृतेन वर्धयामसि ।
बृहच्छोचा यविष्ठ्य स्वाहा ।
इदमग्नयेऽङ्गिरसे इदन्न मम ॥४॥ **यजु० ३-३**

The third woodfuel should be added to with this above cited hymn.

With woodfuels and *ghee* we further inflame that fire which is present in all the organic and inorganic bodies and encourage this powerful fire to blaze more and more. Whatever is uttered herein is right. This offered oblation is meant for thc *angiras angi* only, it is not for me.

FIVE OBLATIONS (Ahutis)

After performing the act of *Samidadhana* (Fuel-adding) the articles accordingly prepared for the purpose of *yajna* should be kept safe in the pots of Gold, silver of *Kansi* or of wood Quantity of an oblation of *ghee* which is molten, warm and mixed with the fragtant herbs etc. and kept in the pots, should not be less then 6 *Mashas*,(5gm)and the quantity of the oblation of *Mohanbhoga* etc, or whichever *samagri* is there, should be utmost one *chhataka*. (50gm) This is the quantity of the oblation.

ओम् अयन्त इध्म आत्मा जातवेदस्तेनेध्यस्व वर्धस्व
चेद्ध, वर्धय चास्मान् प्रजया, पशुभिर्ब्रह्मवर्चसे—
नान्नाद्येन, समेधय स्वाहा ॥
इदमग्नये जातवेदसे इदन्नमम ॥आश्व० गृ० १।१०।१२

This hymn has alcrady been translated on page 36

From this molten *ghee* the spoon which is prepared to contain only 5 gm should be filled and five oblations should be offered by pronouncing the following *mantra*,

Sprinkling of Water Round the *Vedi* containing Fire ablaze

Afterwards taking palmful water the performers of *yajna* should sprinkle it on the four directions including east etc. around the *vedi* and the *mantras* assigned for this purpose are as follows.

ओम् अदिते अनुमन्यस्व

With this *mantra* in the east direction.

O Indivisible Divinity ! Please let us be according to you.

ओम् अनुमतेऽनुमन्यस्व

With this in the west direction

O Irrefragable Divinity ! Please let us be according to you.

ओं सरस्वत्यनुमन्यस्व **गोभिल गृ० १।३।१-३**

With this in the North directon

O Divine Power (the Source of Knowledge) please let us be according to you.

ओं देव सवितः प्र सुव यज्ञं प्र सुव यज्ञपतिं भगाय ।
दिव्यो गन्धर्वः केतपूः केतं नः पुनातु वाचस्पतिर्वाचं न स्वदतु । यजुः ३०-१

And with this (above cited) hymn water should be sprinkled in all the four directions round the *Vedi.*

O ye Savitar ! (All-impelling Lord) for the sake of attain ing felicity, speed onward our self-sacrificing acts and speed him onward who is engaged in protecting our self-sacrifieing act. May the Self-refulgent Lord, the upholder of the earth and other worlds who is the Purifier of reason purify our thoughts and may the Lord of speech sweeten our words which we utter.

AGHARAVAJYABHAGAHUTAYAH

After this the performance of water sprinkling.

It is positively required that the common *homahutis*(oblation of the yajna) should be done in the principal sacraments like *Garbhadhana* etc.

Among the *Ahutis*(oblations)offercd in the beginning and the end of the principal *homa*, the first oblation offered in the narth side of *yajna kunda* and the second oblation offered in the south side of the *yajna kunda* are named as *agharavajyahuti*. The oblations offered in the centre of *yajna kunda* are called *Ajabhagahuti*. After filling the spoon with molten *ghee* preserved in the pot, holding it with thumb and first and the central second fingers the following hymn shoulp be prononced:—

ओं अग्नये स्वाहा । इदमग्नये इदन्न मम ।।

With this *mantra* the libation of molten *ghee* should be poured on the fire in the *Vedi* in the northern side.

I offer this oblation in the praise of self-refulgent God of thc fire, the positive electricity. Whetever is uttered herein is right, This offered oblation is meant for *agni* only. it is not for me.

ओं सोमाय स्वाहा । इदं सोमाय इदन्न मम ।।

गो० गृ० १।८।३-४

With this *Mantra* the libation of molten *ghee* should be poured on fire in the south side of the Vedi.

I offer this oblation in the praise of *Soma*, the negative electricity. Whatever is uttered herein is right. This offered oblation is meant for *Soma* only, it is not for me.

Afterwards:—

ओं प्रजापतयें स्वाहा । इदं प्रजापतये इदन्न मम ।।
ओं इन्द्राय स्वाहा । इदमिन्द्राय इदन्न मम ।।

कात्याय० श्रौ० ३।१२, ३।१९

Two oblations should be offered on the fire in the centre of the *Vedi* with these two above mentioned *Mantra.*

I offer this oblation in the praise of ***Prajapati.*** Whatever uttered herein is right. This offered oblation is meant for Prajapati only, it is not for me.

I offer this oblation in the praise of Indra. whatever is uttered herein is right, This offered oblation is meant for *Indra* only, it is not for me.

After offering the four *Agharavajyabhaghautis* and then performing the principal *Homa,* i. e. completing the desired and required *Homa* to be performed, as the final oblations the four *Agharavajyabhagahutis* should be again offered by the *yajmana.* Again from that pot of the purified molten *ghee* the four oblations of *Vyahriti* should be offered on the burning fuels with the full spoon.

The *Vyahriti* A*hutis* are the following :—

ओं भूरग्नये स्वाहा । इदमग्नये-इदन्न मम ॥
ओं भुवर्वायवे स्वाहा ॥ इदं वायवे इदन्न मम ॥
ओं स्वरादित्याय स्वाहा ॥ इदमादित्याय इदन्न मम ॥
ओं भूर्भुवः स्वरग्निवाय्वादित्येभ्यः स्वाहा ।
इदमग्निवाय्वादित्येभ्यः इदन्न मम ॥

(1) I offer this oblation to know the *bhuh* which is closely connected with *Agni.* Whatever is uttered herein is beautiful and true. This oblation is meant for *Agni* only and it is not for me.

(2) I offer this oblation to know the *bhuvah* which is closely connected with *Vayu* the firmament. Whatever is uttered herein is beautiful and true. This oblation is meant only for *Vayu* and it is not for me.

(3) I offer this oblation to know the *svah* which is closely connected with the *Aditya* the sun. Whatever is uttered herein is beautiful and true. This oblation is meant only for *Aditya* and it is not for me.

(4) I offer this oblation to know *bhur bhuvah* and *svah* collectively which are closely eonnected with *Agni*, *Vayu* and *Aditya*. Whatever is uttered herein is beautiful and true. This oblation is meant collectively for *Agni*, *Vayu* and *Adityg*, and it is not for me.

With these *mantras* four oblations of *ghee* should be offered in the *Vedi*.

SVISTAKRIDAHUTI

The *svista-Kridahuti* is only one. It should be either of *ghee* or of cooked rice. The *mantra* with it should be given is as follows:—

ओं यदस्य कर्मणोऽत्यरीरिचं यद्वान्यूनमिहाकरम् ।
अग्निष्टत् स्विष्टकृद् विद्यात् सर्वं स्विष्टं सुहुतं करोतु मे । अग्नये स्विष्टकृते सुहुतहुते सर्वप्रायश्चित्ताहुतीनां कामानां समर्द्धयित्रे सर्वान्नः कामान्त्समर्द्धय स्वाहा ॥ इदमग्नये स्विष्टकृते इदन्नमम ॥

Whatever in this performance, I have done going out of the procedure, whatever I have left of it with negligence let all that be traced out and corrected by the learned man who knows to perform the act in noble way. May He perfect our act to befit them in the procedure adopted to serve the *yajnagni* which fulfils the desired end of *yajmana*, for which sake all the oblations of resipisence are offered and which is the source of producing good and is eater of the offered oblation. May He fulfil our aspirations. Whatever is uttered herein is right. The oblation offered in the fire of *Vedi* is meant for *Swistakrit* agni, it is not for me.

OBLATION OF PRAJAPATI

The *Prajapati* oblation should be offered in the fire of the Vedi with the following *mantra* which should be pronounced only in mind, not by the organ of speech.

ओं प्रजापतये स्वाहा । इदं प्रजापतये इदन्न मम ॥

PAVAMANAHUTIS, THE OBLATIONS OF PAVAMANA

One oblation with one *mantra* and thus amounting four oblations of *ghee* should be offered with the following hymns:—

But these oblations are principal in the sacraments—*Mundana samavart ana Vivaha*

ओं भूर्भुवः स्वः । अग्न आयूंषि पवस आ सुवोर्जमिषं च नः । आरे बाधस्व दुच्छुनां स्वाहा । इदमग्नये पवमानाय इदन्न मम ॥ २ ॥

ओं भूर्भुवः । अग्निर्ऋषिः पवमानः पाञ्चजन्यः पुरोहितः । तमीमहे महागयं स्वाहा । इदमग्नये पवमानाय इदन्न मम ॥

ओं भूर्भुवः स्वः अग्ने पवस्व स्वपा अस्मे वर्चः सुवीर्यम् । दधद् रयिं मयि पोषं स्वाहा । इदमग्नये पवमानाय इदन्न मम ॥३॥ ऋ० ९, ६६, १९-२१

ओं भूर्भुवः स्वः प्रजापते नत्वदेतान्यन्यो विश्वा जातानि परिता बभूव । यत्कामास्ते जुहुमस्तन्नो अस्तु वयं स्याम पतयो रयीणां स्वाहा । इदं प्रजापतये-इदन्न मम ॥४॥

ऋ० १०, १२१, ११

God is existent, conscious and all-blissful. By His grace may the fire be means of protection for us, may it give to us strength and grains and keep away from us all sorts of evils and persons of evil designs. Whatever is uttered herein is right. The oblation offered in the fire of the *Vedi* is meant for *Pavamana Agni* only. it is not for me.

God is existent, conscious and all-blissful. It is by His grace that this fire becomes the source of our seeing; it is best purifier applicable in *yajna* by five kinds of men : four *varnas* and those who do not come in *varna* category; it is present in every thing from very beginning and may we know to utilize this powerful element in our work. Whatever is uttered herein is right. The oblation offered in the fire of the *Vedi* is meant for the *Pavamana Agni*, it is not for me.

God is existent, conscious and all-blissful. By His grace may this fire which serves multifarious purposes, being the source of wealth and energy for us, give us strenth and physical radiancy. Whatever is uttered herein is right. The oblation offered in the fire of the *Vedi* is meant for *Pavmana Agni*, it is not for me.

God is existent. conscious and all-blissful. It is by HIs grace and power that the fire protecting all the subjects of the world has none as its equal to over-power those worldly objects which are created. May this fire used in *yajna* be the means of fulfiill-ing our those aspirations for which we enkindle it and we may be the possessors of all kinds of riches. Whatever is uttered herein is right. The oblation offered in the fire of the *Vedi* is meant for the *Prajapati* only, it is not for me.

After offering four oblations of *ghee* by these for *mantras* one should offer *eidht Ajyahutis.*

EIGHT AHUTIS of *Ajya*

These eight oblations of *ghee*, one by each, should be offered at the time of all the auspicious rites with the following eight *mantras*:—

ओं त्वन्नो अग्ने वरुणस्य विद्वान् देवस्य हेडोऽवयसिसीष्ठाः यजिष्ठो वह्नितम शोशुचानो विश्वा द्वेषांसि प्र मुमुग्ध्यस्मत् स्वाहा । इदमग्निवरुणाभ्याम् इदन्न मम ॥ १ ॥

ओं स त्वं नो अग्नेऽवमो भवोती नेदिष्ठोऽअस्या उषो व्युष्टौ । अवयक्ष्व नो वरुणं रराणो वीहि मृडीकं सुहबो न एधि स्वाहा । इदमग्निवरुणाभ्याम् इदन्न मम ॥२॥ ऋ० ५-१-४,५

ओं इमं मे वरुण श्रुधी हवमद्या च मुडय । त्वाम वस्युराचके स्वाहा । इदं वरुणाय इदन्न मम ॥ ३ ॥ १-२५-१९

ओं तत्त्वा यामि ब्रह्मणा वन्दमानस्तदाशास्ते यजमानो हविर्भिः ।
अहेडमानो वरुणेह बोध्युरुशंस मा न आयुः प्रमोषी स्वाहा ॥ इदं वरुणाय-इदन्न मम ॥ ४ ॥ ऋ० १-२४-११

ओं ये ते शतं वरुणये सहस्र यज्ञियाः पाशा वितता महान्तः तेभिर्नोऽद्य सवि-तोत विष्णुर्विश्वे मुञ्चन्तु मरुतः स्वर्क्काः स्वाहा ॥ इदं वरुणाय सवित्रे विष्णवे विश्वेभ्यो देवेभ्यो मरुद्भ्य स्वर्क्केभ्यः- इदन्न मम ॥५॥

ओम् अयाश्चाग्नेऽस्यनभिशस्तिपाश्च सत्यमित् त्वमयासि । अया नो घेहि भेषजं ऽ स्वाहा ॥ इदमग्नये अयसे इदन्न मम ॥६॥ का० २५-११

ओं उदुत्तमं वरुण पाशमस्मदवाधमं विमध्यमं श्रथाय । अथा वयमादित्य व्रते तवानागसो अदितये स्याम स्वाहा ॥ इदं वरुणायादित्यायादितये च इदन्न मम ॥७॥
ऋ० १-१४-१५

ओ भवतं नः समनसौ सचेत सावरेपसौ । मा यज्ञꣳ हिꣳ सिष्टं मा यज्ञपतिं जातवेदसौ शिवौ भवतमद्य नः स्वाहा ॥ इदं जातवेदोभ्याम् इदन्न मम ॥८॥
यजु० ५।३

Agni, the animal heat functioning in the body four our benefit does not deviate from the course adopted by the vital air which is also an important functionary in our body. This as the source of corporeal and corpuscular organization, and most powerful force of subsistence strengthening all our activities keeps away from us all kinds of diseases. Whatever is uttered herein is right. The oblation offered in the fire of *Vedi* is meant for *Agni* and *varuna*, it is not for me,

That this Agni is our protector by its operations of protection, resident in our bodys nearest to us it enlivens our vital air. Strengthing our activities it keeps everything right to give us pleasure. It is fit for our good worlds. Whatever is uttered herein is right. The oblation offered in the fire of the *Vedi* is mean for *Agni* and *Varuna*, it is not for me.

Varuna, the air communicates our words to others to make it audible to them, it gives us pleasure by its activities. We desirous for our well-being praise its various properties to take into our use. Whatever uttered herein is right. The oblation offered in the fire of the *Vedi* is meant for only *varuna*, it is not for me.

We desire to attain long life from the *Varuna*, the vital air, performer of *yajnas* pronouncing Vedic hymns desires to attain that by offering oblations, and keeps in balance, this praiseworthy *Varuna* fulfils our desires and gives to us long life. Whatever is uttered herein is right. The oblation offered in the fire of the Vedi is meant for *Varuna*, it is not for me.

The *Savita*, *Savita Prana*, the *Vishnuh*, The *Vaishnava prana* and the briliant *Maruta*, the *Maruta prana* save us to day from those hundred and those thousand great bodily and worldly obstacles of the *Varuna* which are extending throughout, Whatever is uttered herein is right. The oblation offered in the fire of the is *Vedi* meant for *Varuna*, *Savita*, *Vishnu* and *Swarkah marutah*, it is not for me.

Agni is pervading in inner world and outer world both, it is the purifier of dirty things; it is for the benefit of all, it is quite true, it carries the substance of oblations to all the physical forces, and it provides us with the remedy through yajna. Whatever is uttered herein is right. The oblation offered in fire of the *Vedi* is meant for *ayasagni*, it is not for me.

Varuna, the Vital air throws away physical impediments developed in the upper part of our body, middle part of our body and lower part of our body. We should adhere to the ways of *Aditya* and obey the laws of nature inviolably. Whatever is uttered herein is right. The obiation offered in fire of the *Vedi* is meant for *Varuna*, *Adijya* and *Aditi*, it is not for me.

May *Jatavedasau* ,the outer and inner *agnis* be the source of our mental concordance, alround consciousness and perfection, may they be source of protection of our *yajna* and the performer of *yajna* and may they be auspicious for us on this occasion. Whatever is uttered herein is right. The oblation offered in the fire of the *Vedi* is meant for the two *Jatavedas*, it is not for me.

In all *Sanskaras* or ritual pronunciation in a sweet tone, neither quick nor in delay but in middle tone according to the pronouncing procedure of each *Veda* be done by *yajmana*. If the *yajmana* is illiterate, he must atleast make these *mantras* by heart. If any man performing the duty of *yajmana* is uneducated, dull in understanding and illiterate, he should be known as unaccomplished or uncultured & due to his being unable in pronouncing the *mantras* the *Purohita* and *Ritvij* should pronounce the *mantras* and the required actions should be made performed by him, the *yajmana*.

Purnahuti the completing Procedure of ahutis

Filling the spoon with *ghee* the performer of *yajna* should perform *purnahuti* with the following *mantra*.

ओ्रों सर्वं बै पूर्णं ॐ स्वाहा ॥

May all this be exactly accomplished.

By this *mantra* one oblation should be offered and it the same manner the second and third oblations should also be offered. Remuneration should be given to him who deserves it and to whom he desires to entertain with food should do this and give remuneration to him and thus all should be given leave. Afterwards the ladies and gentlemen of the family first eat the remaining *ghee* cooked rice or *Mohanbhoga* which is remaining after offering oblations. Afterwards they eat good food according to their choice.

Vamdevya ganam

The following *Vamdevy gana* of Samved as well as *mahavamedevam* should be performed positively in the sacraments from *Garbhadhana* to *Sanyasa*.

ओ्रों भूर्भुवः स्वः । कया नश्चित्र आभुवदूती सदा वृधः सखा । कया शचिष्ठया वृता ॥१॥

ओ्रों भूर्भुवः स्वः । कस्त्वा सत्यो मदानां मंहिष्ठो मसदन्धसः । वृढ़ा चिदारुजे वसु ॥२॥

ओ्रों भूर्भुवः स्वः । अभी षु णः सखीनामविता जरित्तृणाम् । शतम्भवास्यूतये

साम, उत्तरार्चिक १-३-१, २, ३

God is existent, conscious and all-blissful. He is always mature, unique and friend of all. May He come to our help with His pleasant protection and in auspicious intelligent manner.

God is existent, conscious and all-blissful. God, the greatest possessor of blessedness is true and all-beatitude. O man ! It is He who may make you happy and courageous with his power to overcome the internal enemies firmly.

O Lord ! you are the protector of the eulogizers who have attained great intimacy with you. Please come to our protection hundred times.

Mahavamdevyam

काऽ ५ या। नश्चा ३ इत्रा ३ आ भुवात् ।
ऊ। ती सदावृधः स । खा । औ ३ होहाई ।
कया २ ३ शचाइ ष्ठयौहो औ ३ हुम्मा २ ।
वा २ तों ३ऽ५ हाइ ॥ १ ॥
काऽ ५ स्त्वा । सत्यो ३ मा ३ दानाम् ।
मा हिष्ठो मात्सादन्धा । सा । औ होहाइ ।
दृढा २३ चिदा । रुजौहो ३ । हुम्मा २ ।
वाऽ ३ सो ३ ऽ ५ हायि ॥२॥
आऽ ५ भी । षु णा ३ : सा ३ खीनाम् ।
आ । विता जरायितॄ । णाम् औ २३ हो ।
हायि शता २३ म्भवा । सियौ हो ३ ।
हुम्मा २ । ताऽ २ यो ३ऽ ५ हायि ॥ ३ ॥
साम० उत्तरार्चिके । अध्याये १ खं० ३ ॥
मं० १, २, ३

HOSPITALITY

House-holding men and women, workers, righteous, prominent, compassionate gentlemen, learned persons, unattached impartial monks who are always engaged in the advancement of knowledge and in doing good of all should be given due respect with provision of obeisance. seat, grain, water, clothes, pots, money and gift according to *yajmana's* own possessions and means.

Those who have participated as spectators should also be given leave with due respect. Those who desire to see the per formance of sacraments should take their seats separately and keep quiet without indulging in any kind of talks or uproar. All should be attentive and of delightful faces. The performers specified act and priests should discharge their functions in peace, tolerance, discrimination and accordance with procedure This common procedure should be performed in all the sacraments.

—Here ends the comman procedure Chapter.

———

Sacrament of Impregnation

निषेकादिश्मशानान्तो मन्त्रैर्यस्योदितो विधिः । मनु० २अ—श्लो० १६

For the fitness and sound development of the physique and spirit of the people there are prescribed sixteen sacraments beginnig from the ceremony of impregnation to the consignment to fire the mortal remains of the dead after death.

From the beginning to the body through impregnation and to the cremation of the body there are 16 *Sansharas* which are very noble acts of refinements. The impregnation is the first of them. *Garbhadhana* is that act or method in or by which the impregnation is ensured or materialized, seed fluid for conception is established or made firm.

As the grains become good and fide by the fertility and soundness of field and seed so the progeny becomes good and refined by the maturity of strong females and males. Therefore, for the fulfilment of thy conditions of this ceremony the girl (wife) should atleast be of 16 years having full blooming youth, having practised the disciplines of celibacy and having completed her education. The man (the husband) surely should atleast be of 25 years. It is better if they possess more ages.

Without attaining the age of 16 years the womb of the female has no capacity for the development of the foetus and her body does not become fit and mature to ensute and preserve the conception. The power of procreation or virility in a man is not ripe unless he attains the age 25 years. In this connection the following is the medical authority.

पंचविंशे ततो वर्षे पुमान्नारी तु षोडशे ।
समत्वागत वीर्यौ तौ जानीयात् कुशलोभिषक् ।।

सुश्रु० ३५ अ० । १३ श्लोक

ऊनषोडशवर्षायामप्राप्तपञ्चविंशतिम् ।
यद्याधत्ते पुमान् गर्भं कुक्षिस्थः स विपद्यते ॥ २ ॥
जातो वा न चिरं जीवेज्जीवेद्वा दुर्बलेन्द्रियः ।
तस्मादत्यन्तबालायां गर्भाधानं न कारयेत् ॥ ३ ॥
सुश्रुत० १० अ० । ५४-५५ श्लोक

These are the *Shlokas* of *Sushruta* (a treaties of *Ayurvedie* sciences). The procedure of growth and declination, maturity and immaturity of body described in the *Ayurveda* treatises has no parallel elsewhere. The fundamental principles of *Ayurveda* in this connection which whould be written in the *Vedarambha Sanskara,* include idea and details of the growth and declination maturity and immaturity of essential ingredients of the body in correspondence with the years of the age. Therefore it is necessary to take special advantage & support of the *Ayurvedic scriptures* in performing these rituals of *Garbhadhana* etc.

Be attentive to this fact that the highest medical authority, the author of the *Sushruta* whose authority is accepted by all the learned persons fixes the time of marriage and impregnation at the completion of atleast 16 years of the age of the female and completion of twenty five years of the age in the case of male. A female of 16 years and a male of 25 years at least are fit for marriage and impregnation. Whatsover copicity and strength in her body a girl acquires at her sixteens correspondingly the same is aquired by a male of twenty five years of age. It is why the medical authorities treat them of equal capacity and strength. 1.

If the male who has not attained the age of 25 years impregnate a female who is less then 16 years in her age the foetus will face decay even in the womb of the mother. 2.

If any child from such an impregnation is born it would not survive long, if any how survives would be weak in its body and limbs. Therefore it is obligatory that one should not any how ever impregnate the woman who is less than 16 years in her age.

In the same treatise of the *Sushruta* it has been also mentioned:—

चतस्रोऽवस्थाः शरीरस्य वृद्धियौंवनं संपूर्णता किञ्चित्परिहाणश्चेति । आषोडशाद्वृद्धिराचतुर्विशतेर्यौवनंमाचत्वारिशतः सम्पूर्णत्ता ततः किञ्चित्परिहाणश्चेति ।

सुश्रुत सूत्रस्थान अ० ३५ । सू० २९

From the age of sixteen onwards all the tissued of the body grow and the youth begins from age of 25th year and it completes at the age of 40 years. At this age the youth becomes perfect and all the tissues of the body attain maturity. Afterwards semen tends towards depletion to some extent. That is at the 40 years of age all the limbs and organs of the body are perfectly developed. Afterwards the semen produced from diet takes the turn towards declination.

Therefore, it is proved that if marriage is to be done soon the age of the girl should be 16 years and of the boy 25 years at least. The girl be of 20 years and the boy be of 40 years, this is the middle cours. The utmost and excellent period of marriage is the time when the girl attains 24 years age and the boy becomes of 48 years.

Those who desire the refined development of the family, good progeny and making it long-lived, characteristic, accomplished in knowledge, strength and ventursome, wise and prosperous should not under any circumstances do the marriage of girl attaining the age less than 16 years and the boy attaining the age less than 25 years. This is the act of progress that observing the discipline of continent in this stage, people impart education and good training to their children, so that progeny be good.

The Time for Impregnation

ऋतुकालाभिगामी स्यात्स्वदारनिरतस्सदा ।
पर्ववर्जं व्रजेच्चैनां तद्व्रतो रतिकाम्यया ॥ १ ॥

ऋतुः स्वाभाविकः स्त्रीणां रात्रयः षोडश स्मृताः ।
चतुर्भिरितरैः सार्द्धमहोभिः सद्विगर्हितम् ॥ २ ॥
तासामाद्याश्चतस्रस्तु निन्दितैकादशी च या ।
त्रयोदशी च शेषास्तु प्रशस्ता दश रात्रयः ॥ ३ ॥
युग्मासु पुत्रा जायन्ते स्त्रियोऽयुग्मासु रात्रिषु ।
तस्माद्युग्मासु पुत्रार्थी संविशेदार्त्तवे शुभम् ॥ ४ ॥
पुमान्पुंसोऽधिके शुक्रे स्त्री भवत्यधिके स्त्रियाः ।
समे पुमान् पुंस्त्रियौ वा क्षीणेऽल्पे च विपर्ययः ॥ ५ ॥
निन्द्याष्वष्टासु चान्यासु स्त्रियो रात्रिसु वर्जयन् ।
ब्रह्मचर्यैव भवति यत्र तत्राश्रमे वसन् ॥ ६ ॥

मनुस्मृति अ० ३, श्लोक ४५-५०

In this way the seers like Manu etc. have decidedly prescribed the time of impregnation. According to them the housholding man should always do the sexual intercourse in the properly prescribed time after the completion of menstrual course. He should keep away the idea of sexual intercourse with any woman other than his own wife. The woman on her own part should always be in this matter far away from any other man except her own husband who has been won through real marriage. The man who is avowed with his wife in nuptial vows and is happy with her, like a wife who is faithful to her husband does not live with another man except her own husband. should leave out the Parva (Purnima, amavasya, Chaturdashi and Astami) nights of the 16 nights prescribed for impregnation when he desires to perform impregnation in these Parva nights the husband and wife ought not to do sexual course.

The impregnation time of woman consists of 16 nights which begins from the commencement of the menstrual discharge and lasts till 16 days thereafter. Among these sixteen nights the first four nights when menstruation starting from the first day continues are abominable and odious for the purpose of sexual function. The husband ought not to touch his wife in these first, seeond, third and fourth nights and should not even drink water from her hands and the wife also on her part should not contact her husband in person. The wife should not do any physical or mental exertion at this time, should sit in segragated placc as in these four nights co-habitation is useless and source of chronical diseases. Rajas, a kind of luke-warm menstrual blood like the pus or suppurated matter from boil, discharges out.

Just like the first four nights, the eleventh and thirteenth night are also prohibited for the purpose of impregnation. The remaining other ten nights are auspicious and excellent for the purpose of impregnation.

Those who desire male child should know that the sixth eighth, tenth, twelfth, forteenth and sixteenth nights are appropriatly good for impregnation and those who desire female* child should realize this fact that these four nights, the fifth, seventh, ninth and fifteenth are well condlucive to their desired aim.[3] Therefore, the husband and wife desirous of male child ought to materialise the function of impregnation in odd nights.[4]

In the case of the man's semen being more and prevalent the male child takes birth while woman's semen being more and prevalent the birth of female child takes place. In the case of the semen of men and woman being proportionate in quantity and prevelancy the impotant boy and baren girl are born. The semen deprived of its normal properties and quantatively less in required proportion materialise no conception or it causes abortion.[5]

The house-holding man who does not carry out the sexual intercourse with his wife in those eight nights which have been previously prohibited for impregnation, is in real sense a celibate leading even the life of house-hold.[6]

उपनिषदि गर्भलम्भनम् ०१

(आश्व० गृ० १।१३।२

This is the word of Ashvalayana Grihyasutra. The procedure of impregnation should be followed in conformity with the procedure laid down in the Upanishad in this matter. The upanishad describes the same procedure as it has been laid down

Nights are counted here to denote that day time is prohibited for impregnation.

previously comprising that after marrying the man of 25 years with a girl of sixteen years and materializing impregnation at its appropriately prescribed time.

अथ गर्भाधान ᳪ स्त्रियाः । पुष्पवत्याश्चतुरहादूर्ध्वं ᳪ स्नात्वा विरुजायास्त-स्मिन्नेव दिवा आदित्यं गर्भमिति' ॥ २ ॥

This is the dictum of Paraskara grihyasutra. Similar to this is the command of Gobhiliya and Shaunakiya Grihyasutras. On the fifth day succceding the fourth one when woman starting menstruation has completed the course of discharging menses and has become totally free from it, or thereafter, on any day preceding the night when the man and woman desire to have sexual course for conception, the ceremony should be held with the letter and spirit of the verse. आदित्यं गर्भम्०

The yajna according to Samanya Prakarna should be performed with the odoriferous things prescribed for the purpose, first and thereafter the oblations with the following verses should be offered. The wife in this ceremony should sit in the left side of her husband and the husband as he likes, should sit in the east direction, of the Vedi keeping his in the west or in south or north directions keeping his face befitingly on his own choice. The priests of the ceremony should sit in four directions of the Vcdi at their ease.

ओं अग्ने प्रायश्चित्ते त्वं देवानां प्रायश्चित्तिरसि ब्राह्मणस्त्वा नाथकाम उपधावामि यास्याः पापी लक्ष्मीस्तनूतामस्या अपजहि स्वाहा ॥ इदमग्नये-इदन्न मम ॥ १ ॥

ओं वायो प्रायश्चित्ते त्वं देवानां प्रायश्चित्तिरसि ब्राह्मणस्त्वा नाथकाम उपधावामि यास्याः पापी लक्ष्मीस्तनूतामस्या अपजहि स्वाहा । इदं वायवे इदन्न मम ॥ २ ॥

ओं चन्द्र प्रायश्चित्ते त्वं देवानां प्रायश्चित्तिरसि ब्राह्मणस्त्वा नाथकाम उपधावामि यास्याः पापी लक्ष्मीस्तनूतामस्या अपजहि स्वाहा ॥ इदं चन्द्राय इदन्न मम ॥ ३ ॥

ओं सूर्य प्रायश्चित्ते त्वं देवानां प्रायश्चित्तिरसि ब्राह्मणस्त्वा नाथकाम उधावामि यास्याः पापी लक्ष्मीस्तनूस्तामस्या अपजहि स्वाहा ॥ इदं सूर्याय इदन्न मम ॥ ४ ॥

ओं अग्निवायुचन्द्रसूर्य्याः प्रायश्त्तियो यूयं देवानां प्रायश्चित्तयः स्थ ब्राह्मणो वो नाथकाम उपधावामि यास्याः पापी लक्ष्मीस्तनूस्तामस्या अपहत स्वाहा ॥ इदमग्निवायुचन्द्रसूर्येभ्यः-इदन्न मम ॥ ५ ।

ओं अग्ने प्रायश्चित्ते त्वं देवानां प्रायश्चित्ति रसि ब्राह्मणस्त्वा नाथकाम उपधावामि यास्याः पतिध्नी तनूस्तामस्या अपजहि स्वाहा ॥ इदमग्नये-इदन्न मम ॥ ६ ॥

ओं वायो प्रायश्चित्ते त्वं देवानां प्रायश्चित्तिरसि ब्राह्मणस्त्वा नाथकाम उपधावामि यास्याः पतिध्नी तनूस्तामस्या अपजहि स्वाहा ॥ इदं वायवे-इदन्न मम ॥ ७ ॥

ओं चन्द्र प्रायश्चित्ते त्वं देवानां प्रायश्चितिरसि ब्राह्मणस्त्वा नाथकाम उपधावामि यास्याः पतिध्नी तनूस्तामस्या अपजहि स्वाहा ॥ इदं चन्द्राय इदन्न मम ॥ ८ ॥

ओं सूर्य प्रायश्चित्ति त्वं देवानां प्रायश्चित्तिरसि ब्राह्मणस्त्वा नाथकाम उपधावामि यास्या पतिध्नी तनूस्तामस्या अपजहि स्वाहा ॥ इदं सूर्याय-इदन्न मम ॥ ९ ॥

ओं अग्निवायुचन्द्रसूर्याः प्रायश्चित्तयो यूयं देवानां प्रायश्चित्तयः स्थ ब्राह्मणो वो नाथकाम उपधावामि यास्याः पतिध्नी तनूस्तामस्या अपहत स्वाहा ॥ इदमग्निवायुचन्द्रसूर्येभ्यः-इदन्न मम ॥ १० ॥

ओं अग्ने प्रायश्चित्ते त्वं देवानां प्रायश्चित्तिरसि ब्राह्मणस्त्वा नाथकाम उपधावामि यास्या अपुत्र्या तनूस्तामस्या अपजहि स्वाहा ॥ इदमग्नये इदन्न मम ॥ ११ ॥

ओं वायो प्रायश्चित्ते त्वं देवानां प्रायश्चित्तिरसि ब्राह्मणस्त्वा नाथकाम उपधावामि यास्या अपुत्र्या तनूस्तामस्या अपजहि स्वाहा ॥ इदं वायवे इदन्न मम ॥ १२ ॥

ओं चन्द्र प्रायश्चित्ते त्वं देवानां प्रायश्चित्तिरसि ब्राह्मणस्त्वा नाथकाम उपधावामि यास्या अपुत्र्या तनूस्तामस्या अपजहि स्वाहा ॥ इदं चन्द्राय इदन्न मम ॥१३॥

ओं सूर्य प्रायश्चित्ते त्वं देवानां प्रायश्चित्तिरसि ब्राह्मणस्त्वा नाथकाम उपधावामि यास्या अपुत्र्या तनूस्तामस्या अपजहि स्वाहा ॥ इदं सूर्याय इदन्न मम ॥१४॥

ओं अग्निवायुचन्द्रसूर्याः प्रायश्चित्तयो यूयं देवानां प्रायश्चित्तयः स्थब्राह्मणो वो नाथकाम उपधावामि यास्या अपुत्र्या तनूस्तामस्या अपहत स्वाहा ॥ इदम ग्नवायुचन्द्रसूर्येभ्यः-इदन्न मम ॥ १५ ॥

ओं अग्ने प्रायश्चित्ते त्वं देवानां प्रायश्चित्तिरसि ब्राह्मणस्त्वा नाथकाम उपधावामि यास्या अपसव्या तनूस्तामस्या अपजहि स्वाहा ॥ इदमग्नये इदन्न मम ॥ १६ ॥

ओं वायो प्रायश्चित्ते त्वं देवानां प्रायश्चित्तिरसि ब्राह्मणस्त्वा नाथकाम उपधावामि यास्या अपसव्या तनूस्तामस्या अपजहि स्वाहा ॥ इदं वायवे इदन्न मम ॥ १७ ॥

ओं चन्द्र प्रायश्चित्ते त्वं देवानां प्रायश्चित्तिरसि ब्राह्मणस्त्वा नाथकाम उपधावामि यास्या अपसव्या तनूस्तामस्या अपजहि स्वाहा ॥ इदं सूर्याय इदन्न मम ॥ १८ ॥

ओं सूर्य प्रायश्चित्ते त्वं देवानां प्रायश्चित्तिरसि ब्राह्मणस्त्वा नाथकाम उपधावामि यास्या अपसव्या तनूस्तामस्या अपजहि स्वाहा ॥ इदं चद्राय-इदन्न मम ॥ १९ ॥

ओम् अग्निवायुचन्द्रसूर्याः प्रायश्चित्तयो यूयं देवानां प्रायश्चित्तयः स्थ ब्राह्मणो वो नाथकाम उपधावमि यास्या अपसव्या तनूस्तामस्या अपहत स्वाहा ॥ इदमग्निवायुचन्द्रसूर्येभ्यः-इदन्न मम ॥ २० ॥

दे० गोभिल गृ० प्रपा० २ ।खं० ५ ।सू० २—६, पार० गृ० कां १ ।कं० ११ । सू० १, २, मन्त्रब्राह्मण १ । ४ । १-५ ॥

इन बीस मन्त्रों से बीस आहुती देनी* । और बीस आहुति करने से यत्किंचित घृत बचे, वह कांसे के पात्र में ढांक के रख देवें ।

---

*इन बीस आहुति देते समय वधू अपने दक्षिण हाथ से वर के दक्षिण स्कन्ध पर स्पर्श कर रक्खे ॥

This Agni (fire), the best purifier by nature is the medium of all sorts of purifications amongst all the physical elements. I, the wisher of all prosperities and believer in the existence of Divinity and His words use this fire in various ways. Let this fire remove the invalid and inauspicious signs or bents of the limbs, if any from this lady. Whatever is uttered herein is true. This oblation offered is meant for Agni and it is not for me.[1]

This Vayu (Air) the best purifier by nature is the medium of all sorts of purifications amongst all the physical elements ..... The oblation offered is meant for Vayu and it is not for me.[2]

This Chandra (Moon), the best purifier by nature is the medium of all sorts of purifications amongst all the physical bodies... ... ...The oblation offered is meant for Chandra and it is not for me.[3]

This Surya (Sun), the best purifier by nature is the medium of all sorts of purification amongst the physical elements ... ... The oblation offered is meant for Surya and it is not for me.[4]

The fire, air, moon and the sun, the exellent purifiers by their nature are the media of all sorts of purifications. I, the wisher of all prosperities and believer in the existence of Divinity and His words use them in various ways. Let them remove the invalid and inauspicious signs and bents of the limbs, if any, from this lady. Whatever is uttered herein is true. The oblation offered is meant for Agni, Vayu, Chandra and Surya and it is not for me.[5]

This Agni (fire), the best purifier by nature is the medium of all sorts of purifications amongest the physical elements. I, the believer in Divinity and His words and the wisher of all prosperities use this fire in various ways. Let this fiire remove the husband-inflicting bents of the limbs, if any, from this lady. Whatever is uttered herein is true. The oblation offered is meant for Agni and it is not for me.[6]

This Vayu (Air), the best purifier by nature... ... The oblation offered is meant for Vayu and it is not for me.'

This Chandra (Moon), the best purifier by nature... ...The oblation offered is meant for Chandra and it is not for me.[8]

This Surya (sun), the best purifier by nature... ... The oblation offered is meant for Surya and it is not for me.[9]

These Agni, Vayu, Chandra and Surya, the excellent purifiers by their nature are the media of all sorts of purifications I, the believer in Divinity and His words, the wisher of all prosperities take advantage from them in various ways Let them remove ... ... The oblation offered is meant for Agni, Vayu, Chandra and Surya and it is not for me.[10]

This Agni (fire), the best purifier by nature is the medium of all sorts of purifications amongst all the physical elements I, the believer in Divinity and His words and the wisher of all prosperities use this fire in various ways. Let this remove the imperfect bents of the limbs, from this lady. Whatever is uttered herein is true. The oblation offered is mean for Agni and it is not for me.[11]

This Vayu (Air), the best purifier by nature... ... The oblation offered is meant for Vayu and it is not for me.[12]

This Chandra (Moon), the best purifier by nature... ... The oblation offered is meant for this Chandra and it is not for me.[12]

This Surya (Sun), the best purifier by nature ... ... The oblation offered is meant for this Surya and it is not for me.[13]

These Agni, Vayu, Chandra and Surya, the excellent purifiers by nature are the media of all sorts of purifications. I the believer in Divinity and His words, the wisher of all prosperities take advantage from them in various ways. Let them remove the anti-proligerous bents of the limbs from this lady. Whatever is uttered herein is true. The oblation offered is meant for is uttered herein is true. The oblation offered is meant for Agni, Vayu, Chandro and Surya and it is not for me.[15]

This Agni (fire), the best purifier by nature is the medium of all sorts of purifications. I, the believer in Divinity and His words and the wisher of all prosperities use this in various ways. Let this remove the imperfect bents of this limbs from this lady. Whatever is uttered herein is true. Thc oblation offered is meant for this fire and it is not for me.[16]

This Vayu (Air), the best purifier by nature... ... The oblation offered is meant for this Vayu and it is not for me[17]

This Chandra (moon), the best purifier by nature... ... The oblation offered is meant for Chandra and it is not for me.[18]

This Surya (Sun) the best purifier by nature... ... The oblation offered is meant for Surya and it is not for me.[19]

These Agni, Vayu, Chandra and Surya, the excellent purifiers by nature are the media of all sorts of purifications. I, the believer in Divinity and His words and the wisher of all prosperity take their advantage in various ways. Let them remove the imperfeet bents of the limbs from this lady. Whatever is uttered herein is true. The oblation offered is meant for Agni, Vayu Chandra and Surya and it is nor me.[20]

The twenty oblations should be offered one by each of the above cited twenty Mantras.* The ghee whieh remains after offering these twenty oblations, should be kept safe and covered in the pot of bronze.

Thereafter this procedure should be adopted to offer the oblations of the cooked rice. The cooked rice should be kept in one pot of silver or bronze and it should remain kept for a little time after mixing ghee, milk and sugar. When these mixtures are totally mixed in the rice, the one oblation with each of the Mantras should be offered on fire and whatever remains in the spoon of libation should be dropped into the water-filled pot of bronze placed before.

At the time of offering the twenty oblations the wife should continue to toueh the right shoulder of her husband throughout.

ओं अग्नये पवमानाय स्वाहा ॥ इदमग्नये पवमानाय— इदन्न मम ॥ १ ॥
ओं अग्नये पावकाय स्वाहा ॥इदमग्नये पावकाय— इदन्न मम ॥ २ ॥
ओं अग्नये शुचये स्वाहा ॥ इदमनग्ये शुचये—इदन्न मम ॥ ३ ॥
ओं अदित्यै स्वाहा ॥ इदमदित्यै इदन्न मम ॥ ४ ॥

पा० गृ० कां० १ । कं० २ । सू० ७ ॥

ओं प्रजापतये स्वाहा ॥ इदं प्रजापतये—इदन्न मम ॥ ५ ॥

पार० गृ० १ । ११ । ३ ॥

ओं यदस्य कर्मणोऽत्यरीरिचं यद्वा न्यूनमिहाकरम् अग्निष्टत्स्विष्ट कृद्विद्यात् सर्वं स्वष्टं सुहुतं करोतु मे । अग्नये स्विष्टकृते सुहुतहुते सर्वप्रायश्चित्ताहुतीनां कामानां समर्धयित्रे सर्वान्नः कामान्त्समर्धय स्वाहा । इदमग्नये स्विष्टकृते—इदन्न मम ॥

आश्व० गृ० १ । १० । २२, तुलना पार० गृ । २ । ११॥

विष्णुर्योनिं कल्पयतु त्वष्टा रूपाणि पिंशतु ।
आ सिञ्चतु प्रजापतिधाता गर्भं दधातु ते स्वाहा ॥ १ ॥
गर्भं धेहि सिनीवालि गर्भं धेहि सरस्वति ।
गर्भं ते अश्विनौ देवावाधत्तां पुस्करस्रजा स्वाहा ।
हिरण्ययी अरणी यं निर्मन्थतो अश्विना ।
तं ते गर्भं हवामहे दशमे मासि सूतवे स्वाहा ॥ ३ ॥

ऋ० मं० १० । सू० १८४ । (मं० १-३) । गोभि०
गृ० २ । ५ ९-१०) ॥

रेतो मूत्रं वि जहाति योनिं प्रविशदिन्द्रियम् ।
गर्भो जरायुणावृत उल्वं जहति जन्मना ।
ऋतेन सत्यमिन्द्रियं विपानं शुक्रमन्धस । इन्द्रस्येन्द्रियमिदं पयोऽमृतं मधु स्वाहा ॥ ४ ॥ यजु० अ० १९ । मं ७६ ॥

यत्ते सुसीमे हृदयं दिवि चन्द्रमसि श्रितम् । वेदाहं तन्मां तद्विद्यात् पश्येम शरदः शतं जीवेम शरदः शतं शृणुयाम शरदः शतं प्रब्रवाम शरदः शतमदीनाः स्याम शरदः शतं भूयश्च शरदः शतात् स्वाहा ॥ ५ ॥
पार० गृ० कां० १ । कं ११ । सू० ९, यजुर्वेद ३६ मं० २४ ॥

यथेयं पृथिवी मही भूतानां गर्भमादधे ।
एवा ते ध्रियतां गर्भो अनु सूतं सवितवे स्वाहा ॥ ६ ॥

यथेयं पृथिवी मही दाधारेमान् वनस्पतीन् ।
एवा ते ध्रियतां गर्भो अनु सूतुं सवितवे स्वाहा ॥ ७ ॥

यथेयं पृथिवी मही दाधार पर्वतान् गिरीन् ।
एवा ते ध्रियतां गर्भो अनु सूतुं सवितवे स्वाहा ॥ ८ ॥

यथेयं पृथिवी मही दाधार विष्ठितं जगत् ।
एवा ते ध्रियतां गर्भो अनु सूतुं सवितवे स्वाहा ॥ ९ ॥

अथर्व० कां० ६ । सू० १७ । (मं० १-४)॥

ओं भूरग्नये स्वाहा ॥ इदमग्नये-इदन्न मम ॥ १ ॥
ओं भुवर्वायवे स्वाहा ॥ इदं वायवे इदन्न मम ॥ २ ॥
ओं स्वरादित्याय स्वाहा ॥ इदमादित्याय-इदन्न मम ॥ ३ ॥
ओं अग्निवाय्वादित्येभ्यः प्राणापानव्यानेभ्यः स्वाहा ॥
इदमग्निवाय्वादित्येभ्यः प्राणापानव्यानेभ्यः इदन्न मम ॥ ४ ॥

(गोभि० गृ० १ । ८ । १५ ।)

पश्चात् नीचे लिखे मंत्रों से घृत की दो आहुती देनी—

ओं अयास्यग्नेर्वषट्कृतं यत्कर्मणोऽत्यरीरिचं देवा गातुविदः स्वाहा ॥ इदं देवेभ्यो गातुविद्भ्यः इदन्न मम॥ १ ॥

(पार० कां० १ । कं २ । सू० ११)॥

ओं प्रजापतये स्वाहा ॥ इदं प्रजापतये-इदन्न मम ॥ २ ॥

(पार० गृ० १ । ११ । ३)॥

इन कर्म और आहुतियों के पश्चात् पृष्ठ में लिखे प्रमाणे "ओं यदस्य कर्मणोऽत्यरीरिचं०' । आश्व० गृ० १ । १० । २२) ॥ इस मन्त्र से एक स्विष्टकृत् आहुति घृत की देवें ।

ओं आदित्यं गर्भं पयसा समङ्ग्धि सहस्रस्य प्रतिमां विश्वरूपम् ।
परिङ्धि हरसा माभि मंस्थाःशतायुषं कृणुहि चीयमानः ॥ १ ॥

(यजु० अ० १३ । मं० ४१) ॥

सूर्यो नो दिवस्पातु वातो अन्तरिक्षात् अग्निर्नः पार्थिवेभ्यः ॥ २ ॥

जोषा सवितर्यस्य ते हरः शतं सवां अर्हति ।
पाहि नो दिद्युतः पतन्त्या ॥ ३ ॥

चक्षुर्नो देवः सविता चक्षुर्न उत पर्वतः । चक्षुर्धाता दधातु नः ॥ ४ ॥

चक्षुर्नो धेहि चक्षुषे चक्षुर्विख्यै तनूभ्यः । सं चेदं वि च पश्येम ॥ ५ ॥

सुसंदृशं त्वा वयं प्रति पश्येम सूर्य । वि पश्येम नृचक्षसः ॥ ६ ॥

(ऋ० मं १० । सू० १५८ । मं १-५)

Agni, the fire present in digestion system is Pavamana, remover of all diseases. Whatever is uttered herein is true. The oblation offered is meant for Agni Pavamana and it is not for me.[1]

Agni, the fire is Pavaka, the disinfectant agent. Whatever is uttered herein is true. The oblation offered is meant for Agni Pavaka and it is not for me.[2]

Agni, the fire is Shuchi, the galvanizing and purifying electrical, property. Whatever is uttered herein is true. The oblation offered is meant for Agni Shuchi and it is not for me.[3]

This Agni is Aditi, the indivisible unit of heat, light and magnitism. Whatever is uttered herein is true. The oblation offered is meant for Aditi and it is not for me.[4]

Prajapati,the wind protecting the creature is the element which preserves. Whatever is uttered herein is true. The oblation offered is meant for Prajapati and it is not for me.[5]

Whatever in this performance I have done going out of the procedure, whatever I have left out of it with negligence let all that be traced out and corrected by the learned man who knows to perform the act in noble way. May He perfect our acts to befit them in the procedure adopted to serve the yajnagni which fulfils the desired ends of the yajmana for the sake of which all the oblations of recipisence are offered and which is the source of producing good and is the consumer of the offered oblations.

May He fulfil our aspirations. Whatever is uttered herein is true. The oblation in the fire of the Vedi is meant for swistakrit Agni and it is not for me.[6]

With these six Mantras cited above the oblations of cooked rice shoul be offered. Afterwards eight oblations should be offered with the eight Mantras of Astajyahutis written in the Samanya Prakarana. Eight oblations with these Astyajyahuti Mantras, one with each and further oblations of ghee should be offered with the following Mantras :—

O lady ! Let Vishnu, the vital air which has direct connection with task of conception develop your womb to facilitate conception- let tvastar, the sunlight help in formation of forms of embryo, let Prajapati, the vital air known as Prana give life and envigoration to it, let Dhatar, the preserving apana perserve the embryo.[1]

O beautiful lady ! let you be conceived, O learned wife ! let you be pregnant and let Ashvinau, the Prana and apana which are present in the space of heart preserve and protect your embryo.[2]

We desire the child in your womb which Ashvinau the Prana and Apana that are respendent and source of bodily motion and purity, come from the womb in the tenth month.[3]

The male organ entering into the organ of female releases genitive fluid while othewise it releases urine. The embryo covered with secundine leaves out the skin-cover of it by taking birth. The soul of the embryo through the law of nature retains the organic power and the protective diet, the essance of eatable the milk and honey etc. which is a nectar for it. Whatever is uttered herein is true,[4]

O Wife ! you are well dressed in your hair. Really your heart is fixed in moon in the sky i. e. you are full of pleasure and I realize this fact and the present tendency of your mind. Let your mind know my mind also. May we both have the sight into our eyes for hundred autumns may we both live hundred autumns, may be both hear hundred autumns, may we both have the power of speech for hundred autumns, may we both enjoy freedom for hundred autumns and if we attain a life longer than this, may all these privileges be granted further. Whatever is uttered herein is truc.[5]

O Wife 1 As this mighty earth in the beginning conceived the germ of all the creatures. So may the germ of life be laid in you and you bear it to give a suitable birth and to gain glamour and grace. Whatever is uttered herein is true.[6]

As this mighty earth has borne and bears the grand forest of these trces so may the germ of life be laid in you and you bear it to give a suitable birth and to gain glamour and grace. Whatever is uttered herein is true.[7]

As this mighty earth has borne and bears the mountains and hills so may the germ of life be laid in you ro give suitable birth and to gain glamour and grace. Whatever is uttered herein is true.[8]

As this mighty earth supports the moving world that dwells thereon, may the germ of life be laid in you to give suitable birth and gain glamour and grace.[9]

After having offered nine oblations of the *ghee* and *Mohan-bhoga* with these above cited *Mantras*, the four oblations should be offered with the following *Mantras* ;—

श्रों भूरग्नये स्वाहा । इत्यादि

(*For the translation of these Mantrns, see Samanya Prakrana*)

Thereafter two oblations of *ghee* should be offered with the following *Mantras.*

श्रोम् अयास्याग्ने० । इत्यादि

O Agni ! the expert of *Yajna Vidya* ! let the *Havana* which has been performed by the medium of fire and whatever has been performed more than the proper procedure, be permanent.[9]

This oblation is meant to obey the command of *Prajapati*,

the Lord of the creation. Whatever is uttered herein is true. This oblation is meant for *Prajapati* and it is not for me.

After this performance and oblations the oblation of *ghee* for *Swistakrit* with the *Mantra* यदस्य कर्मणो० should be offered.

The wife should take that remaining *ghee* which has been dropped in the waterfilled bronze pot put before and which is the remaining part of the libations which have been offered with these *mantras* and going to the bath room should rub it on her body from the foot-nails to head and take bath. Thereafter she should rub the body with clean cloth and wearing on neat and clean clothes come near the *yajna kunda*. The wife and husband both should circum-ambulate the *Kunda* and see sun. Seeing the sun they should pronounce the following *mantras* and meditate God through them.

ओम् आदित्यं गर्भम्०

O Almighty Divinity ! make powerful and beautiful with the milk, juice of the fruits and herbs eaten by mother the child in the womb who is the measurement of the wordly objects and the model of the universe. Please remove the obstacles in its way by your power and save it from infliction. Make the daily growing embryo to live the life of hundred years.

O God ! by Thy grace may the sun save us from the troubles and tragedies of the heavenly region. May the air save us from the troubles and tragedies of firmaments and may the fire from the troubles and catastrophes of earthly regions.[2]

O All-creating God ! pour Thy mercy upon us. May your strength whieh is the powerful source of performing hundreds of *yajnas* and good deeds, protect us. O Lord ! protect us from the lightnings falling from the clouds.[3]

Let the sun be full of light and lustres for us, let the cloud be resplendent for us and let the air give us sight.[4]

O God ! please grant us sight to see through eye and grant us light for making our limbs illuminated with their natural functions so that we may see the world of multifarions varieties.[6]

O All-inspiring Lord ! may we see Thee who is the watching observer of all the creature and may we look at the things which are discerniblc by the men.[6]

Meditating God· with above cited *mantras* the wife pronounce as:

ओम् अमुक[1] गोत्रा शुभदा, अमुकदा[2] (नाम्नी)
अहं भो भवन्तमभिवादयामि। (तु० गोभिल गृह्य० २।४।११)

and salute her husband. She should, afterwards, also offer her best compliments to father, grand father etc. of her husband and respectable men and women, family members and old ladies of relations including the mother of her husbaud.

Thus, after the bride have belonged to the *gotra* of her husband, i.e. after the bride assuming wife-hood and the husband husband-hood, the wife and husband both sitting on a nice seat in the west of the *Vedi* keeping their facces eastward should sing the *Vamddevyagana.*

Afterwards both[3] should take their meal as has been described in the *Shastras* and give leave to priests etc. including the gathering with due respect entertaining them with food according to their own circumstances.

---

1. At this place bride should pronounce the Gotra or Kula of her husband.
2. At this place bride should pronounce her name.
3. The main cause of making the progeny good is dependent on the prescribed diet of wife and husband. Therefore, the wife and husband should use all the herbs which increase strength and intellect, for the vigour of body and spirit. These herbs are :—

   Two pieces of आंवा हल्दी, हल्दी, (turmeric) चन्दन, (Sandal) मुरा (this name is prominent in Southern India), कुष्ठ or (Costus speciosus Aralucus,) जटामासी, Asparagus Racemosus, मीवबेल (this is also prominent in Southern India), शिलाजीत (Rock-exudation कपूर (Camphor), मुस्ता (Cyperus Rotundus) भद्रमोथ a kind of Cyperus.

All these herbs should be powdered and taking all of them in equal proportlon mixing with a considerable quantity of cow milk should be curoled to form curd in the pot made of the wood of उदुम्बर (Ficus Glomerata), This curd should be churend by the churning wheel of उदुम्बर and by this process butter should be drawn away from that. The butter thus prepared should be turned to **ghee**. In **ghee** should be mixed flagrant things like केसर (Crocus Sativus or saffron), कस्तूरी (Musk), जायफल (Nutmeg), इलायची (Feronia Elephantum) and जावित्री. The proportion should be 50 gm of the herb's powder in one seer of cow milk. When the **ghee** from this milk has been made by the previously prescribed procedure. ·05 रत्ती musk, gm Saffron and one gm of each of the **Jayphal** (Nutmeg) etc. should be mixed therein (i.e. in the **ghee**). Every day in the morning the four oblations fo **Agharavajyabhagahuti** (beginning with भूरग्नये स्वाहा) and seven oblations with the seven **Mantras** of this impregnation ceremony (beginning with विष्णुर्योनिं० and ending with अनुसूतुं सवितवे) of the seventh **Mantra** arranged in serial order should be offered by adding the word स्वाहा to each of them if not already added to, and the night in which the function of impregnation is to be performed this **Havana** should be performed in the day which the impregnation night follows. The both of the wife and husband should eat the same **ghee** by mixing it in खीर or rice according to their choice and liking.

If the impregnation is performed in conformity to this method there may be born a characteristsc, long-living, brilliant strong and wholesome male child, If thera arises the desire of female child the rice should be boild in water and should be eaten by them with the curd curdied in the pots of Udumbar wood according to the procedure described provïously. By doing so a good female child may be born. The reason for this is :

"आहार शुद्धौ सत्त्वशुद्धिः सत्त्वशुद्धौ ध्रुवास्मृति."

(छान्दो० उप० प्रपा० ७। खण्ड २६। प्रवाक २॥)

This is the words of **Chandogya**. This means that the pure diet quite free from the intoxicants, meats etc. like **ghee**, milk etc. rice, wheat etc. when taken purifies the internal organic

Afterwards at a fixed time in the night when the body of both (the wife and husband) is in a wholesome state, both of them feel exceedingly hilarious and find them in a state of exuberant love, they should perform the act of sexual intercourse. The time of impregnation may be fixed at any time between the period from three houre passing of night and three hours remaining to pass. The wife and husband ought to keep their bodies stable, their face delighted, their mouths face to face of each others mouth, their noses vis-a-vis, their whole body straight at the time when the discharge of semen in the womb tends to nearest proximity. The germinating fluid be dropped by the husband. The wife realizing that the semen fluid has been dropped in her womb should contract the bottom of her rectum and uterous upward and establish the semen fluid in her womb by indraught.

Thereafter with temporary stop the wife should take a bath. If their is a cold season first they (wife and husband) should sleep separately after drinking, to their desire, the cold milk which had been boiled and prepared in Rotcleria Tinctaria (केशर) musk (कस्तूरी) nutmeg (जायफल) Mace (जावित्री) and Feronia Elephantum (इलायची) If the wife and husband are assured that

---

system and gives strength, perseverance, wholesomess and intellect. Therefore, man and woman enjoying the fully bloomed youth marry and after being married perform the procedure strictly and do the impregnation with love the progeny and the family would be refined accomplished day by day. When twelve or thirteen days remain in the time of menstruation in the moon-light part of the month the wife and husband should eat खीर mixed wtth this previously preseribed **ghee** upto twelve days and keep a striet discipline of celibacy fcr 12 day and living on restricted limited diet should perform impregnation functian in the previously prescribed period and thus attain very good progeny. This is the science of ennobling and excelling the progeny likc the sciences of refining, reforming and elevating the things. Men should pay an infallible attention on this matter as the absence of this brings deterioration, backwardness in the family while the presence thereof fatches the sure advancement and excellence of family.

the germitating fluid has been established they on the second day of the night of impregnation and if they are not assured of pregnancy, then after a month at the time of menstruation (that is on the second day at the beginning of the second month should offer the oblations with following *Mantras**. Here it should be borne in mind that in absence of menstruation it is sure that the lady has got pregnant. The *Mantras* of oblation run as follows :—

---

*If two times prescribed for impregnation, i.e. two times within two months, fail without conception and there be no pregnaney assured the husband, in the third month when the time prescribed for impregnation comes with the coincidence of **Pushya nakshatra**, at the first morning, taking two **mashas of the** curd of the cow of first proereation and two **mashas** of crushed roasted barley and mixing them should put into the hand of wife and should then ask her ("किं पिबसि" आश्व० १।१३।३) What do yon drink ? He should ask her thrice likewise, The wife should repply three times pronouncing. 'पुंसवनम्' आश्व० १।१३।३ and should eat that mixture. This procedure should be repeated thricc (in three days). Afterwards the husband should crush solanum (कण्टकारी) plant of white flower In water and sieve the liquid and drop it in the right nostril of his wife and pronounce this **Mantra :—**

ओम् इयमोषधी त्रायमाणा सहमाना सरस्वती ।

अस्या अहं वृहत्याः पुत्रः पितुरिव नाम जग्रभम् ॥

पार० गृ० कां० १ । कं० १३१

This herbacious plant is a safeguard against diseses, this overpowers them and is the product of the water which are the causes of it. By the effect of this powerful herb I like, a son, have got the name and light of my father and in the similar way the child take birth and grasp my name and splendour.

With this **Mantra** the husband praying God who controls and ordains the whole universe, proceed on with the procedure and course of impregnation prescribed in the scripture. This is the opinion of the author of above quoted **Sutra.**

यथा वातः पुष्करिणी समिङ्ग्यति सर्वतः ।
एवा ते गर्भ एजतु निरैतु दशमास्यः स्वाहा ॥१॥
यथा वातो यथा वनं यथा समुद्र एजति ।
एवा त्वं दशमास्य सहावेहि जरायुणा स्वाहा ॥२॥
दश मासाञ्छशयानः कुमारो अधि मातरि ।
निरैतु जीवो अक्षतो जीवो जीवन्त्या अधि स्वाहा ॥३॥

ऋ० मं० ५ । सू० ७८ । मं० ७ । ८ । ९ ॥

एजतु दशमास्यो गर्भो जरायुणा सह ।
यथायं वायुरेजति यथा समुद्र एजति ।
एवायं दशमास्यो अस्रज्जरायुणा सह स्वाहा ॥१॥
यस्यै ते यज्ञियो गर्भो यस्यै योनिर्हिरण्ययी ।
अङ्गान्यह्रुता यस्य तं मात्रा समजीगमँ् स्वाहा ॥२॥

यजु० अ० ८ मं० २८ । २९ ॥

पुमांऀसौ मित्रावरुणौ पुमांऀसावश्विनावुभौ ।
पुमानग्निश्च वायुश्च पुमान् गर्भस्तवोदरे स्वाहा ॥१॥
पुमानग्निः पुमानिन्द्रः पुमान्देवो बृहस्पतिः ।
पुमांऀसं पुत्रं विदस्व तं पुमाननु जायतां स्वाहा ॥२॥

सामवेदे ॥ (मन्त्रब्राह्मण १ । ४, ७, ९)

O Wife ! as the wind moves, on the sides, as the rivers so move your embryo in and come out from the womb as being ten month old.[1]

O ten month old soul in the womb ! as the wind freely moves, as the forest freely flourishes, and as the ocean moves without obstruction, so you take birth out of the womb with cover of embryo.[2]

O Lord of Universe ! may the soul, to be called *Kumar* in time, sleeping in the womb of the mother for ten months come out of the womb of the mother living alive and unmortified.[2]

May the embryo of ten months move and grow with his cover. As the wind moves without any obstruction and so this ten months old embryo take birth with secundine.

O lady of fortune ! the embryo that you have in your womb is the custodian of good knowledge and actions, your womb having such as embryo inside is free from all darkness, misfortunes, may I, the husband receive that embryo whose limbs are free from all kinds of infirmities. Whatever has been uttered herein is true.[3]

The two vital airs called *Prana* and *apana* are full of masculine power, the two electricities are also endowed with masculine power, the fire is full of masculine power and the wind is also united with masculine power may the embryo in your womb be male endowed with masculine strength.

This fire is endowed with manly vigour. *Indra*, the all- pervading electricity also possesses the manly vigour,*Brihaspati.* the Sun is the embodiment of manly vigour, may you get the male child, O lady and may by God's gruce the progeny succeeding him also be vigorous. Whatever has been uttered herein is true.

Having offered the oblations with these above cited *mantras* and also the oblations with afore—mentioned *mantras* of the *Samanya Prakarane* for the purpose of peace and tranqulity they should perform the procedure of *Purnahuti* as has been described in the *Samanya Prakapana.*

He should restrict the diet of his wife. Any kind of intoxicants purgatives like Terminailia Chebula हरीतकी etc., things of acidity like excessively saltish eatables etc, more sour things; dry grain etc,, pungeant things like chillies etc. should be avoided by her always. But she should eat *ghee*, milk, sweet, *Somalata* i.e. *Guduchi* (गुड़ची) etc. herbs; rice, sweet curd; wheat; *Urad* (उड़द), मूंग, तुआर etc. grains, the vegetables giving strength. In these eatables she should mix the spices according to seasons of cold and summer and eat them. In the summer season she should eat cold white Feronia Elephantum etc. and in cold season the saffron, musk etc. Always she should depend on restricted good diets. The woman in the time of pregnancy should particularly use dry ginger root and (ब्राह्मी) herb in milk. So that the child be intelligent, healthy and endowed with good qualities, actions and nature.

—Here ends the procedure of ceremony of impregnation.

Punsavanam

Here begins the ceremony procreating male or vigorous child.

The time of the *Punsavana* sacrament should be fixed in the second or third month from the period when it is known that pregnancy has been assured. The ceremony should be performed at the time so that there be advantage of vigour, Unless two months after the birth of child are elapsed the man (husband should remain intact in continence without spoiling the semen fluid even in dream, He should conduct the affairs of eating, clothing, sleeping, awaking etc. in such a manner as it could save the semen intact and help in making the other progeny noble.

Scriptural authourities on the subjeet :

अत्र प्रमाणानि—

पुमाꣳसौ मित्रावरुणौ पुमाꣳसाश्विनावुभौ ।
पुमानग्निश्च वायुश्च पुमान् गर्भस्तवोदरे ॥१॥
पुमानग्निः पुमानिन्द्रः पुमान् देवो वृहस्पतिः ।
पुमाꣳसं पुत्रं विन्दस्व तं पुमाननु जायताम् ॥२॥

सामवेदे (मं० ब्रा० १ । ४ । ८,९) ॥
(गो० गृ० प्र० २ । खं० ६ । सू०३, ११) ॥

Translation af these mantras has been given in Garbhadhan Ceremony :

शमीमश्वत्थ आरूढ़स्तत्र पुंसवनं कृतम् ।
तद्वै पुत्रस्य वेदनं तत्प्रजापतिरब्रवीत् ॥१॥
पुंसि वै रेतो भवति तत्स्त्रियामनु सिच्येत ।
तद्वै पुत्रस्य वेदनं तत्प्रजापतिरब्रवीत् ॥२॥
प्रजापतिरनुमतिः सिनीवाल्यचीक्लृपत् ।
स्त्रैं षूयकन्यत्र दधत्पुमांसमु दधदिह ॥३॥

अथर्व का० ६ । ११ । (मं० १-३)

This is the purport of these *mantrās* the man should be full of vigour.

This is the authority of Ashvalayana Grihyasutrā :—

अथास्यै मण्डलागारच्छायायां दक्षिणस्यां नासिकायामजीतामोषधी नस्तः करोति ॥१॥

प्रजावज्जीवपुत्राभ्यां हैके ॥२॥

आश्व० गृ० अ० १ । खं० १३ । सू० ५, ६ ॥

The husband in second or third month, make the pregnant wife smell the hairy root and new leave of banyan in her right nostril and other powerful herbs like Cocculus Cordicolius (गुड्ची) and (ब्राह्मी) should be given to her to eat. Similar is the authority of *Paraskara Grihyasutra.*

अथ पुंसवनं पुरा स्पन्दत इति मासे द्वितीये तृतीये वा ॥१॥

पार गृ० कां० १ । कं० १४ । सू० १,२ ॥

This is the proof from *Paraskara Grihayasutra.*

The *Punsavana* sacrament is that ceremony which is performed in the second or third month after impregnation tbe conception being assured.

So has been written in the *Gobhiliyā* and *Saunak Grihya Sutra.*

If the tree of Ficus Religiosa (अश्वत्थ) is mounting or climbing on the tree of Mimosa Suma (शमी) the use of this *Ashvattha* as a medicine in *Punsavana* make one able to have a male or vigorous child. We the house-holders perform these functions in our wives.

The male has semen and it is dropped in woman. Through this child is to be had it is the saying of *Prajapati,* the householding man.

Prajapati, the year or time keeps up female creating germ in other, i.e. in female and in male it maintains the male creating germ. This time of year, full moon night, dark moon night make the embryo perfect.

Now begins here the procedure

The priest and the performer of thc Ceremony should do the procedure of prayer, स्वस्तिप्रकरण and शान्तिप्रकरण. In doing prayer with the *Vedic mantras* विश्वानि देव० etc. the performer of *yājna* and the priest should pray God and the men present there should pay their attention to in meditation of God. They afterwards pronounce the *mantras* of *Svastivachana* and *Shantiprakarana* respectively. They making all sorts of arrengements place of *yajna*, *yajnashala*, *yājnakundā*, *yajnasamidha*, *yajnpatras* and other utensils of *yājna* should perform the procedure of अयन्त इध्म आत्मा०, ओमदिते०, four आघावाराज्याभागाहुति, four *Vyahriti* oblations, two oblations of and यदस्यकर्मणो०. ओं प्रजापतये स्वाहा Thereafter they should offer the oblations of *ghee* with the following two *mantras* :—

ओम् आते गर्भो योनिमेतु पुमान् वाण इवेषुधिम् ।
आ वीरो जायतां पुत्रस्ये दशमास्यः स्वाहा ॥१॥

आश्व० १।१३।६
अथर्व० ३।२३।२

ओं अग्निरंतु प्रथमो देवतानां सोऽस्यै प्रजां मुञ्चतु मृत्युपाशात् । तदयं राजा वरुणोऽनुमन्यतां यथेयं स्त्री पौत्रमघं न रोदात् स्वाहा ॥२॥

आश्व० १।१३।६

O lady ! may your vigorous embryo like arrow in its quiver go to the womb and hecoming ten month old may your strong child take birth smoothly and normally. Whatever is uttered herein is truc.

Agni, the fire first amongst all the physical elements by grace of God come to her protection and it save the offspring of this lady from the hold of immature death. *Varuna* the vital air may come to its co-ordination in this matter and this lady may not ever wail for the grief of her child. Whatever is uttered herein is true.

After offering oblations with the above two *mantras* duly pronounced, the husband keeping his hand on the heart of his wife in a lonely place should pronounce the following *mantra.*

ओं यत्ते सुसीमे हृदये हितवम्तः प्रजापतौ ।
मन्येऽहं मां तद्विद्वांसम् माहं पौत्रमघन्नियाम् ॥१॥

O well dressed lady ! Whatsoever embryo is present in the interior of your child protecting heart I feel myself the knower of it. I pray God that I might not ever receive the grief of immature death of son or child.

Afterwards they should sing the song of *Mahāvamadevya* which has been given at the end of *Samanyaprakarana* and give eave to men and women who came on the oecasion of this ceremony,

Then the husband crushiug very minutely new leaves of banyan and Coculous Cordicolius (गिलोय) and sieving the same with a cloth piece, put it to the right nostril of the pregnant wife to inhale it. Thereafter the husband should pronounce these two mantras as follows and put his hand on the womb of her wife—

हिरण्यगर्भः समवर्ततताग्रे भूतस्य जातः परिरेक आसीत् ।
स दाधार पृथिवीं द्यामुतेमां कस्मै देवाय हविषा विधेम ॥१॥
य० अ० १३ । मं० ४ ॥ —पार० गृ० १।१४।२

अद्भ्यः संभृतः पृथिव्यै रसाच्च विश्वकर्मणः समवर्ततताग्रे ।
तस्य त्वष्टा विदधद्रूपमेति तन्मर्त्यस्य देवत्वमाजानमग्रे ॥२॥
य० अ० ३१ । मं० १७ ॥ पार० गृ० १ । १४ । ३॥

The Divine Power who possesses all the luminous world with in Himself and exists from the very eternity, is the only one conspecuous Lord of all the created objects. He is sustaining this earth and the heaven, to that All-blissful Divinity we offer our humble worship.

God, the creator of the universe. creates in the beginning with His urge this world nourished by waters. earth and sun fixing its form, He assigns in the beginning the wisdom and duties of mankind.

Placing his hand on the womb of his pregnant wife the husband should pronounce the following *Mantra*—

सुपर्णोऽसि गरुत्मांस्त्रिवृत्ते शिरो गायत्रं चक्षुर्बृहद्रथन्तरे पक्षौ ।
स्तोम आत्मा छन्दस्यायङ्गानि यजूँषि नाम ।
साम ते तनूर्वामदेव्यं यज्ञायज्ञियं पुच्छं धिष्ण्याः शफा ।
सुपर्णोऽसि गरुत्मान्दिवं गच्छ स्वः पत ॥१॥
य० अ० १२ । मं ४ ॥ पा० गृ० १।१४·५ ॥

O soul in the womb ! may you have the swiftness of nice-winged swift bird, may there arise in your head the trio of action, contemplation and learning. *Gayatrt* be your eye, ***Brihat*** and *Rathantara* like your sides, *Rtgveda* your soul, metres your limbs, The hymns of *yajuh* are your name. The *Vamadevya* is your body. The deeds worth-doing and shunning are your hind part, The *yajnas* are like your hooves, the feet. You are a noble soul, and master of noble qualities. Acquire knowledge and attain to happiness in life and beyond.

After this the pregnant lady should live in a disciplined way and lead the life of restricted diet and confined movements. She should eat in a small quantity the cocculus cordiclius (गिलोय) ब्राह्मी herb, and dry ginger (सूंठ) with milk. She should not sleep more, should not talk more, should not eat more saltish preparations, should avoid to eat sour, pungent, bitter things and purgatives like Termunallia Chebula (हरीतकी) She should not be involved in the evils like anger, aversion, greed etc. and should always keep her mind delighted and thus such good conduets she should lead.

—Here ends the procedure of Punsavan*a *Ceremony.

Simantonnayana

Here begins the sacrament of Simantonnayana.

Now we tell you the third sacrament called *Simantonnayana* through which the mind of pregnant woman be made satisfied and healthy, conception firm and noble and grow day by day, Now we quote here the authorities :—

चतुर्थे गर्भमासे सीमन्तोन्नयनम् ॥१॥

आपूर्यमाणपक्षे (यदा) पुंसा नक्षत्रेण चन्द्रमा युक्तः स्यात् ॥२॥

अथास्यै युग्मेन शलालुग्रप्सेन (शलाटुग्लप्सेन) त्र्येण्या च शलल्या त्रिभिश्च कुशपिञ्जूलैरुर्ध्वं सीमन्तं व्यूहति भूर्भुवः स्वरोमिति त्रिः चतुर्वा ॥

यह आश्वलायनगृह्यसूत्र (अ० १। कं० १४। सू० १, २, ४, ५)

पुंसवनाप्रथने गर्भे मासे षष्ठेऽष्टमे वा ॥

(पार० गृ० कां १। कं० १५। सू० २, ३)

This is the quotation of *Pāraskara Grihyasutta* and this has been similarly written in *Gobhiliya* and *Shaunāka Grihyasutras.*

The meaning—

In the fourth month after time of pregnancy, on the day of moonlight when moon is connected with the stars which have masculine names *viz, Punarvasu ; Pushya, Anurvdhas; Mula; Shravana; Ashvini and Mrigshiras,* the procedure of *Simantonnayana* should be performed. Or like the *Punsavana* sacrament in the sixth or eighth month in the moonlight fortnight when the moon is connected with these *Nakshatras* the *Simantonnyana* be performed.

The Procedure—

After performing prayer, *Svastivachana, Shantikarana* and *Samanyaprakarana,* the water should be sprin led in the east ete. sides of the *yajnavedi* with the *mantras* अदितेऽनुमन्यस्व० and with the fallowing *mantra* on the four sides of the *Vedi*—

ओं देव सवितः प्रसुव यज्ञं प्रसुव यज्ञपतिं भगाय इत्यादि ।

After sprinkling the water on four sides of the *yajnavedi* the four oblations of *Agharavajyabhagahuti* and four oblations of *Vyahriti Ahuti*, (thus amounting to eight oblations in all) should be offered according to procedure mentioned in *Samanya Prakarnam.*

Thereafter pronouncing the *mantra* "ओम् प्रजापतये त्वा जुष्टं निर्वपामि the performers of the *Sanskura* should take rice. Sesamum Indicum (तिल) and Phaseolus Mungo in equal quantity (abbut 6 gm each) and wash it with water with *Mantra*— "ओम् प्रजापतये त्वा जुष्टं प्रोक्षाचि" After washing the ingredients he s hould cook them into one and mixing sufficient ghee in this cooked hotch-potch, he should offer eight oblations of this hotch-potch with the following *Mantras* :

ओं धाता ददातु दाशुषे प्राची जोवातुमुक्षितम् ।
वयं देवस्य धीमहि सुमतिं वा जिनवति स्वाहा ॥
इदं धात्रे इदन्न मम ॥१॥

अथर्व० कां० ७ । सू० १७ । मं० २, आश्व० गृ० १ । १४, १३
ऋ० खिल सू०।३ । मं० ७, निरुक्त अ११ । खं० ११) ॥

ओं धाता प्रजानामुत रायऽईशे धात्रेदं विश्वं भुवनं जजान ।
धाता कुष्ठीरनिमिषाभिचष्टे धात्रऽइद्धव्यं घृतवज्जुहोत स्वाहा ॥
इदं धात्रे-इदन्न मम ॥२॥

—आश्व० गृ० १ । १४ । ३, ऋ० खिल सूक्त सं० ३ मं ६ ॥

ओं राकामहं सुहवां सुष्टुती हुवे शृणोतु नः सुभगा बोधतु त्मना ।
सीव्यत्वपः सूच्या चिछद्यमानया ददातु वीरं शतदायमुक्थ्यं स्वाहा ॥
इदं राकायै-इदन्न मम ॥३॥

यास्ते राके सुमतयः सुपेशसो याभिर्ददासि दाशुषे वसूनि ।
ताभिर्नो अद्य सुमनाउपागहि सहस्रपोषं सुभगे रराणा स्वाहा ॥
इदं राकायै-इदन्न मम ॥४॥
ऋ० मं० २ । सू० ३२ , मं. ४।५ ॥

नेजमेष परा पत सुपुत्रः पुनरापत ।
अस्यै मे पुत्रकामायै गर्भमाधेहि यः पुमान्स्वाहा ॥५॥
यथेयं पृथिवी मह्यु त्ताना गर्भं मा दधे ।
एवं तं गर्भमा धेहि दशमे मासि सूतवे स्वाहा ॥६॥
विष्णोः श्रेष्ठेन रूपेणास्यां नार्या गवीन्याम् ।
पुमांसं पुत्राना धेहि दशमे मासि सूतवे स्वाहा ॥७॥
आश्व० गृ० १ । १४ । ३, ऋ० खिल सूक्त सं० ३४ । मं० १-३

O lady of vigorous progeny ! May God who sustains the universe provide the giver with life-giving herbs full of juice. We including you grasp and retain unto us good knowledge of that mighty power. Whatever is uttered herein is true, The Oblation offered is meant only for *Dhatar* and it is not for me.

The all sustaining Lord is the master of all the creatures and wealth. This whole universe has come into being by his power and wisdom. He, the upholdes of all is witnessing every moment the acts of all men. O men ! offer the oblation full of *ghee* for obeying the command of Lord, the sustainer of the universe. Whetever is uttered herein is true. The oblation offered is meant only for *Dhatar* and it is not for me.

I, the husband ! call my wife who is as beautiful as full moon night and possesses the good words for me, in all the functions of prayer and praise. Let her, the lady of good fortunes, listen to my words and understand them with her spirit. May she perform the functions of progeny in such a good way as she sews the clothes etc, with the needle which does not pierce the fingers at the time of sewing. May she give me a brave son. Whatever is uttered herein is true. The oblation offred is meant for *Raka* and it is not for me.

O full-moon-like beautiful lady ! Let you come to me with delighted heart accompanied by your those praise-worthy advices through which you give various physical and spiritual wealth to me who is of munificent nature. O lucky one ! come to me giving thousand kinds of fortunes, Whatever is uttered herein is true. The oblation offered is meant for *Raka* and it is not for me.

My husband who is potentially vigorous has established the germ fluid in me, who is desirous of a son or vigorous child. May my husband be free from all evils and accompany me with noble son.

As this grand earth in straight position contains in her the seed of various things so you, O lucky lady I establish in you the embryo to give it birth in the tenth month.

O house-holding man ! by the good grace of God you get the male child or vigorous child in this lady who is the owner of the animals like cow etc. born in the tenth month.

The seven oblations of hotch-potch offered by the above quoted mantras and one should be offered by the *mantra* 'प्रजापते न त्वदेतानन्यो', thus these become eight oblations. Again one oblation of cooked rice should be offered with the *mantra* 'ओं प्रजापतये स्वाहा' Afterwards one oblation of hotch-potch previously prepared should be offered by the *mantra*—यदस्य कर्मणो०

Thereafter offering eight oblations of *ghee* with the eight *mantras* beginning with त्वन्नो अग्ने० etc. and four oblations of *ghee* with the four *mantras* of *Vyahriti Ahuti* (ओं भूरग्नये०) the husband and wife should go to a lonely place and seat them on a good seat in order that the seat of husband be in the back of the wife.

ओं सुमित्रिया न आप ओषधयः सन्तु दुर्मित्रियास्तस्मै सन्तु योऽस्मान्द्वेष्टि यञ्च वयं द्विष्मः ॥१॥

यजु० अ० ६ । मं० २२

मूर्द्धानं दिवो अरतिं पृथिव्या वैश्वानरमृत आ जातमग्निम् ।
को वदं सम्राजमतिथिं जनानामासन्ना पात्रं जनयन्त देवाः ॥२॥
यजु० अ० ७ । मं० २४ ॥

ओं अयमूर्ज्जावतो वृक्ष ऊर्ज्जीव फलिनी भव ।
पर्णं वनस्पते नु त्वा नु त्वा सूयतां रयिः ॥३॥
पा० गृ० १ । १५ । ६, मन्त्र ब्रा० १ । ५ । १ ॥

ओं येनादितेः सीमानं नयति प्रजापतिर्महते सौभगाय ।
तेनाहमस्यै सीमानं नयामि प्रजामस्यै जरदष्टिं कृणोमि ॥४॥
मन्त्र ब्रा० १ । ५ । २ ॥ गो० गृ० २ । ७ । ६ ॥

ओं राकामहं सुहवां सुष्टुती हुवे शृणोतु नः सुभगा बोधतु त्मना ।
सीव्यत्वपः सूच्या छिद्यमानया ददातु वीरं शतदायमुक्थ्यम् ॥५॥

ओं यास्ते राके सुमतयः सुपेशसो याभिर्ददासि दाशुषे वसूनि ।
ताभिर्नो अद्य सुमना उपागहि सहस्रपोषं सुभगे रराणा ॥६॥

किं पश्यसि प्रजां पशून्त्सौभाग्यं मह्यं दीर्घायुष्ट्वं पत्युः ॥७॥
मं० ब्रा० १ । ५ । ३-५ । गो० गृ० २ । ७ । ८-१० ।

May the waters and herbs be friendly to us. May they be unfriendly or destructive to those diseases which harm us and whom we also dislike.

Just as masters of the science of archery, who are at the top of the learned, like the sun, that stands highest in the space, know the qualities of ores inside the earth, are well known for their good behaviour in the path of righteousness afford delight to all and are respected by all like a guest, protect mechanical arts by their selfless life, establish the qualities of lustrous fire as a king establishes the greatness of his country in the world so should all do.

O lady ! as this tree of Ficus glomerata (उदुम्बर) is full plenty of ripe fruits, so you become prolific with the arrival of good child. O proliferous lady ! may we be praising frequently your bud like child produce wealth with your co-operation.

The fifth and the sixth *mantras* are translated previously in this chapter.

Asks the husband. O lady ! what do you see here ? Really you are seeing in it progeny, animal, good fortune for me, and a long life for me, the husband.

Pronouncing these above cited seven *mantras* the husband should drop odiferous oil in the hair of his wife with his own hand and dress the hair with a comb. Afterwards he, taking the small smooth branch piece of अर्जुन tree, or the branch of smooth *Kusha* (कुशा) or the quill of porcupine (शाही पशु का कांटा) clean the hair of his wife, make two parte of hair-bunch and make a nice hair-bunch on her hind part of head. Afterwards both should come to the *yajnashala*. At this time the sounding instruments like वीणा etc. should be sounded. Afterwards song of the *Samveda Mantras* as has been given in the end of *Samanyu Prakarana* should be sung. In singing the *Mantras or Samvada* first they should sing the following *mantra* and other *Mantra* thereafter :

ओं सोम एव नो राजेमा मानुषीः प्रजाः।
अविमुक्तचक्र आसीरस्तीरे तुभ्यम असौ* ॥

पार० गृ० कां १ । कं० १५ । सू० ८ ।

May our King be possessed of peace and tranquility, may this human subject be blessed with happiness and prospe. rity. This is the river on the vast bank of which the people dwell.

Afterwards the pregnant wife, pouring plenty of ghee in the hotch-potch remaining from the offer of oblations, should see the reflected face of her in that *ghee.*

This time the husband should ask—"किं पश्यसि" what do you see ?

The lady should reply— "प्रजां पश्यामि" I am seeing progeny.

Then, thereafter the old noble ladies of own family of pregnant lady who possess good fortunes, who have children, sit

*Here the name of a river should be pronounced.

together and talk together and talk delightfully and pregnant bride should eat that hotch-potch and old ladies sitting near should shower blessing on her in this manner :—

ओं वीरसूस्त्वं भव, जीवसूस्त्वं भव, जीवपत्नी त्वं भव ॥

गो० गृ० २ । ७ । १२ ।

You give birth to brave child, you give birth to living child, you remain the wife of living husband.

These auspicious words should they speak. Afterward giving full respect and entertaining to participants of the ceremony ladies should see the ladies off and gents should see the gents off.

—Here ends the procedure of Simantonnayana

Jatakarma

Here begins the ceremony of Newly born child

The time, the scriptural authorities and the procedure of this ceremony should be followed as this :—

सोष्यन्तीमद्भिरभ्युक्षति ।

पा० गृ० कां० १ । कं० १६ । सू० १

The persons concerned sprinkle waters on the woman giving birth to a child.

This is the authority from Paraskar Grihya sutra and thus the same has been written in the Ashvalayana, Gobhiliya and Shaunakiya Grihya Sutra.

The procedure. At the time when delivery is going to take place the sprinkling of water on the body of the pregnant woman should be done with the *mantra* written belaw :—

ओं एजतु दशमास्यो गर्भो जरायुणा सह ।
यथायं वायुरेजति यथा समुद्र एजति ।
एवायं दशमास्यो अस्त्रज्जरायुणा सह ॥

य० अ० ८ । मं० २८, पा० गृ० १ । १६ । ३।

Let, still born, the ten-month old child move with the secundines, just as the wind moves, as the ocean moves uninterruptedly. so may this ten-month child come forth together with the secundines,

After sprinkling the water with the *mantra* the following *mantra* should be pronounced in mind and the *Marjana*, the water sprinkling act should be done again.

ओं अवैतु पृश्निशेवलं शुने जराय्वत्त वे । नैव मांसेन पीवरीं न कस्मिश्चनायतनमव जरायु पद्यताम् ॥

पा० गृ० १ । १६।२

कुमारं जातं पुरान्यैरालम्भात् सर्पिर्मधुनी हिरण्यनिकासं हिरण्येन प्राशयेत् ॥ आश्व० गृ० १ । १५ । १

O birth giving woman ! Let the cover of the foetus which has many forms and is somewhat stiff come out for the purpose of devouring by dog etc. Let not this spreading and swelling with flesh etc. fall down, O strong lady. By God's grace may not the secundine of any pregnant woman fall down abnormally to cause pain to her.

The father of the newly-born child should make the child to suck the *ghee* and honey rubbad in gold by giving it in the mouth of the child with the bar of gold, before the child born is being taken away with others (in their laps).

When the child has got born, the woman like the nurse etc, should first remove the secundine (the cover with which the child was covered in the womb) from the body of the child born aud clean at once the dirt from his mouth, nose, ears, eyes etc. and should put the child in the lap of its father cleansing it with a smooth cloth and thus making the child clean and neat.

The father of the child born sitting in the place where the wind and cold waves could not enter in, should cut the (नाल) navel-string of the newly born child by binding this (navel string) with a thread on the point of about nine inches above from the root of this navel string and in cutting this navel-string he should carefully cut the part of it above the tie of the thread leaving the nine inches part of it from the root place to the tie of the thread. He afterwards should bathe the child with luke-warm water, clean it with clean cloth, dress this child with new clean cloth and should come to the place of *yajna kunda* which should be prepared out of the house of the maternity or the place where the *yajna kunda* made of copper has been arranged. He should arrange the wood fuel in the *kunda* according to the method prescribed previously in the (*Samanya Prakarana*). He should perform the procedure of *Agnyadhana* and *Samidadhana* as has been described in the *Samanyaprakarana*. Afterwards, he enkindling the fire keeping safely the fragrant articles liek *ghee* etc. near the *yajnavedi*, washing hands, feet, should provide with one nice seat meant for ceremony-conducting priest in the southern side of the *yajnavedi* and the priest (*Purohita*) should sit on that keeping his face northward.

Yajmana, the father of the child born, should take his seat stretched in the west of the *Vedi* having washed his hands and feet, wearing a small cloth piece known as *upvastra.* keeping his face eastward. He, keeing all the things required for *yajna* near him and the priest, should for the acceptance of priesthood by the priest, pronouce—

ओं श्रा वसो सदने सीद ॥ (Please sit on the seat).

The priest should speak—ओं सीदामि (yes. I sit) and take his seat. Thereafter the priest should offer *yajna-sticks* of sandal wood in the *Vedi* with the four *mantras* prescribed in the *Samanya prakarona* beginning with the *Mantra* अयन्त इध्म. He should offer the four oblations of *Agharavajyabhagahutis* and four oblations of *Vyahriti Ahutis* on the fire flaming in the *Vedi*. Afterwards two oblations of molten *ghee* should be offered by following two *Mantras* :—

श्रों या तिरश्ची निपद्यते श्रहं विधरणी इति तां त्वा घृतस्य धाराया यजे सँराधनीमहम् । सँराधिन्यै देव्यै देष्ट्र्यै स्वाहा ॥ इदं संराधिन्यें--इदन्न मम ॥१॥

श्रों विपश्चित्पुच्छमभरत्तद्धाता पुनराहरत् । परेहि त्वं विपश्चित्पुमानयं जनिष्यतेऽसौ नाम स्वाहा ॥ इदं धात्रे इदन्न मम ॥२॥

मन्त्रब्राह्मण १ । ५ । ६, ७ ॥ गोभिल २ । ७ । १५, १६ ॥

I, thc husband, make happy, with offering the pour of *ghee* in the fire of the *Vedi* my wife who understanding her custodian of house-hold affairs, becomes fully concordant with me. I think, you, O lady ; the accomplisher of all the domestic purposes. I hail the glory of this lady who accomplishes homely works, gives all the dcsired things and is mighty force of the house. The oblation offered is meant for this accomplishing factor and it is not for me.

The wisemen call the progeny a point of family honour. God, who is the preserver of the universe also treats the child a point of family's honour. Therefore, O learned men ! you always come to us and preach for our well being, so that this my husband who bears such a name and is strong with vigour may again produce a child endowed with all admirabilities.

After offering these oblations with the above cited two *mantras* he should sing the *Vamadevya-gana* given in the end of *Samanyuprakarana* and perform the prayer of God as has been described in the beginning of *Samanyaprakarana*. thereafter, the father of the child should write ओ३म् syllable on the tongue ef the child with the already prepared golden bar dipped in the *ghee* and honey mixed properly. Doing so he should whisper वेदोऽसीति (your confidential name is *Veda*) in the right car of the child and then, with the bar of the gold make the child lick a little of the mixed *ghee* and honey with the following *Mantras* :

ओं प्र ते ददामि मधुनो घृतस्य वेद सवित्रा प्रसूतं मघोनाम् ।
आयुष्मान् गुप्तो देवताभिः शतं जीव शरदो लोके अस्मिन् ॥१॥

आश्व० गृ० १ । १५ । १ ॥

ओं भूस्त्वयि दधामि ॥२॥ ओं भुवस्त्वयि दधामि ॥३॥ ओं स्वस्त्वयि दधामि ॥४॥ ओं भूर्भुवस्स्वस्त्वयि दधामि ॥५॥

पार० गृ० कां० १ । कं० १६ सू० ४ ॥

ओं सदसस्पतिमद्भुतं प्रियमिन्द्रस्य काम्यम् ।
सनिंमेधामयासिषं स्वाहा ॥६॥

यजु० अ० ३२ । मं० १३,—गृ० २ । ७ । २१

O child ! for you I give this *ghee* and honey, I know that this *ghee* and honey has been produced by God who is the producer of all the wealth of the world, so you preserved and protected by learned men and parent attain long life and live in this world for hundred autumns.

I establish in you the idea of God who is the giver of life.

I establish in you, O child ! the idea of God who is all-beatitude. [3]

I establish in you, O child ! the idea of God who is the source of all movements. [4]

I establish in you the idea of God who is the life of all, all-beatitude and the source of all movements. [5]

May I attain Divinity who is the master of all the assembled masses of the world, who is wondrous and eternal, who is desired and attainable by individual souls and also the wisdom of discrimination.

After giving *ghee* and honey six times to the child to lick with these above cited six *mauiras*, the rice and barley in a very meagre quantity should be cleaned and crushed with water and the liquid thus prepared be seathed out through a cloth-piece and be kept in a pot. The father of the child or person concerned should drop a drop of this liquid in the mouth of child with thumb and the last finger taken together, pronouncing the Mantra as follows :

ओं इदमाज्यमिदमन्नमिदमायुरिदममृतम् ॥

मं० ब्रा० १।५, गो० गृ० २।७।२०।

This is *ghee*, this is grain or cerial, this is for life and this is immortality or the nectar of eatables.

This is the opinion of only *Gobhiliya Grihya-sutra* not of all others. Afterwards. the father of the child born, should keep his mouth with the right ear of child and pronounce the following Mantras :

ओं मेधां ते देवः सविता मेधां देवी सरस्वती ।
मेधां ते अश्विनौ देवावाधत्तां पुष्करस्रजौ ॥१॥

आश्व० गृ० १ । १५ । २ ॥

ओम् अग्निमायुष्मान् स वनस्पतिभिरायुष्मांस्तेन० त्वाऽऽयुषाऽऽयुष्मन्तं करोमि ।।२।।

ओं सोम आयुष्मान् स ओषधीभिरायुष्मांस्तेन०* ।।३।।

ओं ब्रह्माऽऽयुष्मत् तद् ब्राह्मणैरायुष्मत्तेन० ।। ४ ।।

ओं देवा आयुष्मन्तस्तेऽमृतेनायुष्मन्तस्तेन० ।। ५ ।।

ओं ऋषय आयुष्मन्तस्ते व्रतैरायुष्मन्तस्तेन० ।।६ ।।

ओं पितर आयुष्मन्तस्ते स्वधाभिरायुष्मन्तस्तेन० ।।७ ।।

ओं यज्ञ आयुष्मान् स दक्षिणाभिरायुष्मांस्तेन० ।। ८ ।।

ओं समुद्र आयुष्मान् स स्रवन्तीभिरायुष्मांस्तेन त्वाऽऽयुषाऽऽयुष्मन्तं करोमि ।।९ ।।

पा० गृ० कां १ । १६ । ६ ।।

O child ! may God the creator of all, bless you with firm wisdom, may Saraswati, the All-knowing God bless you with firm wisdom, may the sun and moon stationed in the space be the source of giving you firm wisdom. [1]

The fire is the source of life, it gains this power from the wood-fuel and I make you attain long life, O child ! with that life of fire. [2]

Soma, the moon is the source of life.........

.........with that life of moon. [3]

The knowledge and wisdom. is the source of life, it gains this power with the Brahmanas, the knower of the Vedas......... with that life of knowledge and wisdom. [4]

The enlightened persons are the source of long life, they gain this power through immortality......with that life of the learned persons. [5]

The seers, possessing penetrative genius are the source of life, they gain this power by the dint of austerity and discipline ....with that life of the seers. [6]

The parents, grandfathers etc. are the source of life, they gain this power from grain and various cerials.........with that life of parents, grandfathers etc. [7]

The yajna is the source of life, it gains this power through qualified ways of performance.........with that life of yajna. [8]

The ocean is the source of life,, it gains this power from the rivers.........with that life of ocean.

In the similar way these nine *Mantras* should again be recited in left ear of the child. There after, the father of the child born, putting his hand very gently on the shoulders of the child without making the it feel any heaviness of his hand, should recite the following Mantras :

ओम् इन्द्र श्रेष्ठानि द्रविणानि धेहि चित्तिं दक्षस्य सुभगत्वमस्मे ।
पोषं रयीणामरिष्टिं तनूनां स्वाद्मानं वाचः सुदिनत्वमह्नाम् ॥ १ ॥

ऋ०मं २ । सू० २१ । मं ६ आ० गृ० १।१५।३।

अस्मे प्र यन्धि मघवन्नृजीषिन्निन्द्र रायो विश्ववारस्य भूरेः ।
अस्मे शतं शरदो जीवसे धा अस्मे वीराच्छश्वत इन्द्र शिप्रिन् ॥ २ ॥

ऋ० मं० ३ । सू० ३६ । नं० १० ॥ शा० गृ० १ । १५ । ३ ।

ओम् अश्मा भव परशुर्भव हिरण्यमस्तृतं भव ।
बेदो वै पुत्रनामासि सं जीव शरदः शतम् ॥ ३ ॥

मं० बा० १ । ५ । १८ । आ० गृ० १ । १५ । ३।

O Lord Almighty ! please grant us excellent wealths, inspire unto us the consciousness of accomplished knowledge and action give the fortune of good children and body's pleasure. grant us the nicety of speech and prosperity of the days. [1]

O Lord Almighty ! Thou art the master of all worldly wealth and the object aimed attain by all. Kindly grant us that plentiful wealth to be desired by all. O Lord give us hundred autumns to live. O omnicient. All powerful Lord ! give us large mumber of brave and strog men.

O child ! by God's grace you become firm and strong like rock. become axe for wickeds and become bright in charactar and knowledge like the gold. You are the son of mine and Veda by confidential name so you live hundred autumns.

Afterwards he should recite in mind the following Mantra thrice.

त्र्यायुषं जमदग्नेः कश्यपस्य त्र्यायुषम् ।
यद्देवेषु त्र्यायुषं तन्नो अस्तु त्र्यायुषम् ॥ १ ॥
यजु० अ० ३। मं ६२, पार० गृ० १।१६।७।

May by God's grace there be three times life of my eyes, three times life of my vital airs, three times life and may that three times life of learned persons be attained by us and may it be three times for us.

There after he should take off the hands from the shoulders of the child and going to the place where the child was born should pronounce in mind the following *Mantra*.

ओं वेद ते भूमि हृदयं दिवि चन्द्रमसि श्रितम् ।
वेदाहं तन्मां तद्विद्यात्पश्येम शरदः शतं जीवेम
शरदः शतं श्रृणुयाम शरदः शतम् ॥ १ ॥
पा० गृ० का १ । कं० १६ । सू० १७।

O lady ! (the ground of child-birth) I know your heart and mind which got fixed in moon in the heavenly region and let it know me. May I and you be able to see hundred autumns, live hundred autnmns and possess the audibility of ears for hundred autumns.

The father of the child pronouncing the following Mantras should sprinkle fragrant water on the body of the lady who has delivered the child :

यत्ते सुसीमे हृदयँ हितमन्तः प्रजापतौ ।
वेदाहं मन्ये तद् ब्रह्म माऽहं पौत्रमघं निगाम् ॥२॥
यत्पृथिव्या अनामृतं दिवि चन्द्रमसि श्रितम् ।
वेदामृतस्याहं नाम माहं पौत्रमघँरिषम् ॥३॥

इन्द्राग्नी शर्म यच्छतं (प्रजायै मे) प्रजापतिः ।
यथायं न प्रमायते पुत्रो जनित्र्या अधि ॥४॥
यददश्चन्द्रमसि कृष्ण पृथिव्या हृदयं श्रितम् ।
तदहं विद्वाँस्तत्पश्यन माहं पौत्रमघं रुदम् ॥५॥
मं० ब्रा० १।५।१-१३, गोभिल गृ० २।८।४-७

O lady of attractive hair-bunch ; I know that of your heart which is fixed in the Lord of the creatures, that is very generous and I also realize this fact. May God be graceful to me so that I could not be subjected to pain caused by the absence of progeny.

O lady ! I know that of your heart which is the substantial product of earth and is fixed in the moon resident in heavenly space. I know it the lusture of immortality in this world. May I not be subjected to the pain caused by absence of progeny.

Let the fire and electricity which are the preserver of worldly subjects give us pleasure, in the way that this child in the lap of mother may not be subjected by immature death.

I knowing that black substance of the earth which is fixed in moon and carefully seeing it may not weep for the pain caused by the absence of progeny.

The father should bless the child with the following Mantras :—

कोऽसि कतमोऽस्येषोऽस्यमृतोऽसि ।
आहस्पत्यं मासं प्रविशासौ ॥६॥

स त्वान्हे परिददात्वहस्त्वा रात्र्यै परिददातु रात्रिस्त्वाहोरात्राभ्यां परिददात्वहोरात्रौ त्वार्द्धमासेभ्यः परिदत्तामर्द्धमासास्त्वा मासेभ्यः परिददतु संवत्सरस्त्वायुषे जरायै परिददात्वसौ ॥७॥

मं० ब्रा० १।५। १४-१५, गोभिल गृ० २।८।१३-१४ ।

O child ! who are you ? Amongst whomsoever are you ? Really you are this one of our souls. You are immortal. May God grace you to enter the month which is produced by the sun.

By God's grace may the sun give you to days, may the days give you for nights, may nights give you to day and night O child ! may day and night give you to half months, may half months give you to months, may the months give you to seasons, may seasons in their turn preserve you upon the full year, may the full year preserve you for life and timely maturity of age.

He again pronouncing the following Mantras should smell the head of the child. In the same manner he should smell the head of the child when he (father) comes from the journey of out stations, so that there grow more love between the son and parents.

अङ्गादंगात्सँस्रवसि हृदयादधिजायसे ।

प्राणं ते प्राणेन सं दधामि जीव मे यावदायुषम् ॥८॥

अङ्गादङ्गात्संभवसि हृदयादधिजायसे ।

वेदो वै पुत्रनामासि स जीव शरदः शतम् ॥९॥

अश्मा भव परशुर्भव हिरण्यमस्तृतं भव ।

आत्मासि पुत्र मा मृथाः स जीव शरदः शतम् ॥१०॥

पशूनां त्वा हिङ्कारेणाभिजिघ्राम्यसौ ॥११॥

मं० ब्रा० १।४।१६-१९, गोभिल गृ० २।८।२१-२२

O child ! you are born from every limb of my body, you have come to exist from my heart. I preserve your vital airs with my vital airs, O child live up to the life span prescribed to live normally.

O child ! you are born from every part of my body and have come to exist from my heart, you are my son and you are Veda in your confidential identity.

May you become firm and strong like rock, may you become like an axe to destory injustice, may you become as bright as gold with knowledge and action, O child you are my soul and spirit die not an immature death and live hundred autumns.

I smell your head with the lowing of animals.

Again, praying God with the following Mantras restoring the lady to a delightful mood father of child should wash the braces of the lady, (the mother of the child) with lukewarm odoriferous water and wipe them ;

ओम इडासि मैत्रावरुणी वीरे वीरमजीजनथाः ।
सा त्वं वीरवती भव याऽस्मान्वीरवतोऽकरत् ॥१॥

पार० गृ० कां० १ । कं० १६ । सू० १६ ॥

O brave lady ! you are like the idapatri of two vital airs, the *prana and apana*, you have given birth to a brave child. May you who has made us the possessors of brave child, be the mother of brave child.

The father of the child pronouncing the following Mantra should put the right brace of the child's mother into the mouth of the child ;—

ओम इमं स्तनमूर्ज्जस्वन्तं धयापां प्रपीनमग्ने सरिरस्य मध्ये ।
उत्सं जुषस्व मधुमन्तमर्वन्त्समुद्रियं सदनमाविशस्व ॥१॥

यजु० अ० १७ । मं ८७, निर्देश-पार० गृ० १ । कां १६ । सू० २० ।

O child ! yon keeping yourself strong and sturdy amongst your men suck this invigorating brace which has got fat with the flow of milk, You throughout your infancy affectionately suck milk from this brace full of palatable milk and thus enjoying the state of blooming strength you attain not only earthly knowledge but also the kuowledge of firmamant and heavenly region.

With the following Mantra he should put the left brace of child's mother into the mouth of the child :

ओं यस्ते स्तनः शशयो यो मयोभूर्यो रत्नधा वसुविद्यः सुदत्रः ।
येन विश्वा पुष्यसि वार्याणि सरस्वति तमिह धातवे कः ॥१॥

शत० ब्रा० १४।६।४।२८, पार० गृ० १। १६ । २१।

O lady of knowledge and wisdom you give to this child that of your brace which is in your body, which is the source of pleasure, by which you grow and strengthen all the limbs of the child, which has in it the qualities and effect of precious metals and intellectual strength and which gives strength and vigour to child, to suck it.

Afterwards, a jug full of water should be put on the earth in the side where the lady having given birth to child keeps her head and thus this jug should be kept there upto ten nights. The lady who delivered child should positively remain there in the place of delivery for ten days. The Mantra with which the jug of water be kept there runs as follows :

ओं आपो देवेषु जाग्रथ यथा देवेषु जाग्रथ ।
एवमस्याँ सूतिकायाँ सपुत्रिकायां जाग्रथ ॥१॥
(पार० गृ० कां० १ कं० १६ । सू० २२)

The water always remain effective amongst all the physical forces, as they remain activated in all the physical powers so they remain effective and activated in the place of maternity where the child has been born.

With the following two Mantras, there should be offered in the fire the oblations of cooked rice mixed with mustard seeds upto ten days in the place where delivery took place at each evening and morning when the night and day meet together :

ओं शण्डामर्का उपवीरः शौण्डिकेय उलूखलः ।
मलिम्लुचो द्रोणासश्च्यवनो नश्यतादितः स्वाहा ॥
इदं शण्डामर्काभ्यामुपवीराय शौण्डिकेयायोलूखलाय
मलिम्लुचाय द्रोणेभ्यश्च्यवनाय-इदं न मम ॥१॥
पा० गृ० कां० १ । कं० १६ । २३ ॥

ओं आलिखन्ननिमिषः किंवदन्त उपश्रुतिर्हर्यक्षः कुम्भीशत्रुः
पात्रपाणिर्नृमणिर्हन्त्रीमुखः सर्षपारुणश्च्यवनो नश्यतादितः स्वाहा ॥
इदमालिखतेऽनिमिषाय किंवदद्भ्यः उपश्रुतये हर्यक्षाय कुम्भीशत्रवे पात्रपाणये नृमणये हन्त्रीमुखाय सर्षपारुणाय च्यवनाय इदं न मम ॥२॥
पार० गृ० कां० १ । कं० १६ सू० २३ ॥

Let the diseases or germs creating diseases like death, inflicting pain, creating discomfiture to the child, the germs which seem like *Ulukhala*, the germs due to dirt etc., the germs which deform the nose, the disease creating general debility flee away from this place by God's grace.

Let the germs or diseases which always bite, making unintelligible sounds, active in approaching the child, having yellow eyes, creating puss in the nose treating like enemies, whose hands are like pot, killing the man, having violent and voracious mouths, red like mustard seed, causing decay, flee away from this place by God's grace. The oblations offered here are meant for these आलिखन् etc. and are not for me.

Thereafter, the highly learned, pious men subscribing to the vedic religion standing outside and the father of the child remaining inside should delightfully pronounce the following Mantras of the blessings :

मानो हासिषुर्ऋषयो दैव्या ये तनूपा ये नस्तन्वऽस्तनूजाः ।
अमर्त्या मर्त्यां अभि नः सचध्वमायुर्धत्त प्रतरं जीवसे नः ॥१॥
अथर्व० का० ६ । अनु० ४ । सू० ४१ । (मं० ३) ॥

इमं जीवेभ्यः परिधिं दधामि मैषां नु गादपरो अर्थमेतम् ।
शतं जीवन्तः शरदः पुरूचीस्तिरो मृत्युं दधतां पर्वतेन ॥२॥
अथर्व० कां० १२ । अनु० २ । (सू० २) मं० २३ ।

विवस्वान्नो अभयं कृणोतु यः सुत्रामा जीरदानुः सुदानुः ।
इहेमे वीरा बहवो भवन्तु गोमदश्ववन्मय्यस्तु पुष्टम् ॥३॥
अथर्व० कां० १८ । अनु० ३ । (सू० ३) । मं० ६१ ॥

Let not the mighty *Rishis*, the organs of our bodies, leave us. let not the protective bodily forces which are stationed in our bodies and which are produced from them leave us. Let these immortal powers remain united with the mortal bodies and let them provide us with a praisworthy life to live.

. I (God) enjoin the guiding principle of life for all living creatures; let not any one violate that principle; may all of us live a life of hundred autumns acting up in various ways and may all of us subdue death by the mighty force of (continent etc.)

May God, who throws away all ignorance and who is excellent protector, giver of everything and invigorator of energy make us free from fear. May there be many brave men in this world and may there be in me the strength and growth accompanied by cows and horses.

Now here ends the procedure of the ceremony of newly born child.

———

The Ceremony of Naming

Now we will speak of the ceremony of naming.

The authority of scripture on the subject :—

अत्र प्रमाणम्—नाम चास्मै दद्युः ॥१॥

घोषवदाद्यन्तस्थमभिनिष्ठानान्तं द्व्यक्षरम् ॥२॥

चतुरक्षरं वा ॥३॥

द्व्यक्षरं प्रतिष्ठाकामश्चतुरक्षरं ब्रह्मवर्चसकामः ॥४॥

युग्मानि त्वेव पुंसाम् ॥५॥

अयुजानि स्त्रीणाम् ॥६॥

अभिवादनीयं च समीक्षेत तन्मातापितरौ विदध्यातामौपनयनात् ॥७॥

तथा पारस्कर गृह्यसूत्रे इत्याश्वलायन गृह्यसूत्रेषु (आश्व० गृ० १।१५।४-१०)

दशम्यामुत्थाप्य पिता नाम करोति ॥ (१) ॥ द्व्यक्षरं चतुरक्षरं वा घोषवदाद्यन्तःस्थं दीर्घाभिनिष्ठानान्तं कृतं कुर्यान्न तद्धितम् ॥(२)॥ अयुजाक्षरमाकारान्तं स्त्रियै (तद्धितम्) ॥(३)॥ शर्म ब्राह्मणस्य वर्म क्षत्रियस्य गुप्तेति वैश्यस्य ॥(४)॥

पार गृ० १। १७। १-४

They (the parent, Acharya etc.) give name to the child.[1] This name should be formed of the letters of *Ghosha* (प्रयत्न) in the begining, अन्तस्थ letters in the middle and (विसर्ग) in the end. This name should be of two vowels or four vowels. This restriction is not applicable in the ease of the numbers of consonant letters. The child who seems endowed with the tendancy or instinct of observing the discipline of continence should have the name of two or four vowels and who similarly desires conspecuity should have the name of two vowels. Or the parent desiring their child to observe the dicipline of continent should give the name of four vowels to the child and those who desire their child to earn fame should give the child name of two vowels.

The name of the male child should be of even numbers of letters while of female child it should be of odd numbers of letters. One name of the child be given by *Acharya* so as it remain till the ceremony of sacred thread and this name be known by father and mother of the child.[7]

This is from the *Ashvalayava Grihya* Sutra.

Now we quote *Paraskara Grihyasutra.*

On the tenth day from the day of delivery of the child the father taking him from the maternity place gives the name to child.

This name be of two vowels or four vowels and the Ghosha (घोष) letter be arranged in begining and अन्तस्थ letters in the middle. The name be arranged in such a manner that दीर्घ letter vowel be in the end or as it be in the ancestral practice but the name should not be formed of तद्धित। The name of the female child be of odd letters and ending with आकार and it aslo could be तद्धित। The name of the child who promises to rise to the state of a *Brahmans* by worth should be followed with the epithet of शर्मा and वर्मा epithet be used for the child who promises to rise to the status of *kshatriya.* In the same manner the title *Gupta* (गुप्त) be used for the child who could be promising to rise to the status of *Vaishya.*

Accordingly it has been written in *Gobhiliya* 2/8/8-18) and the *Shaunaka Grihyasutra* that a very sound meritoriously attractive name should be given to child born.

The time of *Namakarana.* The name should be given to child on the 11th day leaving ten days from the day of the birth of child or on hundred-first day (101st day) or on the very day of the birth of child in the begining of the second year.

On the day fixed for giving name to the child the *yajmana* (the father of the child) and the priests of the yajna inviting cordially the gentlemen, friends and well-wishers and giving respect to them should start the procedure of ceremony.

After performing the procedure of prayer of God as prescribed in 8 mantras of *Samanya prakarana*, *Svastivachana*, *Shanti karana*, aad the complete procedure of *Samanya prakarana*, four oblations of *Aghavarajyabhagahuti*; four *Vyahriti* oblations, eight oblations with eight *mantras* beginning with त्वन्नो अग्ने as has been given in the *Samanya Prakarana*, should be offered. *Agharavajyabhagahuti* four, Vyahriti four and with eight Mantras of त्वन्नो अग्ने are totalled 16 oblations of *ghee*.

Afferwards, the mother of the child bathing the child with clean water, dressing him with nice and clean clothes, coming near the *yajnakunda* and passing behind the father of the child, standing on the right side of him (child's father) keeping the head of the child in north direction should hand over the child into the hands of the child's father and she herself returning from the back side of her husband (the child's father) should take her seat in the north side keeping her face in the east.

Afterwards the father of the child keeping the child's head in north direction and feet in south direction, should give the child to his wife (the mother of the child). Afterwards they should performed the procedure which has been mainly prescribed for the same ceremony and treated to be main *yajna* performance of it. Filling the spoon with *ghee* from the prepared and properly arranged *yajna-samagri* etc., *yajmana*, the father of the child should offer one oblation pronouncing this *mantra*:—

"ओं प्रजापतये स्वाहा" (गो० गृ० २/८/१२)

Thereafter four oblations—one oblation with each of the *Tithi*, *Nakshotra*, *Tithi devata* and *Nakshatra-devata*, should be offered. These *Tithis* and *Nakshatras* are ment and taken here in this context are the lunar dates and the stars on which the birth of the child took place.

These four oblations are counted in this manner:—first oblation in the name of *Tithi*, the second in the name of *Tithi devata* the third in the name of *Nakshatra* and the final fourth in the name of the *Nakshatra-devta*. The oblations should be offered by adding the *chaturthi Vibhakti* (i. e. making *sampradana*) in the names of the *Tithis, Nakshatras* and their*Devatas.* For example if the birth of child took place on *Pratipada* (the first lunar date) and there was in the sky the presence of *Ashvini Nakshatra* the oblations should be offered like thus:—

ओं प्रतिपदे स्वाहा ।

ओं ब्रह्मणे स्वाहा ।

ओं अश्विन्यै स्वाहा ।

ओं अश्विभ्यां स्वाहा ॥

गो० गृ० २।८।१२

Afterwards one oblation with the स्विष्टकृत् मंत्र which is written in *Samanya prakarana* and four *Vyahriti* oblations (see *Samanya prakarna*) and thus totalling five oblations in all should be offered.

Then the mother taking the child in her lap should sit on a nice seat and the father of the child should touch (examine) the

---

Foot Not : The *devatas* of the Tithis (the lunar dates) *nakashtras are as follows:—*

तिथि-देवताः- १-ब्रह्मन् । २-त्वष्टृ । ३-विष्णु । ४-यम । ५-सोम । ६-कुमार । ७-मुनि । ८-वसु । ९-शिव । १०-धर्म । ११-रुद्र । १२-वायु । १३-काम १४-अनन्त । १५-विश्वेदेव । ३०-पितर ।

नक्षत-देवताः—अश्विनी-अश्वि । भरणी-यम । कृत्तिका-अग्नि । रोहिणी-प्रजापति । मृगशीर्ष-सोम । आर्द्रा-रुद्र । पुनर्वसु-अदिति । पुष्य-बृहस्पति । आश्लेषा-सर्प । मधा-पितृ । पूर्वाफाल्गुनी-भग । उतराफाल्गुनी-अर्यमन् । हस्त-सवितृ । चित्रा-त्वष्टृ । स्वाति-वायु । विशाखा-इन्द्राग्नी । अनुराधा-मित्र । ज्येष्ठा-इन्द्र । मूल-निर्ऋति । पूर्वाषाढ़ा-अप् । उतराषाढ़ा-विश्वेदेव । श्रवण-विष्णु । धनिष्ठा-वसु । शतशिषज्-वरुण । पूर्वभाद्रपदा-अजपाद् । उत्तराभाद्रपदा-अहिर्बुध्न्य । रेवती-पूषन् ॥

breaths being exhaled out from the nostrils of the child should pronounce the following mantras:—

कोऽसि कतमोऽसि कस्यासि को नामासि ।
यस्य ते नामामन्महि यं त्वा सोमेनातीतृपाम ।
भूर्भुवः स्वः सुप्रजाः प्रजाभिः स्याँ सुवीरो वीरैः सुपोषः पोषैः ॥

य० अ० ७ मं २९ ॥

ओं कोऽसि कतमोऽस्येषोऽस्यमृतोऽसि ।
आहस्पत्यं मासं प्रविशासौ ॥

मं० ब्रा० १।५।१४॥ गो० २।८।१३॥

O Child ! you are the source of pleasure and delight, you are most delighting factor, you belong to God, the Lord of creatures. You are of the good and pleasant name. You are the entity whose name we know; name we satisfy with the nice sipping milk etc., may God bless you to make us satisfied, may God who is existent, conscious and all-blissful make us belong good progeny, make us belong brave children and make us rich with all the means of protection and preservation.

O Child ! who are you ? Whom do you belong to ? Really you are immortal and you belong to all-blissful God. May you enter into the months after monthes in the reign of God.

In the place of word असौ used in the end of the second Mantra the name given to child should be pronounced. In the fixing of name the procedure should be adopted that if the child is male he should be given the name of two vowels or four vowels and the *Ghosha varnas* and *Antastha varnas* and the third, fourth, and fifth letters of the alphabetical orders of Sanskrit should also get place in the formation of names.*

Foot Note : ग, घ, ङ, ज, झ, ञ, ड, ढ, ण, द, ध, न, ब, भ, म these, स्पर्श वर्ण य, र, ल, व these four अन्तस्थवर्ण and ह (ऊष्मा) should also get place in the formation of names. There is no restriction about vowels. anyone of them can be used but vowels here are meant the स्वर of Sanskrit. The males names should be formed as :—
भद्रः भद्रसेनः, देवदत्तः, भवः, भवनाथः, नागदेवः, रुद्रदत्तः हरिदेवः etc. But in forming the names rules of even numbers of letters in the case of males and odd numbers of letters in case of females, should be positively applied to, In the case of female names the दीर्घ and तद्धितान्त also applied. These females names are like thus :—श्रीः, ह्रीः, यशोदा, सुखदा, गान्धारी, सौभाग्यवती, कल्याणक्रोडा, etc.

But ladies should not be given the names which are like under-mentioned ones:—

नर्क्षवृक्ष नदी नाम्नीं नान्त्यपर्वतनामिकाम् ।
न पक्ष्यहि प्रेष्यनाम्नीं न च भीषणनामिकाम् ॥

मनु: ३ । ९ ॥

Names formed on the names of stars—रोहिणी, रेवती, etc., names formed on the names of trees and plants like चम्पा, तुलसी etc., names formed on river's names as:—गंगा, यमुना, सरस्वती etc. names formed on the basis lowering merit like चाण्डाली, names formed on the names of mauntain like विन्ध्याचल, हिमालया names based on the names of birds like—कोकिला, हंसा etc., names based on the snake's names like सर्पिणी,नागी etc., names formed on the ground of orderly and menial servants like दासी, किङ्करी etc., and the names which create an awe and fear like भीमा, भयंकरी, चण्डिका etc,, are prohibited to take place in naming a female child.

This distinguishing but not discriminating factor should bear full attention, consideration in giving names. For example the names—देव, जयदेव, can be given to the children. But—in the case of the child possessing a promising tendency of becoming Brahamana, or the parents desiring to make their child a Brahmana should geves him the name as देव शर्मा and similarly in the case of Kshatriya, Vaishya and Shudra, the names be respectively given to children as देव बर्मा. देव गुप्त. and देवदास etc. if the child is a female the name should be of one or three or five letters like श्री, ह्री:, यशोदा, सुखदा, सौभाग्यप्रदा etc. Pronouncing first the name fixed it should be used in the place of असौ in the Mantra, and again the Mantra—कोऽसि कतमोऽसि० as given above be repeated.

By the following Mantras as it has been mentioned in the *Jatkarma* ceremony the child should be blessed accordingly by the father.

ओं स त्वाह्ने परिददात्वहस्त्वा रात्र्यै परिददातु रात्रिस्त्वाहोरात्राभ्यां परिददात्वहोरात्रौ त्वार्द्धमासेभ्यः परिदत्तामर्द्धमासास्त्वा मासेभ्यः परिददतु मासास्त्वर्त्तुभ्यः परिददत्वृतवस्त्वा संवत्सराय परिददतु संवत्सरस्त्वायुषे जरायै परिददातु, असौ ॥

मं० ब्रा० १ । ५ । १५ ॥ गो० गृ० २ । ८ । १५ ॥

The translation of this has been given in the Jatkarma ceremony.

By this authoritative procedure having given the name to child and announcing the name to the people who are participating in the ceremony the performers of ceremony should sing the *Vamdevya gana* as has been described in the end of *Samanaya prakarana.*

Afterwards giving full respect to the people who graced the occasion by their presence, the leave be give to them. All people who are to leave this place should perform adoration, prayer and meditation of God with the Mantras prescribed for this purpose and give blessings to the child as follows:

"हे बालक ! त्वमायुष्मान् वर्चस्वी तेजस्वी श्रीमान् भूयाः ।"

O Child ! may you be long-lived, learned, pious, famous. perseverant, influential, philonthropic and prosperous.

Here ends the procedure of ceremony of naming.

———

Niskraman

Here we will speak of the procedure of

Niskramana Sacrament

The *Niskramana Sanskara* is the name of Vedic sacrament in which the child is brought from the house to place of pure fresh air and climate to take him round. When the time is suitable the parente should take the child outside to turn him round or they should positively take him round in the fourth month.

Authorities—

चतुर्थेमासि निष्क्रमणिका । सूर्यमुदीक्षयति तच्चक्षुरिति ॥

This is also in the *Gobhil Grihyasutra* (2.8.1)

जननाद्यस्तृतीयो ज्योत्स्नास्तस्य तृतीयायाम्

There are two alternatives regarding the time of *Niskramana* The first time is the third lunar date of the third full-mooned fort-night from the birth date of the child. The second time is the birth *Tithi* of the child in the fourth month from the date of birth to perform this ceremony.

On the day of the celebration of this sacrament, in the morning after sunrise the parents should bathe the child with clean water and dress him in clean nice clothes. Afterward, the mother of child bring the child in *yajnashala*, passing from the right side of her husband and coming in front of him should give the child into the hands of him (her husband) keeping the head of child in north direction and chest straight upward. Then, she returning from behind her husband should sit in the left of the husband keeping her face eastward.

ओं यत्ते सुसीमे हृदयं हितमन्तः प्रजापतौ ।
वेदाहं मन्ये तद् ब्रह्म माहं पौत्रमघं निगाम् ॥१॥
ओं यत्पृथिव्यामनृतं दिवि चन्द्रमसि श्रितम् ।
वेदामृतस्याहं नाम माहं पौत्रमघं रिषम् ॥२॥

ओम् इन्द्राग्नी शर्म यच्छतं [प्रजायै मे] प्रजापती।
यथायं न प्रमीयेत पुत्रो जनित्र्या अधि ॥३॥

मं० ब्रा० १।५।१०-१२ ॥ गोभिल गृ० २।८।१-५ ॥

(The english translation of these Mantras has been given in the *Jatkarma Sanskar*.)

Praying God with these above mentioned three Mantras, the procedure of prayer of God by eight *mantras* of *Prarthanopasana* स्वस्तिवाचन, शान्तिकरण and complete Havana of *Samanyaprakarana* as described in the *Samanya prakarna* should be performed. The father of the child be-holding the child touch the head of the child with the following three Mantras:—

ओम् अङ्गादङ्गात्संभवसि हृदयादधिजायसे।
आत्मा वै पुत्रनामासि सं जीव शरदः शतम् ॥१॥
ओं प्रजापतेष्ट्वा हिङ्कारेणावजिघ्रामि।
सहस्रायूषाऽसौ जीव शरदः शतम् ॥२॥
गवां त्वा हिङ्कारेणावजिघ्रामि।
सहस्रायुशाऽसौ जीव शरदः शतम् ॥३॥

पार० गृ० का० १। कं० १८। २-४ ॥

O Child! you come into existence from all of the parts of my body (i.e. the semen from all my bodily parts come and materialize the embryo) and take birth from my heart. You are my soul. May you not die before me and may you enjoy the life of hundred autumns.

O Child! I smell your head with the affectionate heart lowing granted to me my God, May you attain very long life and live hundred autumns.

O Child! I smell your head with sentiment affectionate cowlowing. May you attain very long life and live hundred autumuns.

The father of child should whisper the following Mantra in the right ear of the child:—

अस्मे प्र यन्धि मघवन्नृजीषिन्निन्द्र रायो विश्ववारस्य भूरेः।
अस्मे शतं शरदो जीवसे धा अस्मे वीराञ्छश्वत इन्द्र शिप्रिन् ॥१॥

ऋ० मं० ३ - सू० ३६। मं १० ॥ पार० गृ० १।१८।४ ॥

The translation of the Mantra has been given in *Jatkarma Sanskara*.

The following Mantra should be whispered in the left ear of the child by his father:—

इन्द्र श्रेष्ठानि द्रविणानि धेहि चित्तिं दक्षस्य सुभगत्वमस्मे ।
पोषं रयीणामरिष्टिं तनूनां स्वाद्मानं वाचः सुदिनत्वमह्नाम् ॥२॥
ऋ० मं० २ । सू० २१ । मं० ६ ॥ पा० गृ० १ । १८ । ५ ॥

The translation of this Mantra has also been given in the *Jatkarma Sanskara*

The father of the child, thereafter, should pass over the child into lap of his wife (child's mother) keeping its (child's head in the north direction and its foot in the south direction and keeping a silence should touch thehead of his wife. Afterwards he standing in delight and gay should display the sun to child and pronounce the following *mantra*:—

ओं तच्चक्षुर्देवहितं पुरस्ताच्छुक्रमुच्चरत् । पश्येम शरदः शतं जीवेम शरदः शतं श्रृणुयाम शरदः शतं प्र ब्रवाम शरदः शतमदीनाः स्याम शरदः शतं भूयश्च शरदः शतात् ॥

यजु० अ० ३६ । मं० २४ ॥ पार० गृ० १ । १७ । ६ ॥

He is all-vision and benevolent to men of wisdom. **He** existed pure and genuine prior to this world and would exist pure and genuine after it, mediating Him a hundred autumns may we see, a hundred autumns may we hear, a hundred autumns my we speak, a hundred autumns may we enjoy full freedom; and longer than hundred autumns we may enjoy all those blessings.

Turning round the child in fresh air for a little he should bring the child to the yajnashala and all people should bless it (the child) pronouncing the following sentence—

"त्वं जीव शरदः शतं वर्धमानः"

O Child ! you growing in health and strength live a hundred autumns.

Afterwards the mother and father of the child according due respect to them should give leave to ladies and gentlemen who participated in the ceremony.

Afterwards, in the night when moon be shining in the sky, the mother of the child dressing the child in nice clothes coming in his front from his right should give the child into the hands of the father (child's father) keeping child's head in north direction and foot in the south direction. The mother of the child turning by the right of her husband and coming on his left standing before the moon face to face with water filled in her hand should pray God with the following Mantra—

ओं यददश्चन्द्रमसि कृष्णं पृथिव्या हृदयं श्रितम् ।
तवहं विद्वाँ स्तत्पश्यन्माहं पौत्रमघं रुदम् ॥

मं० ब्रा० १।५।१३॥ गो० गृ० २।८।६।७॥

Performing the prayer of God by this above-mentioned Mantra the mother should drop the water filled in her hands on the ground. Afterwards she, passing from the back side of her husband and coming before him by his right should take the child from him and again passing behind the husband should come by his left and stand keeping the head of the child in north direction and foot in the south direction. The father of the child, then filling his hand with the water perform the prayer of God with the *mantra* "ओं यददश्चन्द्रमसि०" and drop water on the ground. Thus both (the wife and husband) go home in a delightfull mood.

Here ends the procedure of *Nishkramana* sacraments.

Annaprashana

Now we will speak of the procedure of *Annaprashana*,

The first feeding of cerial to child

This *Annaprashana* ceremony should be performed at the time when child gains strength to digest cerial and its preparation.

Herein stands the authority of *Ashvalayans Grihyasutra* (1.16 1,4,5):—

षष्ठे मास्यन्नप्राशनम् ॥१॥
घृतौदनं तेजस्कामः ॥२॥
दधिमधुघृतमिश्रमन्नं प्राशयेत् ॥३॥

There are similar authorities of *Paraskar grihyasutra* etc.

In the sixth month child be fed cerial. He who desires his child to be brilliant and famous should feed cooked rice mixed with *ghee* or the rice mixed with honey, curd and *ghee* according to the following procedure. That is, after having performed the complete procedure of Prayer of God, *Svastivachna, shantikarana* and complete *Samanya prakarana*, the person concerned should perform the the ceremony on the day on which the child was born. The rice should be prepared by the following method :

श्रों प्राणाय त्वा जुष्टं प्रोक्षामि । श्रोंश्रपानाय त्वा० । श्रों चक्षुषे त्वा० । श्रों श्रोत्राय त्वा० । श्रों श्रग्नये स्विष्टकृते त्वा० ।

This is the purport of these above-cited *Mantras* that the rice be washed, cleaned, cooked nicely, *ghee* in proper quantity be mixed in the rice when it is in cooking process. When this rice has been cooked properly and has become cold it should put in *Homasthali*, the pot of Homa. He should then distribute some of this rice in the pots of *yajmana*, the *Purohita*, and *Ritvij*, the priests with the following five *Mantras*:—

ओं प्राणाय त्वा जुष्टं निर्वपामि । ओं अपानाय त्वा० । ओं चक्षुषे त्वा० । ओं श्रोत्राय त्वा० । ओं अग्नये स्विष्टकृते त्वा० ॥

Thereafter the *yajmana* should performd *Agnyadhana*, *Samidadhana* etc. and then should offer eight oblations in total, that is, the four oblations of *Aghavarajyabhagahuti* and four oblation of *Vyahriti*. Afterwards the oblation of that cooked rice (kept in the pots of *Purohita* etc.) should be offered with the following *Mantras*:—

देवीं वाचमजनयन्त देवास्तां विश्वरूपाः पशवो वदन्ति ।
सा नो मन्द्रेषमूर्जं दुहाना धेनुर्वागस्मानुप सुष्टुतैतु स्वाहा ॥
इदं वाचे-इदन्न मम ॥१॥

[ऋ० मं० ८ । सू १०० मं ११ ॥ पार० गृ० १ । १९ । २ ।

वाजो नोऽद्य प्र सुवाति दानं वाजो देवाँ ऋतुभिः कल्पयाति ।
वाजो हि मा सर्ववीरं जजान विश्वा आशा वाजपतिर्जयेयं स्वाहा ॥
इदं वाचे वाजाय इदन्न मम ॥१॥

यजु० अ० १८ मं० ३३ ॥ पा० गृ० १ । १९ । ३ । १ ।

The physical forces of the nature give rise to the mighty and forceful speech which the men of various stature speak. That original speech created by the physical forces praised and having got pleasant come to us pouring knowledge, food, etc. like a milch cow. Whatever is uttered herein is true. The oblation offered is meant for *Vach* not for me.

This grain gives us now the power of giving gift, this also makes strong the learned man with seasons, this is the corn which makes us possess children, may I possess corn and food and conquer all the directions. Whatever is uttered herein is true. The oblation offered is meant for only this *Vaj* and t is not for me.

Afterwards more *ghee* should be poured in this cooked rice and the four oblations should be offered with the following *Mantras*:—

ओं प्राणेनान्नमशीय स्वाहा ।। इदं प्राणाय-इदन्न मम ।।१।।

ओं अपानेन गन्धानशीय स्वाहा ।। इदमपानाय-इदन्न मम ।।२।।

ओं चक्षुषा रूपाण्यशीय स्वाहा ।। इदं चक्षुषे-इदन्न मम ।।३।।

ओं श्रोत्रेण यशोऽशीय स्वाहा ।। इदं श्रोत्राय-इदन्न मम ।।४।।

पार० गृ० कां० १ । कं० १९ ।४।।

I through vital breath take the corn[1]
I through *apana* take the things other than corn[2]
I through eyes see the forms.[3]
I through ears here the words of fame.[4]

Afterwards one oblation of स्विष्टकृत् should be performed with the यदस्य कर्मणो० *Mantra* as written in the *Samanya Prakarna*. Thereafter giving four oblations of the व्याहृति, eight oblations with त्वन्नो अग्ने etc. *Mantras* should be offered. Thus, four oblations of व्याहृति, and eight oblations of eight *Mantras* of "त्वन्नो अग्ने" group become twelve oblations in total.

Thereafter the *yajmana* mixing curd, honey and *ghee*, in a small quantity, in the rice which remains after oblations and mixing in it a little other cooked rice which be fragerant, should give into the mouth of the child in a very minute quantity according to the desire of the child with the following *Mantra*:—

ओम् अन्नपतेऽन्नस्य नो देह्यनमीवस्य शुष्मिणः ।
प्र प्र दातारं तारिष ऊर्जं नो धेहि द्विपदे चतुष्पदे ।।

यजु० अ० ११ । मं ८३ ।। आश्व० गृ० । १ । १६ । ५ ।।

O Lord of plenty of Food ! vouchsafe us a share of food that invigorates us, and brings no sickness, Onward, still onward lead the giver. Grant us maintenance both for quadrupeds and bipeds.

After feeding the rice to the child to his desire his mouth should be washed. Then washing his own hands and singing the *Vamdevyagana* as described in the end of *Samanya prakarna* the mother and father of the child and other old ladies and gentlemen praying God should bless the child with the sentence :

'त्वमन्नपतिरन्नादो वर्धमानो भूयाः'

O Child ! may you by God's grace become master of corn, eater or consumer of corn, growing in strength and life.

Afterwards the father of the child should give respect to the gents and his mother to the ladies who have participated in the ceremony and thus delightfully should give them leave.

Here ends the procedure of *Annaparashana*.

Chudakarma

Now we will speak of the procedure of the Sacramental ceremony of crest or Tuft.

This ceremony of tuft is the eight of all the Sacraments. It is also called the ceremony of cutting or shaving the hair. In this matter the opinion of the *Ashvalayana Grihyasutra* is like thus :—

तृतीये वर्षे चौलम् ।।१।। उत्तरतोऽग्नेर्व्रीहियवमाषतिलानां पृथक्पूर्ण शरावाणि निदधाति ।।२।। आश्व० गृ० १।१७।१-२।।

In the same manner we find authority in the *Paraskara Grihyasutra* :—

सांवत्सबरिकस्य चूडाकरणम् ।। पार० २।१।१

Coincide with the same authority and opinion of *Gobhiliya Grihyasutra* (गो० गृ० २।८।१० ६ ।।)

This ceremony of crest should be performed in the third or the 1st yaers from the date of the child's birth. On the day of delight and choice in the full-mooned fortnight in north solstice this ceremony should be celebrated.

The procedure. In the beginning the performances of *Samanya prakarna* should be performed. The four earthenware pots (शरावे)one of them full of rice, the second one full of barley, the third one full of Phaseolus mungo (मूंग) and the fourth full of Sesumum (तिल)—should be put in the north direetion of the *yajnavedi*. Afterwards the procedure of sprinkling water on the four sides of the Vedi with *Mantros* commencing as ओं अदितेऽनुमन्यस्व० and ending with 'ओं देव सवितः प्रसुव' in the way that with three *Mantras* in three sides and with one ओं देव सवितः in the four sides—should be performed Afterwards by *Agnyadhana*, *Samidadhana* the fire of ihe *Kunda* should be kept ablaze. Keeping in mind the enkindled fuel-wood of the Vedi the 16 oblations which includes four *Agharavajyabhagahuti*; four *Vyahriti*

Ahutis, and eight oblations of *ghee* with the eight *Mantras* of (त्वन्नो अग्ने) etc. as described in the *Samanya prakarana*, should be offered. Afterwards four oblations of *ghee Mantras* beginning with ओं भूर्भुवः स्वः । अग्न आयूँषि० ete- be offered. Again offering four *Vyahriti Ahutis* one oblation of *Svistkrit* with *Mantra* यदस्य कर्मणो० should be offcred.

After having performed the procedure the performer of the ceremony remember God, glancing first at the barber should recite the following *Mantra* :

ओम् आयमगन्त्सविता क्षुरेणोष्णेन वाय उदकेनेहि । आदित्या रुद्रा वसव उन्दन्तु स चेतसः सोमस्य राज्ञो वपत प्रचेतसः ॥

अथर्व० कां० ६ । सू० ६८ । मं० १ । गो० २ । ९। १०॥

This barber who is competent and swift has come with hi razor. Let him come with lukewarm water. May the learned men known as *Rudra*, *Vasus* make it wet with utmost care and let the learned others cut the hair like the king of the *Soma*, the herbs etc.

Afterwards the father of the child sitting behind the child taking a little hot water in one pot and a little cold water in the other pot should mix the waters of both the pots pronouncing the *Mantra* ओम् उष्णेन वाय उदकेनेहि—i.e. let the hot water be mixed with cold water. Afterwards he taking a little water, a little butter or the curd should moisten the hair of the child by turning his hand three times in the hair (on the head) of the child and pronounce the following *Mantras* in doing so—

ओम अदितिः श्मश्रु वपत्वाप उन्दन्तु वर्चसा ।
चिकित्सतु प्रजापतिदीर्घायुत्वाय चक्षसे ॥

अथर्व० कां० ६। सू० ६८। मं २॥ आ० गृ० १। १७। ७॥

ओं सवित्रा प्रसूता दैव्या आप । उन्दन्तु ते तनू दीर्घायुत्वाय वर्चसे ॥२॥

पार० गृ० २। १। ९॥

Let this unbreakable razor cut the bunch of hair, let the waters with their moistening power drench the hair of the child, may the Lord of the creatures (God) remove diseases from this child to make him attain a long life and knowledge.

O Child ! Let the mighty celestial waters produced by sun drench your head to attain a long life and knowledge.

Afterwards the father of the child taking a comb in his hand comb the hair and make them collected in bunch, i.e. the hair be not disturbed. Thereafter, he pronouncing the *Mantra* ओम् ओषधे त्रायस्वैनम्, गो० २।६।१४ (let the herb protect this child) should take three दर्भ and should slightly press the bunch of the hair of right side with these *darbhas* and should glance at the razor pronouncing the *Mantra*—विष्णोर्द ष्ट्रोऽसि ॥ गो० २।६।१३ मं० ब्रा० १।६।४ razor is the means in performance of this *yajna* of *chudakarma.*

Afterwards he should hold the razor in his right hand pronouncing the following *Mantra*—

ओम् शिवो नामासि स्वधितिस्ते पिता नमस्ते (ऽअस्तु) मा मा हिंसीः ॥

यजु० अ० २। मं० ६३॥ पा० गृ० २। १। ११॥

This razar is for auspiciousness, the steel which is so strong as *Vajra* is its producing material, let it be fit for cutting the hair, let it not anyhow cause pain.

Thereafter the father of the child should bring the razor and the कुशा near the hair-bunch of the child pronouncing the following *Mantras* :—

ओं स्वधिते मैनं हिंसीः ।

यजु० अ ४। मं १॥ आ० गृ० १. १७। ६

ओं निवर्त्तयाम्यायुषेऽन्नाद्याय प्रजननाय रायस्पोषाय सुप्रजास्त्वाय सुवीर्याय ॥

यजु० अ० ३। मं० ६३। पार० गृ० २।११॥

Let not this constant steel razor inflict any harm to this child.

O Child ! I perform this tuft-ceremony to make you attain life, constructive power, strength of wealth, good proginy and strength and Vigour.

He (the father of the child) should cut[1] the hair-bunch with *Kusha* (कुश) and pronounce the following *Mantra* :—

श्रों येनावपत्सविता क्षुरेण सोमस्य राज्ञो वरुणस्य विद्वान् ।
तेन ब्रह्माणो वपतेदमस्य गोमानश्ववानयमस्तु प्रजावान् ॥

अथर्व० कां० ६ । सू० ६८। मं० ३ ॥ श्रा० गृ० १। १७ ।१०॥
पा० गृ० २ । १। ११।

O priest and learned ! this competent barber shaves this child by the same razor whereby he shaves the glorious king and man of merits. May this child be pessessor of cows, horess and children.

The hair cut by the razor or scissor, the *Kushas* and the leaves of Mimosa (शमी) which should be arranged to collect there previosly should be kept safe in onc earthendish (शरावा) by the father or the mother of the child, If any hair has flown hither and thither at the time of shaving or cutting should be picked up throug the cow-dung and put in the शरावा with him of her.

Afterwards in the same manner the second the other hair-bunch of another side should be cut and kept in शरावा with the following *Mantra* :—

श्रों येन धाता बृहस्पतेरग्नेरिन्द्रस्य चायुषेऽवपत् ।
तेन त श्रायुषे वपामि सुश्लोक्याय स्वस्तये ॥

श्राश्व० १। १७। १२॥

O Child ! I cut your hair for your long life. fame and prosperity through that power by which the All-sustaining Divinity

1. The method of cutting the hair is that it be cut in the middle by holding it with two *Kushah* on both sides. If the scissor is used instead of razor it is also better.

has cut the grossness of material objects to maintain the longivity of the air, fire and electricity.

In the same manner the third time the hair-bunch should be removed by the following *Mantra* :

ओं येन भूयश्चरात्य ज्योक् च पश्यति सूर्यम् ।

तेन त आयुषे वपापि सुश्लोक्याय स्वस्तये ॥

आश्व० १। १७ । १२॥

O Child ! I cut your hair for your long life. fame and prosperity through that power by whieh this kingdom of creatures sees again and again the objects in the night and the sun till the time of dissolution.

Afterwards with the above mentioned three *Mantras*—"ओं येनावपत् ०" 'ओ येन धाता०', ओं येन भूयश्च० and the fourth *Mantra* as it is being given below (ओं येन पूषा०) the father of child should cut the hair-bunch for the fourth time in similar manner :—

ओं येन पूषा बृहस्पतेर्वायोरिन्द्रस्य चावपत् ।

तेन ते वपामि ब्राह्मण जीवातवे जीवनाय दीर्घायुष्ट्वाय वर्चसे ॥

गोभिल २ । ६ । ११-१६॥

O child ! I cut your hair for your living, life and prolonged life through that power by which the All-sustaining Divinity maintains the life of the sun, air and the electricity.

This is the procedure of the cutting of right side hair-bunches of the child and completing thus, this procedure, the procedure of cutting the hair-bunches of the left-side should be followed. Thereafter the father of the child should cut the hair-bunches of hind side of the head- But in cutting the hair-bunch at the fourth time the following *Mantra* should be pronounced instead of येन पूषा० :-

ओं येन भूरिश्चरा दिवं ज्योक् च पश्चाद्धि सूर्यम् ।

तेन ते वपामि ब्रह्मणा जीवातवे जीवनाय सुश्लोक्याय स्वस्तये ॥

पार० २ । १ । १६ ॥

O Child ! I cut your hair for your living, life, fame, and prosperity through that power by which the moving air moves in heavenly region, the sun thereafter, till the time of dissolution.

Thus having completed the cutting of the hair-bunch of left side with the above mentioned *Mantra* at the fourth time the father of the child should cut the hair-bunch of hind head once again with this following one *Mantra* :—

ओं त्र्यायुषं जमदग्नेः कश्यपस्य त्र्यायुषम् ।
यद्देवेषु त्र्यायुषं तन्नो अस्तु त्र्यायुषम् ॥

यजु० अ० ३। मं ६२। पार० २। १। १४॥

May our eesy attain three times life, may our ears attain three times life, may our other organs attain three times life, may our life be increased three times more as the learned men attain three-times prolonged life.

Afterwards pronouncing the *Mantra* ओं त्र्यायुषं जमदग्नेः० the father of the child should pass over h s hand-palm on the head of the child from hind part of the head and when the *Mantra* is finished he give the razar to barber.

He should, then pronounce the following *Mantra* :—

ओं यत्क्षुरेण मर्चयता सुपेशसा वप्ता वपसि केशान् ।
शुन्धि शिरो मास्यायुः प्र मोषीः ॥

आश्व० १। १७। १५।

O barber ! you are the cutter of the hair, you cleanse the head of the child with that swift soft razor by which you cut his hair and do not decrease his life.

After pronouncing this above-mentioned *Mantra*, he (the father of the child) making the barber sharp the razor on his stone should advise him (the barber) that he (the barber) nicely drench the child's head with hot and cold water very smoothly, do the shaving attentively and with smooth hand, and avoid any cut from the razor. Saying so he take the barber in the north direction of the *yajnakunda* and seat the child in his front keeping child's face eastward and get the child shaved leaving only the hair which he (the father of the child) does not want to get shaved. But the hair should be kept a little unshaved on five sides or on any one side or once it should get completely shaved as the keeping of tuft at the second time is proper and good.

When the shaving of the child has got eompletd the child's father should give the barbar whetever to be given is lying near the *yajnakunda* and the four cerial-filled earthen dishes previously kept by the north side of *yajnakund.* The barber should be given some money and clothes also. The barber be advised by child's father to carry the cut-hair दर्भ, शमीपत्र and गोबर in the jungle, dig a pitch and burry all this therein by filling the soil or burry those hair etc. near cow-home, river to tank, Either he should advise the barber to do so or send some one with him to get the needful done through the barber.

After shaving is complete, the father of the child taking curd or butter in his hand and rubing it on the head of the child should bathe the child. Thereafter dressing the child with nice dress, the father should keep the child with him and sit on a nice seat keeping his own face eastward and perform the singing of M*ahavamdeva Gana.* Afterwards the mother of the child giving due respect to ladies and child's father to the gentlemen leave them. All leaving and father and mother of the child remembering God should bless the child with the sentence—"ओं त्वं जोव शरद: शतं वर्धमान: (ie." O Child ! you live hundred autumns growing in strength and vigour.) Thus all should go their homes and father and mother delighted themselves keep the child delighted and happy.

Here ends the procedure of *Chudakarma.*

Karnavedha

Now we will speak of the ceremony of Piercing the ears.

The Scriptural authority:—

कर्णवेधो वर्षे तृतीये पंचमे वा ॥१॥

This is the saying of *Katyayana Grihyasutra* (1.2). The time of the piercing the ear or nose of the child is the third or the fifth year from the date of birth.

On the day when the piercing of ears or nose of the child is fixed, the mother of the child should take the child to the *yajnashala* after bathing him in the morning with clean water and getting him dressed with clothes and ornaments. The procedure of *Samanya Prakaran* should be completely performed. Afterwarde puting some eatables or toys before the child by the experienced physician who is specialist in the treatisses of *Charaka* and *Sushruta* and who can do the work saving sinews etc., should be materialized the piercing of ears and nose, He should pierce the right ear first with the following *Mantra*:—

ओं भद्रं कर्णेभिः श्रृणुयाम देवा भद्रं पश्येमाक्षभिर्यजत्राः ।
स्थिरैरङ्गैस्तुष्टुवां सस्तनूभिर्व्यशेमहि देवहितं यदायुः ॥१॥

यजु० २५ । २१

O ye enlightened persons ! you are fit for our association, may we ever hear with our ear such words which are beneficial to all, and may we ever see with our eyes whatever is good. Ever praying with our firm limbs may we attain such state of life through our bodies which will be help-ful to the cause of the enlightened persons.

He should pierce the left ear with the following *Mantra*:—

वक्ष्यन्ती वेदा गनीगन्ती कर्णं प्रियं सखायं परिषस्वजाना ।
योषेव शिङ्क्ते वितताधि धन्वञ्ज्या इयं समने पारयन्ती ॥२॥

यजु० २९ । ४० ॥ पार० १। १७

This bow-string strained on the bow whispers like a woman, and preserves us in the combat, as a wife, fain to speak, offering advice, embraces her affectionate praiseworthy husband.

Thereafter the same physician should put bar or wire in the holes of the piercing so that the holes could not be filled up and he should apply such medicine on the holes that the ears be not rotten and be cured soon.

Here ends the procedure of the ceremony of piercing the ears.

Upanayana

Now we will speak[1] of the Procedure of Investiture of Sacred Thread.

Scriptural Athorities :

अष्टमे वर्षे ब्राह्मणमुपनयेत् ॥१॥ गर्भाष्टमे वा ॥२॥ एकादशे क्षत्रियम् ॥३॥ द्वादशे वैश्यम् ॥४॥ आषोडशाद् ब्राह्मणस्यानतीतः काल ॥५॥ आद्वाविंशात्क्षत्रियस्य, आचतुर्विंशाद्वैश्यस्य, अत ऊर्ध्वं पतितसावित्रीका भवन्ति ॥६॥

This is the authority of *Ashvalayana Grihyasutra* 1-19-1-6). Similar saying is found in the *Paraskara Grihya*sutra etc.

The *Brahmana* the child of *Brahmana* or the child promising to be *Brahmana* should be invested with the sacred thread in the eighth year from the date of birth or from the date of conception; Kshatriya, the child of Kshatriya or the child promising to be Kshatriya should be invested with the sacred thread in the eleventh year from the date of birth or from the date of conception; *vaishya*, the child of *vaishya* or the child promising to be *vaishya* should be invested with the sacred threrd in the 12th year from the date of his birth or from the date of conception. Positively the children of *Brahmana*, *Kshatriy*a and *Vaishya* should respectively be invested with sacred thread before the years 16th, 22nd and 24th of their age. If they are not invested with saered thread in these years they are treated befallen from their duties.

ब्रह्मवर्चसकामस्य कार्यं विप्रस्य पञ्चमे ।
राज्ञो बलार्थिनः षष्ठे वैश्यस्येहार्थिनोऽष्टमे ॥

मनु २।३७

This is the word of *Manusmriti,* The child of the *Brahmana* whose parent wish him attain learning, strength and application

---

1. *Upa* here means near and *Nayana* means to go or to be brought.

of knowledge soon and who by himself be promising in study should be invested with sacred thread in the fifth year of his age from the date of birth or from the date of conception (his mother materialized in her womb), in the same manner the child of *Kshatriya* in the sixth year of his age from the date of birth or from the date of conception and the child of *Vaishya* in the eighth year of his age from the date of birth or from the date of conception be invested with sacred thread. But this thing is possible only under the conditions that the parent of the child had been married after having completed the strict discipline of continent on their parts. It is only such kinds of the parent who can have such exellent child who could promise genuine wisdom and swiftness of advance capacity. Generally the parants or the men concerned should arrange to get the child invested with sacred thread when the child possesses such a grasping power that he would learn and study smoothly.

The time of *yajnopavita*—The winter solstice and

वसन्ते ब्राह्मणमुपनयेत् । ग्रीष्मे राजन्यम् ।
शरदि वैश्यम् । सर्वकालमेके ।।

This is the injunction of *Shatpath Brahmana* (2.1.3.5).

That is. the child of *Brahmana* in the spring season, the child of *Kshatriya* in the summer season and the child of *Vaishya* in autumn be respectively invested with sacred thread. Or the investiture of sacred thread can be held in all seasons and the morning time is the best time for holding this ceremony,

पयोव्रतो ब्राह्मणो यवागूव्रतो राजन्य आमिक्षाव्रतो वैश्यः ।।

Three or one day prior to the day when the ceremony is fixed to be held the child to be invested with sacred thread, should have three or one fasts. In the time of fastings the child of *Brahmana* can take only milk once or many times; the child of *Kshatriya* can take barley gruel (यवागू) (whieh is Prepared of crushed barley by mixing sugar and boiling in water). This barley gruel should be given to him to drink. The child of

Vaishya should complete his fast by taking आमिक्षा once or many times. This आमिक्षा (*Amiksha*) is sometimes called *Shrikhanda* or *Sikhanda*. This is prepared from curd four parts, milk one part, sugar in proportionate quantity and saffron (केशर). This preparation is made after sorting these curd etc. through the cloth-Piece. The children of three *Varnas*, as described above should eat only things prescribed above for them respectively when they feel hungry and they should not eat and drink any thing else.

The procedure—The utensils to be used in the *yajna* etc. should be collected and appropriately sorted and cleansed out day before the sacred thread investiture is going to be held, On the day of ceremony every thing needed as has been mentioned in the *Samanya Prakarana* should be arranged near the *yajna Kunda* The child to be vested with sacred thread should be shaved and bathed with clean water and dressed in nice dress Either the father of the child or the Acharya[1] having fed the child with sweets, eatables etc. seat him on a comfortable seat in the west of the *yajnavedi* keeping his face eastward, The father of the child and the priests of the *yajna* who are mentioned in the *Samanya* prakarana, taking their respective seats in the previously described manner should properly perform acts of *yajna* like sipping of water etc.

Afterwards the Acharya conducting the cremony should make the child pronounce the following sentence from his child's own mouth

May I observe the disipline of celibacy and thus may I be a celibrate.

---

*Acharya is he who knows the words, meanings, their relations and the application of the Vedas with their limbs and joint limbs, is free from pretention, deceit, given of knowledge to all with great affection, alruist buisy in ameliorating the pleasure of all with body, mind and wealth, is magnaminous impartial, expounder of truth, well-wisher of all, righteous and free from carner desires.

The Acharya pronouncing the following *Mantra* should give to the child a dress and a *upvastra* to put on:—

श्रों येनेन्द्राय बृहस्पतिर्वासः पर्यंदधादमृतम् ।

तेन त्वा परिदधाम्यायुषे दीर्घायुत्वाय बलाय वर्चसे ॥

पार० गृ० २। २। ७

O Child ! I for your health, long-life, strength and Vigour give this dress to you to wear, through the method by which an Acharya gives strong and durable dress to his disciple.

Afterwards the child taking the sacred thread in his hand should sit in front of Acharya and Acharya pronouncing the following *Mantra* should invest with sacred thread which he puts on in such a manner that it could be on the left shoulder near the throat hanging below the right hand side upto belt and the head be in the middle:—

यज्ञोपवीतं परमं पवित्रं प्रजापतेर्यत्सहजं पुरस्तात् ।

श्रायुष्यमग्र्यं प्रतिमुञ्च शुभ्रं यज्ञोपवीतं बलमस्तु तेजः ॥१॥

यज्ञोपवीतमसि यज्ञस्य त्वायज्ञोपयवीतेनोपनाह्यामि ॥२॥

This sacred thread is very sacrosanct. This normally and naturally extends out befor the *Prajapati*, the *Prajapati yajna* performed to enter into the *Ashram* of *Sanyasa*. I invest you with this white *yajnopavlta* which being a main thing, is meant for strength and vigour.[1]

This sacred thread is really a sacred thread. I tie you with this for the purpose of performing *yajna*.

Afterwards the Acharya seating the child on his right with him, should perform the adoration, supplication and meditation of God *Svastivachana*, *Shantikarana*, *Samidadhana* and *Agnyadnana*. Afterwards pouring water in the four sides of the *yajna Kunda* with the *Mantras* begenning with ओम् अदिते ऽनुमन्यस्व० etc. as the procedure has been mentioned in the *Samanyaprakarana* the preparation should be made to offer *Ajyahutis.*

He taking into mind the woodfuels blazing and taking *ghee* in spoon from the pot of *ghee* should offer sixteen oblations in total consisting four oblations of *Agharavavajyabhagahuti*, four oblations of *Vyahriti Ahutis* and eight oblations of *Astajyahuti*, should be offered. Thereafter the oblations of principal *Homa* (होम) with the special *Shakalya* (शाकल्य) prepared for the purpose, should be offered by the child himself with the following *Mantras*:—ओं भूर्भुवः स्वः । अग्न आयूंषि पवस० etc. four *Mantras.* Thereafter the five oblations be offered with the following five *Mantras*:—

ओं अग्ने व्रतपते व्रतं चरिष्यामि तत्ते प्रब्रवीमि तच्छकेयम् ।

तेनर्ध्यासमिदमहमनृतात्सत्यमुपैमि स्वाहा ।। इदमग्नये-इदन्न मम ।।१।।

ओं वायो व्रतपते० स्वाहा ।। इदं वायवे-इदन्न मम ।।२।।

ओ सूर्य व्रतपते० स्वाहा ।। इदं सूर्याय-इदन्न मम ।।३।।

ओं चन्द्र व्रतपते० स्वाहा ।। इदं चन्द्राय-इदन्न मम ।।४।।

ओं व्रतानां व्रतपते० स्वाहा ।। इदमिन्द्राय व्रतपतये-इदन्न मम ।।५।।

मं० ब्रा० १ । ६ । ९-१३।। गोभिल २ । १०। १६

O Self-refulgent God ! Thou art the master of vows; I will observe the vows and disciplines of celibacy, I declare before you. May I be able to observe that my vow. May I prosper with that vow and I attain highest truth rising above from the untruth. Whatever has been uttered herein is true. The oblation offered is meant for *Agni* and it is not for me.[1]

O All-moving God.!...
...............The oblation offered is meant for *Vayu* and it is not for me.[2]

O All-impelling soul ! ....
........The oblation offered is meant for *Surya* and it is not for me.[3]

O All blissful God !.. ....The oblation offered is meant for *Chandra* and it is not for me.[4]

O Lord of all the Vows and laws !................................ ....The oblation offered is meant for Indra and it is not for me.

Tnereafter, the six oblations consisting four oblations of Vyahriti Ahutis; one of Svistakrit, and one of Prajapatyahuti should be offerd.

All these fifteen oblations stated above (four oblations of अग्न आयूंषि० etc., four Mantras; five obletions of अग्ने व्रतपते० etc. *Mantras*; and six oblations of *Vyahriti,Svistakrit* and *Prajapatya*) should be offered by the child himself who is being invested with sacred thread

Afterwards, the Acharya should sit in the north of the *Yajna Kunda* kceping his face eastward and the child should sit in front-of Achary keeping his face westward.

Afterwards, the Acharya looking at the child should recite the following Mantra:—

ओम् आगन्त्रा समगन्महि प्र सु युयोतन ।
अरिष्टाः संचरेमहि स्वस्ति चरतादयम् ॥

मं० ब्रा० १। ६ । १४ ॥ गोभिल २ । १० । २०-२२ ।

O Self refulgent God ! We have got on a very good term with this boy. Kindly lead to the company of good men and teachers. This lad as well as we follow the path of know-ledge and ease. May this lad do whatever is auspicious for him and for all.

माणवकवाक्यम्— ओं ब्रह्मचर्यमागामुप मानयस्व ॥

मं ब्रा० १ । ६ । १६॥ गोभिल २ । १० । २०-२२ ।

आचार्योक्तिः···को नामासि ॥

मन्त्र ब्रा० १ । ६ । १७ ॥ गोभिल २। १०। २२

बाल्कोक्ति···एतन्नामास्मि ॥

मं० ब्रा० १ । ६ । १८ ॥

The student (child, says—"O teacher ! I have—acepted to observ the discipline of continence, now kindly admit me and invest me with sacred thread" says Acharya— What is your name ? Replies the student— Sir, My name is so and so. Or I bear such a name.

Afterwatds, the Acharya should fill up the right अञ्जलि, (the hollow of the hand) with clean and pure water and pronouce the following Mantras in doing so:—

ओम् आपो हिष्ठा मयोभुवस्ता न ऊर्जे दधातन ।
महे रणाय चक्षसे ॥१॥

यो वः शिवतमो रसस्तस्य भाजयतेह नः ।
उशतीरिव मातरः ॥२॥

तस्मा अरं गमाम वो यस्य क्षयाय जिन्वथ ।
आपो जनयथा च नः ॥३॥

ऋ० मं १० । सू० ६ । म० १-३ ॥ पार० २ । २ । १४

The waters are the source of happiness, may they be helpful for us in attaining grain and may they help us to have a nice sight. [1]

Let the pleasant essence of waters be useful for us like the mothers who, for the well-being of their children, give their breast to them to suck. [2]

Let us acquire those cereals for the growth of which the waters help herbacious plants and let them be helpful in welfa re of our progeny. [3]

Afterwards, the Acharya, filling his own handful with water

should drop the water of his handful in the handful of the child pronouncing the following *Mantra*:—

ओं तत्सवितुर्वृणीमहे वयं देवस्य भोजनम् ।

श्रेष्ठं सर्वधातमं तुरं भगस्य धीमहि ॥

ऋ० मं ५ । सू० ८२ । मं० १ ॥ आ० १ । २० । ४

We, for our maintenance, accept whatever good food has been provided by God who is the mighty power and creator of the world. We also accept the strength and might of all-powerful God who maintains and preserves the existence of all the objects of creation.

Afterwards the Acharya, holding the handful of the child filled with water, including child's thumb, there with should get the child pour down the handful of water in a pot pronouncing the following *Mantra*:—

ओं देवस्य त्वा सवितुः प्रसवेऽश्विनोर्बाहुभ्यां पूष्णोहस्ताभ्यां

हस्तं गृह्णाम्यसौ* ॥

य० अ० ५ मं० २६ ॥ आ० १ । २० । ४

O child! I admit you in this life to make you attain the power and prosperity of God, who is the creator of the world. I hold your hand in my own with the firmness and strength of the vital breaths called *Prana* and *apana* and with the firmness and strength of *Pushan*, the all preserving vitality of the body.

In the similar way again for the second time the Acharya filling water in his own handful and pouring the same in the अजलि of the child and holding child's *Anjali* together with his thumb, get him drop the water in the pot. The Acharya should pronounce the following sentence in doing so:—

ओं सविता ते हस्तमग्रभीत् असौ ॥

आश्व० १ । २० । ५

---

*The name of the child be pronounced everywhere in the place of असौ ।

O Child ! your hand has been grasped by *Savitar*, the mighty teacher who is the preserver of all knowledge .

Again for the third time the Acharya filling water in his own handful and pouring it in the *Anjali* of the child and holding his hand together with his thumb should get the water dropped in the pot . In doing so he should pronounce the following *Mantra* :—

अग्निराचार्यस्तव, असौ ॥

मं० ब्रा० १ । ६ । १५ ।, आश्व० १ । २० । ५ ।

O Child ! Again, the self-refulgent God is your Acharya.

Afterwards, Acharya going out standing in front of the sun, should show the sun to the chid and should pronounce the following two *Mantras* in complying with this procedure :—

१ ओं देव सवितरेष ते ब्रह्मचारी ते गोपाय
समामृता ॥ आ० १ । २० । ६

२ तच्चक्षुर्देवहितम्० इत्यादि

O All-creating Lord ! this child is the *Bruhmacharin* of Thine: Please protect and preserve him, so that he may perform his duties well.

2. Translation has been given in *Shantikarana* and *Sandhya*.

Thereafter, the Acharya returning to *yajna Mandapa* with the child and sitting in the north of the *yajnakunda*, should pronoun the following two *mantras* and the child should take a round of the Acharya and sit before him:—

ओं युवा सुवासाः परिवीत आगात्स उ श्रेयान् भवति जायमानः

ऋ० मं० ३ । सू० ८ । मं० ४ ॥ आ० १ । २० । ८

ओं सूर्यस्यावृतमन्वावर्त्तस्व, असौ ॥

गोभिल २ । १० । २८

This child possessing strong physique, dressed in nice dress, wearing the sacred thread comes before me. He taking the second birth in the domain of study enjoy dignity.[1]

O Child ! you circum-ambulate your Acharya who is the sun of knowledge.

After this, the Acharya should touch the right shoulder of the child with his (Acharya's) right hand and thereafter covering his (Acharya's) hand with a piece of cloth should pronounce this following *Mantra*:—

ओं प्राणानां ग्रन्थिरसि मा विस्रसो ऽन्तक इदं ते
परिददामि, अमुम्* । गो० २ । १० । २८

Let not this navel which is a tie of vital airs be displaced from its proper place, O Lord ! (the Annihilator of all) I, the Acharya give it to your cautious care and I declare this keeping this child in my mind.

Thereafter Acharya pronouncing the following *Mantra* should touch the belly of the child:—

ओम् अहुर इदं ते परिददामि. अमुम् । २ ॥

O God ! Thou art the mover of wind. I, the Acharya··· etc.

Acharya should touch childs heart and pronounce :—

ओं कृशन इदं ते परिदामि, अमुम् ॥ ३

O God ! Thou art invigorator of the fire. I, the Acharya··· etc.

The Acharya should touch child's right shoulder and pronounce:—

ओं प्रजापतये त्वा परिददामि, असौ ॥ ४ ॥

---

*Everywhere the name of the child should be pronounced in the place of असौ and अमुम् in their respective cases.

O Child ! I appoint you to attain the knowledge of God and follow his commands.

The Acharya should touch child's left shoulder and should pronounce :—

ओं देवाय त्वा सवित्रे परिददामि, असौ ॥ ५ ॥

मं० ब्रा० १ । ६ । २१-२४ ॥ गोभिल २ । १० । ५८-३४ ॥

O Child ! I appoint you to attain All-creating God and obay His commands.

Thereafter, the Acharya keeping his hand on the child's breasts, should pronounce the following *Mantra*:—

ओं तं धीरासः कवय उन्नयन्ति स्वाध्योऽ३ मनसा देवयन्तः ॥

ऋ० मं० ३ सू० ८ । मन्त्र ४ ॥ ब्रा० १ । २० । ६

The learned men of firm intentions and swift intellects attaining the highest feats of knowledge through their mind and spirit raise this student to high status of geneus and charater.

Thereafter, tht Acharya keeping him in front of the child and putting his hand on the right breast of the child should pronounce the following *Mantra* of the sacred pledge :—

ओं मम व्रते ते हृदयं दधामि मम चित्तमनुचित्तं ते अस्तु ।

मम वाचमेकमना जुषस्व बृहस्पतिष्ट्वा नियुनक्तु मह्यम् ॥

पार० कां० २ । कं० । १६

Thereafter Acharya should order the child to pronounce this *Mantra* ओं मम व्रते० ॥

O disciple ! I make your mind and heart into my own control, let your mind be concordant with my mind always, you being fully attentive grasp my words with affection and attain the meaning of these words and May God who is the master ef Vedic speech, unite you with me in thought and action according to your vow from this very day, to day.

Similarly the disciple should also request the Acharya to take the vew. I hold your mind and heart in me for the advancement of my study and learning and good action. May your mind be accordant with that of my mind. Please listen to my words with attention and may God keep you always engaged in task of my well-being.

Thus both should complete the procedure of taking vow.

आचार्योक्ति :—को नामाऽसि ।

Says Acharya—What is your name ?

बालकोक्ति :—असौ ।

Says student—Sir, my name is so and so.

आचार्य :—कस्य ब्रह्मचार्यसि ॥

Acharya says—Whose *Brahmachari* are you ?

बालक :—भवतः ॥ पार० कां० २ । १७-२०

Says student—your, Sir.

The Acharya should pronounce the following *Mantra* for the safety of the child:—

इन्द्रस्य ब्रह्मचार्य्यस्यग्निराचार्यस्तवाहमाचार्यस्तव असौ ॥

पार० कां० २ । कं० २ । २१

O child ! You are the *Brahmachari* of Almighty God. The Self- refulgent God is your Acharya. I am your Acharya (as His representative).

एतन्नामास्मि, असौ:—।

Everywhere the name of the child should be pronounced in the place of असौ Acharya should again pronounce these following two Mantras for child's safety and should instruct the child to be active in attaining the knowledge of Prana etc.

ओं कस्य ब्रह्मचार्य्यसि प्राणस्य ब्रह्मचार्यसि कस्त्वा कमुपनयते काय त्वा परिददामि ॥ १ ॥ आश्व १ । २० । ७ ॥

ओं प्रजापतये त्वा परिददामि । देवाय त्वा सवित्रे परिददामि । अद्भ्यस्त्वोषधीभ्यः परिददामि । द्यावापृथिवीभ्यां त्वा परिददामि । विश्वेभ्यस्त्वा देवेभ्य परिददामि । सर्वेभ्यस्त्वा भूतेभ्यः परिददाम्यरिष्टयै ॥ २ ॥

पार० कां० २ । कं० २ । २१

O Child ! you are the *Brahmachari* of *Prajapati*; you are the *Brahmachri* of *prana,* God who is the soul of all. *Prajapati* in vest you with sacred thread for your happiness. I also appoint you to follow the command of *prajapati*.

O Child ! I appoint you for attaining the knowledge of *Prajapati,* the Lord of the creatures; I. appoint you to attain the knowledge of the mighty sun, I appoint you for attaining the knowledge of liquids and herbs; I appoint you for attaining the knowledge of .he earth and heavenly region; I appoint you for attaining the knowledge of all the physical and spiritual forces; I appoint you for maintaianing peace and tranquility among all the living beings.

After this *Upanayanaa* ceremony is finished, the father of the child and Acharya, if they think fit, should hold the *Vedarambha* ceremony on the very day and if they think to hold *Vedarambha* on other day they should sing *Mahavamdevya* as has been prescribed in the end of *Samanyprakavna.* The mother of the child paying full respect to ladies give them leave and the father of the child give respect to gentlemen and give them leave.

The mother and father of the child, the Acharya, other relatives, friend etc, should say together—

ओं त्वं जीव शरदः शतं वर्द्धमानः ।

आयुष्मान् तेजस्वी वर्चस्वी भूयाः ॥

O Child ! you, growing in strength and vigour live hundred autumns. You become long-lived, brillant and radiant.

Here ends the procedure of the *uapnayana* ceremony.

VEDARAMBHA

Now here is prescribed the procedure of *Vedarambha*, the beginning of the study of Vedas

To undertake to observe the discipline and rules for studying the four Vedas with all their systems and limbs (Sangopanga*) beginning from the *Mantra* of *Gayatri*—is called the *Veda rambha*.

Time-the day of the investiture of sacred thread is also the time of *Vedarambha*. If the same could not be performed on the day of *Ubanayana* or it is anyhow not desired to be done on the same day, this be performed on the next day. If this next day is also not suitable the ceremony of *Vedarmaha* be performed on any day within one year (from the date of *Upanayana* performed).

Procedure—On the day fixed for the *Vedarambha* ceremony the performer of the ceremony, i. e. father of the child or in absence of father the *Acharya* bathing the child with pure clean water and dressing him in nice dress should sit with the child on a good seat in the west of the *Yajnavedi* keeping faces eastward.

Thereafter, the adoration, supplication and meditation of God with the eight[1], *Mantra*, *svstivachan*, *Santikarana* should be performed. *Agnyadhana* with ओं भूर्भुवः स्वः० *Samidadhana* with ओम् अयन्त इध्म० इत्यादि three *Mantras* and the sprinkling of water on the four sides of the *yajanakunnda* with ओम् अदिते०········ ओं देव सवितः० etc. four *Mantra* should be performed.

---

*Angas of the vedas are:—**Shiksha**, **Kalpa**, **Vyakarana**, Nirukta, chhandas and Jyotisha, Upangas are —Purvamimansa, Vaisheshika, Nyaya, Yoga, Sankhya and Vedanta. Upvedas are —Ayurveda, Dhanurveda, Gandharvaveda, Arthveda. The science of art. Brahmanas are:—Aitreya, Shatapatha, Sam, Gopath, Vedas are—RK, Yajur, sam and Atharva. The student should learn them systemetically and in their order.

1. He who holds the Vedarambha on the day of Upanayan after its performance has not to do these prayers etc, again.

Thereafter the fire of the *Yajnakunda* should be inflamed ablaze with ओम् उदबुध्यस्वाग्ने० and on the enkindled woodfuel four oblations of *Agharavajyabhagahuti*, four *Vyahriti Ahutis*, and eight *Ajyahutis* with (ओं त्वन्नो अग्ने etc, eight *Mantras*) (all totalling 16) should be offered. Then principal *Homa* should be Performed (with the four *Mantras* ओं भूर्भुवः स्वः अग्न आयूंषि० etc.). There after, four oblations of *Vyahriti Ahuti*, one oblation of *Svistakrit Ahuti* and one *Prajapatya Ahuti* (thus totalling six in all), should be made offered from the hand of the child.

Afterward the fire of the *Yajnakunda* should be gathered in the *Kunda with* following *Mantra*—

ओम् अग्ने सुश्रवसं मा कुरु । ओं यथा त्वमग्ने सुश्रवः सुश्रवा असि । ओम् एवं मां सुश्रवः सौश्रवसं कुरु । ओं यथा त्वमग्ने देवानां यज्ञस्य निधिपा असि । ओम् एवमहं मनुष्याणां वेदस्य निधिपो भूयासम् ॥

पार० कां० २ । कं० ४ । २

O famous *Acharya* ! please make me earn fame in the field of education. O *Acharya* ! as you are enjoying prominence and are highly learned so you make me enjoy prominence and become highly learned. O *Acharya* ! as you among the learned men, are the preserver of the treasure oi knowledge, *Yajna* etc. so I become amongst the men, the preserver of the treasure of the Vedic knowledge and speech,

Afterward the child taking round of the *Yajnakuada* should sprinkle water round the *Yajnakunda* with the procedure and pronouncement of ओम् अदिते 'अनुमन्यस्व०' etc. four *Mantras.*

Thereafter the child standing on the south side of the *Yajnakunda* keeping his face northward should take one wood-stick (समिधा) dipped in *ghee* and should offer it in the middle of fire of the Vedi after pronouncing the following *Mantra*:—

ओम अग्नये समिधमाहार्षं बृहते जातवेदसे । यथा त्वमग्ने समिधा समिध्यस एवमहमायुषा मेधया वर्चसा प्रजया पशुभिर्ब्रह्मवर्चसेन समिन्धे जीवपुत्रो ममा-

चार्यो मेधाव्यहमसान्यनिराकरिष्णुर्यशस्वी तेजस्वी ब्रह्मवर्चस्यन्नादो भूयासं स्वाहा ॥

पार० कां० २ । कं ४ । ३

I have brought the wood-fuel for the enkindlement of *Yajna* fire which is mighty in nature and is present in all the created object of the world. As this fire blazes with wood-fuel so I shine with long life, wisdom, vigour, progeny, animals and the knowledge of Veda and *Brahman.* May my *Acharya* have his sons alive and may I be enriched with high intellectual power. May I not be arrogant to anyone. I may be prominent, vigorous, possessed of the Divine merits and the master of grain and food.

In the same manner the second and third wood-stick should be offered. Thereafter the fire of the *Vedi* should be accumulated by pronouncing the *Mantra*—'ओम् अग्ने सुश्रव: सुश्रवसं०' and water should be sprinkled in the four side of the *Vedi* with ओम् अदिते ऽनुमन्यस्व० इत्यादि four *Mantras.* The child sitting in the west of the *Vedi* keeping his face in the east warm his hand palms a little and touching a little water should touch his mouth seven times with each of the following *Mantras* likewise :—

Here the word likewise means that procedure of warming of hand palms and touching of water with them should be done at each time.

ओं तनूपा अग्नेऽसि तन्वं मे पाहि ॥ १ ॥

ओम् आयुर्दा अग्नेऽस्यायुर्मे देहि ॥ २ ॥

ओं वर्चोदा अग्नेऽसि वर्चो मे देहि ॥ ३ ॥

ओम् अग्ने यन्मे तन्वा ऊनं तन्म आपृण ॥ ४ ॥

ओं मेधां मे देवः सविता आदधातु ॥ ५ ॥

ओं मेधां मे देवी सरस्वती आदधातु ॥ ६ ॥

ओं मेधां मे अश्विनौ देवावाधत्तां पुष्करस्रजौ ॥ ७ ॥

पार० कां० २ । कं० ४, ७, ८ ॥

This fire is the preserver of body let it preserve my body.[1]

This fire is the giver of life let it grant me long life.[2]

This fire is the giver of brilliancy let it give me brilliancy.[3]

Whatever has exhausted in my body let this fire recuperate.[4]

May the creator of the universe grant me wisdom.[5]

Let the all-flourishing knowldge give us wisdom.[6]

Let the teacher and preacher wearing garlands give us knowledge.

Afterwards the child should touch the limbs described in each *Mantra* by pronounceing the concerned following *Mantras* in the manner given below:—

ओं वाक् च म आप्यायताम् ॥ १ ॥—touch the mouth
ओं प्राणश्च म आप्यायताम् ॥ २ ॥—touch the nose
ओं चक्षुश्च म आप्यायताम् ॥ ३ ॥—touch the eyes
ओं श्रोत्रञ्च म आप्यायताम् ॥ ४ ॥—touch the ears
ओं यशो बलञ्च म आप्यायताम् ॥ ५ ॥—touch the both arms

O God ! may my organ of speech be sound and well developed.[1]

O God ! may my nose be sound and well developed.

O God ! may my eyes be sound and well- developed.

O God ! may my ears be sound and well-developed.

O God ! may my arms which are the source of fame and strength grow appropriately.

The child should meditate God with the following *Mantras*:—

ओं मयि मेधां मयि प्रजां मय्यग्निस्तेजो दधातु । मयि मेधां मयि प्रजां मयीन्द्र इन्द्रियं दधातु । मयि मेधां मयि प्रजां मयि सूर्यो भ्राजो दधातु । यत्ते अग्ने

तेजस्तेनाहं तेजस्वी भूयासम् । यत्ते अग्ने वर्चस्तेनाहं वर्चस्वी भूयासम् । यत्ते अग्ने हरस्तेनाहं हरस्वी भूयासम् ।

आश्व० अ० १ कं० २१ । सू० ४

May Agni, the self-refulgent God give me wisdom, progeny and strength. May Indra, The Almighty God bestow upon me the favour of wisdom, progeny and the organic power, May *Surya*, The All-Controlling God grant me wisdom, progeny and brilliance, May I be effulgent with the effulgence Thou possessest in Thee my Lord ! May I be powerful with the power Thou hast in Thee my Lord ! May I be an overpowering force with the force wherewith Thou art endowed my Lord !

Afterwords the child walking to the north side of the *Yajnaknuda* should sit his knees supported on the ground keeping his face in the east and *Acharya* should sit in front of the child keeping his face westward.

बालकोक्ति :—अधीहि भूः सावित्री भो अनुब्रूहि ॥

आश्व० १ । २१ ।४

Says the child—O *Acharya* instruct me the *Gayatri Mantra* the subject-matter of which is *Savitar*, the sun. Please teach me.

Here it is meant by the term अधीहि and 'अनुब्रूहि' that first Om be pronounced, at the next step the भूर्भुवः स्वः be pronounced and at the third step the portion of *Mantra* be pronunced. The trio of *Om Mahabyahriti* and the portion if *Mantra* explain the nature and characteristics of God and it is, therefore, the demand of child that this be pronounced in the specific manner,

Thereafter, *Acharya* putting a cloth piece on the shoulder of him and on the shoulder of the child and holding the fingers of both of the hands of the child into his own hand should teach *Gayatri Mantra* to child in three parts.

First time

श्रों भूर्भुवः स्वः तत्सवितुर्वरेण्यम् ।

This part be got pronounced by the child word by word correctly.

Second time

श्रों भूर्भुवः स्वः । तत्सवितुर्वरेण्यं भर्गो देवस्य धीमहि ।

This should be repeated by the child slowly and correctly word by word.

Third time

ओं भूर्भुवः स्वः । तत्सवितुर्वरेण्यं भर्गो देवस्य धीमहि । धियो यो नः प्रचोदयात् ।

Acharya getting this repeated by the child slowly should tell the short meaning of this *Mantra* to the child.

Meaning—*Om* is the prime name of God in which all other names somehow are contained; He is *Bhuh* because of his being the life of life; He is *Bhuvah* as He is the protector from all the pains; He is *svah* because of His being all-bliss and giver of bliss to His devotees. To that creator of all the worlds, the illuminator of all the luminous bodies like the sun etc; the giver of wisdom and wealth we establish in our heart as our worshipable Lord. We concentrate in our hearts the excellent attainable, thinkable quality and power of God who is desired by all and who is most predominating, pure, sanctimonious by nature and the destroyer of all sorts of pains. May he lead our intellects and actions towards excellent quality. acts and natures. Far this purpose only the Lord of the universe should be eulogized, prayed and premeditated. None else but Him should be treated as the object of worship and choice and be known as like Him and superior to Him,

Afterwards the child and *Acharya* should take a firm vow as has been taken previonsly in the sacred-thread ceremony with the following *Mantra*:—

श्रों मम व्रते हृदयं ते दधामि मम चित्तमनुचित्तं ते अस्तु ।
मम वाचमेकव्रतो जुषस्व बृहस्पतिष्ट्वा नियुनक्तु मह्याम् ॥

पा० १ । २१ । ७

This *Mantra* has been translated in the sacred thread ceremony.

The *Acharya* should tie in the belt of the child the girdle (मेखला)* previously prepared, beautiful and smooth one by the following *Mantra* :—

ओम् इयं दुरुक्तं परिबाधमाना वर्णं पवित्रं पुनती म आगात् ।
प्राणापानाभ्यां बलमादधाना स्वसा देवी सुभगा मेखलेयम् ॥

पार० कां० २ । कं० २ । ८

This is the girdle which is as sacred and pleasant as the sister. It is Devi; the sing and symbol of purity and chastity. This obstructing evil thought and action, preserving the sanctity of *Varna* system, giving strength for our inhailing and exhaling breath has come into my possession.

The *Acharya* pronouncing the following *Mantra* should give the *Brahmachari* (the child) two clean कौपीन, two अंगोछे, one उत्तरीय (चादर) and two कटिवस्त्र. Of thesse clothes one कौपीन, one कटिवस्त्र, and one अंगोछा should be put on by the child with the advice of *Acharya*: |

यों युवा सुवासाः परिवीत आगात् स उ श्रेयान् भवति जायमानः
तं धीरासः कवय उन्नयन्ति स्वाध्यो३ मनसा देवयन्तः

ऋ० मं०३ । सू० ८ । मन्त्र ४ ॥ पार० २ । २ ६

The translation of this Mantra has been given in *Upanayana*.

Afterwards the Acharya having a दण्ड*, stick in his hand should stand up before the chid and the child standing in the

---

*Foot note : The girdle of Darbha or Munja be appropriated for Brahmna, the Khastriya be provided with the girdle of Dhanusa Grass or Valkala and the Vaishya with wooden or jute girdle.

*The child to be worthy of Brahmanship would take the stick of पलाश or बिल्व which be as long as it extends from the ground to hair of fore head, the child to be worthy of Khatriya ship take the stick of बद or खदिर as long as it could reach to his brows, the child to be worthy of Vaishyaship take of पीपल or गूलर as long as it could reach upto projectile part of his nose. These sticks should be made smooth, straight, free from fire burnt, bending and worm-eaten :—

One piece of deer skin for each to sit, one water-pot, one small pot and one आचमनीय should be given to the Brahmacharis front of Acharya with folded hand should take the stick from his hand pronouncing the folloing *Mantra*:—

ओं यो मे दण्डः परापतद्वैहायसोऽधिभूम्याम् ।

तमहं पुनरादद आयुषे ब्रह्मणे ब्रह्मवर्चसाय ॥

पा० कां० २ । कं० २ । १२ ॥

This stick which has come into my possession is based on the ground standing straight in the space. I again accept it specially for the attainment of long life, knowledge of the *Veda* and discipline and strength of continence.

Afterward the father should give a general information to celibate regarding the life of chastity and preech him the code of conduct as follows :—

ब्रह्मचार्यसि असौ ॥ १॥ अपो ऽशान ॥ २ ॥ कर्म कुरु ॥ ३ ॥ दिवा मा स्वाप्सीः ॥ ४ ॥ आचार्याधीनो वेदमधीष्व ॥ ५ ॥

आश्व० १ । २२ । २, ॥

द्वादश वर्षाणि प्रतिवेदं ब्रह्मचर्यं गृहाण वा ब्रह्मचर्यं चर ॥ ६ ॥

[तु० आश्व० गृ० १ । २२ । ३, ४ ॥ तथा पा० गृ० २ । ५ । १३-१५]

आचार्याधीनो भवान्यत्राधर्माचरणात् ॥ ७ ॥ क्रोधानृते वर्जय ॥ ८ ॥ मैथुनं वर्जय ॥ ९ ॥ उपरि शय्यां वर्जय ॥ १० ॥ कौशीलवगन्धाञ्जनानि वर्जय ॥ ११ ॥ गो० गृ० ३ । १ । १५१-९

अत्यन्त स्नानं भोजनं निद्रां जागरणं निन्दां लोभमोहभयशोकान् वर्जय ॥ १२ ॥ प्रतिदिनं रात्रेः पश्चिमे यामे चोत्थायावश्यकं कृत्वा दन्तधावनस्नान-सन्ध्योपासनेश्वरस्तुतिप्रार्थनोपासनायोगाभ्यासान्नित्यमाचर ॥ १३ ॥ क्षुरकृत्यं वर्जय ॥ १४ ॥ मांसरूक्षाहारं मद्यादिपानं च वर्जय ॥ १५ ॥ गवाऽश्वहस्त्युष्ट्रा वियानं वर्जय ॥ १६ ॥ अन्तर्ग्रामनिवासोपानच्छत्रधारणं वर्जय ॥ १७ ॥ अका

मतः स्वयमिन्द्रियस्पर्शेन वीर्यस्खलनं विहाय वीर्यं शरीरे संरक्ष्योर्ध्वरेताः सततं भव ॥ १८ ॥ तैलाभ्यङ्गमर्दनात्यम्लातितिक्तकषायक्षाररेचनद्रव्यमि मा सेवस्व ॥ १९ ॥ नित्यं युक्ताहारविहारवान् विद्योपार्जने च यत्नवान् भव ॥ २० ॥ सुशीलो मितभाषी सभ्यो भव ॥ २१ ॥ मेखलादण्डधारणभैक्ष्यचर्यसमिधादानोदकस्पर्शनाचार्यप्रियाचरणप्रातःसायमभिवादनविद्यासंचयजितेन्द्रियत्वादीन्येते ते नित्य धर्माः ॥ २२ ॥

तु० गोभिल ३ । १ । १५-२६

You realize it that you are celibate (ब्रह्मचारी) from to day.[1] You always perform the act of sipping clean pure water before taking meals and performing daily prayers.[5] Always be away from evil acts and do the pious and righteous acts.[3] You do not ever sleep in day time.[4] Remaining under the guidance and control of your Acharya you always persever in learning the *Vedas* with their limbs and sub-limbs.[5] You lead the life of celibate throughout till 48 years in proportion to 12 years for each of the four *Vedas* with its limbs and sub-limbs or you observe this disciplne without any failure unless you complete the study of the four *Vedas* with limbs and sub-limbs.[6] You always follow the rules of *Dharma* under your Acharya but you do not ever obey the advice of your Acharya if he preaches you anything of *Adharma* and desire you to act according to that.[7] You do abstain from anger and telling a lie. Always you keep yourself away from the habit of the eight kinds of passionate* acts.[9] You do sleep only on ground never sle:p on *charpoy* etc. Never be in the habit of *Kaushilava*, i. e. bad song, playing on musical instruments, dance etc. abominable acts, use of perfumery and *Anjana*.[11] Always keep you away from much-bathing, much-eating, much-sleeping, much-awaking, reproach, greed. undue indulgence, fear, grief.[12] Rise in the fourth part of night, alway-

---

**Foot note*:—To think of woman, to gossip about woman, to touch woman, to play with woman, to gaze at woman to embrace woman, to stay separate with woman, to have cohabitation—are the habits of eight kinds of passionate acts.

do needful acts like clearance of bowls etc. brushing the teeth with *Dantadhavana*, washing the mouth, bath daily, two times meditations, euiogium, prayer and communion with God and the practice of ***Yogic*** systems.[13] Do not eat meat, dry, coares cerials and do not ever drink intoxicant drinks.[15] Never you do the rIdind on bullock, horses, elephant, camel etc.[16] You never live in a village (Except in *Gurukula*), never use shoses and ambrella.[17] Except in the case of urine-discharge never touch the organ of urine to cause the discharge of semen and restrining the semen in body always try to become 'उर्ध्वरेता'; the man whose semen is never discharged and has thus become the source of attaining knowldge by taking uptrends towards mind and thus do your work with all such cares.[18] Do not ever use massage with oil etc., do not use mustard-plaster for the beauty of body, do not take ever the eatables which are very sour like tamerind etc. very pungent like red chillies etc., astringant like (हरड़) Terminalia chebula; purgative like (जमालगोटा) Clerodendum Phlomoides aciditic like more saltish things. Daily you do your work of eating and other dealings with great care and thought and be active in learning knowledge.[20] You always possess good character, be not extravagant in talk and cultivate behaviour and courtesies of sitting in meetings and assemblies. You keep yourself bound by the duties of wearing girdle, keeping the stick, mendicancy* performance of *Agnihatra*: bath,daily meditation of God, good sentiments for Acharya and salutation to Acharya every morning and evening. These are the deeds of your daily performance and whatever has been prohibited, you should abstain from doing.

**Foot note*:—The Brahamana's child in asking for alms from a man should address him भवान् भिक्षां ददातु in asking alms from woman he shoud address भवती भिक्षां ददातु; the kshatriya's child should address men and ladies respectively as—भिक्षां भवान् ददातु; भिक्षां भवती ददातु; Vaishya child should address men and women respectively भिक्षां ददातु भवान्, भिक्षां ददातु भवती ।

As father has completed his preaching the child salute him, should say him with folded hand. "I would no doubt, act according to whatever you have preached me"

Afterward the celibate circumambulating the fire of the *Yajnakunda* should stand in the west of that and ask alms from mother, father, sister, brother, maternal uncle, mother's sister, uncle etc. who do not hesitate in giving alms and thus alms accumuluted should be surrendered to Acharya. Afterwards Acharya taking some-what cerial from that return the alms to the celibate and he (the child) should keep it safe for his own food.

Afterwards seating the child on a nice seat the song of *Vamdevya* as has been prescribed in *Samanya Prakarana* should be performed. Thereafter the child should eat the alms which he had kept for him.

Afterwards there should be rest till evening and then (in the evening) Acharya should get the prayer and meditation as discribed in Grihashrama Sanskara, performed by the child with his own hands.

Afterwards Acharya with the Brahmachari should sit in the west of the kunda keeping faces eastward and should prepare *SthaliPaka* (स्थालीपाक) according the method described in Samanya Prakarana and sprinkling *ghee* on it should keep it safe there. They should perform समिधादान and keeping the *samidhas* ablaze they should offer the four oblations of Agharavajyabhagahutis and four oblations of Vyahriti Ahutis totalling eight in all.

Thereafter the Brahmachari standing up should offer three समिधा with the Mantra श्रोम् श्रग्ने सुश्रवः० etc. Again he warming his hand-palms on the fire of *Agnikunda* should touch his limbs having touched his mouth according to the procedure previously described in this *Vedarambha* Sanskara. Afterwards the child

(ब्रह्मचारी) should hand over *Acharya* the previously prepard rice for offering oblations and eating thereafter, Then Achrrya taking into press the prepared rice in the proportion desired for offering oblations and spirinkling *ghee* on it, should offer three oblations with the following Mantras:—

ओं सदसस्पतिमद्भुतं प्रियमिन्द्रस्य काम्यम् ।
सनिं मेधामयासिषँ स्वाहा ॥ इदं सदसस्पतये-इदन्न मम ॥ १ ॥
[यजु० अ० ३२ । मं० १३ ॥]

तत्सवितुर्वरेण्यं भर्गो देवस्य धीमहि ।
धियो यो नः प्रचोदयात् [स्वाहा] ॥ इदं सवित्रे इदन्न मम ॥ २ ॥
[यजु० अ० २२ । मं ९ ॥]

ओं ऋषिभ्यः स्वाहा ॥ इदं ऋषिभ्यः इदन्न मम ॥२ ॥
[आश्व० अ० १ । कं० २२ । सू० १४ ॥]

May I attain God who is self-effulgent, the master of knowledge, wondrous, dear to all, desirable by human spirit and also the discriminatory wisdom. Whatever has been uttered herein is true. The oblation offered is meant for obeying the command of *Sadasaspati* and it is not for me.

I hold into me the praisworthy qualities and light of allcreating God who is almighty. May he lead our intellects and acts towards good qualities. Whatever has been uttered herein is true. the oblation offered is meant for *Savitar* and it is not for me.

We describe the qualities of seers who study *Veda* and see their meanings. Whatever has been uttered herein is true. The oblation offered is meant for the *Rishis* and it is not for me.

After having offered these three above mentioned oblations the *Acharya* should offer fourth oblation with the *Mantra*—ओं यदस्य कर्मण: ete. Thereafter he should offer four oblations of *Vyahriti Ahutis* and eight oblations of *Ajyahutis* totaling twelve in number. Thereafter the *Brahmachri* sitting on a nice seat, keeping his face eastword should do *Vamdevyagana* as has been discribed in *Samanya Prakarna* with the Acharya. Then saying— अमुक गोत्रोत्पन्नो ऽहं भो भवन्तमभिवादये (गोभिल० २/१०/२५) i. e; I born in the geneology of so and so salute you, O my teacher—should salute the Acharya.

Acharya says—आयुस्मान् विद्यावान् भव सौम्य ॥

O my dear diciple ! may you be long-lived and celebrated with knowledge.

When Acharya has given his blessing to the *Brahmachari*, he should eat the cerials remaining from *yajna* and also other sweets etc. with Acharya sitting separately. Afterwards washing hand and mouth they entertain the people invited to grace the occassion with food according to their satisfaction. Afterwards ladies give leave to ladies affectionately and gents to gents. All the people leaving the place should give blessing to the child with the following Sanskrit sentence and go their home:—

हे बालक ! त्वमीश्वरकृपया विद्वान् शरीरात्मबलयुक्तः कुशली
वीर्यवानरोगः सर्वा विद्या अधीत्याऽस्मान् दिदृक्षुः सन्नागम्याः ॥

O child ! you, by the grace of God become learned. strong in body and soul, blessed with pleasure, vigorous, healthy and having attained all the branches of knowledge come from (*Gurukula*) with the deisre of seeing us.

Afterwrads the *Brahmachari* (child) should sleep on the ground for the three days. The Acharya should get performed by the *Brahmachari* the procedure of three *Samidha* with *Mantra* ओम् अग्ने सुश्रवः etc. and the *Angasparsha* procedure as has been desribed in the *Vedarambha*. He should also get performed by the hand of *Brahmachari* the four oblations of the स्थालीपाक by the *Mantra* (सदसस्पति०). the *Brahmachari* should take for three days only the food which are free from acidity and salt.

Afterwards he should go to *Pathshrla* and perform the pledge and vows of the time of education near him and Acharya also do take pledge.

ग्राचार्य उपनयमानो ब्रह्मचारिणं कृणुते गर्भमन्तः ।
तं रात्रिस्तिस्र उदरे विभर्ति तं जातं द्रष्टुमभिसंयन्ति देवाः ॥ १ ॥
इयं समित्पृथिवी द्यौर्द्वितीयोतान्तरिक्षं समिधापृणाति ।
ब्रह्मचारी समिधा मेखलया श्रमेण लोकांस्तपसा पिपर्ति ॥ २ ॥
ब्रह्मचर्येति समिधा समिद्धः कार्ष्णं वसानो दीक्षितो दीर्घश्मश्रुः ।
स सद्य एति पूर्वस्मादुत्तरं समुन्द्रं लोकान्संगृभ्य मुहुराचरिक्रत् ॥ ३ ॥
ब्रह्मचर्येण तपसा राजा राष्ट्रं वि रक्षति ।
ग्राचार्यो ब्रह्मचर्येण ब्रह्मचारिणमिच्छते ॥ ४ ॥
ब्रह्मचर्येण कन्या३ युवानं विन्दते पतिम् ॥ ५ ॥
ब्रह्मचारी ब्रह्म भाजद् विभर्ति तस्मिन्देवा अधि विश्वे समोताः ।
प्राणापानौ जनयन्नाद व्यानं वाचं मनो हृदयं ब्रह्म मेधाम् ॥ ६ ॥

अथर्व० का० ११ । सू० ५ । [मं ३, ४, ६, १७, १८, २४]

Purport. The Acharya having solemnized the vow concerned with the scriptural ceremony of *Vedarambha* keeps the celibate near him for three days. He makes him a celebrated scholar by keeping him (the celibate) in his own control to establish the knowledge in the spirit of student and teaching him the performance of *Sandhyopasana* as described in the *Grihasthashram* chapter and imparting him the knowledge of the conduct of the learned righteous persons. All the learned men approach the celibate to see and admire and respect him when he completing his education and strict full discipline of continence return back home.[1]

The *Brahmachari*, who at the time of *Vedarambha* offering three sticks in the fire of *Homa*, observing the complete strict dicipline of celibacy regularly gain courage to complete education, in reality protects all the humanity like the earth, the sun and the firmament as he satisfies all by wearing the signs of *girdle* etc. offering the *Samidhas*, completing the education and excercising the austerity of continence and with the good qualities and pleasure.[2]

The *Brahmaehari*, when shining with knowledge becoming initiated in attaining knowledge wears the dear skin etc. and does not shave beards, moustache, etc. five Keshas and becomss full fledged celebate, completing in *Gurukula* the state of *Brahmacharya* called as *Purvasamudra* enters immediately into the house-hold life called as *uttarsamudra*. He organizes all the people to achieve their goal and exerting continuously achieves the goal of life and makes happy the world with his speech of righteousness and truth.[3]

Only that is the king who by the dint of observing the austerity, strict celibacy becomes a perfect learned man, perfectly educated, symbol of good conduct, and self-controlled and rules the country in various ways. In the same manner only that learned Acharya who with the observation of complete strict diseipline of continence has attained the perfect knowledge of all sciences can desire a learned celibate to teach and become the Acharya in real scnse.[4]

As the boys completing the life of perfect *Brahmachari*, attaining the complete knowledge of all branches of science and bloomed with full youth wed to a girl so the girls completing and bloomed with full youth wed to a girl so the girls completing the courses of all sciences with perfect discipline of continence and becoming fully young should attain matchful young husband.[5]

When *Brahmachari* retain the *Brahma*, the four *Vedas* with all their limbs and sub-limbs with the knowledge of their words, meaning and the links between these two, he shines and all the virtuous qualities abide in him and all the men of wisdom treat him friend, This *Brahmachari* only through the power of celibacy attains vigour, long life, freedom from pains and sorrows, dexcterity in all branches of knowledge, good speech, purity of soul, purity of consecence, God and excellent intellect dissiminates all sciences for the good of all men.[6]

The period of Brahmacharya

Here is the authority of *Chhandogyopnishad* 3/16:—

मातृमान् पितृमानाचार्य्यवान् पुरूषो वेद ॥ १ ॥

शत० १४। ६ । १०। २

पुरूषो वाव यज्ञस्तस्य यानि चतुर्विꣳशतिवंर्षाणि तत् प्रातः सवनं चतुर्विꣳ
शत्यक्षरा गायत्री गायत्रं प्रातःसवनं तदस्य वसवोऽन्वायत्ताः प्राणा वावव सव
एते हीदꣳसर्वं वासयन्ति ॥ २ ॥

तं चेदेतस्मिन् वयसि किञ्चिदुपतपेत् स ब्रूयात् प्राणा वसव इदं मे प्राताः
सवनं माध्यन्दिनꣳ सवनमनुसन्तनुतेति माहं प्राणानां वसूनां मध्ये यज्ञो विलोप्सी
येत्युद्धैव तत एत्यगदो ह भवति ॥ ३ ॥

अथयानि चतुश्चत्वारिꣳशद्वदर्षाणि तन्माध्यन्दिनꣳसवनं चतुश्चत्वारिꣳ
शदक्षरा त्रिष्टुप् त्रैष्टुभं माध्यन्दिनꣳसवनं तदस्य रुद्रा अन्वायत्ताः प्राणा वाव
एते हीदꣳ सर्वꣳ रोदयन्ति ॥ ४ ॥

तं चेदेतस्मिन् वयसि किञ्चदुपतपेत् स ब्रूयात् प्राणा रुद्रा इदं मे माध्य-
न्दिनꣳसवनं तृतयोसवनमनुसन्तनुतेति माहम्प्राणानाꣳ रुद्राणां मध्ये यज्ञो विलो
प्सीयेत्युद्धैव तत एत्यगदो ह भवति ॥ ५ ॥

अथ यान्याष्टाचत्वारिꣳशद्धर्षाणि तत् तृतीयसवनमष्टाचत्वारिꣳशदक्षरा
जगति जागत् तृतीयसवनं तदस्यादित्या अन्वायत्ताः प्राणा वावादित्या एते हृीदꣳ
सर्वममादवते ॥ ६ ॥

तं चेदेतस्मिनं वयसि किञ्चदुपतपेत् स ब्रूयात् प्राणा आदित्या इदं मे
तृतीयसवनमायुरनुसन्तनुतेति माहंप्राणानामादित्यानां मध्ये यज्ञो विलोप्सी यत्युद्धै
व तत एत्यगदो ह भवति ॥ ७ ॥

[छादोग्य० अ० ३ ख० १६ । १-६

Become in the matter of achieving Dharma, Arth, Kama and *Moksha* excellently clever celebrated with knowledge only those men and women who respectively have got the education and instruction till five years of age from mother, five to eight from father and eight to 48, 44, 40, 36, 30, 25 from Acharya (आचार्य) and 8, 10, 24, 22, 20, 18. 16 from Acharya (आचार्या).[1]

The smallest side to keep this *yajna*, the human body fully bloomed with long life, vigoure etc, is that the man should keep a strict celibate life till 24 years of his age and woman till 16 years of her age taking in mind the similarity of the 24 letters of the *Gayatri* metre. That is the first phase (प्रातः सवन) of the human body when the vital airs known as *Vasus* come to it and gaining vigour make reside all the meritorious qualities in body, spirit and mind.[2]

If any one preaches to *Brahmachari* that he should execute marriage or enjoy carnal pleasure or passion before 25 years of his age he should reply to the man that he whould not be able to observe the strict discipline of *Brahmachrya* of 44 years, the middle one had he not got his vital air, mind and organs strong by adhering to he discipline of celibacy till 25 years. He should say the *Brahmacharya* of first cetegory approves the *Brahmacharya* of middle category. Am I a fool like you who quickly destroying the body which is the organization of vital airs, bodies, inner organs, soul and the medium of all good qualities, good acts and good nature, become deprived of the fruits of assumption of the human body ? Why do I sink into the deep sea of great pains by breaking the discipline and pledge of the state of celibacy which is the root of all *Ashramas* and most excellent act among all the nice deeds and the main cause of all virtues ? He who observes the diseipline of *Brahmachrya* in the first age becomes free from all diseases, attaining knowledge through the power of *Brahmacharya.* Therefore I whould not break the pledge of *Brahmacharya* under influence of the exhortations of you fools"[3]

The *Brahmchari* who observe the strict disciplines of the 44 years *Brahmcharya* known as middle category and symbolized by the 44 letters of the Tristup metre, holds into him the vital and he always leave the wickedness to weep and cry.[4]

If any one say to the Brahmachari who is going to observe the discipline of the continence of middle category to leave this and gain pleasure with marriage the Brahmachari should thus—"Whatever happiness can be attained by observing the first category of Brahmacharya and even whatever more carnal pleasure can be obtained by it—may not be attained even in dream without observing the celibate life. It is only Brahmachari who can attain the full worldly and unworldly happiness and no one else. Therefor, I would achieve the complete happiness enjoying wisdom, strength, long life and righteousness without breaking the pledge of observing the celibacy which is the excellent source of gaining pleasure and happiness. I won't spoil and destroy myself and family by doing marriage early, acting under the persuasive of you fools."[5]

The student observing the discipline of the celibacy till 48 years of age which has been symbolized on the similarity of the 48 letters of the Jagati metre and is the first category, attains complete knowledge, perfect strength, perfect intellect, perfect good qualities, acts and nature and shining like sun he learns all the sciences.[6]

If anyone desires to deviate him from the path of first category of continence, the Brahmachari should replying say, "O lads of lads ! keep away from me. I always remain far off from your words of bad-smelling and spoiling. I would never break this excellent Brahmacharya. I will be equipped with the good qualities, acts, nature like knowledge etc. by completing this Brahmacharya. May God fulfil my this auspicious pledge through his kindness so that I could specifically make your children happy by preaching and educating you uneducated.[7]

चतस्रोऽवस्थाः शरीरस्य वृद्धियौवनं संपूर्णंता किञ्चित्परिहाणिश्चेति । तत्रा शोडशाद् वृद्धिः । आपञ्चविंशतेर्यौवनम् । आचत्वारिंशतस्सम्पूर्णंता । ततः किञ्चित्परिहाणिश्चेति ॥ १* ॥

पञ्चविंशे ततो वर्षे पुमान्नारी तु षोडशे ।
समत्वागतवीर्यौ तौ जानीयात् कुशलो भिषक् ॥ २ ॥

This is the authority quoted here from the *Sushruta* of *Dhanvantari*.

There are four stages of this human body—. The first growth, the second youth, the third maturity and the fourth gradual decay. The growth stage begins from the age of 16 and completes in 25th. If any one spoils the marrows in the stage of growth he is destroying his all like the axed tree and broken Jug, would repent on his act and there would remain nothing in his hand to recuperate this loss. The second stage known as youth begins from the age of 25 years and finishes at 40 years. He who does not preserve this stage thoroughly would exterminate his fortune. The third stage which is of maturity is completed at 40th year. Any one who having observed Brahmacharya would in household life) not become *Rtugami*, free from the discourse of other lady, desirous to his own wife as pledged and Brahmachari for one year after the wife being pregnant would spoil all good he had earned previously and really he would demolish every thing to dust. The fourth stage begins from 40th years and remains till any one becomes semenless. This is known as the stage of gradual decay. Any one who will destroy his semen more than whatever decay takes place in this stage would fall the victim of tuberculosis, fistula etc. diseases. He who keeps these four stages well balanced and safe, would earn pleasure for always and would make all the world happy.[1]

Here a little variety should be realized and this is that there is not the equal period of the four stages of the bodies of male and female. Whatever strength and power is available in the body of male in his age of 25 years, is available in the female body in her sixteens. If the marriage is desired to be celebrated early it should be known that male of 25 years and the female of 16 years have equal strength and power.[2]

Therefore the marriage in this stage is of the marriage of low grade merit. The marriages respectively of female 17 and the male 30, female 18 and male 36, female 19 and male 38 should be treated as of middle grade merits. The marriages between female and male respectively in the ages 20, 21, 22, 24 female and 40, 42, 46, 48 male is of first grade merit. O celibate ! you bear in your mind all these things and these will serve your purpose well in the other *Ashramas*.

Those men who desire to promote their families, progenies and relatives and their countries should keep the following things in their minds:—

श्रोत्रं त्वक् चक्षुषी जिह्वा नासिका चैव पञ्चमी ।
पायूपस्थं हस्तपादम् वाक् चैव दशमी स्मृता ॥ १ ॥

बुद्धीन्द्रियाणि पञ्चैषां श्रोत्रादीन्यनुपूर्वशः ।
कर्मेन्द्रियाणि पञ्चैषां पाय्वादीनि प्रचक्षते ॥ २ ॥

एकादशं मनो ज्ञेयं स्वगुणेनोभयात्मकम् ।
यस्मिन् जिते जितावेतौ भवतः पञ्चकौ गणौ ॥ ३ ॥

इन्द्रियाणां विचरतां विषयेष्वपहारिषु ।
संयमे यत्नमातिष्ठेद्विद्वान् यन्तेव वाजिनाम् ॥ ४ ॥

इन्द्रियाणां प्रसङ्गेन दोषमृच्छत्यसंशयम् ।
संनियम्य तु तान्येव ततः सिद्धिं नियच्छति ॥ ५ ॥

वेदास्त्यागश्च यज्ञाश्च नियमाश्च तपांसि च ।
न विप्रभावदुष्टस्य सिद्धिं गच्छन्ति कर्हिचित् ॥ ६ ॥

वशे कृत्वेन्द्रियग्रामं संयम्य च मनस्तथा ।
सर्वान् संसाधयेदर्थानाक्षिण्वन् योगतस्तनुम् ॥ ७ ॥

(मनु० अ० २ । ९०-९२, ८८, ९३, ९७, १००)

यमान् सेवेत सततं न नियमान् केवलान् बुधः ।
यमान् पतत्यकुर्वाणो नियमान् केवलान् भजन् ॥ ८ ॥

(मनु० ४ । २०४)

अभिवादनशीलस्य नित्यं वृद्धोपसेविनः ।
चत्वारि तस्य वर्द्धन्ते आयुर्विद्या यशो बलम् ॥ ९ ॥

अज्ञो भवति वै बालः पिता भवति मन्त्रदः ।
अज्ञं हि बालमित्याहुः पितेत्येव तु मन्त्रदम् ॥ १० ॥

न हायनैर्न पलितैर्न वित्तेन न बन्धुभिः ।
ऋषयश्चक्रिरे धर्मं योऽनूचानः स नो महान् ॥ ११ ॥

न तेन वृद्धो भवति येनास्य पलितं शिरः ।
यो वै युवाप्यधीयानस्तं देवाः स्थविरं विदुः ॥ १२ ॥

यथा काष्ठमयो हस्ती यथा चर्ममयो मृगः ।
यश्च विप्रोऽनधीयानस्त्रयस्ते नाम बिभ्रति ॥ १३ ॥

संमानाद् ब्राह्मणो नित्यमुद्विजेत विषादिव ।
अमृतस्येव चाकाङ्क्षेदवमानस्य सर्वदा ॥ १४ ॥

वेदमेव सदाभ्यस्येत्तपस्तप्स्यन् द्विजोत्तमः ।
वेदाभ्यासो हि विप्रस्य तपः परमिहोच्यते ।। १५ ।।

योऽनधीत्य द्विजो वेदमन्यत्र कुरुते श्रमम् ।
स जीवन्नेव शूद्रत्वमाशु गच्छति सान्वयः ।। १६

यथा खनन् खनित्रेण नरो वार्यधिगच्छति ।
तथा गुरुगतां विद्यां शुश्रूषुरधिगच्चति ।। १७ ।।

श्रद्दधानः शुभां विद्यामाददीतावरादपि ।
अन्त्यादपि परं धर्मं स्त्रीरत्नं दुष्कुलादपि ।। १८ ।।

विषादप्यमृतं ग्राह्यं बालादपि सुभाषितम् ।
विविधानि च शिल्पानि समादेयानि सर्वतः ।। १९ ।।
(मनु० अ० २ । श्लो० १२१, १५३, १५४, १५६, १५७, १६२, १६६ १६८, २१८, २३८ २३९ पूर्वार्द्धं २४० उत्तरार्द्धं ।)

These are the shlokas from Manusmriti.

The ears, skin, eyes, tongue, nose, rectum, phalus, hands, feet and speech are the organs of the body. Amongst them five, the ears etc. are the cognitive organs while remaining others are called the active organs.[2]

The eleventh organ is the mind. It has its relation with both the sets of organs in its qualities and functions. By the control of this mind the both sets of organs are controlled.[3]

The Brahmachari and learned men should always control their organs when they go to enjoy the external objects and their reactions in the manner as a chariot-holder controls the horses running amuck and astray.[4]

Thc Brahmachari implying his mind with the organs in the function of their hunting becomes blamable undoubtedly. He can gain the accomplishment after keeping these above-mentioned organs in his control.[5]

The study of the *Vedas*, renunciation (*Sanyasa*) performance of *yajna—Agnihotra* etc., observance of celibacy etc., Austerity including the tolerance of blame, praise, loss, profit etc., of the man who has lost his main quality of keeping away from praise and respect and control of organs and has fallen lacking in the duties, qualities etc. of *Varanashrama*, do not succeed to perfection. Therefore it is the duty of the Brahmachari to succeed in attaining perfection by scruplously discharging the duties of his *Ashrama.*[6]

The celibate should keep all his organs in control. He should concentrate his mind with his inner spirit. He should succeed in reaching at his aim by excercising the principles and practices of *yoga* and thereby giving a very minute pain to his body[7]

The wise celibate ought to observe the principles of *yamas,** not only of *niyamas* as without observing *yamas* and observing only *niyamas*‡ anyone becomes fallen from his duties. Therefore it is necessary to observe *yamas* with the observance of *niyamas* daily.[8]

He who cultivates the habit of paying respect (Salutation) and serves the men older in age and in knowledge, prolongs his life, knowledge, fame and strength always. Therefore it is incumbent on the Brahmachari to salute and serve Acharya, mother, father, guest and man of spirituality.[9]

An ignorant one is called *Bala*, the child or innocent in knowledge, the man who gives idea too thers, and is educated and mature in sciences and thought is called *Pita*, the father

---

Foot Note:—Non-violence, truth, non.stealing, continence and indifference or discard in wordly attachments.

Purity, contentment, austerity, self-study and surrender o actions in Divinity.

*अहिंसासत्यास्तेयब्रह्मचर्यापरिग्रहा यमाः। (योग द० २। ३०)। सत्य बोलना, चोरीत्याग, वीर्यरक्षण, श्रौर विषयभोग में घृणा ये ५ यम हैं।

शौचसन्तोषतपः स्वाध्यायेश्वरप्रणिधानानि नियमाः। योग द० २। ३२)। शौच, सन्तोष तप (हानि लाभ आदि द्वन्द्व का सहना) स्वाध्याय (वेद का पढ़ना), ईश्वरप्रणिधान (सर्वस्व ईश्वरार्पण) ये पाँच नियम कहाते हैं।

as the learned persons have called the ignorant man as *Bala* and manof intellet as *Pita.* Therefore every one should become learned and wise by accomplishing the principle of celibacy.[10]

The teachers of piety, righteousness and duty have note counted years, white hair, loosing limbs, wealth and family as the standard of greatness but they have established that he who is competent in answering the debate and is an orator may be called great. Therefore it is obligatory on the Brahmachari to become learned by attaining perfection in the observance of Brahmacharya and attain greatness and fame and dexterity in answering the questions from others.[11]

A man does not become *Briddha,* the mature or perspieacious one as his is trembling in oldness and his hair have grown gray. But a youth who is educated and dexter has been treated as *Briddha,* the old or mature by the men of learning. Therefore completing the discipline of continence one ought to learn and study.[12]

The Brahman or learned by name and not in reality having no education is treated to be like a doll of wood and a lion of eather, Such elephant. lion and Vipar are not the same in reality but the only bear the names alike.. Therefore it is a pressing need that knowledge be attained by observing the discipline of celibacy.[13]

A Brahman, the man desirous to learn the *Veda* and know God should be indifferent from the respect treating it like poison and desire disrespect taking it as Amrit or nectar or boon and he should never expect respect even if he is asking for alms in obeying the rules of the *Ashramas* like *Brahmacharya* etc.[14]

The persons superior amongst the men of Brahmana, Kshatriya and Vaishyas practising austerity should always study the *Vedas.* As the study of the Vedas by Brahmana or learned man has been called a great austerity in this world so one should learn the sciences of the *Vedas* acomplished in the Brahmacharyashrama.[15]

The Brahmana, the kshatriya and the Vaishya who does study the *Vedas* and engage him earnestly in the study of other scriptures, goes down to the state of *Shudra* in his life time and with his children. So it is incumbent on every one to study *Veda* by observing the discipline of Brahmacharyashrma.[16]

As a man digging the earth with spade finds out water in the same manner a student serving his teacher habitually attains the knowledge acquired by him (the teacher). Therfore it is an obligation for student to take instrucation from teacher to take educaton and education by serving him and study the *Veda* with the observance of discipline of the Brahmacharyashrama.[17]

The man having faith in the attainment of perfect knowledge should take instruction from the man might he be low in rank. The teachings of a true Dharma should be taken from even the man of low status and in the same manner good woman (in-marriage) should be accepted from a blamed family also. This is the prcctical norm of morality. Therefore a Brahmachari observing discipline of continence should acquire good knowledge from any quarter before entering into the house-hold life. He should learn the canons of true dharma and completing the Brahmacharyashrama marry a suitable woman in house-hold life.[18]

Because, the Amrit should be taken from within the poison good words should be grasped even from a child and all sorts of arts should be learnt from every one. Therefore, observing Brahmacharya one should learn good qualities by touring one country to other.[19]

यान्यनवद्यानि कर्माणि । तानि सेवितव्यानि । नो इतराणि । यान्यस्माकं सुचरितानि । तानि त्वयोपास्यानि नो इतराणि । ये के चास्मच्छ्रेयाँसो ब्राह्मणा । तेषां त्वयासनेन प्रश्वसितव्यम् ॥ ११ ॥

तैत्तिरीय० प्रपा० ७ । अनु० ११ :

ऋतं तपः सत्यं तपः श्रुतं तपः शान्तं तपो दमस्तपश्शमस्तपो दानं तपो यज्ञस्तपो ब्रह्मभूर्भुवः सुवर्ब्रह्म तदुपास्वैतत्तपः ॥ २ ॥

तैत्तिरी० प्रपा० १० । अनु० ८

O disciple ! you do attend to and follow only those acts which are unblamable, sinless i. e. free from injustice and unrighteousness and concordent with justice and righteousness and do not follow the acts otherwise contaminated with unright eousness· O disciple ! you do take into action and attend to only those acts of your Acharya ! mother and father like us which are right, true and full of righteousness and you never translate into action those acts of ours which are bad and blameworthy, O Brahmachri ! you sit only near those persons amongst us who are pious, righteous, learned and celebrated with the knowledge of Divinty and sit in their company and do have faith in them only.[1]

O diciple ! you embrace only whatever is true and in reality, accept only truth, speak truth, hear and study the true scriptures like the *Vedas*; abstain your mind from its attending to unrighteouness, control your organs like ears etc. from doing bad acts and employ them in good acts, become calm and quiet by renouncing anger etc.. dissiminate good qualities like knowledge etc; enjoy the company of learned and perfrom *Agnihotra* etc; aequire to your best the knowledge of all the objects found in the locality of the earth, firmament and the sun etc.; do practies of *yoga*, *Pranayam* and worship only one God who is second to none. The performance of all such acts is called austerity (*Tapas*).2

ऋतञ्च स्वाध्यायप्रवचने च। सत्यञ्च स्वाध्यायप्रवचने च। तपश्चस्वाध्या०। दमश्च स्वाध्या०। शमश्च स्वाध्या०। अग्नयश्च स्वाध्या०। अग्निहोत्रं च स्वाध्या०। सत्यमिति सत्यवचा राथीतरः। तप इति तपोनित्यः पौरुशिष्टिः। स्वाध्यायप्रवचने एवेति नाको मौद्गल्यः। तद्धि तपस्तद्धि तपः ॥ ३ ॥

तैत्तिरी० प्रपा० ७। अनु० ६।

O Brahmachari ! you do accept truth, learn and teach others. Always preach truth, speak truth, learn and teach others Leave out pleasure and grief etc; practies *yoga* and *Pranayama*, learn and teach others. Obstruct your organs from bad things, empoly them in good acts, acquire knowledge and give it to others also, Abstain your conscience and spirit from unjust actions, employ them in just actions, persuade others to do good and just actions; learn and teach others. Learn and make other learn acquiring the science of *Agni*. Learn and teach others performing *Agnihotra*. To be a truth-teller is austerity according to Acharya *Rathitara*, a truth-teller. To suffer pain in acting according to the terms of justice is the austerity according to Acharya *Paurushisti*, the great austere one, to learn and teach others according to the dictates of Dharma and preach truth is the austerity—this is the opinion of Naka Maudgalya. In the opinion of other Acharyas this is the austerity whatever has been previously revealed and revealed before—this you do bear in mind. This preaching should be put into the mind of the child within three days by the Acharya or by the father of the child.

Afterwards leaving the home the child should be sent to *Gurukula*. If male, should be sent to the *Gurukula* of boys and if girl, should be sent to the *Kanya gurukul*.

If the children have not been taught the pronunciation of the alphabats the Acharya to boy and female Acharya to girl should teach this in the period of a month. For this end the *Panini's Varnochcharana Shiksha* should be utilized. Again teaching the *Ashtadhyayee* of *Panini* with the division of words and meaning within eight months or an year the derivations and from of the 10 *Lakars*, tenses etc. of the roots should be taught with the making of all forms of the Verb and their grammatical operations. Afterwards they should teach the *Ling-anushashana* of *Panini Unadipatha* and *Ganapatha* as well as the forms of cases and derivataives from the root mentioned in the *Astadhyayee* as ण्वुल and तृच् suffics within the period of six months. There are concerned with noun in cases and noun forms derived from root directly by the procedure of *Kridanta*. Then there should be the second teaching of the *Astadhyayee* specially with reference to *Padarthokti*; compounds, questions and answers, *utsarga* exception and *Anvaya* etc. Effort should be made to make student competent in speaking in *Sanskrit*. This syllabus should be completed within 8 months.

Thereafter the *Mahabhashya by Patanjali Muni* which is the commentary of *Varnochcharana Shiksha, Astadhyayee Dhatuptha, Ganapatha, Unadigana and Linganushashana* etc. six treatises should be studied and taught within 18 months i, e, one and a half year. Thus completing the study of Shiksha and Grammar within three yearsand 5 months or 3 years 9 month, or within four years should gain the knowledge of sanskrit language and attain competency in understanding the vital contexts thereof.

Afterwards having studied the *Nighantu Nirukta* of *yaska*, the *Koshas* of Katyayana Muni within one and half year should correctly know the meaning of *Avyaya* and etymology of the words and meaning with special context of *yaugika, yogarudhi* and *Rudhi* the *kinds* of words, Afterwards student should study the *Pingalsutra* by *Pingalacharya* with its commentary within three months and within other three months should learn the art of framing or constructing *Shlokas*. Thereafter the *Kavyalankar Sutra* of *yaska* with *Vatsayana's* commentry with special reference of *Akanksha, yogyata*, Asatti and *Tatparyarth* with the *Anavaya* should be studied, Manusmriti Vidurniti and 10 cantos of any chapter of the Ramayana of Valmiki should be studied. All this should be completed within one year.

Thereafter from any *Siddhanta* of the *Suryasiddhanta* Mathematics including Algebra, Geometry, Arithmatic should be learnt and taught in one year. The students should study *Vedangas* from Nighantu to *jyotisha*, the Astronomy should be studied within four years. Afterwards the *Jaiminiya sutras* of *Purvamimansa* with *Vyasas* commentary; *Vaisheshika Sutras* of *Kanada* with the commentary of Gotama know as *Prashastapada* commentary; the Nyayasutra of Gotama with the commentary of Vatsyayana Muni, the *yogasutras* of *Patanjali* with Vyasa's commentary, the *Sankhya Sutras* known as *Sankhya Shastra* by the Kapilacharya with the commentary of Bhaguri Muni and the *sharirikasutra* of Vyasa with the commentary of Jaimini or Bauddhayana and Isha, *Kena, Katha, Prashna, Mundaka, Mandukya, Aitareya, Taittiriya, Chhandogya* and *Brihadaranyaka* ect. 10 *Upanisheds* and *Vedanta* with the commentary of Vyasa etc. should be studied within two years.

Afterwards within the period of three years should be studied and taught the *Rigveda* with the specific knowledge of metres, accents (स्वर) meanings of the words, *Anvaya*, purport with the help of grammar including Bahvricha, Aitaraya Brahmanas of *Rigveda*, the *Shrauts* and *Grihya** *sutras* of Ashvalayana known as *Kalpa*. In the same way the *yajurveda* with Shatapath Brahmana and knowledge of words and meanings in two years, the *Sama veda* with word-meaning, *Sambrahmana* and knowledge of its singing details in two years and with Gopatha Brahmana and knowledge of words and meaning the *Atharvaveda* within two years—should be studied. The four *Vedas* including its auxilliary treateses should be thus studied and taught in nine years Thereafter the *Ayurveda*, the *Upaveda* of *Rigveda* which is the. scripture of medical sciences, and wherein are included the treatises like Sushruta and Nighantu of Dhanvantari and charaka etc. of Patanjali which are the treatises written by *Rishis* should be studied within three years. The operational instruments given in the *shushruta* should be prepared accordingly and students should examine the parts of body by postmartuming the dead body and dissecting it. They should verify carefully the sciences of anatomy etc. given in them by practical demonstration.

Thereafter, Dhanurveda, the upaveda of the yajurveda which is known as the treatise on weapons, arms and amunitions and are written by Angira etc. seers, not generally available now, should be studied and taught within three years. Thereafter, the student should be taught *Gandharvaveda*, the *upaveda* of the *Samveda* in which are included the Narada-samhita etc. with the knowledge of *Svara*, *Raga*, *Ragini*, *Samaya*, *Vaditra*, *Grama*, *Tala* and *Murehhana* etc. within three years.

Afterwards, *Arthveda* the *upaveda* of *Atharvaveda* which is known as the scripture of the various arts and in which are included the various treatises of *Vishvakarma*, *Tvastar* and Maya

---

***Foot note:**—Brahmanas or the Sutras which seem to inculcate the spirit of violence should not be treated as authority.

should be studied within six years and thus thereby the sciences of Aircraft, telegraphy, geology should be acquired and experimented. In this way completing the syllabus begining from Shiksha and ending at *Ayurveda* etc. which are known as the 14 Arts and sciences in 31 years, the students becoming celebrated scholars should engage them always in the welfare of their own and all the world.

Here ends the ceremony of *Vedarambha*.

□□□

Samavartana

Here we would prescribe the procedure of Samavartana, the covocation.

The Samavartana sacrament is that sacrament in which the student having completed the discipline of Brahmacharya and the study the Vedas with their limbs and sub-limbs and having fully attained good knowledge with the learning of phyislical sciences, returns to the parental home leaving the Gurukula with the idea of entering into house-hold life after doing a legitimate marriage in conformity to scriptural dictates.

Authorities:—

वेदसमाप्तिं वाचयीत । कल्याणैः सह सम्प्रयोगः । स्नातकायोपस्थिताय । राज्ञे च । आचार्यश्वशुरपितृव्यमातुलानां च दधनि मध्वानीय । सर्पिर्वामध्वलाभे । विष्टरः पाद्यमर्घ्यमाचमनीयं मधुपर्कः ॥१॥

आश्वलायनगृह्यसूत्र (१ । २२ । १६ । १ । २३ । २० १ । २४ । २-७) तथा
पारस्करगृह्यसूत्र (२ । ६ । १-२ ॥ १ । ५ । ३२ में—)

वेदं समाप्य स्नायाद् । ब्रह्मचर्यं वाष्टचत्वारिंशकम् । त्रय एव स्नातका भवन्ति । विद्यास्नातको व्रतस्नातको विद्याव्रतस्नातकश्चेति ॥२॥

The ceremony of Samavartana be performed when the study of the Vedas are finished. Always should be a partner in the dealings of the pious persons. At the time when there come these dignitories viz, the student after graduation and completion of discipline of Brahmacharya from Gurukula. King, Acharya, father-in- law, uncle and maternal uncle, the water for washing feet first, water for washing mouth thereafter and then water for sipping should be given to them and they be given a nice seat to sit. Thereafter honeymixed curd, if not available, the ghee-mixed curd in a clean pot should be given to them. This is called *Madhuparka*. There are three categories of *Snatkas*, the graduates of Gurukulas. These are *Vidyasnataka*, *Vratasnataka* and *Vi-*

dyavratasnataka. Therefore a student who takes the bath* of Samavartana after having completed his education as well as the discipline of Brahmacharya vows for 48 years is fully competent for this ceremony.

तं प्रतीतं स्वधर्मेण धर्मदायहरं पितुः ।
स्रग्विणं तल्प आसीनमर्हयेत् प्रथमं गवा ॥३॥
(मनु० ३ । ३ ॥)

The Brahmachari Student who is the son of learned parent, should seat the Acharya, who is pious and like his father on a good seat, garland him and give the gift of cow, the dress according to his status, money etc, and thus respect the Acharya.

तानि कल्पद् ब्रह्मचारी सलिलस्य पृष्टे तपोऽतिष्ठत्तप्यमानः समुद्रे ।
स स्नातो बभ्रुः पिङ्गलः पृथिव्यां बहु रोचते ॥४॥
(अथर्व० कां० ११ । सू० ५ । मं० २६ ॥)

That Brahmachari who is as grave as the calm ocean, who abiding by the disciplines of strict celibacy and thus practises a hard austerity who completing the discipline of controlling his semen and acting according to the desires of the Acharya acquires and ratains all the perfect sciences, bathing according to the procedure of Samavartana enjoys the possition of a good Varna and thus shines on the earth endowed with various good qualities, actions and nature, deserves all thanks.

Period:—The period of Samavantana be known as has been prescribed in the *Vedarambha* ceremony in the context of the discription of the categories of Brahmacharya. But the man and woman desire to enter into the life of house-hold only when they have completed the education, handicrafts, and pledge of continence. There are two Places of settling marriage. One is the home of the Acharya and the other is ones own house. At any

---

Footnote—He who takes bath completing his study without completing Brahmacharya vows is Vidyasnataka He who takes bath completing vows of Brahmacharya without completing study is called Vratasnataka. He who takes both after having completed education and Brahmacharya vows both is known as Vidyavratasnataka.

one of these places according to the procedure prescribed in marriage should be executed after having completed the procedure of Samavartana.

The procedure:—On the day fixed for the Samavartana the *Kunda* etc. for *yajna* as has been prescribed in the *Samanyaprakarna* should be made in the house of the Acharya. All the utensils required in the *yajna* should be collected and arranged one day before. The *SthaliPaka* having been prepared, *ghee* etc. and pots etc, should be kept safe in the *yajnashala*, near the *yajnavedi*. The persons concerned with he yajna and *Sanskara* should take their respective seats according to procedure prescribed on four sides of the yajnakunda and do prayer of God, *Svastivachana*, *Shantikarana* and the men and women who have come to participate should concentrate their mind in the meditation of God attentively. Afterwards the procedure of *Agnyadhana*, *samidhadana* as prescribed in *Samanya prakarana* having been duty performed the sprinkling of water on four sides should be done. The Acharya taking his seat in the west and keeping his face eastward should offer Agharavajybhagahuti[4], Vyahriti Ahutis[4] Svistakrit[1], Prajapatya[1], Ajyahutis[8] totaling 18 in all. Afterwards, the Brahmachari should heap together the fire in the middle of the *Kunda* with the *Mantra* (ओमग्ने सुश्रवः०) Thereafter he offering three sticks in the fire of the *Kunda* with the *Mantra* (ओम् अग्नये समिध०) should touch first his mouth with (ओं तनूपा०). Thererfter his limbs in accordance with the procedure prescribed in the Vedarambha for this purpose with the seven *Mantras* (ओ वाक् च म०) etc., heating his hand-palm on the fire of yajna and sprinkling a little water on it. Then taking one jug from the eight jugs previously kept in the north of the *Vedi* of perfumes and herbacious substance, the Brahmachari take water from it and in doing so he should pronounce the following *Mantra*;—

ओं ये अप्स्वन्तरग्नयः प्रविष्टा गोह्य उपगोह्यो मयूषो मनोहास्खलो विरुजस्तनदुषूरिन्द्रियहा तान् विजहामि यो रोचनस्तमिह गृह्णामि ॥

पार० कां० २ । कं० ६ । १० ॥)

I renounce here the eight kinds of fire present in the waters including which is concealed, which heats the body, which distroys the strength, which reduces the power of mind, which brings out constipation etc. which creates various pains, which spoils the body and which kills the organs and accept only that fire which is auspicious and destroyer of the diseases.

With this water he should then bathe and pronounce the following *Mantra*:—

ओं तेन मामभिषिञ्चामि श्रिये यशसे ब्रह्मणे ब्रह्मवर्चसाय ॥

(पार० कां २। कं० ६। सू० ११ ॥)

I take bath with this water for the sake of beauty, spread of Vedic knowledge and propagation of Vedic rites and rituals.

Afterwards the Brahmachari pronouncing the *Mantra* (ओं ये अप्स्वन्तर०) should take water into his pot from the second jug of the above mentioned eight jugs. Thereafter he should bathe and pronounce the following *Mantra*:—

ओं येन श्रियमकृणुतां येनावमृशताꣳ सुराम् ।
येनाक्ष्यावभ्यसिञ्चतां यद्वां तदश्विना यशः ॥

(पार० कां० २। कं० ६। सू० १२ ॥)

May I attain by the grace of God that fame of the *Ashvinis*, the surgeon and physician whereby they accomplish the beauty of the organs and whereby they increase pleasure of the organs, whereby they keep moistened the eyes always.

Afterwards he should first pronounce the *Mantra* (ओम् अप्स्वन्तर०) and take water from three jugs and should take bath pronouncing the *Mantras* beginning with (ओम् आपो हिष्ठा०) written in the *Upanayana*. Thereafter he should take other three remaining jugs of the eight jugs and should bathe pronouncing into mind the three *Mantras* (ओम् आपो हिष्ठा०)

Afterwards the Brahmachari pronouncing the following *Mantra* should relinquish his girdle and stick:—

ओम् उदुत्तमं वरुण पाशमस्मदवाधमं वि मध्यमꣳश्रथाय ।
अथा वयमादित्य व्रते तवानागसोऽअदितये स्याम ॥

(यजुः० १२ । २)

This has been translated in the *Samanya prakarana.* Standing before the sun he should meditate God with the following *Mantra*:—

ओम् उद्यन् भ्राजभृष्णुरिन्द्रो मरुद्भिरस्थात् प्रातर्यावभिरस्थाद्दशसनिरसि दशसनिं मा कुर्वाविदन् मा गमय । उद्यन् भ्राजभृष्णुरिन्द्रो मरुद्भिरस्थाद्दिवा यावभिरस्थाच्छतसनिरसि शतसनिं मा कुवाविदन् मा गमय । उद्यन् भ्राजभृष्णुरिन्द्रोमरुद्भिरस्थात् सायंयावभिरस्थात् सहस्रसनिरसि सहस्रसनि मा कुर्वाविदन् मा गमय ॥

(पार० कां० २ । कं ६ । १६ ॥)

O God ! Thou art shining like Sun pervading with light every where, Thou art firm in thy powers followed by the various physical forces, Thou art worshipped by all the men of sharp-sightedness in the morning. Thou art pervading in ten directions. Make me able to serve the mankind abiding in ten corners of the world. Thou give me power to attain thee as thou knowest my all the acts.

The snataka Brahmachari, then, should eat curd and sesmum (तिल) and removing his hair of head, hair of mouth and cutting his nails should brush his teeth with the dantdhavana of Flcus Glomerata (उदुम्बर) and doing so pronounce the following *Mantra*:—

ओम् अन्नाद्याय व्यूहध्वं सोमो राजाऽयमागमत् ।
स मे मुखं प्रमाक्ष्यंते यशसा च भगेन च ॥

पार० कां० २ । कं० ६ । १७ ॥

O men ! brush and wash your teeth to take grain and preparations of cerial. This you know purifies and washes my teeth and mouth and would make me crowned with fame and prosperity in the society.

Afterwards the Brahmachari smearing perfumes on his body and bathing with clean water and having washed his body should wear *Dhoti* or yellow cloth should plastar perfumes of sandals etc. He should then touch the holes of the eyes, mouth and nose with the follwing Mantra:—

ओम् प्राणापानौ मे तर्पय चक्षुर्मे तर्पय श्रोत्रं मे तर्पय ॥

(पार० कां० २ । कं० ६ । १८ ॥)

O Almighty God ! make my *prana* and *apana* full of vitality, make my eyes full of sight, make my ears full of audibillity.

Thereafter, he taking water in his hand, moving a little in the left side and keeping his face southward should pronounce the following Mantra and drop the water on the ground :—

ओम् पितरः शुन्धध्वम् (पार० कां० २ कं० ६ १६ ॥)

Let the *Pitarah*, the preserving or protecting powers of the nature be firm, and pure.

Then the *Brahmachari* moving a little right recite in mind the following *Mantr*a ;—

ओंम सुचक्षा अहमक्षीभ्यां भूयासं सुवर्चा मुखेन ।
सुश्रुत्कर्णाभ्यां भूयासम् ॥ (पार० कां० २ । कं० ६ । १६)

O God ! may I be normal and good eye-sighted with my eyes, may I be handsome with my mouth and may I be a man of normal and good audibillity with my ears.

He. then should put on a nice and precious cloth and pronounce the following *Mantra*:—

ओं परिधास्यै यशोधास्यै दीर्घायुत्वाय जरदष्टिरस्मि ।
शतं च जीवामि शरदः पुरुची रायस्पोषमभिसंव्ययिष्ये ।

(पार० कां० २ । ६ । २८)

This *Mantra* has been translated in the *Vivaha Sanskara*.

He should dress him with precious and nice *upavastra* pronouncing the following Mantra:—

ओं यशसा मा द्यावापृथिवी यशसेन्द्राबृहस्तो ।
यशो भगश्च मा विन्दद्यशो मा प्रतिपद्यताम् ।

(पार० कां० २ । कं० ६ । २१)

This has been also translated in the *Vivaha Sanskara.*

The *Brahmachari* should take a garland of flowers in his hand pronouncing the following Mantra :—

ओं या आहरज्जमदग्निःश्रद्धायै मेधायै कामायेन्द्रियाय ।
ता अहं प्रतिगृह्णामि यशसा च भगेन च ॥
(पार० कां० २ । कं० ६ । २३)

I with fame and prosperity accept the garland made of those flowers which the man avowed to perform *yajna*, brings for the sake of expressing faith, attaining mental pleasure fulfilling desire and gaining pleasure for limbs—by garlanding a great one.

Thereafter he should pronounce the following Mantra and wear the garland which he had previously taken in his hand :—

ओं यद्यशोऽप्सरसामिन्द्रश्चकार विपुलं पृथु ।
तेन सङ्ग्रथिता, सुमनस आबध्नामि यशो मयि ॥
(पार० कां० २ । क० ६ । २४)

Whatever great fame a *King* earns by using these flowers amongst his workers with that fame I tie to my naek this garland which has artistically prepard,

Afterwards he should put on turban, sheet and cap or taking crown in his hand he should pronounce the Mantra (ओं युवा सुवासः given in *Upanayana Sanskara* and put it on his head, Then, he should take an ornament in his hand and should wear it with the following Mantra :—

ओं अलङ्करणमसि भूयोऽलङ्करणं भूयात् ॥
(पार० कां० २ कं ६ । २६)

This is an ornament and let it become the article of ornamentation.

He should apply ointment in the eyes with the following Mantra:—

ओं वृत्रस्यासि कनीनकश्चक्षुर्दा असि चक्षुर्मे देहि ॥

(यजु० अ ४ । मं । ३ ॥ पार० कां० २ । कं० ६ । २७)

O God ! Thou art the illuminator of the black eye. Thou art the giver of eyes so please give me normally fit eyes. He should see his face in the mirror and pronounce :—

ओं रोचिष्णुरसि । (पार० कां० ४ । कं० ६ । २८)

This glass is transparent and beautiful. Thereafter he should have *Umbrella* and pronounce the folloing Mantra :—

ओं बृहस्पतेश्छदिरसि पाप्मनो मामन्तर्धेहि तेजसो यशसो माऽन्तर्धेहि ॥

(पार० कां० २ । कं० ६ । २९)

This *Umbrella* is the cover of the *King* and learned, let it conceal me as ever from sins, and let it not conceal me from the fame. He should, then wear shoes with the following Mantra:—

ओं प्रतिष्ठे स्थो विश्वतो मा पातम् ॥

(पार० कां० २ । कं० ६ । ३०)

These shoes save one from thorn etc. and let them serve me in this matter.

Afterwards he should take a smooth stick of bamboo etc. with the following Mantra:—

ओं विश्वाभ्यो मा नाष्ट्राभ्यस्परिपाहि सर्वतः ॥

[पार० कां० २ । कं० ६ । ३१]

Let this stick protect me from all the wickeds.

The father and mother etc. of the *Brahmachari* should receive him cordially when he come from the house of the *Acharya*. They receive him with great affection and gaeity. On his coming to the house, his father, mother, brother and relatives entertain him according to the procedure of *Madhupark* given in the *Vedarambha Sanskara*. Again *Brahmachari*, the father and mother etc. of the *Brahmachari* entertaining the *Achaarya* and the other participants of the *Sanskara* with nice food and drink respectfully and seating the Acharya on a nice seat respect him with the procedure of *Madhupark*, good garland, gift of clothes and cow accordig to their pecuniary condition. They should praise the Acharya for his good characteristics before the other people and express their gratefulness for the education he had imparted to the student. They should address the people in the following manner :—

"Here you gentle men ! This honourable Acharya has done a great good to me. He has saved me from brutality and has made me a celebrated scholar. I cannot compensate to him for whatever he has done for me, For this I only offer many thanks to my Achary and with great respect salute him. I further pray him to make other students successful and accomplished as he had made me by imparting good educotion and instrucation, As you have blessed me with imparting good eduction I, in the same manner would make accomplished and happy other students, O Acharya, I can never forget the good you have done for me."

May Almighty Divinity, the Master of the universe showing mercy on me, the other students and the whole world make all the men cultured, learned and blessed with the physical and spiritual strength and make all long-lived, healthy, industrious and courageous in discharging the duties and fulfilling the task of philanthropy the act of good quality, So that all of us in the creatim of *God* moulding our own qualities, acts and nature in correspondence to the quality, action and nature of *God* and accomplishing the fulfilment of *Dhrama*, *Artha*, *Kama*, and *Moksha* abide in pleasure and happiness for always.

Here ends the procedure of the convocation.

———

Marriage Ceremony

Here-undar we would prescribe the procedure of Marriage Ceremony

Vivaha, the marriage ceremony is that procedure of rites and performance in which the man and woman having completed the perfect disciplines of the continence, having attained the education, strength, having suited matchfulness and compatibillity in good qualities, acts and natures and having sentiment of love. join together in a bond of relation to produce a good progeny according to the authority and standard mentioned hereunder and to discharge duties of their *Varnashram* conducive to good acts :—

Authorities—

उदगयन आपूर्य्यमाणपक्षे पुण्ये नक्षत्रे चौलकर्मोपनयन गोदानविवाहा: ॥ १ ॥ सार्वकालमेके विवाहम् । २ ।

आश्वलायन गृह्यसूत्र (१, ४ । १, २) और—

आवसथ्याधानं दारकाले ॥ ३ ॥पारस्कर [१ । २ । १]

और

पुण्ये नक्षत्रे दारान् कुर्वीत ॥ ४ ॥

लक्षणप्रशस्तान् कुशलेन ॥ ५ ॥

गोभिलीय [२ । १ । १, २ [गृह्यसूत्र और इसी-प्रकार शौनक गृह्यसूत्र में भी है ।

The marriage should take place on the day which is in the light-mooned half of lhe month and in winter solstice, i. e. On the day which falls in choice and when parties are cheerful. Many Acharya accept that the marriage ceremony be celebrated at any time throughout the year. The fire which is established at the time of marriage is called *Avasathya*.

The hand-grasping of a women accomplished with al:

———

The imagination of star etc. is nothing but a fancy. It has no validity.

perfect qualities, be celebrated on the day when both the parties feel them pleased and happy.

Period: The time of the marriage ceremony is that which has been described in the *Vedarambha* in the context of the categories of *Brahmacharya*. The age, family, residing place, body and nature of the bride and bride-groom, should be examined cerefully i. e. the bride and bride-groom both be mature in sense etc. and both be willing for marriage. The age of the bride-groom should be one and half time more then the age of the bride which is a minimum requirement but maximum age of the bride-groom should be double of the age of bride. The authorities on the subject are :—

वेदानधीत्य वेदौ वा वेदं वापि यथाक्रमम् ।
अविप्लुतब्रह्मचर्यो गृहस्थाश्रममाविशेत् ।। १ ।।
गुरुणानुमताः स्नात्वा समावृत्तो यथाविधि ।
उद्वहेत द्विजो भार्या सवर्णा लक्षणान्विताम् ।। २ ।।
असपिण्डा च या मातुरसगोत्रा च या पितुः ।
सा प्रशस्ता द्विजातीनां दारकर्मणि मैथुने ।। ३ ।।
महान्त्यपि समृद्धानि गोऽजाविधनधान्यतः ।
स्त्रीसम्बन्धे दशैतानि कुलानि परिवर्जयेत् ।। ४ ।।
हीनक्रीयं निष्पुरुषं निश्छन्दो रोमशार्शसम् ।
क्षय्यामयाव्यपस्मारिश्वित्रिकुष्ठिकुलानि च ।। ५ ।।
नोद्वहेत् कपिलां कन्यां नाधिकाङ्गीं न रोगिणीम् ।
नालोमिका नातिलोमां न वाचाटां न पिङ्गलाम् ।। ६ ।।
नर्क्षवृक्षनदीनाम्नीं नान्त्यपर्वतनामिकाम् ।
न पक्ष्यहिप्रेष्यनाम्नीं न च भीषणनामिकाम् ।। ७ ।।
अव्यङ्गाङ्गीं सौम्यनाम्नीं हंसवारणगामिनीम् ।
तनुलोमकेशदशनां मृद्वङ्गीमुद्वहेत स्त्रियम ।। ८ ।।
ब्राह्मो दैवस्तथैवार्षः प्राजापत्यस्तथासुरः ।
गान्धर्वो राक्षसश्चैव पैशाचश्चाष्टमोऽधमः ।। ९ ।।
आच्छाद्य चार्चयित्वा च श्रुतिशीलवते स्वयम् ।
आहूय दानं कन्याया ब्राह्मो धर्मः प्रकीर्त्तितः ।। १० ।।
यज्ञे तु वितते सम्यगृत्विजे कर्म कुर्वते ।
अलङ्कृत्य सुतादानं दैवं धर्मं प्रचक्षते ।। ११ ।।

एकं गोमिथुनं द्वे वा वरादादाय धर्मतः ।
कन्याप्रदानं विधिवदार्षो धर्मः स उच्यते ॥ १२ ॥

सह नौ चरतां धर्ममिति वाचानुभाष्य च ।
कन्याप्रदानमभ्यर्च्य प्राजापत्यो विधिः स्मृत ॥ १३ ॥

ज्ञातिभ्यो द्राविणं दत्त्वा कन्यायै चैव शक्तितः ।
कन्याप्रदानं विधिवदासुरो धर्म उच्यते ॥ १४ ॥

इच्छायाऽन्योन्यसंयोगः कन्यायाश्च वरस्यच ।
गान्धर्वः स तु विज्ञेयो मैथुन्यः कामसम्भवः ॥ १५ ॥

हत्वा छित्वा च भित्त्वा च क्रोशन्तीं रुदतीं गृहात् ।
प्रसह्य कन्याहरणं राक्षसो विधिरुच्यते ॥ १६ ॥

सुप्तां मत्तां प्रमत्तां वा रहो यत्रोपगच्छति ।
स पापिष्ठो विवाहानां पैशाचश्चाष्टामोऽधमः ॥ १७ ॥

ब्रह्मादिषु विवाहेषु चतुर्ष्वेवानुपूर्वशः ।
ब्रह्मवर्चस्विनः पुत्रा जायन्ते शिष्टसंमताः ॥१८ ॥

रूपसत्त्वगुणोपेता धनवन्तो यशस्विनः ।
पर्याप्तभोगा धर्मिष्ठा जीवन्ति च शतं समः ॥१९ ॥

इतरेषु तु शिष्टेषु नृशंसानृतवादिनः ।
जायन्ते दुर्विवाहेषु ब्रह्मधर्मद्विषः सुताः ॥ २० ॥

अनिन्दितैः स्त्रीविवाहैरनिंद्या भवति प्रजा ।
निन्दितैर्निन्दिता नृणां तस्मान्निन्द्यान् विवर्जयेत् ॥ २१ ॥

(मनु० अ० ३ । २, ४-१०, २१, २७-३४, ३९-२४)

After completing systematically the study of 4 *Vedas* or 3 *Vedas* or 2 *Vedas* or One *Veda* with observance of the discipline of continence and strictly having observed the rules and practice of *Brahmacharya* without any failure the man and woman enter into the life of house-holding affairs.[1]

The men of *Brahman*, *Kshatriya* and *Vaishya varnas* should marry the compatible girl of their own *varna* with the permission of the preceptor performing the *Samavartan* and having systematically completed the vows of *Brahmacharya* and attained the knowledge.[2]

The girl of good qualities who does not fall within the six

geneological orders of the mother and is not of the geneology of the father is legitimately marriageable by the *Dvijas.*[3]

The girls from the ten undermentioned families, may these be superior in the riches of cow etc. animals and wealth should not be accepted for matrimonial relations.[4]

The 10 families are :—

1. The family deprived of good conduct and behaviours. 2. The family in which any good and characteristic personality has not taken existence. 3. The family wherein there is no man of distinguished intellect and wisdom. 4. The family the members of which have more long hair on their bodies. 5. The family which has virus of piles in heritance. 6. The family which has the affection of tuberculosis. 7. The family which is the victim of the abdominal diseases caused by the defect of indigestion. 8. The family which is affected with the fit. 9. The family with white spots on skin and. 10. The family which has leporosy. The girls and boys of such families should not ever be accepted for matrimony.

The girl who is of yellow, colour, who has over-grown limbs as six fingers etc. who has diseases, who is deprived of hair on her body, who has long hair on her body, who is too much talkative and has her eyes as yellow as the the eyes of a cat, should not be accepted as bride.[6]

The girl bearing her name based on the stars like *Revati*, *Rohini* etc. who has her name in the name of river like *Ganga*, *Yamuna* etc. who has the name of mountains like *Vindhyachala*, whose name is based on the birds like *Kokila*, *Hansa* etc. whose name is the name of venomous raptiles like *Dasi* etc. and whose name is dreadful and fear-provoking should not be accepted as bride.[7]

But the girl of beautiful limbs, good name, possessing the movement of a female elephant, having very little and rare hair rare head-hair, rare teeth and who has all the body parts tender ones should be accepted for marriage.[8]

There are eight kinds of marriages named as—*Brahma, Daiva, Arsha, Prajapatya, Asura, Gandharva, Rakshasa* and *Pishacha.*[9]

1. The *Brahma* marriage is that marriage in which the learned, characteristic, compatible man is married with a girl who is well-dressed and ornamented and for whom the bride-groom is selected and accepted by herself.[10]

2. After performing a great *yajna* by calling the great learned men to participate therein to give the well-dressed and well-ornamented and beautiful girl to the learned man conducting the *yajna*—is called *Daiva* marriage.[11]

3. In the marriage wherein taking one pair* or two pairs of cow and bullock from the bride-groom, the bride is given to bridegroom is known as *Arsha* marriage.[12]

4. The marriage wherein with the performance of *yajna* and ritual procedure the bride and bride-groom both are preached, before all, to discharge the duties of the house-hold life in union systematically and thus the hand-grasping being performed with pleasure and acceptance of both—is *Prajapatya* marriage. These four marriages are superior to other four.[13]

5. To give the girl with the gift of wealth to girl and the party of bride-groom with performance of *Homa* is called *Asura* marriage.[14]

6. The union of girl and boy on their own mutual accord and the acceptance of the fact in their minds by them that they are now wife and husband—is *Gandharva* marriage which is based on the sentiments of passion.[15]

7. To kidnap the girl physically by killing, cutting and

---

* This is not true as it has been prohibited in the Manusmriti itself and is also against the rules of logic and morality. Therefore, without taking from and giving to anything the either party the marriage performed on the acceptance of both is **Arsha** marriage.

cleaving the men opposing such an act and marry her in condition of her crying, trembling, fearing and abusing—is *Rakshasa* marriage.[16]

8, To defile a girl in sleep, in lunacy, in the state of intoxication in lonely place is known as *Paishacha* marriage and it is very low and most demoralised and full of all sorts of blames and blemishes among all the marriages.[17]

The offsprings issuing out from the couples married under the procedure of first four marriages become superior in quality and nature and shine with the knowledge of the *Veda* and are admired by the learned persons.[18]

Such boys and girls attaining nice beauty, form, strength vigour, clear intellect etc. good qualities, plentiful wealth, piousness and fame, complete enjoyment of the pleasure and extensive righteousness live hundred years.[19]

The progeny produced by the couple married under the procedure of other remaining four marriages but the first four become blameworthy, lie-teller, antagonist of *Vedic* religion and of very low nature.[20]

Therefore, it is proper for people that they should leave out the marriage low norms which give wicked progeny and they should always accept the marriages of high norms which become the source of excellent progeny.

उत्कृष्टायाभिरूपाय वराय सदृशाय च ।
अप्राप्तामपि तां तस्मै कन्यां दद्याद्विचक्षणः ॥ १ ॥
काममारणात्तिष्ठेद् गृहे कन्यर्त्तुमत्यपि ।
न चैवैनां प्रयछेत्तु गुणहीनाय कर्हिचित् ॥ २ ॥
त्रीणि वर्षान्युदीक्षेत कुमार्यृतुमती सती ।
ऊर्ध्वन्तु कालादेतस्माद्विन्देत सदृशं पतिम् ॥ ३ ॥

(मनु० अ० ९ । ८८-९०

If parent of a girl desire to marry their daughter they should prefer to select only bride-groom who is superior to her in good qualities, actions and nature and is matchful to her in beauty, radiance and form. In spite of her being within the six geneological order of mother, she should be given to that bridegroom only and to none else, so that the both of them delightfully promote the life of house-hold and produce good progeny.[1]

The parents of the girls should never marry their daughter to a man who is inferior, unmatched and wicked might she remain in the house of her father unmarried till death and the same standard is applicable to a man that he should marry a bride compatible with him.[2]

The marriage of girl when she desires to do so should be arranged in the fourth year leaving the three years period from the day of menstruation.

Question—If so, what will be the situation of the *shlokas* 'अष्टवर्षा भवेद् गोरी नववर्षा च रोहिणी' etc. ?

Answer—'Nothing but a miserable fate to them and to their composers. 'That is, those who according to these *Shlokas* do the marriage of their children in immature age or child-hood make them spoiled, ruined, diseased and of very short life. In reality they destroy their family and clan. If anyone desires to marry his children earlier he should do their marriage according to whatever has been mentioned in the *Vedas* and in the context of category of continence. They should never do the marriage of girl less than 16 years minimum and a boy less than 25 years minimum. More long period they will extend to observe the discipline of continence greater will they enjoy the pleasure.

Questions—Should marriages be arranged in the near vicinity or distance ?

Answer—दुहिता दुहिता दूरे हिता भवतीति ॥

निरु० ३/४

This is the authority of *Nirukta*. It says that marriage of a girl in distant place is more beneficial.

Question—Why do not marriage take place between male and female of the same *gotra* or between brother and sister ?

Answer—The first defect which comes in the light is that there remains always lack of love between them. As much love in found in distant thing, the same is notf ound in the nearest one. The both of them are acquainted with the merits and evils of each other and they do not have any fear from each other. The second defect is that unless the marriage is arranged in a distant family the body does not become strong. The third benefit of the distant marriage is that it increases the mutual love, progress and supremacy. The marriage of near family does not give this benefit.

The *Vedic* proofs pro to the marriage of youth :—

तमस्मेरा युवतयो युवानं मर्मृज्यमानाः परियन्त्यापः ।
स शुक्रेभिः शिक्वभी रेवदस्मे दीदायानिध्मो घृतनिर्णिगप्सु ॥ १ ॥

अस्मै तिस्रो अव्यथ्याय नारीर्देवाय देवीर्दिधिषन्त्यन्नम् ।
कृता इवोप हि प्रसर्स्रे अप्सु स पीयूषं धयति पूर्वसूनाम् ॥ २ ॥

अश्वस्यात्र जनिमास्य च स्वर्द्रुहो रिषः सम्पृचः पाहि सूरीन् ।
आमासु पूर्षु परो अप्रमृष्यं नारातयो वि निशन्नानृतानि ॥ ३ ॥

ऋ० मं० २ । सू० ३५ । मं ४-६

वधूरियं पतिमिच्छन्त्येति य ईं वहाते महिषीमिषिराम् ।
आस्य श्रवस्याद्रथ आ च घोषात्पुरू सहस्रा परि वर्त्तयाते ॥ ४ ॥

ऋ० मं० ५ ।सू० ३७ मं० ३

उप व एषे वन्द्येभिः शूषैः प्र यह्वी दिवश्चितयद्भिरर्कैः ।
उषासानक्ता विदुषीव विश्वमा हा वाहतो मर्त्याय यज्ञम ॥ ५ ॥

ऋ० मं० ५ । सू० ४१ । मं० ७

The girls of 20 to 24 years accomplished with good educations and vows of *Brahmacharya* win to us (the bride-grooms) who are one and half-time older or 2 times older than her and have attained the complete knowledge, discipline of *Brahmacharya*, and good merits and are in blooming youth, in marriage according to their choice, like the river or waters which go to the ocean. The *Brahmchari* embellished with vigour etc. and pure qualities attaining all sorts of praiseworthy things win the girl who is full of youth. As the automatically refulgent water-purifying electricity resides in the firmament or the water-purifying electricity resides in the firmament or the water-purify self-shining marine fire resides in the ocean so the wife and husband in whose heart the love is not refulgent externally but is shining internally, obtain good and marvellous pleasure.[1]

O women and men ! as the learned wives of enlightened persons having the nature of first, second and third grade acquire grain etc. for the purpose of the *Kama*, which is painless and full of delight. The wife like a trained and educated lady has union with husband and husband equally with wife to employ them in dealings of affection and love. As a child sucking the milk of woman of first delivery increases the nectar of water in the same manner the chaste man and chaste woman increase the prosperity of their children.[2]

As the *King* and other people can never destroy the good education and instruction etc. in their cities and in their house born children knowing the value of such things and as the internal enemies can not destroy the body which has been attained by the observance of *Brahmacharya* and is equipped with the physical and spiritual strength and falsehood etc. can not touch it so the sentiments of inamicability, evils and violence can not have any contact with them who in their blooming youth delightfully and legitimately do marriage and bring out children. The good children take birth in such families. Therefore, O lady of the house ! You give all protection to learned men. No doubt this house-hold life of yours would flourish with happiness and delightment.[3]

Prospers in the house-hold life with knowledge, wealth etc. from all sides that marrried couple amongst whom the man blooming with youth, with careful examination wins the hand of a woman who is born in nice family, is educated, beautiful, meritorious, characteristic, desirous to have a good husband and lovely to husband and amongst whom the woman wins the hand of a man as her husband who is compatible to her in all respect and selected and desired by her. They can carry on the burden of house-hold exchanging good talk with each other like a *Chariot*. They can solve multifarious purposes and problems facing them from all sides.[4]

O men ! if you do the marriage of your children according to their own choice after making them perfect in the discipline of continence, education etc. they in return would give you all pleasure and happiness equipping them with the various qualities, praise, various knowledge, various acts of good performances and different kinds of strength inclusive of physical and spiritual maturity. They can discharge satisfactorily the duties of household life like the night and day and learned lady and learned man who perform their task smoothly. The marriage in its sanctity is beneficial and auspicious for men and women. The men and women of good nature and culture can attain the desired benefit of house-hold life.[5]

As the observance of celibacy by a girl is the dictum of the *Veda* in the same manner the men should also observe the discipline of continence, through it attain perfect knowledge and becoming full fledged youth marry the girls whom they like with full examinations. The marriage of boy or girl should always be settled only with the girl and boy respectively whom both of them mutually like. This is the best marriage. Those who do not do marriage of girls or boys in full youth and do the marriage in their child-hood and settle an incompatible marriage between boys and girls violate the commandments of God revealed in *Veda*,

Why would they not sink in the deep ocean of great sufferings thus violating the dictates of *God*? Those persons who do and get done marriages according to aforementioned procedure attain perfect happiness as their act is accordant with the dictates of Divinity.

Question—Should marriage take place in one own *Varna* or in other *Varna* also ?

Answer—Marriage should take place in their own *Varnas* But the *Varnavyavastha* be based on quality, action and culture, not on the birth. He or she who is well-learned, pious, benevlent, self controlled, free from the evils like telling lie etc. ready in desssemінating education and religious tenets and possessed of excellent characteristics, may respectively be called *Brahmana* and *Brahmani*. The *Kshatriya* or *Kshatriya* is he or she who possesses the qualities of knowledge, strength, bravery, and dispensation of justice. The *Vaishya* and *Vaishya* is he or she who is learned, does agriculture, domestication of animals, trade and has efficiency in the languages of countries. He or she who has no education or learning, is *knaiva*, is called *Shudra* or *Shudra*. This order and standard of *Varna* should be counted and maintained in setting and materializing the marriage. That is *Brahman* should marry *Brahmani*, *Kshatriy Kshatriya*, *Vaishya Vaishya* and *Shudra*, *Shudra* and the pleasure and delight flow out in such marriages not other-wise.

The authority in *Varnavyavastha* :—

धर्मचर्यया जघन्यो वर्णः पूर्वं पूर्वं वर्ण मापद्यते जातिपरिवृत्तौ ॥ १ ॥

अधर्मचर्यया पूर्वो वर्णो जघन्यं जघन्यं वर्णमापद्यते जातिपरिवृत्तौ ॥ २ ॥

(आपस्तम्ब प्र० २ । ५ । ११ । १०, ११ ॥)

शूद्रो ब्राह्मणतामेति ब्राह्मणश्चैति शूद्रताम् ।

क्षत्रियाज्जातमेवन्तु विद्याद्वैश्यात्तथैव च ॥ ३ ॥

मनुस्मृतौ (अ० १० । ६५)

Through the righteous conduct an individual of inferior *varna* might be he or she aspires and rises to the status of a superior *varna* and adopts, discharges authorized duties of qualities and right of action etc. of that *varna*.

In the same manner in absence of *Dharmacharana* and the prevalence of *Adharmacharana* an individual of excellent *varna*, might be he or she, falls down to the status of an inferior *varna* and adopts and practises authorized right and duties of that *varna*.[2]

The *Shudra* of good quality, action and culture rises to the status of *Vaishya*, *Kshatriya* and *Brahman Varnas* and adopts and practises their respective rights and action. Equally the *Brahmans* of evil quality, act and culture may fall down to the status of *Kshatriya*, *Vaishya* and *Shudra*, *Kshatriya* to the status of *Vaishya* and *Shudra* and *Vaishya* to the status of *Shudra* and enjoys the rights and action of these respective *Varnas*.

On being established such a standard of *Varnavyavavastha* there arises nothing of partiality to anyone and all the *Varnas* maintain their status to remain always persons of excellent *Varna*. They also try to become superior *Varna* for always. The men of Superior *Varna*, with a fear that we might not fall to the status of low *Varna*, stop to do any bad deed and do always good acts. This leads the world towards a great progress. In *Aryavarta* till the time when such a *Varnavyavastha* was prevailing, the institution of marriage was well-maintained on self-chosen be rothal system after completion of education, and perfect discipline of *Brahmacharya* the country was advanced in all respects. The should continue even now so that the country of *Aryavarta* securing its previous ancient position attain happiness and prosperity.

Examination of compatibility—The bride and bride-groom should examine mutually the qualities, actions and nature of one another in this way——the characteristic behaviour of both be equal, intellectual maturity of both be equal, the demeanour of both be equal, the form and beauty etc, qualities of both be equal, both of them be equally non-violent, truth-speaking and sweet-speaking, both be possessed of the sense of gratitude, mercifulness and free from egoism malignance, heart-burning, passion, anger, both be equally free from covetousness and be bedewed with the sentiments of country-reform, knowledge, attainment. intrapedity in truth-preaching, enthusiasm, renouncement of the evils of deception, gambling, theft, intoxicant drinking, eating of meat etc. and both the equally clever in domestic affairs.

Whenever at morning or at evening they meet together coming from distant places should exchange salutation between one another pronouncing नमस्ते. The wife should touch the feet of her husband wash his feet and give seat to him. Thus both of them should enjoy the pleasure with the reciprocation of affectionate speech and dealing between them. The body of the wife should be slimer than the body of the husband. She should be so tall as her head could reach upto the shoulder of the husband. The internal test should be done by women and men through the confabulation etc.

ओम् ऋतमग्रे प्रथनं जक्षे ऋते सत्यं प्रतिष्ठितम् । यदियं कुमार्य्यँभिजाता तदियमिह प्रतिपद्यताम् । यत्सत्यं तद्दृश्यताम् ॥

(आश्व० गृ० अ० १ । कं० ५ । ५ ॥)

When the time of marriage be fixed the girl should get the bride-groom carefully examined through the experienced men indirectly and in the same manner the bride-groom should get the bride tested indirectly through experienced ladies. Afterwards there should be held a metting of intelligent women and men and both (the girl and the boy) should converse together with one another. They start 'O woman' or O man. *Mahattatva*, the resolution, which is a reality came first out of matter in the beginning of creation. The real, indestructibe matter endowed with its three qualities and substances was permeating the *Mahattava*. As this universe has come into existence with the union of matter and *Purusha*, the eternal individual soul so we, the virgin and bachelor take this vow now to wed together both of us. Let us win each other i.e. virgin to bachelor and bachelor to virgin. Let us have a firm courage to make this vow a reality by fulfiling it.

Procedure—When the girl after discharge of monthly course comes to normalcy and on the day and night of which is decided for impregnation all the utensils and necessary articles of *yajna* etc. should be arranged before hand to celebrate marriage. All the *samagris* should be kept safe after cleansing them and *yajnashala*, *vedi*, *yajna*, priests of *yajna*, *yajnapatra* etc. be settled and arranged as has been mentioned in the *samanya-prakarana*.

Afterwards, when one hour not passes* away the bride and bride-goom taking the jugs full of perfumed clean water should take bath.

Afterwards the bride dressed in nice dress and decorated in ornaments should sit on a nice seat keeping her face east-wards. In taking jugs of perfumed waters and taking their bath they should pronounce the following *Mantras* :—

ओं काम वेद ते नाम मदो नामासि समानयामुं सुरा ते अभवत् । परमत्र जन्माग्ने तपसो निर्मितोऽसि स्वाह ॥ १ ।

ओं इमं त उपस्थ मधुना संसृजामि प्रजापते मुखमेतद् द्वितीयम् । तेन पुंसोभिभवासि सर्वानवशान्वशिन्यसि राज्ञी स्वाहा ॥ २ ॥

ओं अग्निं क्रव्यादमकृण्वन् गुहानाः स्त्रीणामुपस्थमृषयः पुराणाः । तेनाज्यमकृण्वं स्त्रैंश्रृङ्ग त्वाष्ट्रं त्वयि तद्दधातु स्वाहा ॥ ३ ॥

(गो० २ । १ । १० ॥)

This *Kama* (the passion) has been known by the whole of the world by its name. It is known as intoxicant. This girl has become an intoxicant one for purpose of *Kama*. Let this make this girl or boy graceful. This heat of *Kama* has excellent birth in woman. This has got its inception from the heat of the body.

O bride ! I, the husband embrace your organ of pleasure with love and affection. This is the second door or the second requirement of a house-holder to house-holder in real sense. Through this organ and pleasure you take all the men who can not be influenced, under your influence and control. You are the subjugating entity and hence mistress of the house.[2]

---

* If the procedure of the marriage cannot anyhow be completed upto midnight, the ceremony should be commend after meridian to get it completed upto midnight.

The ancient seers of high penetration call the organ of women as the fire which eats the flesh (as it causes the discharge of semen which is the rarest form of flesh and comes from it from all the parts of the body). They accept the semen of men which flows from the organ of men as the *Ajyam*, the *ghee*. Let that semen grow strong and productive in you.[3]

Afterwards. according to the procedure described in the *Samanyprakarana* eulogium, prayer and contemplation of God, recitation of *Svastimantras*, recitation of *Shanti Mantras* should be performed. Thereafter, *Agnyadhana*, *Samidadhana* should be done and cerial preparations already prepared should be kept aside on the *Vedi*. In the same manner the bride-groom also, at his home, going in separate corner should put on nice dress and ornaments etc. and sit on a nice seat in the *yajnashala* keeping his face eastward. He performing the procedure of eulogium,* prayer and contemplation of God according to the method prescribed in the *Samanyaprakarna* should prepare to him to go to the house of bride. Afterwards the men of bride's party and of beide-groom's party take him with respect to the house of bride. At the time when bride-groom enter into the house of bride, the bride and the person arranging the marriage ceremony should receive the bride-groom with *Madhuparka* etc. in the following manner. The manner of reception is that the bride-groom entering the house of bride stand there keeping his face eastward the bride and people of bride's party stand near bride groom keeping their faces in north direction. The bride and her party-men should say.

साधु भवान् ग्रास्तामर्चयिष्यामो भवन्तम् । पार० कां० १ कं० ३ सूत्र ४

Kindly stay here, we would receive you. Replies bride-groom.

ओमर्चय ।। Thanks; please do.

Taking the *assana*, the seat in her hand standing in front of the bride-groom bride says :

ग्रों विष्टरो विष्टरो विष्टर: प्रतिगृह्यताम् । पा० १ । १६

* The men and women participating in the marriage ceremony should contemplate God with concentrated mind in thoughtful manner.

Here is the seat, kindly accept it. Bride-groom replies :

श्रों प्रतिगृह्णामि ॥

Thanks, I accept it. The bride-groom, taking the seat from brides' hand and stretching it on the ground of the *mandapa*, sitting on it with his face in the east direction pronounce the following *mantra* :

श्रों वर्ष्मोऽस्मि समानानामुद्यतामिव सूर्यः ।
इमन्तमभितिष्ठामि यो मा कश्चाभिदासति । पा० १ । ३ । ८

I, at this juncture hold superiority amongst my equal like the sun amongst, shining planets and stars. To Him who tries to humiliate me I will make down like this seat upon which I sitting.

Men from brides' party should give a small pot full of water in the hand of bride should say :

ओं पाद्यं पाद्यं पाद्यं प्रतिगृह्यताम् ॥ पार० १।३।६

Here is water to wash feet. kindly accept it. Bride-groom replies :

श्रों प्रतिगृह्णामि ।

Thanks, I accept it.

Bride-groom should take the pot of water from the hand of bride and wash* his feet and pronounce the following *mantra* :

श्रों विराजो दोहोऽसि विराजो दोहमशीय मयि पाद्यायै विराजो दोहः ।
पार० कां० १ । ३ । १२

This water is the essance of the wordly nabulae. May I obtain it for the removal of diseases. It is here at hand for washining my feet.

श्रोमर्घोऽर्घोऽर्घः प्रतिगृह्यताम् ।

* If the door for entry in the house be in the east the bride-groom should keep his face northward and bride and her partymen eastward. If bride-groom is Brahman varna he should first wash his right foot and thereafter left. If the bride-groom of Kshatrya etc. Varna he should fistwash left foot and right thereafter.

Afterwards men of the brides' party should give another pot full of clean water to bride and she should say :

Here is water to wash the face, kindly accept it. The bride-groom taking water from brides' hand replies :

ओं प्रतिगृह्णमि ।

Thanks, I accept it.

The bride-groom should wash his face and pronounce the folloiwng *Mantra.*

ओमापस्थ युष्माभिः सर्वान्कामानवाप्नवानि । १

ओं समुद्रं वः प्रहिणोमि स्वां योनिमभिगच्छत ।

अरिष्टास्माकं वीरा मा परासेचि मत्पयः ।।२

पार० कां० १ । कं०३ । १३, १४ ।।

This is water. Through it I obtain the health, I send this water to Ocean or the atmospheric Ocean. This could reach to its primal source. Our children enjoy health and pleasure. By grace of God this water may not leave us.

Afterwards, the bride-groom should take his seat in the west of the *mandapa* keeping his face in east direction. Bride's men should give a small pot full of clean and pure water to the bride, keeping an *Achamani*, sipping spoon in the pot and the bride should offer it to the bride-groom pronouncing the following *Mantra*:

ओं आचमनीयमाचमनीयमाचमनीयं प्रतिगृह्यताम् ।

Here is water for sipping, kindly accept it. The bride.groom taking the pot from bride replies :

औं प्रतिगृह्णमि ।।

Thanks, I accept it.

The bride-groom should take the pot of water from the bride and put it before him. Taking water in the cavity of the palm of right hand the bride-groom should pronounce the following mantra and sip it. He should pronounce the mantra thrice and sip water thrice,

ओमामागन् यशसा सꣳसृज वर्चसा । तं मा कुरु प्रियं प्रजानामधिपतिं पशूनामरिष्टिं तनूनाम् ।

पार० कां० १ । ३ । १५

O God ! Please come to us with your great splendours, make us accomplished with your refulgence. by the grace, may we be affectionate to our children, master of animals like cow etc. and well-wisher of our body and limbs.

Afterwards bride's worker should give the pot of *Madhuparka** to her and she extending it towards bride-groom should say:—

ओं मधुपर्को मधुपर्को मधुपर्कः प्रतिगृह्यताम् ।

Here is *Madhuparka* (Curd and honey put together) kindly accept it.

The bride-groom taking the pot of *Madhuparka* from the hand of bride replies :—

ओं प्रतिगृह्णामि । —

Thanks, I accept it.

The bride-groom should pronounce the following sentence and minutely look at *Madhuparka.*

ओं मित्रस्यस्त्वा चक्षुषा प्रतीक्षे ॥

पार० १ । ३ । १६

I look at you with the eye of friend.

The bride-groom pronouncing the following *Mantra* should take the pot of *Madhuparaka* in his left hand :—

ओं देवस्य त्वा सवितुः प्रसवेऽश्विनोर्बाहुभ्यां पूष्णो हस्ताभ्यां प्रतिगृह्णामि ॥

यजु० १ । १० पार० १ । ३ । १७

I take it through the active for of *Prana* and *apana*, the

---

* *Madhuparka* is that in which the ghee or honey is mixed in curd. The quantity of this be in 12 tolas of curd four tolas honey or ghee be mixed and this should be kept in bronze pot.

two vital airs and through the now functions of digestive system for attaining the extension of our inner self.

The bride-groom should pronounce the following three montras and see the *Madhuparka* carefully :—

ओं भूर्भुवः स्वः । मधुवाता ऋतायते मधु क्षरन्ति सिन्धवः । माध्वीर्नस्सन्त्वोषधीः ॥

यजुः १३ । २७

ओं भूर्भुवः स्वः । मधु नक्तमुतोषसो मधुमत्पार्थिवं रजः मधु द्यौरस्तु नः पिता ॥ २ ॥

ओं भूर्भुवः स्वः । मधुमान्नो वनस्पतिर्मधुमां अस्तु सूर्यः । माध्वीर्गावो भवन्तु नः ॥ ३ ॥

God is exsitent, conscious and all-bliss. For us who strictly adhere to the laws of nature and dictates of God, sweet are the breaths of winds, sweet is the flow of rivers and herbs are full of sweetness

God is existent,conscious and all-bliss. Night is sweet and so is the dawn. Sweet is the earth and sweet is for us the heaven which is the protector of all,

God is existent, conscious and all-bliss. The vegetable is sweet for us and so is the Sun. Rays of sun are also sweet for us.

Afterwards the bride-groom should mix the honey into curd thrice with the second finger and the thumb of the right hand and pronounce the following mantra :

ओं नमः श्यावास्यायान्नशने यत्त आविद्धंतत्ते निष्कृन्तामि ॥

पार० १ । ३ । १८

This *madhuparka* is food for the heat which operates the digestive system. I take away from it if there is any thing uneatable mixed herein.

The bride-groom taking very slight part of *madhuparka* at each time should sprinkle it through the medium of second finger with the thumb of right hand with the following *mantras* in all the direction mentioned below the *mantras* :

ओंवसवस्त्वा गायत्रेण छन्दसा भक्षयन्तु ॥ १ ॥

By this in the East.

ओं रुद्रास्त्वा त्रैष्टुभेन छन्दसा भक्षयन्तु ॥ 2 ॥

By this in the South

ओमादित्यास्त्वा जागतेन छन्दसा भक्षयन्तु ॥ ३ ॥

By this in the West.

ओं विश्वे त्वा देवा आनुष्टुभेन छन्दसा भक्षयन्तु ॥ ४ ॥

By this in the north.

ओं भूतेभ्यस्त्वा परिगृह्णामि ॥ ५ ॥

By this in the above direction three times.

The learned men known as *vasus* should take it with the *gayatri* metre.

The learned men known a *Rudra* should take it with *tristubha* metre.[2]

The learned men known as *aditya* should take it with *jagati* metre.[3]

The otner learned men known as *Vishvedevas* should take it with *anustubha* metre.[4]

I accept it for all the creatures.[5]

Afterwards the bride-groom dividing the *madhuparka* in three parts, should put these parts in three bronze dishes one in each. He should put these three dishes in front of him and pronouncing the following mantra he should eat a little or the whole of the *madhuparka* from each of three dishes. Whatever remains in the dishes should be given to servant or be dropped in water :—

ओं यन्मधुनो मधव्यं परमं रूपमन्नाद्यम् तेनाहं मधुनो मधव्येन परमेण रूपेणान्नाद्येन परमो मधव्योऽन्नादोऽसानि ॥

पार० १ । ३

O ye learned men ! may I be pure, sweet-tongued and the consumer of all cereals through the purity, sweetness and cereal essance pertaining to whatever is the pure, sweet and eatable form of honey.

Thereafter the bride-groom should sip water twice by the following *mantras* one by each :

ओममृतापिधानमसि स्वाहा ॥ १ ॥

आश्व० १ । २४ । २१

ओं सत्यं यशः श्रीर्मयि श्रीः श्रयताम् स्वाहा ॥ २ ॥

आश्व० । २४ । २२

This water is protection to creatures, and this my utterance is quite true.

This bring unto us the truth, fame, beauty and fortune. Whatever is being uttered herein is quite true.

After this the bride-groom should touch his limbs like eyes etc. with water by the *mantras* prescribed for this purpose in the *Havana* i. e.

ओं वाङ्‌म आस्ये अस्तु इत्यादि ।

Thereafter the bride should give to the bride-groom the cow or money etc. according to her circumstances pronouncing the following sentence :

ओं गौर्गौर्गौः प्रतिगृह्यताम् ॥

आश्वला० । २४ । २२

Here is Cow or money, kindly accept it.

The bride-groom should accept it by pronouncing the following formula :

ओं प्रतिगृह्णामि । पारस्कर १ । ३

Thanks, I accept it.

The person entrusted to accomplish the ceremonial work of the bride's party should take the bride-groom to *sabhamandapa* or the other room of the house joining the *madhuparka* place and seat him keeping his face in the east direction and seat the bride before him (the bride-groom). He himself sit there keeping his face in the north direction and pronounce the following sentence :

ओममुकगोत्रोत्पन्नामिमाममुकनाम्नीमलंकृतां कन्यां प्रतिगृह्णातु भवान् ॥

Kindly accept this girl named so and so, born in such and such family :

In the place of अमुकगोत्र bride's गोत्र should be pronounced. In the place of words अमुकं नाम्नीं the name of the bride should be pronounced in objective case.

Pronouncing the sentence ओममुकगोत्रोत्पन्नाम् the entrusted person of bride's party (Parent or other relatives) stretching right palm of the bride-groom put the palm of bride therein and then bride-groom say as follows :

ओं प्रतिगृह्णामि ॥

Thanks, I accept her.

Thereafter the bride-groom should give to bride the *uttama* cloth and the *upavastra* respectively with the following *mantras* :

ओ जरां गच्छ परिधत्स्व वासोभवा कृष्टीनामभिशस्तिपावा । शतं च जीव शरदः सुवर्चा रयिं च पुत्राननुसंव्ययस्वायुष्मतीदं परिधत्स्व वासः ।

पारस्कर १ । ४ । १२

ओं या अकृतन्नवयन या अतन्वत याश्च देवीस्तन्तूनभितो ततन्थ । तास्त्वा देवीर्जरसे संव्ययस्वायुष्मतीदं परिधत्स्व वासः ।

पार० गृ० १ । ४ । १३

O bride ! you attain the indefectible maturity of oldness with me, put on this cloth and be well-wisher of mankind, endowed with the resplendency of household life, acquire wealth accompanied with boon of children and O lady ! blessed with long life, you put on this cloth.

O bride ! blessed with long life, put on also this *upavastra*.

These ladies of my household family who prepared fabrics, spun the thread and wove this cloth, and who in the process of weaving stretched and arranged the knot of warp and weft, may provide you the cloth till the attainment of indefectible maturity of oldness.

The bride-groom should dress himself with the *vastra* and *upavastra* respectively by the following *mantras* :

ओं परिधास्यै यशोधास्यै दीर्घायुत्वाय जरदष्टिरस्मि ।
शतं च जीव शरदः पुरूची रायस्पोषमभि संव्ययिष्ये ।

पार० २. ६ । २०

ओं यशसा मा द्यावापृथिवी यशसेन्द्राबृहस्पती ।
यशो भगश्च मा विन्दद्यशो मा प्रति पद्यताम् ॥

पार० २ । ६ । १०

May I be possessed of maturity of age and blessed with wealth, children etc. I will put on this cloth which is symbolic to weal and nourishment for the sake of dressing, fame and long life. May I live hundred autumns.

May the earth and heaven find me attended by fame, may the air get me accompanied with fame, may the Sun find me enriched with fame and may fame always visit me.

During the period in which the bride and brid-groom are engaged in changing their dresses the preparation should be made and the following items should be arranged :

1. Wood-fuel for *yajna* should be kept reserved in sufficient quantity.
2. With Camphor or ghee the fire in the *Kunda* should be inflamed.
3. Ghee should be molten and perfumed with the necessary *yajna dravyas*.
4. Spoon for dropping oblation and other pots of *yajna* should be arranged.

5. *Havana Samagri* should be kept safe for the yajna.
6. One man from the party of bride-groom dressed neatly and cleanly, taking a jug full of water should circumambulate the *yajna kunda* and should sit in the south direction keeping his face in the north and having placed the jug in his front. He should sit there till the completion of marriage ceremony.
7. Similarly another person from the bride-groom's party taking a stick in his hand should sit in the south direction keeping his face in the north.
8. Bride's akin brother or cousin brother or the son of maternal uncle, or the son of mother's sister as the case may be should sit there in the west direction of the *Vedi* keeping four handful of roasted paddy mixed with dry *shami patra* in *a surpa*.
9. One squared small stone and two seats (*asanas*) for bride and bride-groom should be kept there.

Afterwards escorted by the person entrusted with the ceremony purpose the bride should come before the bride-groom and both the bride and bride-groom should pronounce the following *mantra* :

ओं समञ्जन्तु विश्वेदेवाः समापो हृदयानिनौ ।
सं मातरिश्वा सं धाता समुदेष्ट्री दधातु नौ ॥

ऋग्वेद १०-८-४७

Let all the learned persons present here know that we are accepting each other voluntarily and pleasantly and our hearts are concordant and united like waters, let the air. let God, let the instructress keep us conjugate.

The bride-groom, taking the right hand of the bride into his own right hand and pronouncing the following *mantra*, should come to the *Yajna Vedi* :

***ओं यदैषि मनसा दूरं दिशोऽनुपवमानो वा हिरण्यपर्णो वैकर्णः स त्वा मन्मनसां करोत्वसौ ॥**

पार० १ । ४

*The name of the bride should be pronounced instead of असौ।

O bride or bride-groom ! you voluntarily and mindfully accept one another like the wind and transplendent Sun which attain the contact of directions from a great distance. May God make both of us of concordant and united mind.

Afterwards the bride-groom should pronounce the following Mantras:

ओं भूर्भुवः स्व। अघोरचक्षुरपतिघ्न्येधि शिवा पशुभ्यः सुमनाः सुवर्चाः।
वीरसूर्देवृकामा स्योना शन्नो भव द्विपदे शं चतुष्पदे ।।

ऋग्वेद १०। ८५-४४

ओंभूर्भुवः स्वः। सा नः पूषा शिवतमामैरय सा न ऊरू उशती विहर।
यस्यामुशन्त प्रहराम शेफं यस्यामुकामा बहवो निविष्टयै ॥

पारस्कर १।४।१६

O bride ! by the grace of God who is existent, Conscious and all-bliss, you may not be ungenial in temperament and riogorous-eyed towards husband. May you be benevolent to animals, and be conscientious, delighted at mind and possessed of gracious energy: May you be procreant of brave offsprings, desirous of *devara* under the circumstances when such emergency arises, and blessed with great pleasure. May you be favourable to our bipeds and kind to our quadrupeds.

May condescending Master of the world make this bride that ideal custodian of maternity who abiding with the sacrosanctity of the procreative function of the household life submits herself to her husband's impregnation and in whom are destined many desired ends of life.

Afterwards bride-groom and bride circum-ambulate the-*yajna kunda* and take their seat at previously fixed place in such a manner as the bride, keeping her face in the east be in the right of the bride-groom and bride-groom in the left side of bride. The bride should pronounce the following *mantras*:

ओं प्र मे पतियानः पन्थाः कल्पताम् शिवा अरिष्टा पतिलोकं गमेयम् ॥
गो० २।१३ मंत्रब्राह्मण १।१।८

May this path of mine leading to husband-hood be auspicious and I unobstructed and free, go husband's home.

The chief *Homa* of marriage ceremony. The following acts should be done in connection with the chief *Homa* of marriage ceremony.

1. *Purohita*. Priest to conduct the ceremony should be selected and employed. He should take seat in the south of the *Vedi* keeping his face in the north direction.

2. *Achamana* (sipping of water) should be done with 'ओममृतोपस्तरणमसि स्वाहा' etc. *mantras.*

3. *Samidadhana* and *agnyadhana* etc. should be done according to *Samanya yajna* procedure.

4. Sprinkling of water round the *vedi* with 'अदिते ऽनुमन्यस्व' etc. four *mantras*.

5. आघारावाज्यभागाहुति, व्याहृति आहुति, and अष्टाज्याहुति should be offered.

After performing all these above acts the bride should touch the right shoulder of bride-groom. Thereafter they should offer the four oblations of molten ghee with the four *mantras* —अग्न आयूंषि पवस० etc. they should offer the fifth oblation with the following *mantra*—:

ओं भूर्भुवः स्वः । त्वमर्यमा भवसि यत्कनीनां नाम स्वधावन्गुह्यं बिभर्षि । अञ्जन्ति मित्रं सुधितं न गोभिर्यद्दम्पती समनसा कृणोषि स्वाहा ॥ इदमग्नये इदन्न मम ॥

ऋ० ५।३।२

God is existent, Conscious and all-bliss. This fire or heat which has its connection with girls is the most controlling power in the body. It consumes the oblations of cereal etc. and has a mysterious name—the *Vaishvanara*. Performers of *yajnas* keep this clandestine fire ablaze with milk, ghee, curd etc. like friend as it makes the married couple of concordant mind.

The *Rashtrabhrit* oblations should be offered in the fire of the *vedi* with the following twelve hymns:

ओमृताषाड् ऋतधामाग्निर्गन्धर्वः । स न इदं ब्रह्म क्षत्रं पातु तस्मै स्वाहा-
वाट् ।। इदमृताषाहे ऋतधाम्ने अग्नये गन्धर्वाय—इदन्न मम ।। १ ।।

Bearing the operation of eternal law and abiding by the eternal law this fire is *gandarva* the force resisting the earth. May it be source of protection to intellectual and defensive power of our society or state. This oblation offered in the fire of the *vedi* is meant for *Rtasat,Rtadhama*, *gandharva agni*, *and it is not for me.*

ओमृताषाड्ऋतधामाग्निर्गन्धर्वस्तस्यौषधयोऽप्सरसो मुदो नाम ताभ्यः स्वाहा
इदमोषधीभ्योऽप्सरोभ्यो मुद्भ्य—इदन्न मम ।। २ ।।

Bearing the operation of eternal law and abiding by the eternal law this fire is *gandharva*, the force resisting the earth and herbs are its *apsaras*, the element extending in water named as *mudah*, the giver of pleasure. This oblation is offered for them. The oblation offered in the fire of the *Vedi* is meant for the *Osadhi*, *apsarar mudah*, it is not for me.

ओं स꣡हितः विश्वसामा सूर्यो गन्धर्वः स न इदं ब्रह्म क्षत्रं पातु तस्मै
स्वाहा वाट् ।। इदं स꣡हिताय विश्वसाम्ने सूर्याय गन्धर्वाय—इदन्न मम ।। ३ ।।

Co-ordinating night and day and maintaining the tune of all the *Saman* this sun is *gandharva*, the power resisting the planets. May it be the source of protection to intellectual and defensive power of our society or state. This oblation is offered for its subsistance. The oblation offered in the fire of the *vedi* is meant for *Samhita*, *Vishvasaman*, *surya gandharva*, and it is not for me.

स꣡हितः विश्वसामा सूर्योगन्धर्वस्तस्य मरीचयोऽप्सरसः आयुवो नाम
ताभ्यः । इदं मरीचिभ्योऽप्सरोभ्य आयुभ्यः—इदन्न मम ।। ४ ।।

Co ordinating night and day maintainig the tune of all *saman*, this Sun is *gandhrava*, the power resisting the planets and the rays are its *apsavas*, the means of evaporation, named *ayuvah*, the power causing expansion. This oblation is offered for them. The oblation offered in the fire of the *Vedi* is meant for *marichi apsara ayuvah* and it is not for me.

ओं सुषुम्णः सूर्यरश्मिश्चन्द्रमा गन्धर्वः। स न इदं बृह्म क्षत्रं पातु तस्मै स्वाहा वाट् ॥ इदं सुषुम्णाय सूर्यरश्मये चन्द्रमसे गन्धर्वाय—

इदन्न मम ॥ ५ ॥

Illuminated by the rays of sun the pleasant moon is *ganharva* the planet which acquires its light from the Sun. May it be the source of protection to the intellectual and defensive power of our society or state. This oblation is offered for its subsistance. The oblation offered in the fire of the *Vedi* is meant for *susumna*, *suryarashmi chandrama gandharava* and is not for me.

ओं सुषुम्णः सूर्यरश्मिश्चन्द्रमा गन्धर्वस्तस्य नक्षत्राण्यप्सरसो भेकुरयो नाम ताभ्यः स्वाहा ॥ इदं नक्षत्रेभ्योऽप्सरोभ्यो भेकुरिम्य—इदन्न मम ॥ ६ ॥

Illuminated by the rays of the Sun the plesant moon is *gandharva*, the planet which acquires light from the Sun and the stars are its *apsaras*, the celestial co-inhabitants, named as *behkurayah*, the bodies emitting light. This oblation offered in the fire of the *Ved is* meant for *Naksatra apsaras bhekuris* and not for me.

ओमिषिरो विश्वव्यचा वातो गन्धर्वः। स न इदं ब्रह्म क्षत्रं पातु तस्मै स्वाहावाट् ॥ इदमिषिराया विश्वव्यचसे वाताय गन्धर्वाय—इदन्न मम ॥ ७ ॥

Expeditious and all-pervading wind is the *gandharva*, highly conductible medium. May it be source of protection to the intellectual and defensive power of our society or state. This oblation is offered for its subsistance. The oblation offered in the fire of the *vedl* is meant for *ishira Vishvavyacha Vata gandharva* and it is not for me.

ओं इषिरो विश्वव्यचा वातो गन्धर्वस्तस्यापो अप्सरस ऊर्जो नाम ताभ्यः स्वाहा ॥ इदमद्भ्यो अप्सरोभ्य ऊर्ग्भ्यः—इदन्न मम ॥ ८ ॥

Expeditious and all-pervading wind is the *gandharva*, higly conductible medium and the waters are its *apsarasas*, atmospheric co-movers named *urjas*, powerful essance produced by heat. This oblation is offered for them. The oblation offered in the fire of *Vedi* is meant for *apah apsaras urjas* and it is not for me.

ओं भुज्युः सुपर्णो यज्ञौ गन्धर्वं । स न इदं ब्रह्म क्षत्रं पातु तस्मै स्वाहा वाट् । इदं भुज्यवे सुपर्णाय यज्ञाय गन्धर्वाय —इदन्न मम ॥ ९ ॥

Giving protection and happiness to its performers and conducive to produce good results, this *yajna* is *gandharva*, the means of knowledge and happiness (worldly and unworldly). May it be the source of protection to intellectual and defensive power of our society or state. This oblation is offered for its subsistence, The oblation offered in the fire of the *Vedi* is meant for *bhujyu suparna yajna gandharva* and it is not for me.

ओं भुज्यु: सुपर्णो यज्ञो गन्धर्वस्तस्य दक्षिणा अप्सरस स्तावा नाम । ताभ्यः स्वाहा । इदं दक्षिणाभ्यो ऽप्सरोभ्यस्तावाभ्यः — इदन्न मम ॥ १० ॥

Giving protection and happiness to its performer and conducive to produce good results this *yajna* is *gandharva*, the means of knowledge and happiness (worldly and unworldly) and *dakshina*, the remuneration for the conducting priests is its *apsaras*, good act of fulfilment named as *stavah*, the praiseworthy performances. This oblation is offered for them. The oblation offered in the fire of the *vedi* is meant for *dakshina apsarasas tavas* and it is not for me.

ओं प्रजापतिर्विश्वकर्मा मनोगन्धर्वः स न इदं ब्रह्म क्षत्रं पातु तस्मै स्वाहा वाट् । इदं प्रजापतये विश्वकर्मणे मनसे गन्धर्वाय — इदन्न मम ॥ ११ ॥

The master of all organs and instrumental in all actions this minds of ours is *gandharva*, the inspiring principle between all organs. May it be source of protection to intellectual and defensive power of our society or the state. This oblation is offered for its subsistance. The oblation offered in the fire of the *vedi* is meant for *Prajapati Vishvakarman manas gandharva* and it is not for me.

ओं प्रजापति विश्वकर्मा मनो गन्धर्वस्तस्य ऋक्स मान्यप्सरस एष्टयो नाम ताभ्यः स्वाहा ॥ इदं ऋक्सामेभ्योऽप्सरोभ्य एष्टिभ्यः—

इदन्न मम ॥ १२ ॥

The master of all organs and instrumental in all actions this mind of ours is *gandharva*. the inspiring principle between all organs and *RK* and *Saman*, are its *apsaras*, the accomplishing factor of knowledge and actions named as *estayah*, the deliberate activities of mind. This oblation offered in the fire of the *vedi* is meant for *RK saman apsarasas estayas* and it is not for me.

N.B. These oblations are entitled as *Rastrabhrita* oblations. These security of *Rashtra* is the main theme of them. The security depends on the coordination of all the units of state. Household life is a small unit of society or state. House becomes an abode of bliss if there is coordination in the wife and husband. This is based on the firmness of conjugal tie. Thus aiming at the security and safety of the state great stress has been laid on the firmness of conjugal coordination through the education of permanent coordination of physical *gandharva* and *apsarasas*. The married couple should lesson from them in maintaining close affinity between them.

With the following *mantras* oblations of *jaya homa* should be offered.

ओं चित्तं च स्वाहा ॥ इदं चित्ताय—इदन्न मम ॥ १ ॥

ओं चित्तिश्च स्वाहा ॥ इदं चित्यै—इदन्न मम ॥ २ ॥

ओमाकूतं च स्वाहा ॥ इदमाकूताय—इदन्न मम ॥ ३ ॥

ओमाकूतिश्च स्वाहा ॥ इदमाकूत्यै—इदन्न मम ॥ ४ ॥

ओं विज्ञातञ्च स्वाहा ॥ इदं विज्ञाताय—इदन्न मम ॥ ५ ॥

ओं विज्ञातिश्च स्वाहा ॥ इदं विज्ञात्यै—इदन्न मम ॥ ६ ॥

ओं मनश्च स्वाहा ॥ इदं मनसे—इदन्न मम ॥ ७ ॥

ओं शक्वरीश्च स्वाहा ॥ इदं शक्वरीभ्यः—इदन्न मम ॥ ८ ॥

ओं दर्शश्च स्वाहा ॥ इदं दर्शाय—इदन्न मम ॥ ९ ॥

ओं पौर्णमासं च स्वाहा ॥ इदं पौर्णमासाय—इदन्न मम ॥ १० ॥

ओं बृहच्च स्वाहा ॥ इदं बृहते—इदन्न मम ॥ ११ ॥

ओं रथन्तरञ्च स्वाहा ॥ इदं रथन्तराय—इदन्न मम ॥ १२ ॥

ओं प्रजापतिर्जयानिन्द्राय वृष्णे प्रायच्छदुग्रः पृतना जयेषु । तस्मै विशः समनमन्त सर्वा स उग्र स इहव्यो बभूव स्वाहा ॥ इदं प्रजापतये जयानिन्द्राय—इदन्न मम ।

पारस्कर १ । ५ । ८

May *Prajapati*, the Master of the universe give us good conscience. The oblation offered is meant for *chitta* and it is not for me. "1"

May *Prajapati*, the master of the universe give us good consciousness of the conscience. The oblatlon offered is meant for *chitti* and it is not for me. "2"

May *Prajapati*, the master of the universe make us competent in forming good opinion. The oblation offered is meant for *akuta* and is not for me. "3"

May *Prajapati*, the master of the universe endow us with the power of right discrimination. The oblation offered is meant for *akuti* and it is not for me. "4"

May *Prajapati*, the master of the universe inspire unto us the tendancy of science. The oblation offered is meant for *Vijnatam* and it is not for me. "5"

May *Prajapati*, the master of the universe inspire unto us the love for arts. The oblation offered is meant for *Vijnatih* and it is not for me. "6"

May *Prajapati* the master of the universe keep our mind alert for ever. The oblation offered is meant for *manas* and it is not for me "7"

May *Prajapati*, the master of the universe give us the strength of mind and body. The oblation offered is meant for *shakvaris* and it is not for me. "8"

May *Prajapati*, the master of the universe keep us conscious of the duties at the time of *darsha* (*amavasya*). The oblation offered is meant for *darsha* and it is not for me. "9"

May *Prajapati*, the master of the universe keepus aware of the duties at the time of full moon. The oblation offered is meant for *Paurnamasam* and it is not for me. "10"

May *Prajapati*, the master of the universe endow us with the knowledge of distinguishing the relation between *Brihat saman* and its counterpart in the physical world. The oblation offered is meant for *Brihat* and it is not for me. "11"

May *Prajapati*, the master of the universe endow us with the knowledge of distinguishing the relation between *Rathantara Saman* and its counterpart in the physical world. The oblation offered is meant for *Rathantara* and it is not for me. "2"

Prajapati, the master of the universe handed over *jayan*, the hymns of victory to *Indra*, the all-pervading electricity; which is the source of rainfall. *Indra* became furiously powerful to have celebrated victory upon the foes in the battle with *vritra*, the cloud. It is why all the subjects of this world subordinate them to *Indra*. *Indra* is deadfully powerful and oblations in the yajna are offered for him. The oblation offered is meant for *Prajapati Jayanindra* and it is not for me,

Afterwards the oblations of *abhyatana homa* should be offered with the following *mantras* :

ओमग्निर्भूतानामधिपतिः स मावत्वस्मिन्ब्रह्मण्यस्मिन् क्षत्रेऽस्यामाशिष्यास्यां पुरोधायामस्मिन् कर्मण्यस्यां देवहूत्यां स्वाहा ।। इदमग्नये भूतनामधिपतये—इदन्न मम ।।

श्रोमिद्रो ज्येष्ठानामधिपतिः······स्वाहा । इदमिन्द्राय ज्येष्ठानामधियतये इदन्न मम ।। २ ।।

श्रों यमः पृथिव्या अधिपतिः······स्वाहा । इदं यमाय पृथिव्याअधिपतये— इदन्न मम ।। ३ ।।

श्रों वायुरन्तरिक्षस्याधिपतिः······स्वाहा । इदं वायवेऽन्तरिक्षस्याधिपतये — इदन्न मम ।। ४ ।।

श्रों सूर्थो दिव्रोऽधिपतिः······स्वाहा । इदं सूर्याय दिवोऽधिपतये – इदन्न मम ।। ५ ।।

ओं चन्द्रमा नक्षत्राणामधिपतिः······स्वाहा । इदं चन्द्रमसे नक्षत्राणामधिप तये—इदन्न मम ॥ ६ ॥

ओं वृहस्पति र्ब्रह्मणोऽधिपतिः······स्वाहा । इदं वृहस्पतये ब्रह्मणोऽधिपतये—इदन्न मम ॥ ७ ॥

ओं मित्रः सत्यानामधिपति·····स्वाहा । इदं मित्राय सत्यानामधिपतये—इदन्न मम ॥ ८ ॥

ओं वरुणोऽपामधिपतिः······स्वाहा । इदं वरुणायापामधिपतये—इदन्न मम ॥ ९ ॥

ओं समुद्र स्त्रोत्यानामधिपतिः······स्वाहा । इदं समुद्राय स्त्रोत्यानामधिपतये—इदन्न मम ॥ १०

ओमन्नं साम्राज्यानामधिपतिः······स्वाहा इदमन्नाय साम्राज्यानामधिप तये - इदन्न मम ॥ ११ ॥

ओं सोम ओषधीनामधिपतिः······स्वाहा । इदं सोमाय औषधीनामधिपतये —इदन्न मम ॥ १२ ॥

ओं सविता प्रसवानामधिपतिः······स्वाहा । इदं सवित्रे प्रसवानामधि पतये— इदन्न मम ॥ १३

ओं रुद्रः पशूनामधिपतिः······स्वाहा । इदं रुद्राय पशूनामधिपतये इदन्न मम ॥ १४ ॥

ओं त्वष्टा रूपाणामधिपतिः······स्वाहा । इदं त्वष्ट्रे रूपाणमधिपतये—इदन्न मम ॥ १५ ॥

ओं विष्णुः पर्वतानामधिपतिः······स्वाहा । इदं विष्णवे पर्वतानामधिप-तये—इदन्न मम ॥ १६ ॥

ओं मरुतो गणनामधिपतयस्ते मावन्त्वस्मिन्—स्वाहा । इदं मरुद्भ्यो गणा नामधिपतिभ्यो—इदन्न मम ॥ १७ ॥

ओं पितरः पितामहाः परेऽवरे ततास्ततामहा इह मावन्त्वस्मिन्—ब्रह्मण्यस्मिन् क्षत्रे ऽस्यामाशिष्यस्यांपुरो धायामस्मिन् कर्मण्यस्यां देवहूत्यां स्वाहा । इदं पितृभ्यो पितामहेभ्यः परेभ्यो अवरेभ्यस्ततामहेभ्यश्च—इदन्न मम ॥ १८ ॥

पारस्कर का० १ । ५ । १०

Agni, the fire is the dominating power among the animate and inanimate creatures, let it be source of protection for us in our intellectual feats and let it be so in our administrative performances, let it be source of protection in this auspicious act, let it be source of protection for this bride. Let it be source of protection in this marriage ceremony and let it be source of protection in this *yajna* wherein the oblations are offered for the *devas*, the physical and spiritual elements. Whatever has been uttered herein is correct. The oblation offered is meant for the *Prajapati agni* and it is not for me.[1]

Indra, the Electricity is the dominating power in all the powers of pre-eminence. Rest is like the previous one. The oblation offered is meant for the *jyestadhipati Indra* and it is not for me.[2]

Yama, the attraction power of the sun is pre-dominating over earth. Rest is like the previons one. The oblation offered is meant for *Prithvipati yama* and it is not for me.[3]

Vayu, the air is predominoting over the atmospheric region. Rest is like previous one. The oblation offered is meant for *antrikshadhipati vayu*, and it is not for me.[4]

Sury,a the sun is predominating over the heavenly region. Rest is like the previous one. The oblation offered is meant for *divoadhipati Surya* and it is not for me.[5]

Chandrama, the Moon is the predominating planet among the stars. Rest is like the previous one. The oblation offered is meant for *Nakshatradhipati Chandrama* and it is not for me.[6]

Brihaspati, the Ether is predominating the sound or speech. Rest is like the previous one. The oblation offered is meant for *Brahmanoadhipati Brihaspati* and it is not for me.[7]

Mitrah, the force of integration is predominent over the existing objects. Rest is like the previous one. The oblation offered is meant for *satyadhipati mitra* and it is not for me.[8]

Varuna, the Vapour is the predominent power of waters. Rest is like the previous one. The oblation offered is meant for *upamadhipati Varuna* and it is not for me.[9]

Samudrah, the Ocean, or atmospheric ocean is the predominating power over the rivers. Rest s like the previous one. The oblation offered is meant for *srotyadhipati samudra*, and it not for me.[1]

Anna, Grain is the predominent protective meensof the is empes. Rest is like the previous one. The oblation offered meant for *samrajyadhipati anna* and it is not for me.[11]

Soma, the lunar substance which flourishes medicinal herbs, is the predominating strength of herbs. Rest is like the previous one. The oblation offered is meant for *oshadhyadhipati soma* and it is not for me.[12]

Savitar, the creative, energy of the sun is the predominating constructive power of the product. Rest is like the previous one. The oblation offered is meant for *Prasavadhipati* savitar and it is not for me.[13]

Rudrah, the animal heat is predominent over the animal kingdom. Rest is like the previous one. The oblation offered is meant for *Pashvadhipati Rudra*, and it is not for me.[14]

Tvastar, the light of the Suu is the predominating source of colours. Rest is like the previous one. The oblation offered is meant for *Rupadhipati Tvastar* and it is not for me.[15]

Vishnuh, the scorching heat of the Sun is the predominent factor of the clouds. Rest is like the previous one. The oblation offered is meant for *Parvatadhipati vishnu* and it is not for me.[16]

Marutah, the forty nine *maruts* are the dominating power which control the bodies collected. Rest is like the previous one. The oblation offered is meant for *Ganadhidati maruts* and it is not for me.[17]

Pitarah, the learned and practical persons playing their respective roles in the family, society and states be our saviors in intellectual feats etc. Rest is like the previous one. The oblation offered is mean for *Pitarah*, *Pitamaha*, *parayara tatas tatamahas* and it is not for me.

Further the oblations should be offered with the following *mantras* :

ओमग्निरैतु प्रथमो देवतानां सोऽस्यै प्रजां मुञ्चतु मृत्युपाशात् । तदयꣳ राजा वरुणोऽनुमन्यमां यथेयꣳ स्त्री पोत्रमघं न रोदात् स्वाहा ।। इदमग्नयेइवं न मम ।। १ ।।

ओमिमाग्निस्त्रायतां गार्हपत्यः प्रजामस्यै नयतु दीर्घमायुः । अशून्योपस्था जीवतामस्तु माता पौत्रमानन्दमभिविबुध्यतामियꣳ स्वाहा ।। इदमग्नये—इनं न मम ।। २ ।।

मंत्र ब्रह्ममण २ । १ । २ ।।

ओं स्वस्ति नोऽग्ये दिव आ पृथिव्या विश्वानि धेह्ययथा यजत्र यदस्यां महि दिबि जातं प्रशस्तं तदस्मासु द्रविणं धेहि चित्रं स्वाहा ।। इदमग्नये—इदं न मम ।। ३ ।।

ओं सुगन्नपन्था प्रदिशं न एहि ज्योतिर्मध्ये ह्यजरं न आयुः । अपैतु मृत्युरमृतं म आगाद्वैवस्वतो नो अभयं कृणोतु स्वाहा ।। इदं वैवस्वताय—इदं न मम ।। ४

ओं परं मृत्यो अनुपरेहि पन्थां यत्र नो अन्य इतरो देवयानात् । चक्षुष्मते श्रृण्वते ते ब्रवीमि मानः प्रजाꣳ रीपिषो मोत वीरान्-त्स्वाहा ।। इदं मृत्यवे-इदं न मम ।। ५ ।।

पार० कां० १ । ५ ११-११

ओं द्यौस्ते पृष्ठं रक्षतु वायुरूरू अश्विनौ च । स्तनन्धयांस्ते पुत्रान्त्सविताभिरक्षत्ववासस: परिधानाद् बृहस्पतिर्विश्वेदेवा अभिरक्षन्तु पश्चात् स्वाहा ।। इदं विश्वेभ्यो देवेभ्य—इदं न मम ।। ६ ।।

ओं मा ते गहेषु निशि घोष उत्थावन्यत्र त्वद्रुवत्यः संविशन्तु । मात्वꣳ रुवत्युपुर आवधिष्ठा जीवपत्नी पतिलोके विराज पश्यन्तीं प्रजाꣳसुमनस्यमानाꣳ स्वाहा । इदमग्नये -- इदं न मम ।। ७

ओमप्रजस्यं पौत्रमर्त्यं पाप्मानमुत वा अघम् । शीर्ष्णः स्रजमिवोन्मुच्य द्विषद्भ्यः प्रतिमुञ्चामि पाशꣳ स्वाहा ।। इदमग्नये इदं न मम ।। ८ ।।
मंत्रब्राह्मण १ । १ १-३, गोभिल २ । १ २३-२६

First amongst all the physical elements Agni, the fire by grace of God come to her protection and it save the offspring of this bride from the hold of immature death. *Varuna*, the vital air may come to its coordination in this matter and this bride may not ever wail for the grief of her child. Whatever is uttered herein is true. The oblation offerad is meant for *agni* and it is not for me.

May the fire of house-hold come to the safety of this bride and may it lead her offspring to long life. May she be free from all defects of barrenness and be the mother of living children. May she ever be conscious of the pleasure of children. Whatever is uttered herein is true. The oblation offered is meant for *agni* and it is not for me.[2]

May *Agni*, the refulgence of vitality which is the means of all voluntary activities, correct our incongruous deeds and make them of our benefit. Whatever is possessed for glory in the broad region of heaven the earth, be given to us. May we attain the various wealth produced in earth as well as the praisworthy wealth hidden iu the refulgence of wlsdom. Whatever is uttered herein is correct. The oblation offered is meant for *agni* and it is not for me.[3]

O enlightened person ! please come to us guiding us the easily passable path of prosperity. bless us with the life full of enlightenmeht and free from the evils of oldness, death may not hunt us, immortality be attained by us and by your blessing the time make us fearless. Whatever is uttered herein is correct. The oblation offered is meant for *Valvasvata* and it is not for me.[4]

Let the death carry unfavourably towards the second path to him who amongst us is other than the man who traveres the path of enlightened persons. I pray god that the death which works out its plan like the man enjoying the possession of sound hearing and seeing, should not destroy our offspring and brave men. Whatever is uttered herein is true. The oblation offered is meant for *mrityu* and it is not for me.[5]

O bride ! let the Sun protect your back, let the vital airs like *Prana* and *apana* and the atmospheric wind protect your belly and waist, let *savitar,* the productiue power of nature protect your children who are infant and sucking the breast, prior to their being able to put on dress and let Brihaspati, the teacher and *vishvedevah,* other learned persons protect them afterwards. Whatever is uttered herein is true. The oblation offered is meant for *vishvedevah* and it is not for me.[6]

O bride ! let there not be wailing of any kind in your home in the night time, let not there weeping women also enter the house not appertaining to you. Let you not weeping punish your attendents in your house and you having your husband alive and seeing your children delightful prosper in your husband's house. Whatever is uttered herein is correct. The oblation offered is meant for *agni* and it is not for me.[7]

O bride ! like a garland from the head I remove from you the evils of barrenness, affection of child's death, dreadful sin and sins caused by foes. Whatever is uttered is true. The oblation offered is meant for *agni* and it is not for me.[8]

After this the four oblations should be offered with *mantras*—भूरग्नये स्वाहा-etc.

The bride-groom standing in front of sitting bride keeping her face in the east direction, should keep his face in west direction and should lift up the bride by taking her right palm into his left hand. He grasping the lifted right hand palm of bride by his right hand should pronounce the following hand-grasping *mantras* to take vow :

ओं गृभ्णामि ते सौभगत्वाय हस्तं मया पत्या जरदष्टिर्यथासः । भगो अर्यमा सविता पुरन्धिर्मह्यं त्वादुर्गार्हपत्याय देवाः १ ॥

ऋ १० । ८५ । ३६ पार १।६।३

ओं भगस्ते हस्तमग्रभीत् सविता ते हस्तमग्रभीत् । पत्नी त्वमसि धर्मणाहं गृहपतिस्तव ॥ २ ॥

ममेयमस्तु पोष्या मह्यं त्वादाद् बृहस्पतिः । मया पत्या प्रजावति शं जीव शरदः शतम् ॥ ३ ॥

त्वष्टा वासो व्यदधाच्छुभेकं बृहस्पतेः प्रशिषा कवीनाम् । तेनेमां नारीं सविता भगश्च सूर्यामिव परिधत्तां प्रजया ॥ ४ ॥

इन्द्राग्नी द्यावापृथिवी मातरिश्वा मित्रावरुणा भगो अश्विनोभा । बृहस्पति-मरुतो ब्रह्म सोम इमां नारीं प्रजया वर्धयन्तु ॥ ५ ॥

अहं विष्यामि मयि रूपमस्या वेददित्पश्यन्मनसा कुलायम् । न स्तेयमद्मि मनसोदमुच्ये स्वयं श्रन्थानो वरुणस्य पाशान् ॥ ६ ॥

अथर्व १४ । १ । ५८

I, the bride-groom hold your hand unto mine for the prosperity of house-hold life. May you attain the age of oldness in pleasure with me as your husband. God who is the master of all drosperity, the administrator of justice, the creator of the universe and all sub-sistidg and the enlightened persons present here are giving you to me for the fulfilment of house-hold life's attainments and obligations,[1]

I possessed of virtues and prosperity grasp your hand I full of inspirations of duty and procreation hold your hand unto mine, you are my wife in the letter and spirit of *dharma* and I your husband accordingly.[2]

O bride ! that you whom the Protector of the universe gave to me, remain supported and nourished by me. O ye procreating lady ! may you live hundred autumns delightfully with me as your husband.[3]

O bride ! the relation of husband and wife is based in this world in contormity to the teachiegs of God and enlightened persons. Just as the electricity is permeating in all the objects so you attain nice dresses, ornaments and happiness from me for the sake of my pleasure. May the all-creating, Super-excellent God bless this my wife with offspring. Similarly I will keep you well-dressed and well-ornamented.[4]

O ye our relatives ! Kindly be helpful in well-being of my wife just as the electricity and fire, the Sun and the earth, atmospheric air, oxygen and hydrogen, good fortune, physician and true preacher, impartial ruler, cultured men, Supreme Being and the moon protect and enhance the lot of subject and this my wife with prosperity, offspring etc.[5]

O bride ! just as I, foreseeing the progress of family through my mind, love your beauty, desire you, so you also be attracted in me. I leave with good intention to conceal any thing from you and I say I would not also eat or use any thing stealthily. I myself even being unsturdy would remove all the obstacles of righteousness and you are also expected to act accordingly.[6]

The vow of hand-grasping should also be taken by the bride. Afterwards the bride-groom accompanied by the bride should circum-ambulate the *agnikunda* and the person who was sitting near the jug full of water and placed in the south direction, carrying the jug should follow the bride-groom and bride. After the circum-ambulation being finished both of them should take the following *mantra* :

ओममोऽहमस्मि सा त्वꣳ सा त्वमस्यमोऽहम् । सामाहमस्मि ऋक्त्वं द्यौरहं पृथिवी त्वं तावेव विवहावहै सह रेतो दधावहै । प्रजां प्रजनयावहै पुत्रान् विदावहै बहून् । ते सन्तुजरदष्टयः सं प्रियौ रोचिष्णु सुमनस्यमानौ । पश्येम शरदः शतम् जीवेम शरदः शतम् शृणुयाम शरदः शतम् ।

पार० १ । ६ । ३

O bride ! I am *amah* and you are *saa* and say in turn that you are *saa* and I am *amah* which form *saam* signifying our coniugal affinity in which I intentionally and voluntarily accept you and you intentionally and voluntarily accept me. I am *sama* and you are like *RK*, I am like *dyauh*, the Sun and you are like *prithivi*, the earth. Both of us are marrying each other pleasantly, let us put our semen together let us procreate children, let us have many sons and let these children live till the expiry of oldness. Both of us loving each other, admiring each other and keeping each other good at heart see hundred autumns, live hundred autumns end hear hundred autumns.

Thereafter, the bride-groom from behind the bribe going near her and standing in the south direction keeping his face in the north, should hold the right palm of the bride in his own right palm and thus both should stand. The man carrying the jug full of water should take his previously accupied seat in the south of the *yajna vedi.* Thereafter the mother or brother of the bride taking the roasted pady or maize kept in the winnowing basket in her or his left hand should lift the right foot of bride and should make her mount it on the small slab of stone. At this time the bride-groom should pronounce the following *mantra.*

ओमारोहेममश्मानमश्मेव त्वँ स्थिरा भव। अभितिष्ठ पृतन्यतोऽवबाधस्व पृतनायतः। १।

पार० १।७।१

O bride ! ascend this stone assume firmness like rock. Resist foes and overcome quarrelsome persons.

Thereafter the bride and bride-groom should stand near the *yajna kunda* keeping their faces in the east direction. In this performance the bride keeping herself in the south should place her folded and kept-together hand palms on the folded and kept-together have palms of the bride-groom. After this the mother or brother of bride, as the case may be, should place the winnowing basket on the ground or give to some one else and should sprinkle pure ghee on the coupled *anjalis* of the bride and bride-groom. In this performance the *anjali* of the bride should be above and the *anjali* of bride-groom should be below. The mother or brother of bride after this should take two handful of roasted paddy or maize from the winnowing basket with her or his right hand, should drop in the coupled *anjali* of the bride and bride-groom and should sprinkle a little pure ghee again on the roasted paddy or maize contained in the *anjali* of the bride and hride-groom. Then, the bride bending her own *anjali* with that of bride-groom should drop three oblations on the blazing fuel, one by each, dividing the roasted paddy in three equal parts, with the following *mantras* :

ओमर्यमणं देवं कन्या अग्निमयक्षत। स नो अर्यमा देवः प्रेतो मुञ्चतु मा पतेः स्वाहा। इदमर्यम्णे अग्नये इदं न मम॥ १॥

ओमियं नार्युपब्रूते लाजानावपन्तिका । आयुष्मानस्तु मे पतिरेधन्तां ज्ञातयो मम स्वाहा । इदमग्नये—इदं न मम ॥ २ ॥

ओमिमाँल्लाजानावपाम्यग्नौ समृद्धिकरणं तव । मम तुभ्यं च संवननं तदग्निरनुमन्यतामियँ स्वाहा ॥ इदमग्नये इदं न मम । पार० १ । ६

The bride offers the oblation in the fire which is controlling the world. May that all-controlling fire be the source of separating me from parentpl family for joining the husband' family but it should not keep me separate from my husband. Whatever is uttered herein is correct. The oblation offered is meant for *aryama agni* and it is not for me.[1]

This lady offering the oblations of roasted paddy in the fire prays," By grace of God my husband attain long life and the members of the family and relations flourish in happiness and prosperity, Whatever is uttered herein is correct. The oblation offered is meant for *Agni* and it is not for me.[2]

O bride-groom ! I drop these grains of roasted paddy in the fire for your prosperity and progress, may there be great affection between you and me for each other's this fire of yajna be the source of help to us. Whatever is uttered herein is eorrect. The oblation offered is meant for *agni* and it is not for me.

Thereafter the bride-groom should pronounce the following *mantra* :

ओं सरस्वति प्रेदमव सुभगे वाजिनीवति । यान्त्वा विश्वस्य भूतस्य प्रजायामस्याग्रतः । यस्यां भूतँ समभवद्यस्यां विश्वमिदं जगत् । तामद्य गाथां गास्यामि या स्त्रीणामुत्तमं यशः ॥ १ ॥ पार० १ । ७ । २

Endowed with excellent powers, treated to be the material cause of all worldly objects, grain etc. this Prakriti, the matter be helpful to save this eonjugal affinity. It is called the procreator of the objects of this present world which remained even prior to the world enveloped in the dissolution. It is that material cause in which this world got rise and wherein the whole of the universe is present now. I will sing that story of the matter which involvest the most excellent worthwhile glory of women.

Afterwards the bride-groom holding the right palm of bride into his own right palm pronounce the following *mantras* and circum-ambulate the *yajnaknnda* :

ओं तुभ्यमग्रे पर्यवहन्त्सूर्या वहतुना सह । पुनः पतिभ्यो जायां दा अग्ने प्रजया सह ॥ १ ॥ ऋ० १० । ८५ । ३८
पार० १ । २ । ४

ओं कन्यला पितृभ्यः पतिलोकं यतीयमपदीक्षामयष्ट । कन्या उत त्वया वयं धारा उदन्या इवाति गाहेमहि द्विषः ॥ मं ब्रा० १ । २ । ५

The natural elements organic and inorganic playing their parts in the body hand over the girl to *agni*, the heat which brings maturity in her. This *agni* in its trun givec her to Soma, the most vital activity of mental maturity just as the light of Sun with its operational power goes to the moon. And consequently in the form of bride she is given to husband for being his wife blessed with children.

This girl leaving her parents and going to join the husband's family has accepted the husband's ereed. She may live with me as her husband. We would dip deen iu happiness like the me as her husband. We would dip deep in happiness like the streams of water crushing and overcoming the obstacles and jealousies.

After this the bride and bride-groom should stand for a littlc in the west of the *yajnkunda* keeping their faces in the east direction. Thereafter they both should circum-ambulate the *yajnakunda* once again followeP by the man carrying the jug of water.

The procedure beginning from stone-climbing with the *mantra* आरोहेममश्मानम्—and ending with the circum-ambulation of *yajnakunda* after pronouncingthe *manrr* ओंकन्यलापितृभ्य: etc., should be rcpeated twice again.

Thus completing the procedure three times in total for the fourth time the bride and bridegroom should stand in the west of the *Vedi* keeping their faces in the east direction. The mother or the brother of the bride, as the case may be, bending obliquely the winnoing basket should drop the remaining roasted pady in the *anjali* of the bride. Then, bride pronouncing the following *mantra* should *offer* one oblation of that who roasted pady in the blazing fire of the Vedi :

ओं भगाय स्वाहा ॥ इदं भगाय इदन्न मम ॥

I offer this oblation for the great fartune. Whatever is uttered herein is correct. The oblation offered is meant for *Bhaga* and it is not for me.

Afterwards bridegroom should sit in the west, keeping his face in the east direction and having the bride seated in his right-side. They should offer one oblation of molten ghee by the spoon with the under-mentioned *mantra* :

ओं प्रजापतये स्वाहा ॥ इदं प्रजापतये इदं न मम ॥

पार० १ । ७ । ६

We offer this oblation for *prajapati,* the fire resisting the world. Whatever is uttered herein is correct. The oblation offered is meant for *Prajapati* and it is not for me.

Thereafter going to a private room the bridegroom should loosen the tied hair of bride with the following *mantras* :

ओं प्रत्वा मुञ्चामि वरुणस्य पाशाद्येनत्वाबध्ना त्सविता सुशेवः । ऋतस्य योनौ सुकृतस्य लोकेऽरिष्टान्त्वा सह पत्या दधामि ॥ १ ॥

ओं प्रेतो मुञ्चामि नामुतः सुबद्धामुतस्करम् । वथेयमिन्द्र मीढ्वः सुपुत्रा सुभगासति ॥ २ ॥

ऋ० १० । ८५ । २४-२५

O bride ! I free you from the restrictions of the law, the life of celibacy by which your good father hitherto bound you. With me as your husband you will live a life of righteousness and charity.

I free this bride from the obligations of her father's family, of course, not from her husband's family. Now she stand well bound, that she, with her valiant husband might have good luck in worthy progeny:

After this the bride and bride-groom should come in the *sabhamandapa* and begin the procedure of seven steps ceremony. At this juncture the dress-sheet of bride should be tied with the *upvaśtra* of the bride-groom. This is called the conjugal tie of couple. Leaving their seats the bride and bride-groom both should stand up. Then the baide-groom holding the right hand *anjali* of the bride in his own right hand and taking her with him should go in the north side of the *yajnakunda*. Then both of them should stand near keeping their faces in the north direction but in this pose the bride-groom should put his right hand on the right shoulder of the bride. The bride-groom pronouncing the under-mentioned *Mantra* should order the bride to walk by raising her right foot :

मा सव्येन दक्षिणमतिक्राम ॥

In order to let her realize importance of consistency and constancy in the life bride-groom says to bride "Let not your left foot surpass your right foot."

Afterwards the bride-groom taking the bride with him should walk and also make her to walk, one step in the north east cornor of the direction with the folloing hymns :

ओमिषे एकपदी भव सा मामनु व्रता भव विष्णुस्त्वानयतु पुत्रान् विन्दावहै
बहूंस्ते सन्तु जरदष्टयः ॥ १ ॥

O bride ! take the first step for the sake of *Isha*, the cereal or food. Follow me in my vows. May God be your guide. May we both get children. Let your progeny be numerous and long-lived.

The second to seventh steps should be with the following hymns :

ओमूर्ज्जे द्विपदी भव-पूर्वंमंत्रवत्

The second step.

श्रों रायस्पोषाय त्रिपदी भव ,,

The third step.

श्रों मयोभवाय चतुष्पदीभव ,,

The fourth step.

श्रों प्रजाभ्यः पंचपदीभव ,,

The fifth step.

ओमृतुभ्यः षट्पदीभव ,,

The sixth step.

श्रों सखे सप्तपदीभव ,,

The seventh step

Take the second step for power...
follow me etc. etc,

Take the third step for the weal and prosperity...
follow me etc. etc,

Take the fourth step for happiness...
follow me etc. etc,

Take the fifth step for progeny...
follow me etc, etc,

Take the sixth step for seasonal equipment...
follow me etc. etc,

Take the seventh step for close union...
follow me etc. etc,

Completing the procidure of seven-step-ceremony the bride-groom and bride, their tie having got tied, should take their previous seats. Thcreafter the man who was sitting in the south of the *yajnaknnda* with the jug full of water, should carry that previously placed jug near bride-groom. The bride taking a little water from that jug should sprinkle it on the bride-groom and he should pronounce the following four hymns at that time :

श्रोमापो हिष्ठा मयो भुवस्ता न ऊर्ज्जे वधातन । महेरणाय चक्षसे । १ ।
योवः शिवतमो रसतस्य भाजयतेह नः । उशीतीरिव मातरः । २ ।
तस्मा श्ररङ्गमाम वो यस्य क्षयाय जिन्वथ । श्रापो जनयथा च नः ॥
ऋ० १० । ९ । १-३ ।

ओमापः शिवाः शिवतमाः शान्ताः शान्ततमास्तास्ते कृण्वन्तु भेषजम् । ४ ।
पार० १ । ८५-८६

The waters are the source of happiness, may they be helpful for us in attaing grain and may they help us to have a nice sight. 1.

Let the pleasant essence of waters be useful for us like the mothers who. for the well-being of their children, give their breast to them to suck. 2.

Let us acquire those cereals for the growth of which the waters help herbacious plants and let then be helpful in welfare of our progeny. 3.

O bride ! These waters are auspicious, and most advantageous. They are sources of peace and most pleasant. Let them make you free from all sort of diseases. 4.

After this the bride and bride-groom see the Sun with the following *mantra* if marriage is being conducted in the day time ;

ओं तच्चक्षुर्देवहितं पुरस्ताच्छुक्रमुच्चरत् । पश्येम शरदः शतं जीवेम शरदः शतꣳ शृणुयाम शरदः शतं प्रब्रवाम शरदः शतमदीनाः स्याम शरदः शतं भूयश्च शरदः शतात् ॥ १ ॥
यजुः ३६ । २४ पार० १ । ८ । ७

He (God) is All-vision and benevolent to men of wisdom. He existed pure and genuine prior to this world and would exist pure and geuine after it, meditating Him a hundred autumns may we see, a hundred autumns may wc live, a hundred autumns may we hear, a hundred autumns may we speak, a handred autumns may we enjoy full freedom and longer then hundred autumns we may enjoy all those blessings.

Afterward the bride-groom putting his right hand on right shouder of bride touch her heart by the same hand and should pronounce the folloing *mantra*:

ओं मम व्रते ते हृदयं दधामि मम चित्तमनुचित्तं ते अस्तु । मम वाचमेकमना जुषस्व प्रजापतिष्ट्वा नियुनक्तु मह्यम् ॥ पार० १ । ८ । ८

I put thy heart into my vowed discipline. Let my mind be concordant with thy mind. Follow my words with concentrated attention. Let God join thee with me.

Here in the similar manner the bride should also touch the heart of the bride-groom with her right hand and should pronounce the hymn मम व्रते ते हृदयं दधामि etc. etc.

Afterward the bride-groom should put his right hand on the forehead of the bride and pronouncing the following *mantra* should look at the people gathered there on this occasion.

सुमङ्गलीरियं वधूरिमां समेत पश्यत । - सौभाग्यमस्यै दत्वा याथास्तं विपरेतन ।

ऋ० १० । ८५ । ३, पारस्कर १ । ८ । ९

This bride is my lucky wife. Come ye and see. Bless her before you go to your house. Be not unfriendly to her.

At this juncture the people gathered on the occasion should bless with the following sentences : (ओं सौभाग्यमस्त : ओं शुभं भवतु ।।)

Let fortune attend you. Let everything be auspicious.

Thereafter the oblation with the *Swistakrita mantra* (यदस्य कर्मणो०)etc. etc. should be offered and further on the *ajahutis* with four *mantras*—भूरग्नये स्वाहा etc. etc. should be offered, And thus (पूर्वंविधि) the first main function of the marriage ceremony comes to an end.

After a short interval the second function of the marriag ceremony should be performed in the following manner :

1. *Agnyadhana*—with ओं भूर्भुवः० etc. etc.
2. Samidadhana—with अयन्त इध्म० etc.
3. Agharavajyahutis with ओमग्नये स्वाहा etc.
4. Vyahriti ahutis—with ओं भूरग्नये स्वाहा etc.

Afterwards main part of the *homa* should be performed by offering oblations with the following hymns :

अ लेखा सन्धिषु पक्ष्मस्वावर्त्तेषु च यानि ते । तानि ते पूर्णाहुत्या सर्वाणि शमयाम्यहं स्वाहा । इदं कन्यायै—इदं न मम ॥१॥

ओं केशेषु यच्च पापकमीक्षिते रुदिते च यत् । तानि ॥२॥

ओं शीलेषु यच्च पापकं भाषिते हसिते च यत् । तानि० ॥३॥

ओमारोकेषु दन्तेषु हस्तयोः पादयोश्च यत् । तानि० ॥४॥

ओमूर्वोरुपस्थे जङ्घयोः सन्धानेषु च यानि ते । तानि ॥५॥

ओं यानि कानि च घोराणि सर्वाङ्गेषु तवाभवन् । पूर्णाहुति-भिराज्यस्य सर्वाणि तान्यशीशमं स्वाहा ॥ इदं कन्यायै— इदं न मम ॥६॥

मंत्रब्राह्मण १ । ३ । १-६, गो० २ । ३ ।५

Whatever defects are seen in the streaks of your forehead and the whatever in the hair of eye-lids and the wholes, navel etc. I allay with this *purnahuti*, the accomplished oblation. Whatever is uttered herein is true. The oblation offered is meant for *kanya* and it is not for me. 1.

Whatever defect has made its place in hair, in sight, and walking etc. I allay with this *purnahut*i. Rest is like previous one. 2.

Whatever defcdt has got its root in culture. habit, in speech and laugh etc. I allay with this *purnahuti*. Rest is like previous one. 3.

Whatever defect has made its place in tooth-wholes, in teeth, in hand and in legs etc. I allay with this *Purnahuti*. Rest is like previous one. 4

Whatever defect has taken its place in thighs, organs, joints of the legs and other joining parts, I allay with this *purnahuti*. Rest is like previous one. 5.

O bride ! Whatever are the greatest defect in your other parts of the body I allay with these *Purnahutis* of the molten ghee. Whatever is uttered herein is true. The oblation offered is meant for *Kanya* and it is not for me.

Afterwards four oblations should be offered with the mantras भूरग्नये स्वाहा ete. etc.

Thereafter the bride and the bride-groom should go out of the *sabhamandapa* in the north direction. And the bride-groom should make the bride to see pole (ध्रुव) if the marriage is being conducted in the night time. The procedure of this is as follows :

The bride-groom pointing out at the Pole-star says ध्रुवं पश्य ।
O bride ! look at the Po le-star.

The bride replies—पश्यामि

Yes, I see,
She further declares :

ओं ध्रुवमसि ध्रुवाहं पतिकुले भूयासम् । अमुष्य असौ ।
गोभिल० २।३।८

The Pole-star is *dhruva*, constant. May I be *dhruva*, constant in my husband's family.

The bride-groom says—
अरुन्धतीं पश्य । गोभिल० २।३।६

O bride ! look at the *Arundhati*, the star bearing this name.

The bride replies : पश्यामि

Yes, I see.

She further declares—

ओमरुन्धत्यसि रुद्धाहमस्मि [अमुष्य असौ] गो २ । ३ । १०

This *Arunhati* is not an obstacle. I am under control but I won't obstruct my husband in his good and righteous ventures.

N.B. Here in the place of असौ, the name of bride should be pronounced and in the place of अमुष्य the name of husband should be pronounced but it should be in possessive case.

Thereafter the bride-groom looking at the bride should place his right hand on her forehead and should pronounce the following two hymns :

ओं ध्रुवा द्यौर्ध्रुवा पृथिवी ध्रुवं विश्वमिदं जगत् । ध्रुवासः पर्वता इमे ध्रुवा स्त्री पतिकुले इयम् ॥

मंत्रब्राह्मण १।३।६। गो० २।३।११ ॥

ओं ध्रुवमसि ध्रुवन्त्वा पश्यामि ध्रुवैधि पोष्ये मयि । मह्यं त्वादाद्बृहस्पति मया पत्या प्रजावती संजीव शरदः शतम् ॥

पारस्कर० १ । ८

Constant is the heavenly region, constant is this earth, contant is this universe, constant are these mountains and constant is this woman in the husband's house.

O bride !

Constant are you and may I always see you constant. Be you constant near me who is your supporter. God has given you to me and having good progeny you may live hundred autumns with me as your husband.

This second *mantra* should be interpreted on bride's part also.

Afterwards the bride and bride-groom should take their seats in the west of the *yajnakunda* keeping their faces in the east. They should perform yajna- procedure :

1. *Achamana*, Sipping of water.
2. Agnyadhana.
3. Samidadhana.
4. Agharavajyahutis.
5. Vyahriti Ahutis.

Afterwards the cooked rice in a small quantity seould be kept in a press and ghee should be sprinkled on it. Ghee and rice should be mixed. The bride and bride-groom should take very little part of that rice in their right hands and offer oblation with the following *mantras* :

ओमग्नये स्वाहा ॥ इदमग्नये—इदं न मम ।

ओं प्रजापतये स्वाहा ॥ इदं प्रजापतये—इदं न मम ।

ओं विश्वेभ्यो देवेभ्यः स्वाहा ॥ इदं विश्वेभ्यो देवेभ्य-इदं न मम ।

ओमनुमतये स्वाहा ॥ इदमनुमतये···इदं न मम ॥

गो० २ । ३ । ११७-१२१

We offer this oblation for *Agni*. Whatever is uttered herein is correct. The oblation offered is meant for Agni and it is not for me.

We offer this oblation for *Prajapati.* Whatever uttered herein is correct. The oblation offered is meant for *Prajapati* and it is not for me.

We offer this oblation for *vishvedevas.* Whatever is uttered herein is correct. The oblation offered is meant for *vishvedevas* and it is not for me.

We offer this oblation for *Anumati.* Whatever is nttered herein is correct. The oblation offered is meant for *Anumati* and it is not for me.

1. Svistakrit,
2. Vyahriti Ahutis,
3. Eight ajyahutis,

Thereafter the remaining cooked rice should be put in a press and ghee should be mixed in it. The bride-groom keeping his right hand on it, should pronounce the following *mantras* in mind and should eat a little of that cooked rice :

ओमन्नप्राशेन मणिना प्राणसूत्रेण पृश्निना । बध्नामि सत्यग्रन्थिना मनश्च हृदयं च ते ॥ १ ॥

ओं यदेतद्धृदयं तव तदस्तु हृदयं मम । यदिदꣳ हृदय मम तदस्तु हृदयं तव ॥ २ ॥

ओमन्नं प्राणस्य षड्विंꣳ शस्तेन बध्नामि त्वा असौ ॥ ३ ॥

मंत्र ब्राह्मण १।३।८-१०, गोभि० २।३।१७-२१

In the place of असौ in the last *mantra* the name of the bride should be used in vocative case.

O bride or bride-groom ! I tie your heart and mind with the thread of vital air of which the grain is food, truth is tie and which like a precious stone, operates the bodily limbs. [1]

O bride or bride-groom ! that which is your heart be my heart and that which is my heart be your heart.[2]

O bride ! tie you with the cereal which is the 26th of the elements supporting the vital air.

Remaining part of the cooked rice of which the small part was eaten by him, should be given to bride by the bride-groom. When bride has eaten it the bride and bride-groom should take their seats in the *yajnamdapa* keeping their faces in the east. They should perform the *maha vamadevya-ganam* of *samaveda.*

Afterwards performing, eulogium, prayer and contemplation of God, *Svastivachna, Shantikarana* as he has been given in the *Samanyaprakarana* the bride and bride-groom should take meal free from saltish and aciditic eatables and enriched with sweet, milk and ghee.

Thereafter, the priests, righteous persons, and the persons who are the participants of the ceremony should be entertained with nice food and then the men be given leave by men and ladies by ladies with due respect and cordiality.

Thereafter, on passing of four hours (१० घटिका) of night the bride-groom and bride arranging their bedding on the ground separately should sleep observing vows and discipline of strict celibacy and this procedure be followed for three nights continually. They should eat such a kind of meal that even in dream there could not be any discharge of semen badly. Then in the night of fourth day they should systematically do the ceremony of impregnation. If there is any difficulty on the fourth day they should perform it on another day according to their choice and desire but they should abide firmly in the vows and practice of *Brahmacharya* for more days in doing so. They can perform the ceremony of impregnation with systematic procedure on the night as has been mentioned previously in the ceremony of *Garbhadhana*.

Thereafter, on the second or third day the people of the bride-groom party take the bride-groom to their home with respect seating them in a chariot.

If the bride's eyes are moistened witd tears when leaving the house of her parents, the following *Mantraj* shonld be pronounced:—

जीवं रुदन्तिविमयन्ते अध्वरे दीर्घामनु प्रसितिं दीधियुर्नरः ।
वामं पितृभ्यो य इदं समेरिरे मयः पतिभ्यो जनयः परिष्वजे ॥
(ऋ० मं० १० । सू० ४० मं० १०)

O learned persons ! women embrace to attain pleasure only those men who take all trouble to reform the life of their wives, inspire into them the spirit of participating in the *yajna*, obey the great sacred laws of the house-hold life and strengther its tle and for the continuity of the race of father and mother accet this *Ashrama* of *Grihastha*.

The bride-groom sitting in the chariot keep the bride sitting by his right side and should pronounce the following *Mantras* and make the chariot move:—

पूषा त्वेता मयतु हस्तगृह्याश्विना त्वा प्र वहतां रथेन ।
गृहान्गच्छ गृहपत्नी यथासो वशिनी त्वं विदथमा वदासि ॥ १ ॥

सुकिंशुकं शल्मलिं विश्वरूपं हिरण्यवर्णं सुवृतं सुचक्रम ।
आ रोह सूर्ये अमृतस्य लोकं स्योनं पत्ये वहतुं कृणुष्व ॥ २ ॥
(ऋ० मं० १० सू० ८५ मं० २६, २०)

O girlie ! your husband who has grasped the hand and has all means to support you, whould bring you home. Let these two horses of the chariot carry you comfortably and you reach the home of your husband safely. Like a mistress of the house you have your husband under your influence and direct the establishment of your husband.

O Sunlike refulgent girlie! you mount on this chariot which is made of wood of *Butra Fondosa* and decorate with the wood of *Bombax Heptaphylium*, which has various colours, which is decorated with decorating things or ornaments and which has qiuck moving wheels. You make your going to your husband's house happy and the place of pleasure and comfort.

If in carryng the bride to her husband's house the need arises out to sit in a boat, the following *Mantra* be pronounced prior to sitting therein:—

अश्मन्वती रीयते सं रभध्वमुत्तिष्ठत प्र तरता सखायः ।

O worldly people ! if you have to cross the river which is full of stones and has risky currents, you invite all your courage, keep your feet firm and cross it. In getting out of the boat the following *Mantra* be pronounced:—

अत्रा जहाम ये असन्नशेवाः शिवान्वयमुत्तरेमाभि वाजान् ॥

[ऋ० म० १० । सू० ५३ । मं० ८]

We leave all the inauspicious things in the boat and get out from it to obtain the auspicious wealth like grain etc.

If in the way there happen to come the cross of paths, river, fear of wild beasts, thief etc, dreadful places, the land full of breaches and digs, grove of tall trees and cremation ground the bride-groom pronounce the following *Mantras*:—

मा विदन् परिपन्थिनो य आसीदन्ति दम्पती ।
सुगेभिर्दुर्गमतीतामपद्रावत्वंरातयः ॥

[ऋ० मं १० । सू० ८५ । मं० ३२[

Whosoever of the wickeds may come in the way of this couple, might not come. The enemies who lurk the men travelling on the easy paths surmounting the unpassable one, may, by God's grace, flee away.

If in the way* any part of the chariot occupied by this

couple breaks out or any unexpected calamity breaks through, the couple may stay at any good place. They should offer the four oblations of ghee with the *Vyahriti Mantras* mentioned in the *Samanya-prakarana*. Afterwards they should sing the song of *Mahavamdevya* as it has been described in the *Samanya-prakarna*.

When the chariot carrying the bride and bride-groom reaches at the front of the house of the bride-groom a cultured, *Brahmni* or family lady who has child and is enriched with her husband-ship should come before the chariot and holding the hand of bride make her get down the chariot with the bride-groom and take her to *Sabhamandap* with him. The bride-groom reaching at the door of the *sabhamandapa* should have a glance on the people who have come for this purpose and pronounce the following Mantra:—

सुमङ्गलीरियं वधूरिमां समेत पश्यत ।
सौभाग्यमस्यै दत्त्वायाथास्तं वि परेतन ॥

[ऋ० मं० १० । सू० ८५ । मं० ३३]

This has been translated previously in the *Vivah Sanskara* in its context. The other comers bless with the following sentences:—

ओं सौभाग्यमस्तु । ओं शुभं भवतु ॥

Afterwards the bride-groom take the bride into the *Sabha-mandapa* having pronounced the following *Mantra*:—

इह प्रियं प्रजा ते समृध्यतामस्मिन्गृहे गार्हपत्याय जागृहि ।
एना पत्या तन्वं १ स सृजस्वाधा जिव्री विदथमा वदाथः ॥

(ऋ० मं० १० । सू०८५ । मं० २७)

May your happiness flourish here in this home. O bride! with progeny, you always be alert in this house or in this *Ashrama*, you unite your body with this husband of yours. O bride and bride-groom you praise each other till attaining old age.

Afterwards the bride and bride-groom should come near

the *Kunda* which has been previously prepared. At this time the bride-groom pronouncing the following *Mantra* should seat the bride on the wood-seat or the seat made of grass in the west of the *Kunda* on his right keeping her face eastward:—

ओम् इह गाव: प्रजायध्वमिहाश्वा इह पूरषाः ।
इहो सहस्रदक्षिणोऽपि पूषा निषीदतु ॥
अथर्व० कां० २० । १२७ । मं० १२

May the cows grow in numbers in this house, may here grow innumerable horses and also increase the number of men. May I the supporter of this house remain here well maintained giving thousands to others in alms.

Afterwards the both of them should do three *Achamanas*, water-sippings with the *Mantras* ओम् अमृतोपस्तरणमसि० etc. One *Achamana* be done with one *Mantra* only.

Afterwards according to the procedure prescribed in the *samanyaprakarana* the fuel in the *Kunda* be arranged and *Agnyadhana* be performed. When the fire is ablaze in the *Kunda* ghee should be warmed and pured on it. Then the procedure of *samidadhana* be performed. Afterwards *Agharavajyabhagahuti* four in number, *Vyahuti Ahuti* four and eight *Ajyahutis* totalling 16 in all, should be offered. These oblations be offered by bride and bride-groom. Afterwards they should perform the chief *homa* by the following *Mantras* and only one oblation by one *mantra* totalling eight in all be offered.

ओम् इह धृतिः स्वाहा ॥ इदमिह धृत्यै-इदन्न मम ॥ १ ॥
ओम् इह स्वधृतिः स्वाहा ॥ इदमिह स्वधृत्यै-इदन्न मम ॥ २ ॥
ओम् इह रन्तिः स्वाहा ॥ इदमिह रन्त्यै-इदन्न मम ॥ ३ ॥
ओम् इह रमस्व स्वाहा ॥ इदमिह रमायै-इदन्न मम ॥ ४ ॥
ओं मयि धृतिः स्वाहा ॥ इदं मयि धृत्यै-इदन्न मम ॥ ५ ॥
ओं मयि स्वधृतिः स्वाहा ॥ इदं मयि स्वधृत्यै-इदन्न मम ॥ ६ ॥
ओं मयि रमः स्वाहा ॥ इदं मयि रमाय-इदन्न मम ॥ ७ ॥
ओं मयि रमस्व स्वाहा ॥ इदं मयि रमाय-इदन्न मम ॥ ८ ॥
(तु० मं० ब्रा० १ । ३ । १४)

May tolerance and constancy reign here in this house. Whatever has been uttered herein is true. The oblation offered is meant for *Ihadhriti* and not for me.1.

May unity in family reign here in this house......2.
May enjoyment reign here in this house......3.
May you enjoy pleasure here O bride ! in this house. 4.
May there reign tolerance and firmness in me. 5.
May the sense of unity prevail in me......6.
May there reign pleasure and enjoyment in me......7.
May you enjoy pleasure in me, O bride !......8.

Afterwards the four oblations, one by each *mantra*; should be offered with the following *Mantras*:—

ओम् आ नः प्रजां जनयतु प्रजापतिराजरसाय समनक्त्वर्यमा । अदुर्मङ्गलीः पतिलोकमा विश शं नो भव द्विपदे शं चतुष्पदे स्वाहा ।। इदं सूर्याय सावित्र्यै-इदन्न मम ।। १ ।।

ओम् अघोरचक्षुरपतिघ्न्येधि शिवा पशुभ्यः सुमनाः सुवर्चाः : वीरसूर्देवृकामा स्योना शन्नो भव द्विपदे शं चचुष्पदे स्वाहा ।। इदं सूर्यायै सावित्र्यै-इदन्न मम ।। २ ।।

ओम् इमां त्वमिन्द्र मीढ्वः सुपुत्रां सुभगां कृणु । दशास्यां पुत्राना धेहि पतिमेकादशं कृधि स्वाहा ।। इदं सूर्यायै सावित्र्यै-इदन्न मम ।। ३ ।।

ओं सम्राज्ञी श्वसुरे भव सम्राज्ञी श्वश्र्वां भव । ननान्दरि सम्राज्ञी भव सम्राज्ञी अधिदेवृषुस्वाहा* ।। इदं सूर्यायै सावित्र्यै-इदन्न मम ।। ४ ।।

(ऋ० मं० १० । सू० मं० ४३-४६)

O bride ! May God who is just and merciful, till our old age make our children cultured, so that we may attain great happiness. All the ladies of the house keep delighted to all. You attain pleasure and enjoyment in the family of mine, your husband. May you be source of happiness to our bipeds and our quadrupeds. Whatevar has been uttered herein is true. The oblation offered is meant for *Surya Savitri* and it is not for me. 1.

This *Mantra* has been translated in the *Vivaha Sanskara* in its context. 2.

O strong and mighty bride-groom ! you are enriched with virile power and make this bride happy and bearing offshoots. You have only ten childre in your wife, not more. O bride ! you also do not desire more children than ten and be content with them counting the husband as eleventh. If you desire more progeny than this you would produce children of short life and deprived of genius and you whould also become short-lived and diseased. Therefore you do not procreate more progeny.

The meaning of the sentence पतिमेकादशं कृधि will be different in the context of *Niyoga*. As God has given commandment for a husband to produce ten children in his married wife in the same manner He has given the commandment for a married lady to have ten children with the married husband or the husband of *Niyoga* after becoming widow. One woman should marry only one man at a time and one man only one women at a time and this is the sanction (*of shastra*). As a women, after being widow can have progeny through the tradition of *Niyoga* so a man can also have children through *Niyoga*. 3.

O bride ! you, in the house of my father who is your father in-law deal impartially and shine like an empress. You enjoy also this status having affection in my mother who is your mother-in-law Having affection in my sister who is your sister-in-law you shine like empress. You also have affection in my brother who is your brother-in-law and shine like an empress. You have affection in all without any opposition and that is what I mean to say.

Afterwards one oblation of *svistakrit*, four oblations of *Vyahriti Ahuti*, and one oblation of *Prajapatyahuti* should be offered, as has been prescribed in the *Samanya prakarana*.

The bride-groom add bride should eat curd pronouncing the following *Mantra*:—

समञ्जतु विश्वे देवाः समापो हृदयानि नौ ।

सं मातरिश्वा सं धाता समु देष्ट्री दधातु नौ ।।

(ऋ० मं० १० सू० ८५ । मं० ४७)

The translation of this *mantra* has been already given in the *Vivaha Sanskara* in its context.

Afterwards the bride-groom and bride should offer their obeisance to father and mother of the bride-groom, and old people pronouncing the following sentence:—

अहं भो अभिवादयामि ।।

(गोभि० २ । ४ । ११)

Thereafter they decorated and dressed, sit on the nice seat and singing *Vamdevyagana,* at once perform the contemplation God as it has been given in the *Samanyaprakarna.* At that time the ladies and gents who have come to grace the occasion should meditate God with concentrated mind and the bride and bride-groom tell to father, mother and *Acharya.*

ओं स्वस्ति भवन्तो ब्रुवन्तु ।।

(आश्वला० गृ० अ० १ । कं० ८ । स० १५ ।। वृत्ति)

"Kindly you all recite the *svastivaahanam-*"

Afterwards father, *Acharya* and *Purohita*, if they are learned and in their absence only bride and bride-groom both, if they are learned or the knower of *Veda* should recite with interest. *Svastivachana matras* have been given in the *Samanyahrakarana*. After the recitation being finished the men and women who have come to participate in the function should pronounce this sentance:—

ओं स्वस्ति, ओं स्वस्ति, ओं स्वस्ति ।।

Thereafter the men holding this function, father, uncle,

---

*More excellent than this is नमस्ते which has been written in the Vedas and is useful daily solutation between father and son, disciple and preceptor. In the morning and evening or whenever in a function there is a meeting this नमस्ते should be applied for the purpose of exchanging salutation.

brother etc. of the bride-groom should give leave to the gents with due respect and mother, aunt, etc. to ladies.

Afterwards if due to some special reason the impregnation ceremony could not be held in the house of father-in law the bride and bride-groom leaving the saltish food and carnal desires and observing the disciplines and vows of celibacy should hold impregnation ceremony on the fourth day from the date of marriage according to the procedure prescribed in *Garbhadhana* ceremony. If on that day the time for impreganation is not suitable they should do it on any other day. If the bride-groom has come frome other place for the purpose of marriage the impregnation ceremony be performed at the place where he stays.

Then husband, mother-in-law, father-in-law, siser-in-law, brother-in-law, wife of brother-in-law, wife of elder brother-in-law and other members of the family should respect the bride. They should always deal mutually with affection and exchange of sweet words between them. They should keep the bride content with dress and ornaments and the bride also should keep them delighted and pleased with her dealings. The bride-groom should treat the bride in confor mity to the vows and piousness of *Patnivarta* and wife should also treat her husband according to the vows of *Pativrata.* The bride-groom should always be cerefully aware in the service and pleasure of his wife and wife always should be obedient to her husband with her fair conduct and dealings.

Now we would prescribe the procedure of house-hold sacrament

The house-hold sacrament is that in which the practice of philanthropy according to one's circumstances is adopted to attain the worldy and ultra-mundane happiness after marrying and in which the prayer and meditation of God at fixed time, house-hold duties, to employ ones mind, body, wealth in the righteousness and procreate progeny according to the dictates of *dhrama* are duely performed.

The authorities on this subject:—

सोमो वधूयुरभवदश्विनास्तामुभा वरा ।
सूर्यां यत्पत्ये शंसन्तीं मनसा सविता ददात् ॥ १ ॥
इहैव स्तं मा वि यौष्टं विश्वमायुर्व्यश्नुतम् ।
क्रीडन्तौ पुत्रैर्नप्तृभिर्मोदमानौ स्वस्तकौ ॥ २ ॥

(अ० कां० १४ । सू० १ । मं० ६, २२)

The bride-groom, tender in constitution, desiring meritorious bride and the bride desiring the bride-groom should acquire knowledge with the observancce of celibacy and both of them be compatible in good quality, action and nature. God, the creator of the universe provides a husband with a wife who is brilliant like the rays of sun and is beautiful and meritorious and praises her husband. He provides the bride with a husband who is similarly and perfectly matchful to her. That is, the match of bride-groom and bride is to be attained with a great good luck. 1

O women and men! I, the Almighty God issue this command to you that you both abide by the vows you have taken previously in your marriage. You never deviate from these vows. You attain a long life, not short of hundred years obeying the rules of disciplined co-habitation without spoiling the semen in vain and according to the law of *dhrama* play your role accompanied by sons, grand-sons and owning own good house, lead the life of house-hold with delight and happiness. 2

सुमङ्गली प्रतरणी गृहाणो सुशेवा पत्ये श्वशुराय शम्भूः ।
स्योना श्वश्र्वै प्र गृहान् विशेमान् ॥ ३ ॥
स्योनास्यै सर्वस्यै विशे स्योना पुष्टायैषां भव ॥ ४ ॥
या दुर्हार्दो युवतयो याश्चेह जरतीरपि ।
वर्चो न्वस्यै सं दत्ताथास्तं विपरेतन ॥ ५ ॥
आ रोह तल्पं सुमनस्यमानेह प्रजां जनय पत्ये अस्मै ।
इन्द्राणीव सुबुधा बुध्यमाना ज्योतिरग्रा उषसः प्रति जागरासि ॥६॥

(अथर्व० कां० १४ । सू० २ । मं० २६, २७, २९, ३१)

O bride ! you performing righteous and auspicious deeds, keeping away from evils and sorrows, possessing cleverness and sincerity in domestic affairs and enjoying happiness become pleasure-giving to your husband, father-in-law and mother-in-law and enter into these houses enjoying delight. 3

O bride ! you become the source of pleasure to your husband, to your father-in-laws etc. and people of your house. You make happy all this subject and be engaged in their protection, 4

The young women of malignant conscience and also the old ladies of this place grant vigour to this bride and thereafter go to their houses not to return again. 5

O bride ! you having a delightful sound sleep on the bed, procreate children for this husband and you educated well, rise always very early like the splendour of the sun which is the first light of dawn and always be alert like this dawn-light in your work and duties. 6

देवा अग्रे न्य पद्यन्त पत्नीः समस्पृशन्त तन्व स्तनूभिः ।
सूर्येव नारि विश्वरूपा महित्वा प्रजावती पत्या सं भवेह ॥ ७ ॥
सं पितरावृत्विये सृजेथां माता पिता च रेतसो भवाथः ।
मर्यइव योषामधि रोहयैनां प्रजां कृण्वाथामिह पुष्यतं रयिम् ॥ ८ ॥
तां पूषञ्छिवतमामेरयस्व यस्यां बीजं मनुष्या३ वपन्ति ।
या न ऊरू उशती विश्रयाति यस्यामुशन्तः प्रहरेम शेपः ॥ ९

[अथर्व० कां १४ । सू० २ । मं० ३२, ३७, ३८,[

O bride ! as learned men, at first, in this house-hold life won their wives and had contact of their bodies with the bodies of their wives in the same manner you beautiful, securing all rs-pect, meeting your husband become the mother of children like the splendour of the sun. 7

O women and men ! you are the procreator of children so you produce good progeny observing the rules of timely impre-gnation. You are to be mothers and fathers so you follow the procedure of timely impregnation in mixing your semens thro-ugh co-habitation, O man ! you as the husband of this woman like the other husbands who have wives promote her position with progeny and you both procreate children in this house-hold life, bringe them and acquire wealth with perservance,8

O man ! you are the strengthener. Yon inspire into this lady well-wisher of you and your family the spirit of procreating children. This woman is such an entity in whom the men sow semen-seed, who desiring progeny spread her thigns fowrards her husband and in whom the husband like you and us thrust organ with the desire of children. 9

स्योनाद्योनेरधि बुध्यमानौ हसामुदौ महसा मोदमानौ ।
सुगू सुपुत्रौ सुगृहौ तराथो जीवावुषसो विभातीः ॥ १० ॥
इहेमाविन्द्र सं नुद चक्रावाकेव दम्पती ।
प्रजयैनौ स्वस्तकौ विश्वमायुर्व्यश्नुताम् ॥ ११ ॥
जनयन्ति नावग्रवः पुत्रियन्ति सुदानवः ।
अरिष्टासू सचेवहि बृहते वाजसातये ॥ १२ ॥

अथर्व० कां० १४ । सू० २ । मं० ४३, ६४, ७२

O women and man ! as the sun comes into rise from splen-did dawn in the same manner you both coming the house full of prosperity and happiness, chearing with smile and delight, pleased with love and affection, treading on the path of pious-ness, having good progeny, possessing nice houses and leading a good life succeed in discharging the duties of house-hold life. 10

O learned man or the King ! you make such rules and regu-lations in the society and state that woman and man should enter into married life according to the dictates of the scripture as has been mentioned in the *Vedarambha Sanskara.* No one could violate the rules laid down for marriage affairs. You instruct and educate them to observe the discipline of *Brahmacharya,* to acquire knowledge to enter into married life and live the house-hold life with love as the pair of *Anus Casarca.* Both of them attain the full longevity of life with children enjoying all sort of happiness. 11

O people ! As the men and women engaged in imparting education and dessiminating knowledge procreate children and desire the birth of son so we both have and we preserving our vitality and strength be always ready for attaining scientific knowledge, grain etc. for the purpose of philanthropy and giving alms. So that our children become good and virtuous. 12

प्र बुध्यस्व सुबुधा बुध्यमाना दीर्घायुत्वाय शतशारदाय ।
गृहान् गच्छ गृहपत्नी यथासो दीर्घं त आयुः सविता कृणोतु ॥ १३ ॥
अथर्व० कां १४ । सू० २ । मं० ७५

सहृदयं सांमनस्यमविद्वेषं कृणोमि वः ।
अन्यो अन्यमभि हर्यंत वत्सं जातमिवाघ्न्या ॥ १४ ॥
अथर्व० कां० ३ । सू० ३० मं० १

O wife ! You having the knowledge of domestic affairs and briliant in intellegence come to my houses for living till hundred autumns. As my wife, the mistress of the house you attain long life and know properly the method of it. May God, the creator of all and the giver of all fortunes fulfil your desires to enable you and me to live in advancement and hippiness. 13

O ye mankind ! I ordain for you to have concordance in your heart, unanimity in your minds and freedom from hatred in your dealings. Everyone of ought to love one another in every way just as the inviolable cow loveth the calf which she hath born. 14

अनुव्रतः पितुः पुत्रो मात्रा भवतु संमना ।
जाया पत्ये मधुमतीं वाचं वदतु शान्तिवाम् ॥ १५ ॥

मा भ्राता भ्रातरं द्विक्षन्मा स्वसारमुत स्वसा ।

सम्यञ्चः सव्रता भूत्वा वाचं वदत भद्रया ॥ १६ ॥

अथर्व० कां० ३ । सू० ३० । मं० २, ३ ॥

येन देवा न वियन्ति नो च विद्विषते मिथः ।

तत्कृण्मो ब्रह्म वो गृहे संज्ञानं पुरुषेभ्यः ॥ १७ ॥

अथर्व० कां० ३ । सू० ३० । मं० ४ ॥

ज्यायस्वन्तश्चित्तिनो मा वि यौष्ट संराधयन्तः सधुराश्चरन्त । अन्यो अन्यस्मै

वल्गु वदन्त एत सध्रीचीनान्वः संमनसस्कृणोमि ॥ १८ ॥

अथर्व० कां० ३ सू० ३० । मं० ५ ॥

समानी प्रपा सह वोऽन्नभागः समाने योक्त्रे सह वो युनज्मि ।

सम्यञ्चोऽग्नि सपर्यतारा नाभिमिवाभितः ॥ १६ ॥

सध्रीचीनान्वः संमनसस्कृणोम्येक श्नुष्टीन्त्संवननेन सर्वान् ।

देवा इवामृतं रक्षमाणाः सायंप्रातः सौमनसो वो अस्तु ॥ २० ॥

अथर्व० कां० ३ । सू० ३० । मं० ६, ७ ॥

Let the son be obedient to his father and in accordance with the mind of his mother. Let the wife speak to her husband calm gentle and sweet words : s honey. 15

Neither a brother should hate his brother nor a sister should be unkind to her sister, you ought to speak to others most gently being united in your mind and keeping the same ideal before you. 6

That path of the *vedas* I ordain in your home against which the enlightened persons never go nor do they bear hatred towards one another, so that it may serve as leading principle for all men. 17

O ye mankind ! who are respectful to the elders possesssing noble hearts, friendly in your understandings of acquiring wealth and walking in the same path bearing in the common yoke together, be never disunited with one another come, I make you one-intenioned and one-minded let each one of you speak sweetly to the other. 18.

Let your place of drinking water be common and let the partaking of your food be together as I yoke you to a common yoke, worship *Agni* (the Self-refulgent God) all of you together attaching yourself to Him) just as the spokes are attached to the nave of the chariot all round. 19.

(O ye mankind !) I (God) enjoin on all of you to be mutually helping one another, to be united in your mind and to have common ideal of life for benefiting one anothr. Like the enlightened persons whoever take care of the immortal principle (in their life) may the friendly feelings amongst you increase morning and evening. 20.

श्रमेण तपसा सृष्टा ब्रह्मणा वित्त ऋते श्रिता: ॥ २१ ॥

सत्येनावृता: श्रिया प्रावृता: यशसा परीवृता ॥ २२ ॥

स्वधया परिहिता: श्रद्धया पर्यूढा दीक्षया गुप्ता यज्ञे प्रतिष्ठिता लोको निधनम ॥ २३ ॥ अथर्व० कां० १२ । सू ५ । मं० १-३ ॥

O women and men ! (God) ordian you that you should be united with labour, austerity and the knowledge of the *Veda* and Divinity. You always be engaged in earning wealth and remain active in impartial conduct, the justice.21.

You be surrounded with righteous deeds on all sides, equipped with the wealth which is the beauty of the life and you be always enveloped with fame. 22.

You possessing grain etc. engage yourself in benefit of others, always be ready in accepting truth, the root of the faith. Preserve yourself with observance and practice of *Brahmacharya* and the pledge of speaking truth. You gain fame in the service of learned men, attainment of knowledge of the various arts and in giving good qualities to others. By the dint of these actions and practices you attain the worldly pleasure and live in happiness till death. 23

ओजश्च तेजश्च सहश्च बलञ्च वाक् चेन्द्रियं च श्रीश्च धर्मश्च ॥ २४ ॥

अथर्व० कां० १२ । सू० ५ । मं० ७ ॥

O man ! You attain energy and vigour and its means the power and might and their means the tolerance in the cases of praise, abusement, lose, profit, sorrow etc. with its means, strenght with its means, truth-speaking, sweet speech and dealings according to it, calm and righteous conscience, purety of soul and control over limbs, the wealth and the right effort to earn it, and impartial just act i. e. the *dharma* as mentioned in the *Veda*, its means and translate them into your action. 24

ब्रह्म च क्षत्रं च राष्ट्रं च विशश्च त्विषिश्च यशश्च वर्चश्च द्रविणं च ॥ २५ ॥

आयुश्च रूपं च नाम च कीर्तिश्च प्राणश्चापानश्च चक्षुश्च श्रोत्रं च ॥ २६ ॥

पयश्च रसश्चान्नं चान्नाद्यं च ऋतं च सत्यं चेष्टं च पूर्तं च प्रजा च पशवश्च ॥ २७ ॥

अथर्व० कां० १२ । सू० ५ मं० ८-१०

O house-holders ! You always do the deed guided by the sense of—the humanity accomplished with perfect knowledge and virtues and *Brahmanatva* full of tranquilty, control over organs, the *Kshatriyatva* celebrated with knowledge, virtues and bravity, the state and its just administration, good subject and its progress, the vigour accompanied by good learnings, health and strength of body and soul and their advancement, fame and the means of its acquisition, the ponderance of learnt sciences and their continuous study and the acquisition of wealth, its protection and its utilization in the cause of philanthropy. 25

O women and men ! you prolong your life and do righteous act throughout the life, renouncing passionate attachments, ill-deiting, diseases and unrighteous dealings make your nature good and also put on dresses and ornaments. You bear good name as has been written in the *Namakarana Sanskara*, also obey the rules prescribed for that. Always earn fame through practice of good actions and always keep away from re-crimations and abusement. For long time you live and take deit etc. suitable to longivity of life. Collect means to get freedom from pains and sufferings and pave ways for this sake. Always utilize the ways and means of perception, conjecture, similarity and authority in deciding the problems.[26]

O house-holders ! you always take and use to take nice clean water, milk with carefulness of its purity etc., you take ghee, milk, honey etc. and use them with almost care. Eat cooked and prepared cereals with nice palatable pulse, vegetable, curry. You speak truth and try everyone to speak truth, you believe in truth and try that everyone believe in truth, perform *yajnas* and encourage everyone to perform *yajna*, collect the articles for *yajna* and make tanks, gardens for recreation etc. and encourage others to materialize such works. Procreate children, bring up them and make them advanced and inspire spirit in others to do the same. Always domesticate the animals like cows etc. and promote the cause of their protection and increasement and encourage others also for this purpose.[27]

कुर्वन्नेवेह कर्माणि जिजीविषेच्छतं समाः ।
एवं त्वयि नान्यथेतोऽस्ति न कर्म लिप्यते नरे ॥ १ ॥

यजु० अ० ४० । मं० २ ॥

I (God) enjoin on the men that everyone strong in body desire to live hundred autumns performing unattached noble deeds. He should not become lazy and drowsy. In doing such good deeds the deeds of sin do not mix with the man and you never become attached in sinful acts. The noble and unattached actions do not bear any pain in their fluctification. You men and women both becoming active for always do excellent deeds and promote cause of your and other's progress.[1]

Again the women and men should always desire and act in conformity to the spirit of following these *Mantras* :—

भूर्भुवः स्वः सुप्रजाः प्रजाभिः स्याꣳसुवीरो वीरैः सुपोषः पोषैः :
नर्यं प्रजां मे पाहि शꣳस्य पशून् मे पाह्यथर्यं पितुं मे पाहि ॥ २ ॥
गृहा मा बिभीत मा वेपध्वमूर्जं बिभ्रत एमसि ।
ऊर्जं बिभ्रद्वः सुमनाः सुमेधा गृहानैमि मनसा मोदमानः ॥ ३ ॥

यजु० अ० ३ । मं० ३७, ४१ ॥

O Woman or Men ! I, with relation of your and mine own enjoying bodily, sonorous and mental happiness, i.e. three kinds of happiness, become the parent of children with the procreation of excellent progeny. May I become attached with good brave children or men accompanied by our children, brothers, relatives and servants. May I have all the vigour accompanied by the means of vigour. O brave and gentle person amongst men ! protect my children. O praiseworthy one ! please protect my animals. O merciful one ! you preserve and save grin etc. for me. O lady ! you always preserve my children, my quadrupeds and my grain etc.[2]

O house-holders ! you never hesitate in entering the house-hold life according to the scriptural procedure prescribed for the same and never tremble in fear in this matter. You become celebrated with good qualities like education etc. and enjoying house-hold life come to us, the learned men who are busy in righteous speech and acts. You support us with food, drinking juice, clothes etc. your house-hold life is good. O lady of the house ! as I delighted in mind, delighted in mood and possessed of excellent intellectual power and having plenty of grain come to you and you, O my parents ! in the same manner become pleased with me and deal witn me.[3]

येषामध्येति प्रवसन्येषु सौमनसो बहुः ।
गृहानुप ह्वयामहे ते नो जानन्तु जानतः ॥ ४ ॥

उपहूता इह गाव उपहूता अजावयः । अथो अन्नस्य कीलाल उपहूतो गृहेष नः । क्षेमाय वः शान्त्यै प्रपद्ये शिवँ शग्मँ शंयोः शंयोः ॥ ५ ॥

यजु० अ० ३ । मं० ४२, ४३ ॥

O house-holders !

We, the learned persons praise and call affectionately near us those house-holders whom the man living in the country other than his own remembers, in whom everyone finds great affection, genial attitude. Let these house-holders know us who are acquainted with them. We, the sanyasins and you, the house-holders unitedly concert our efforts in the attainment of worldly and non-worldly progress and advancement.[4]

O house-holders ! in our houses we should make effort in the way so as the cows be available, so as the goats and sheep be available, so as the substantial quantity of grain be available. I, the preacher or the ruler approach to you in this house-hold life for yonr safety and peace. I and yon both attain happiness and pleasure of worldly nature and of unworldly nature and we always promote thc pleasure of others.[5]

सन्तुष्टो भार्यया भर्त्ता भर्त्रा भार्या तथैव च ।
यस्मिन्नेव कुले नित्यं कल्याणं तत्र वै ध्रुवम् ॥ १ ॥
यदि हि स्त्री न रोचेत पुमांसं न प्रमोदयेत् ।
अप्रमोदात् पुनः पुंसः प्रजनं न प्रवर्त्तते ॥ २ ॥

[मनु० अ० ३ । श्लो० ६०, ६१]

Surely the happiness and prosperity prevails in the home where the husband is contented with his wife and wife with her husband and the state of quarrel prevails otherwise in the house where the both are not at good terms.[1]

If the wife has not affection with her husband and does not make him delighted there never rises up the inclination of passion in the husband and absence of this causes the childlessness. If still there come issues they enjoy very short life.[2]

स्त्रियान्तु रोचमानायां सर्वन्तद्रोचते कुलम् ।
तस्यां त्वरोचमानायां सर्वमेव न रोचते ॥ ३ ॥

[मनु० अ० ३ । श्लो० ६२]

पितृभिर्भ्रातृभिश्चैताः पतिभिर्देवरैस्तथा ।
पूज्या भूषयितव्याश्च बहुकल्याणमीप्सुभिः ॥ ४ ॥

यत्र नार्यस्तु पूज्यन्ते रमन्ते तत्र देवताः ।
यत्रैतास्तु न पूज्यन्ते सर्वास्तत्राफलाः क्रियाः ॥ ५ ॥

शोचन्ति जामयो यत्र विनश्यत्याशु तत्कुलम् ।
न शोचन्ति तु यत्रैता वर्द्धते तद्धि सर्वदा ॥ ६ ॥

जामयो यानि गेहानि शपन्त्यप्रतिपूजिता : ।
तानि कृत्याहतानीव विनश्यन्ति समन्ततः ॥ ७ ॥

[मनु० अ० ३ । श्लो० ५५-५८]

If the husband does not please his wife the whole family becomes displeased because of her displeasure. If the wife is pleased with her husband the whole family seems to be pleased.[3]

The father, brother, husband and *Devarah*, the brother-in-law of the bride should give due respect to daughter, sister, wife and sister-in-law, the wife of the brother. That is, they should keep them contented and delighted with sweet speech, food, cloth, ornaments. Those who desire the good should never give any pain or trouble to ladies.[4]

In the family where the women are adored i.e. given due respect abide and arrive good qualities, good pleasure etc. and good progeny and in the family where these women are treated otherwise or are not respected all the acts and efforts of prosperity become infructuous, this should be borne in mind.[5]

The family in which women are pinched and perturbed by the bad acts of their husbands like prostitution or other kinds of deboucherous deeds, goes downward to destruction. The family otherwise where the ladies are delightful and happy by the good acts of their husbands, enjoys all sorts of progress and advancement.[6]

The house and family in which the women being dissatisfied and ill-treated use the words of malediction and imprecation to house-holders, fall to degeneration and destruction on all sides like the army of persons poisoned through artistic means.[7]

तस्मादेताः सदा पूज्या भूषणाच्छादनाशनैः ।
भूतिकामैर्नरैर्नित्यं सत्कारेषूत्सवेषु च ॥ ८ ॥

[मनु० अ० ३ । श्लो० ५९]

Therefore it is obligatory to the persons desiring good and prosperity to keep always these women well-treated, respected and delighted with ornaments, clothes, food and juice etc. on the occasion of respect and festivity.[8]

सदा प्रहृष्टया भाव्यं गृहकार्येषु दक्षया ।
सुसंस्कृतोपस्करया व्यये चामुक्तहस्तया ॥ ९ ॥

[मनु० अ० ५ । श्लो० १५०]

The woman should always be engaged in the homely affairs with pleasure and versed action and should always be ready and glad in dealing with and managing expenditure etc. of cooking the food, pots, cloth, the homely hospitality, family's mess etc.[9]

एताश्चान्याश्च लोकेऽस्मिन्नपकृष्टप्रसूतयः ।
उत्कर्षं योषितः प्राप्ताः स्वैः स्वैर्भर्तृगुणैः ॥ १० ॥

[मनु० अ० ९ । श्लो० २४]

Many women having bad habits and deeds attained, attains and would attain excellence in this world by the good qualities and characteristics of their husbands. If the men are good the women become good, if the men bad the women bad. Therefore it is the duty of men to become good by themselves and make their wives good and excellent.[10]

प्रजनार्थं महाभागाः पूजार्हां गृहदीप्तयः ।
स्त्रियाश्रियश्च गेहेषु न विशेषोऽस्ति कश्चन ॥ ११ ॥

उत्पादनमपत्यस्य जातस्य परिपालनम् ।
प्रत्यहं लोकयात्रायाः प्रत्यक्षं स्त्री निबन्धनम् ॥ १२ ॥

अपत्यं धर्मकार्याणि शुश्रूषा रतिरुत्तमा ।
दाराधीनस्तथा स्वर्गः पितृणामात्मनश्च ह ॥ १३ ॥

[मनु० अ० ९ । श्लो० २६-२८]

यथा वायुं सामश्रित्य वर्तन्ते सर्वजन्तवः ।
तथा गृहस्थमाश्रित्य वर्त्तन्ते सर्व आश्रमाः ॥ १४ ॥

[मनु० अ० ३ । श्लो० ७७]

The women in the house-hold life are for the production of

progeny, O man ! they are the fortunes of the house, they are able to be adored, i.e. respected and the light of homes. They are treated to be the wealth of the house as there is no difference between Lakshmi, the weal, the beauty, wealth and women.[11]

The lady of the house is the direct managing authority of the production of children, their bringing up and the worldly affairs that is the affairs of house-hold life.[12]

The function of producing progeny, discharge of religious duties, good service, pleasure, the happiness of self and parents—all these are under the control of woman.[13]

As the support of air serves the purpose of the living of creatures so the house-hold life give shelter and protection to the persons of all the other *Ashramas* like *Brahmacharya*, *Vanaprastha* and *Sanyasa*,[14].

यस्मात्त्रयोऽप्याश्रमिणो दानेनान्नेन चान्वहम् ।
गृहस्थेनैव धार्यन्ते तस्माज्ज्येष्ठाश्रमो गृही ॥ १५ ॥

सः संधार्यः प्रयत्नेन स्वर्गमक्षयमिच्छता ।
सुखं चेहेच्छता नित्यं योऽधार्यो दुर्बलेन्द्रियैः ॥ १६ ॥

[मनु० अ० ३ । श्लो० ७८-७८]

सर्वेषामपि चैतेषां वेदस्मृतिविधानतः ।
गृहस्थ उच्यते श्रेष्ठः सः त्रीनेतान् बिभर्त्ति हि ॥ १७ ॥

[मनु० ६ । ८९]

Because of giving protection through gift and grain etc. to the persons of three other *Ashramas* daily the house-holder is holder of excellent *Ashrama*.[15]

O men and women ! if you desire *Akshaye**, an indestructible or eternal happiness of emancipation you enter compitently

---

*Here Akshaya stands to mean the long period of salvation which is fixed in length of time. It does not stand in the sense of eternal. The happiness of salvation is not mixed with pains. It is not like the carnal happiness.

into the life of house-hold which is not acceptable by the men of weak organs and men deprived of wisdom.[16]

According to the authority of *Veda* and *Smritis* the household life is most excellent among all the *Ashramas* as it foster the *Ashramas* of *Brahmacharya*, *Vanaprastha* and *Sanyasa*.[17]

यथा नदीनदाः सर्वे सागरे यान्ति संस्थितिम् ।
तथैवाश्रमिणः सर्वे गृहस्थे यान्ति संस्थितिम् ॥ १८ ॥

[मनु० अ० ६ । श्लो० ६०]

उपासते ये गृहस्थाः परपाकमबुद्धयः ।
तेन ते प्रेत्य पशुतां व्रजन्त्यन्नादिदायिनाम् ॥ १९ ॥
आसनावसथौ शय्यामनुव्रज्यामुपासनाम् ।
उत्तमेषूत्तमं कुर्याद्धीनं हीने समे समम् ॥ २० ॥

[मनु० अ० ३ । १०४, १०७]

पाषण्डिनो विकर्मस्थान् वैडलाव्रतिकान् शठान् ।
हैतुकान् वकवृत्तीश्च वाङ्मात्रेणापि नार्चयेत् ॥ २१ ॥

[मनु० अ० ४ । श्लो० ३०]

O men ! As the rivulets and rivers fall in the ocean to find their final resort in the same manner men of all the *Ashramas* other than that of *Grihasthashram* go to house-holder and get support and means.[18]

The foolish house-holders who enjoying the life of a *Grihastha* desire to take their meals etc. in the house of others become after death the animal of the men who give grain etc. in gift as they are the doers of the sin of *Pratigraha*, the acceptence of something without doing anything for the good of giver. To accept food etc. from others is allowed only for guests not for the house-holder who is not in the position of a guests.[19]

When guests come to a house-holder he should give them due respect with the provision of seats, resting place, bed, going after them with respect and sitting near them in conformity to their superior, middle and inferior rank and positions and should always be aware of such specific courtesy.[20]

He should not give even lip-barren respect to hypocrites who discard the *Vedas*, do not believe in *Veda*, God and *Dharma*, are engaged in doing impions acts, are violent, brutal, indulged in false arrogance, vain-hair-splitters, engaged in taking the things of others by cheating and bamboozling others like a heron and like guest in disguise.[21]

दशसूनासमं चक्रं दशचक्रसमो ध्वजः ।
दशध्वजसमो वेशो दशवेशसमो नृपः ॥ २३ ॥

[मनु० अ० ४ । श्लो ८५]

न लोकवृत्तं वर्तेत वृत्तिहेतोः कथंचन ।
अजिह्मामशठां शुद्धां जीवेद् ब्राह्मणजीविकाम् ॥ २३ ॥

[मनु० अ० ४ । श्लो० ११]

सत्यधर्मार्यवृत्तेषु शौचे चैवारमेत्सदा ।
शिष्यांश्च शिष्याद्धर्मेण वाग्बाहूदरसंयतः ॥ २४ ॥
परित्यजेदर्थकामौ यौं स्यातां धर्मवर्जितौ ।
धर्मं चाप्यसुखोदर्कं लोकविक्रुष्टमेव च ॥ २५ ॥

[मनु० अ० ४ । श्लों० १७५, १७६]

The ten slaughterings are equal to wheel i.e. the profession depending on wheel like wheel-potters and the carting etc. ten wheel is equivalent to one *Dhvaja*, the earning of living by distillery or the washer-mans' profession, ten *Dhvaja* is equivalent to *Vesha*, that the earning of living in decorated and prostitution house like the profession of prost (the moral traffic) men of prosts, men who earn their living on cutting jokes, funs and changing dress, mimics, the priest of a temple who worships idol etc. and ten *Vcshas* are equivalent to one despotic ruler. The guests should always avoid food etc. from these persons.[22]

The house-holder for earning living should never adopt the method and policy of local type and tradition which do not stand in conforming to the dictates of religious scriptures. He should earn his living through the method and policy accordant to the religion, dictates of the *Vedas*, devoid of all sorts of transgression, ignorance, false-hood and unrighteousness.[23]

The men of house-hold life should always adopt the method of their dealing which are true, honest and concordant with the dealings of *Aryas*, the noble men, pure and sanctimonious. They should always teach children and disciples and make them fellow the code of conduct quite concordant with right speech, ungreediness in food etc., proper pious act through the hands, feet and other limbs.[24]

If the occasion and possibility arise to attain the plenty of wealth, kingdom and self-aspirations through the irreligious dealings they should always renounce the irreligious method and should never be involved in the acts which are against the dictates of the *Vedas*, which are pseudo-religious and in doing of which there will come pain afterwards and will result in the degeneration of the world. They should not perform such acts which are *Dharma* and *Karma* in name not in essance.[25]

सर्वेषामेव शौचानामर्थंशौचं परं स्मृतम् ।
योऽर्थे शुचिर्हि स शुचिर्न मृद्वारिशुचिः शुचिः ॥ २६ ॥

क्षान्त्या शुध्यन्ति विद्वांसो दानेनाकार्यकारिणः ।
प्रच्छन्नपापा जप्येन तपसा वेदवित्तमाः ॥ २७ ॥

अद्भिर्गात्राणि शुध्यन्ति मनः सत्येन शुध्यति ।
विद्यातपोभ्यां भूतात्मा बुद्धिर्ज्ञानेन शुध्यति ॥ २८ ॥
(मनु० अ० ५ । श्लो० १०६, १०७, १०९)

दशावरा वा परिषद्यं धर्मं परिकल्पयेत् ।
त्र्यवारा वापि वृत्तस्था तं धर्मं न विचालयेत् ॥ २९ ॥

(मनु० अ० १२ । श्लो० ११०)

दण्डः शास्ति प्रजा सर्वा दण्ड एवाभिरक्षति ।
दण्डः सुप्तेषु जागर्त्ति दण्डं धर्मं विदुर्बुधाः ॥ ३० ॥

तस्याहुः संप्रणेतारं राजानं सत्यवादिनम् ।
समीक्ष्यकारिणं प्राज्ञं धर्मकामार्थकोविदम् ॥३१॥

(मनु० अ० ७ । श्लो० १८, २६)

To earn the things through righteousness is the best cleanliness amongst all cleanliness i.e. hc who does not acquire any thing through injustice and dishonesty is really a man of purity. The purity secured through water, soil etc. does not stands commensurate with that of religious sanctity.[26]

The learned gain purity through forgiveness, the man of wicked acts through good company and munificence good qualities and knowledge etc., the sinner in disguise or clandestine sinner through renouncing the idea of committing, sins and the learned and masters of the *Vedic* speech through the practice of celibacy, truta speeking etc.[27]

The outer parts of the body becomes clean with water, not the mind and spirit. The mind becomes pure through the acceptance of truth, speaking of truth and doing of truth. The soul or spirit becomes pure by attaining knowledge, practising *yoga* and acting according to truth. The intellect gains purity through attainment of wisdom it does not become pure with water, soil etc. [28]

In the accomplishment of small or great dealings and the affairs of the ruling the country or kingdom the men of household life follow the act of doing or not-doing and religious affairs according to decision of the committee constituted by and consisted of ten learned—one having mastery of over *Rigveda*, one over *Yajurveda*. one over *Samveda*, one over *Atharvaveda*, one logician, one learned in the *Nirukta*, one teacher of *Vedic* religion, *Brahmachari*, *Snataka* and *Vanaprastha* appropriately or at least the competent men having mastery over three *Vedas* respectively in their right order.[29]

As the wise men treat the *Dandah*, the sanction of the state as *dharma*, in the same manner every one should take it. It is only the sanction which rules over the subjects and controls them, protects the people from all sides, keeps itself always awaken amongst all the people in sleep and frightens the theives etc. to leave the acts of offence with its fear.[30]

This sanction is appropriately issued by the king who is righteous, considerate, wise, learned and conversant with the principles of *Dharma*, *Artha*, *Kama* and *Moksha*.[31]

सोऽसहायेन मूढेन लुब्धेनाकृतबुद्धिना ।
न शक्यो न्यायतो नेतु शक्तेन विषयेषु च ॥ ३२ ॥

शुचिना सत्यसन्धेन यथाशास्त्रानुसारिणा ।
प्रणेतु शक्यते दण्डः सुसहायेन धीमता ॥ ३३ ॥

(मनु० अ० ७ । श्लो० ३०, ३१)

अदण्ड्यान् दण्डयन् राजा दण्ड्यांश्चैवाप्यदण्डयन् ।
अयशो महदाप्नोति नरकं चैव गच्छति ॥ ३४ ॥

(मनु० अ० ८ । श्लो० १२८)

The administrator who has not any good assistant, is fool, greedy and has not any progress in learning and knowledge through the practice of celibacy, is absorbed in evils can not use the sanction justly and honestly.[32]

Only that king who is pure, assisted with good men, apt to act according to the rules of politics, cooperated by the righteous men and clever in affairs can issue and utilize sanctions correctly.[33]

The king who awards punishment to the innocent and discharges accused and guilty persons without any punishment attains defame in this life and great pain and torture after death.[34]

मृगयाक्षा दिवास्वप्नः परिवादः स्त्रियो मदः ।
तौर्यत्रिकं वृथाट्या च कामजो दशको गणः । ३५ ।
पैशुन्यं साहसं द्रोह ईर्ष्याऽसूयार्थदूषणम् ।
वाग्दण्डजं च पारुष्यं क्रोधजोऽपि गणोष्टकः । ३६ ।
द्वयोरप्येतयोर्मूलं यं सर्वे कवयो विदुः ।
तं यत्नेन जयेल्लोभं तज्जावेतावुभौ गणौ । ३७ ।

(मनु० अ० ७ श्लो० ४७, ४८, ४९)

Mrigaya, the hunting, gambling and plays of gambling nature for pleasure, day-sleeping, to talk and laugh loudly in or making false-gossips etc. to be passionate in compuny of the women, to use intoxicant drinks etc. undue singing, unduly playing with singing instruments, dancing or seeing of dance and to wander aimlessly—are the ten evils which are the offshoots of *Kama*, the passion or sex.[35]

Back-biting, to do the thing without thinking over pros and cons, to invite quarrel in vain, to be involved in burning of heart seeing the progress and prosperity of others, to find fault in other's good things and find correctness in others faults, to use money in bad things and habits, to speak very roughly and angrily and to award rigorous punishment to any one without fault—are the eight evils which come out of the anger and take their existence in the man of angry habit. These eighteen evils enumerated in these two verses always surely be renounced by a king.[36]

The root-cause of these two groups of evils or the twain of *Kama* and *Krodha* is the covetousness and it is described so by the men of high learnings. The king should over-come this covetousness with all effort at his disposal, as it is this evil which creates the above-mentioned eighteen evils and others. Therefore, O house-holders ! you do not elect and select the king to a person of such evils might he be the elder son of the king for the kingshig of the kingdom. If by mistake you have him king you must remove him from the rank and make another person of the kings family the king of the state. Then and there only the happiness and progress would prevail in the subjects.[37]

सैनापत्यं च राज्यं च दण्डनेतृत्वमेव च।
सर्वंलोकाधिपत्यं च वेदशास्त्रविदर्हति। ३८।
(मनु० अ० १२। श्लो० १००)

मौलान् शास्त्रविद: शूरान् लब्धलक्षान्कुलोद्गतान्।
सचिवान् सप्त चाष्टौ वा प्रकुर्वीत परीक्षितान्। ३९।
अन्यानपि प्रकुर्वीत शुचीन्प्राज्ञानवस्थितान्।
सम्यगर्थसमाहर्तृनमात्यान् सुपरीक्षितान्। ४०।
(मनु० अ० ७ श्लो० ४५, ६०)

दूतं चैव प्रकुर्वीत सर्वशास्त्रविशारदम्।
इङ्गिताकारचेष्टज्ञं शुचि दक्षं कुलोद्गतम्। ४१।
अलब्धमिच्छेद्दण्डेन लब्धं रक्षेदवेक्षया।
रक्षितं वर्धयेदवृद्ध्या वृद्धं पात्रेपु नि:क्षिपेत्। ४२।
(मनु० अ० ७। श्लो० ११, १०१)

Only the man who is competent in the Vedas and scriptures, righteous, continental, just and endowed with spiritual will, should be made to assume the helm of affairs of militia civil administration, department of justice and presiding power, not the others undesirable and mean.[38]

Of the seven or eight persons who are accomplished in all respects, conversant with the scriptnres, brave and interpid. of high family status; righteous, the lover of freedom and whose thinking and stretegy ever succeeds the ministerial cabinet be made after careful test and the king should be the nineth in it. They should collectively think over and decide whatever should he done and whatever should not.[39]

In this same manner the other dignitaries of the state and army, upto the number sufficiently required to shoulder the responsibility of the affairs of the state, be appointed. They all should besaure, pious, learned, clever firm in mind and endowed with acumen of increasing the wealth of the state.[40]

The man who is dexter in all the scriptures, skilled in recognizing and knowing inner intentious of others by inclination of eyes etc. face and actions, conscientious, great endowed with unique sensorial power, possessed with the knowledge of the circumstances, time and locality, good in personality, good orator and is main figure of his family should be appointed as principal Ambassador and other Ambassadors entrusted with the duties of giving information of home department and foreign countries should be appointed as Ambassadors.[41]

All the authorities of state including the king should be ever engaged in the progress and betterment of the state. They should desire the kingdom not attained through sanction, guard safety of the country through careful preserving means, they increase the wealth of the well guarded country by trade, interests etc. and they should dissiminate the education, right knowledge and propagate religious truth by utilizing the wealth of the state in such good works.[42]

Procedure : Always women and men should go to bed at 10 p.m. in the night and rise up at 4 a.m. in the last period of night. They should at first-remember God and ponder over the *dharma* and *artha*. In the attainment of *dharma* and *artha* if there comes any trouble they should not ever renounce their righteous and honest effort. They always protecting their bodies and souls by good food and healthy walking, use of strength—giving medicines and maintaining their affort should perform prayer and contemplation of God for the accomplishment of their worldly and ultramundane duties. God is that powerful entity through whose grace and help most difficult tasks are easily done. For the purpose of this the following mantras are prescribed :—

प्रातरग्निं प्रातरिन्द्रं हवामहे प्रातर्मित्रावरुणा प्रातरश्विना
प्रातर्भगं पूषणं ब्रह्मणस्पतिं प्रातस्सोममुत रुद्रं हुवेम । १ ।
प्रातर्जितं भगमुग्रं हुवेम वयं पुत्रमदितेर्यो विधर्ता ।
आध्रश्चिद्यं मन्यमानस्तुरश्चिद्राजा चिद्यं भगं भक्षीत्याह । २ ।
भग प्रणेतर्भग सत्यराधो भगेमां धियमुदवा ददन्नः ।
भग प्रणो जनय गोभिरश्वैर्भग प्र नृभिर्नृवन्तः स्याम । ३ ।

उतेदानीं भगवन्तः स्यामोत प्रपित्व उत मध्ये अह्लाम् ।
उतोदिता मघवन्त्सूर्यस्य वयं देवानां सुमतौ स्याम ।
भग एव भगवाँ अस्तु देवास्तेनं वयं भगवन्तः स्याम ।
तं त्वा भग सर्व इज्जोहवीति स नो भग पुरएता भवेह । ५ ।

ऋ० मं० ७ । सू० ४१ । (मं० १-५)

In this way the prayer and contemplation of God should be performed.

Translation

At dawn we invoke *Agni*, self-refulgent God, at dawn we invoke *Indra*, God of supreme power, at dawn we invoke *Mitra*, God, the friend of all, *Varuna*, God the only object of our choice and at dawn we invoke *Ashvina*, the creator of the sun and the moon. At down we invoke *Bhaga*—God the only Being to be served, at dawn we invoke *Pusan*—God, the Nourisher of the universe and *Brahmanspati*, God, the Lord of mighty object, at dawn we invoke *Soma*—All-impelling God and at dawn we invoke *Rudra*—the chastiser of evil-doers.[1]

At dawn we invoke the Victorious Mighty *Bhaga*—God the only object of adoration, the creator of the sun which is situated in the atmosphere and the Upholder of the universe and sustainer of all, the knower of all beings, the Imperial Ruler, the Chastiser of evilrdoers. He admonishes us to worship Him so we invoke Him above.[2]

O *Bhaga* ! (God, the only object of adoration) thou art the Leader of all beings and O Bhaga ! (God, the only object of adoration) Thou art Lord of all eternal substances, please confer on us this supreme wisdom and shield us from danger. O Bhaga! (God, the only Object of adoration) please dugment our earthly, possession by bestowing on us kine and horses and O Bhaga ! (God, the only object of adoration) let us become rich in men and horses.[3]

O Generous one ! through Thy grace let us become prosperous at present, at the approach of day and at noon time and let us attain felicity at the rising of the sun and at evening too, so that we may enjoy the loving-kindness of the enlightened persons.[4]

O *Bhaga* ! (God, the only object of adoration) please be our only Object of service so that we, the enlightened persons may attain felicity through Thy grace for this purpose. O Bhaga ! (God, the only object of adoration, all men invoke These as such be thou our Leader here.[5]

Afterwards clearing the bowls, doing *Dantadhavana* (the brushing of teeth), washing the mouth one should take bath. Afterwards one should go in lonely jungle two miles or three miles far and performing the act of communion with God there according to the method and practice of yoga, upto the time of sun-rise or one or half hour later at the day-break return back to home and should always use to perform daily-prayer (Sandhya) and contemplation of God (upasana) etc. at proper according to the procedure given below. The meaning of the *mantras* of daily-prayers and also their authority be known with reference to *Panchmaha Yajna-Vidhi*.

First having done the task of cleaning the body i.e. the bathing *Sandhya* and *Upasana* be commenced. In the beginning taking the water in the hollow of the right hand's palm three sipping with following *mantras* one by each be done.

ओम् अमृतोपस्तरणमसि स्वाहा । १ ।
ओम् अमृतापिधानमसि स्वाहा । २ ।
ओं सत्यं यशः श्रीर्मयि श्रीः श्रयतां स्वाहा । ३ ।

(आश्वलायन गृ० सू० अ० १ । कं० २४ । १२, २१, २२)

Washing the both hands, touching the ears, eyes, nose etc. with pure and clean water, sitting on a nice clean seat in the undisturbed and cleanly place keeping the face towards the direction of wind blowing then and there, constraining the Muludriya upward from below the navel, and throwing out the wind of the stomach and heart forcibly one should obstrut it outside according to his strength and power. Afterwards the breath struck outside be slowly taken inside and be stopped a little there. This is the performance of one *Pranayama*. In this way one should perform three *Pranayamas* at least. In doing so ones hould not hold his nose with hand. At this juncture adoring, praying and contemplating God in the conscience or heart should do three *achamanas* pronouncing the following Mantra only once :—

ओं शन्नो देवीरभिष्टय आपो भवन्तु पीतये।
शंयोरभि श्रवन्तु नः॥ यजु० अ० ३६। मं० १२॥

May the Omnipresent self-refulgent and Blissfull God be gracious unto us in the attainment of our desired end and may He ever shower over us the blessedness and peace from all sides.

Afterwards touching the water from the pot with the middle big finger of the right hand the limbs should be touched with the following Mantras and the order of the touching of limbs should be from right to left :—

ओं वाक् वाक्। ओं प्राणः प्राणः। ओं चक्षुः चक्षुः। ओं श्रोत्रम्-श्रोत्रम्। ओं नाभिः। ओं हृदयम्। ओं कण्ठः। ओं शिरः। ओं बाहुभ्यां यशोवलम्। ओं करतलकरपृष्ठे।

Blessed be Thy name O Lord I By thy grace may my organ of speech be real and strong organ of speech, May my respiratory organ be real and strong respiratory organ, May my organ of sight be real and strong organ of sight. May my organ of hearing be strong and real organ of hearing, May my navel be real and strong navel, May my heart be real and strong heart, May my throat be real and strong throat, May my brain be real and strong brain, May my arms and hands attain fame and strength and May my palms be real and strong palms.

Afterwards Marjan, the purification be done (with the following Mantras :—

ओम् भूः पुनातु शिरसि। इस मंत्र से सिर पर
ओम् भुवः पुनातु नेत्रयोः। इस मंत्र से दोनों नेत्रों पर
ओं स्वः पुनातु कण्ठे। इस मंत्र से कण्ठ पर।
ओम् महः पुनातु हृदये। इस मंत्र से हृदय पर।

ओं जनः पुनातु नाभ्याम् । इससे नाभि पर ।
ओं तपः पुनातु पादयो । इससे दोनों पगों पर ।
ओं सत्यं पुनातु पुनः शिरसि । इससे पुनः मस्तक पर ।
ओं खं ब्रह्म पुनातु सर्वत्र । इस मन्त्र से सब अंगों पर छींटा देवे ।

May the Supreme Being who is identified as *bhuh*, existent purify my brain, may the Supreme Being who is identified as *bhuvah*, conscious purify my eyes, May the Supreme Being who is identified as *svah*, all-bliss purify my throat. May the Supreme Being who is identified as *mahah* all-power purify my heart, May the Supreme Being who is identified as *janah*, the creator purify my navel, May the Supreme Being who is identified as *tapah*, the Ever-active and just purify my feet, May the Supreme Being who is identified as *satyam*, imperishable purify my brain again and May the Supreme Being who is identified as kham Brahma, Omnipresent Great Lord purify the rest of the body and limbs.

Afterwards the procedure of *Pranayama* be performed and the following Mantra be recited in mind :

ओं भूः, ओं भुवः, ओं स्वः, ओं महः, ओं जनः' ओं तपः, ओं सत्यम् ।
(तैत्तिरियारण्य० प्र० १० । अनु० २७)

The Supreme Being is called *bhuh*, self existent. The Supreme Being is called *bhuvah*, conscious. The Supreme Being is called *svah*, all-bliss, The Supreme Being is called *mahah*, all-power, The Supreme Being is called *janah*, creator, of all, The Supreme Being is called *tapah*, ever-active and just, The Supreme Being is called *satyam*, imperishable.

In this way at least three and utmost 21 Pranayamas be performed.

Afterwards the devotee think over the order of the creation and God, the Creator of if with the following *mantras* and determining God the master of the universe as Omnipresent dispenser of Justice and always everywhere sure observer of the actions of the *Jivas* should not let loose his mind and soul towards sin and make them always engaged in righteous acts :—

ओम् ऋतं च सत्यं चाभीद्धात्तपसोऽध्यजायत ।
ततो रात्र्यजायत ततः समुद्रो अर्णवः ॥१॥
समुद्रादर्णवादधि संवत्सरो अजायत ।
अहोरात्राणि विदधद्विश्वस्य मिषतो वशी ॥२॥
सूर्याचन्द्रमसौ धाता यथा पूर्वमकल्पयत् ।
दिवं च पृथिवीं चान्तरिक्षमथो स्वः । ३ ॥

ऋ० मं० १० । सू० ९० । (मं० १-३)

From the self-illuminating active force of or the all-pervading heat caused by Divinity became manifest the Law eternal together with the subtle matter, Thence the dissolution after creation was produced, and thence the atmospheric ocean containing the cosmic principles came into existence.

After the manifestation of the atmospheric ocean containing the cosmic principles the operation of time became manifest and then the mighty controller of the universe by his very nature made possible the division of days and nights.

As God, the upholder of the worlds created the sun and the moon just as he had created them in the previous cycles. He created in the same order the heaven and the earth, the atmosphere and the realm of light.

8. *Manasaparikrama mantrah, hymns of mental circumspection.* Devotee should pray with the following hymns of mental circumspection :

Afterwards three *Achamans* be performed again with the Mantra—शन्नो देवीः०. He should eulogyze and supplicate God with the following Mantras :—

ओं प्राची दिगग्निरधिपतिरसितोर क्षितादित्या इषवः । तेभ्यो नमोऽधिपतिभ्यो नमो रक्षितृभ्यो नम इषुभ्य नम एभ्यो अस्तु । यो३स्मान्द्वेष्टि यं वयं द्विष्मस्तं वो जम्भे दध्मः ॥ १ ॥

दक्षिणा दिगिन्द्रोऽधिपतिस्तिरश्चिराजी रक्षिता पितर इशव । तेभ्यो ॥ २ ॥

प्रतीची दिग्वरुणाऽधिपतिः पृदाकू रक्षितान्नमिषवः ।
तेभ्यो० ॥ ३ ॥
उदीची दिक्सोमोऽधिपतिः स्वजो रक्षिताशनिरिषवः ।
तेभ्यो० ॥ ४ ॥
ध्रुवा दिग्विष्णुरधिपतिः कल्माषग्रीवो रक्षिता वीरुध इषवः ।
तेभ्यो० ॥ ५ ॥
उर्ध्वा दिग्बृहस्पतिरधिपतिः श्वित्रो रक्षिता वर्षमिषवः ।
तेभ्यो० ॥६ ॥

अथर्व० कां० ३ । सू २७ । सं० १-६ ॥

The above-mentioned Mantras be recited by the devotee and he should remain fearless, indubious, enthusiastic, pleased and diligent knowing in mind God pervading all from outside and from within.

The self-refulgent God is the Lord of the east, His unfettered powers are his protection for us, the vital airs are His arrows, we pay our compliment to Lord Paramount, we pay our compliment to His unfettered protective powers, we pay our compliment to His arrows, whosoever ignorantly envies us and whomsoever we ignorantly envy, we place him in the jaws of His arrows, the vital airs.

The Omnipotent God is the Lord of the South, His rows of insects and moths are protection for us; rays of the luminous bodies are His arrow; we pay our compliment to the Lord Paramount; we pay our compliment to His protective powers; we pay our compliment to His arrows, whosoever ignorantly envies us and whomsoever we ignorantly envy, we place him in the jaws of His arrows, the rays of the luminous bodies.

The most Exalted God is the Lord of the west, the venomous crawling reptiles are His protection for us; efficacious estables like ghee etc. are His arrows; we pay our compliment to Lord Paramount, we pay our compliment to His protective powers, we pay our compliment to His arrows, whosoever ignorantly envies us and whomsoever we ignorantly envy, we place him in the jaws of His arrows.

The All-impelling Blissful God is the Lord of the north, natural forces under His control are his protection for us;

lighting is His arrows; we pay our compliment to Lord Paramount, we pay our compliment to His protective powers; we pay our compliment to His arrows, whosoever ignorantly envies us and whomsoever we ignorantly envy, we place him in the jaws of His arrows.

The Omnipresent God is the Lord of the regions down below us; various gases are His protection for us; plants and trees and His arrows; we pay our campliment to Lord Paramount, we pay our compliment to His protective powers, we pay our compliment to His arrows, whosoever ignorantly envies us and whomsoever we ignorantly envy, we place him in the jaws of His arrows.

God who is the Lord of speech and vast space etc. is the Lord of the regions above us; powers of His innate Omniscience are His protection for us; drops of rain are His arrows; we pay our compliment to Lord Paramount, we pay our compliment to His protective powers, We pay our compliments to His arrows. Whosoever ignorantly envies us and whoms over we ignorantly envy, we place him in the jaws of his arrows.

Afterwards devotee should perform the *upasthana* of God i.e. he should realize that he is near to God and God is nearest to him and follow the procedure :—

जातवेदसे सुनवाम सोममरातीयतो नि दहाति वेदः ।
स नः पर्षदतिदुर्गाणि विश्वा नावेव सिन्धु दुरतात्यग्निः ॥ १ ॥

ऋ० मं० १ । सू० ९९ । मं० १ ॥

चित्रं देवानामुदगादनीकं चक्षुर्मित्रस्य वरुणस्याग्ने ।
आ प्रा द्यावापृथिवी अन्तरिक्षँ सूर्यआत्मा जगतस्तस्थुषश्च ।१ ॥

यजु० अ० १३ । मं० ४६ ॥

उदुत्यं जातवेदसं देवं वहन्तिकेतव । दृशे विश्वाय सूर्यम् । २ ।

यजु० अ० ३३ । मं० ३१

उद्वयं तमसस्परि स्वः पश्यन्त उत्तरम् ।
देवं देवत्रा सूर्यमगन्म ज्योतिरुत्तमम् । ३ ।

यजु० अ० ३५ । मं० १४ ।

तच्चक्षुर्देवहितं पुरस्ताच्छुक्रमुच्चरत् । पश्येम शरदः शतं जीवेम शरदःशतं शृणुयाम शरदः शतं प्रब्रवाम शरदः शतमदीनाः स्याम शरदः शतं भूयश्च शरदः शतात् । ४ ।

यजु० अ० ३६ । मं० २४

We offer our prayer to God who is present in all the worldly and unworldly objects. He burns out our intentions of doing any evil. He makes us able to cross over the difficulties and obstacles like boat which makes one cross over the sea.

The wondrous Divine Power is manifest in this universe and is the force of integration, regulation and disintegration, it is this power which is permeating the whole heaven, earth and the atmospheric region and is the impelling force of all, acting as the inner-most self of all animate and inaminate creation.

The luminous rays of the universal laws ordained by Divinity make Him thoroughly known so that all may have a glance of the Jatvedas surya-God, the all-pervading, all-knowing soul of all that moveth and that moveth not.

We have realized the most excellent light of *Surya* God, the soul of all-that moveth and that moveth not by ever keeping in view the Divine splendour which is beyond darkness and which persists even after the dissolution of the world.

He is all-vision and benevolent to wisdom, He existed pure and genuine prior to this world and would exist pure and genuine after it, meditating Him a hundred autumns may we see a hundred autumn may we live, a hundred autumns may we hear; a hundred autumns may we speak; a hundred autumns may we enjoy full freedom; and longer than hundred autumns we may enjoy all those blessings.

After performing the act of *upasthana* of God three *Achamanas* should be done again with the *mantra* शन्नो देवीः Again he should adore, pray and contemplate God taking into mind the meaning of the Gayatri *mantra* as has been written in *Vedarambha* Sanskara and *Panchmaha-yajna vidhi* Again:—

ओं नमः शम्भवाय च मयोभवाय च नमः शङ्कराय च मयस्कराय च नमः शिवाय च शिवतराय च ।५ ।

O God almighty, Infinite treasurer of Mercy, by Thy grace, may we attain soon success in accomplishment of righteousness, acquisition of wealth, fulfilment of noble desires and emancipation through the performance of this recitation, meditation and communion.

We bow in reverence to God who is All-bliss; we bow in reverence to God who is the eternal source of happiness, we bow in reverence to God who is giver of peace; we bow in reverence to God who is All-beatitude; we bow in reverence to God who is benevolent by nature; we bow in reverence to God who is most benevolent.

After saluting God with the above *Mantra* three *Achamanas* be done with शन्नो देवी: mantra

This is the end of the *Sandhyopasana* procedure in short.

अथाग्निहोत्रम्

Now Begins *Agnihotra* :

As the house-holder men and women* perform Sandhya, *Upasana* at the conjunction of the period of *Sandhis* of night and day so they should positively perform the *Agnihotra* daily at both the times (Morning and Evening). Thereafter performing the procedure of *Agnyadhana Samidadhana* according to the method prescribed in the *samanya prakarana* and sprinkling water on the four sides of *yajnakunda* with ओमदितेऽनुमन्यस्व etc. four mantras, heating the ghee which has been made pure and mixed with odiferous substances and taking ghee etc. in pots, sitting in the west direction of the *yajnakunda*, keeping their face eastward they after offering the four oblations of the Agharvajyabhagahuti should do the morning Agnihotra, with the following mantras :—

ओं सूर्यो ज्योतिर्ज्योतिः सूर्यः स्वाहा । १ ।
ओम् सूर्यो वर्चो ज्योतिर्वर्चः स्वाहा । २ ।
ओम् ज्योतिः सूर्यः सूर्यो ज्योति स्वाहा । ३ ।
ओम् सजूर्देवेन सवित्रा सजुरुषसेन्द्रवत्या ।
जुषाणः सूर्यो वेतु स्वाहा । ४ ।

I offer this oblation for the well-being of mankind in obedience of the Command of God who resides in everything that moves or is stationary, who is the illuminer of all luminaries and who is the life of all.[1]

I offer this oblation for the well-being of mankind in obedience of the Command of God who, on account of His being the indwelling ruler of all instructs the wise in truth and who resides in the self of all.[2]

---

*If husband wife both could not attend the yajna due to circumstances beyond control any one of the both can perform the yajna on behalf of both. But under this condition the two oblations be offered with one mantra pronounced twice.

I offer this oblation for the benefit of the mankind in obedience of the Command of God who is self-luminous, the illuminer of the whole world and the Lord of the universe.[3]

I offer this oblation for the benefit of mankind in obedience of the Command of God, who pervades the luminous orb of the Sun and *Jiva*, who dwells within the dawn illuminated by Sun's light and in the mental faculties of the *Jiva*, who is the self (ie) the enlivener of all. May he with his divine love and kidness make us wise by endowing us with the excellent qualities of knowledge.

The following *mantras* should be known as the mantras of oblation in evening.

ओम् अग्निर्ज्योतिर्ज्योतिरग्निः स्वाहा । १ ।
ओम् अग्निर्वर्चो ज्योतिर्वर्चः स्वाहा । २ ।
ओम् अग्निर्ज्योतिर्ज्योतिरग्निः स्वाहा । ३ ।

The third oblation be offered with this mantra recited in mind not through organ of speech.

ओम् सजूर्देवेन सवित्रा सजूरात्र्येन्द्रवत्या ।
जुषाणो अग्निर्वेतु स्वाहा । ४ ।

(तु० यजु० अ० ३ । मं० ६, १०)

With the following *mantras* the oblations be offered at both the times—i.e morning and evening :—

ओम् भूरग्नये प्राणाय स्वाहा । इदमग्नये प्राणाय-इदन्न मम । १ ।
ओं भुवर्वायवेऽपानाय स्वाहा । इदं वायवेऽपानाय इदन्न मम । २ ।
ओं स्वरादित्याय व्यानाय स्वाहा । इदमादित्याय व्यानाय इदन्न मम । ३ ।
ओं भूर्भुवः स्वरग्निवाय्वादित्येभ्यः प्राणापानव्यानेभ्यः स्वाहा । इदमग्नि-वाय्वादित्येभ्यः प्राणापानव्यानेभ्यः इदन्न मम । ४ ।

ओं आपो ज्योती रसोऽमृतम् ब्रह्म भूर्भुव, स्वरों स्वाहा । ५ ।

ओं यां मेधां देवगणा पितरश्चोपासते ।
तया मामद्य मेधयाऽग्ने मेधाविनं कुरू स्वाहा । ६ ।

यजु० अ० ३२ । मं० १४

ओं विश्वानि देव सवितर्दु रितानि परा सुव ।
यद्भद्रं तन्न आ सुव स्वाहा । ७ ।

यजु० अ० ३० मं० ३

ओं अग्ने नय सुपथा राये अस्मान्विश्वानि देव वयुनानि विद्वान् ।
ययोध्यस्मज्जुहुराणमेनो भूयिष्ठां ते नम उक्तिं विधेम स्वाहा । ८ ।

यजु० अ० ४० । मं० १६

The oblations are offered by the above-mentioned *mantras* one by each one.

The purnahuti then be offered with

ओं सर्वं वै पूर्णं स्वाहा ।

The procedure of Purnahuti is that three oblations be offered with the mantra pronouncing the *mantra* in offering each oblation.

This is the end of the Agnihotra procedure in short form.

Atha Pitriyajnah

Now here we begin the *Pitriyajnah*.

After finishing the procedure of Agnihotra the house-holding men and women should do the *Pitriyajna* ie, the proper service of living parent etc. is called the *Pitriyajnah*.[3]

Atha Balivaishvadeva vidhih

Now here we begin the procedure of *Balivaishvadeva*

ओं अग्नये स्वाहा । १ । ओं सोमाय स्वाहा । २ ।
ओं अग्नीषोमाभ्यां स्वाहा । ३ । ओं विश्वेभ्यो देवेभ्यः स्वाहा । ४ ।
ओं धनवन्तरये स्वाहा । ५ । ओं कुह्वै स्वाहा । ६ ।
ओं अनुमत्यै स्वाहा । ७ । ओं प्रजापतये स्वाहा । ८ ।
ओं द्यावापृथिवीभ्यां स्वाहा । ९ । ओं स्विष्टकृते स्वाहा ।१०।

1.	We know the property of fire.				It is praiseworthy.
2.	,,	,,	,,	Soma	,,
3.	,,	,,	,,	Agni-Soma	,,
4.	,,	,,	,,	All the physical and spiritual forces	
5.	,,	knowledge		of medical science	,,
6.	,,	,,	,,	the dark-night	,,
7.	,,	,,	,,	Anumati	,,
8.	,,	,,	,,	Prajapati the master of universe	,,
9.	,,	,,	,,	Earth and heaven	,,
10.	,,	,,	,,	Good deeds and its methods	,,

the ten oblations of cooked rice mixed with ghee, if it is not prepared, of other preparation without sour and shalty substance, be offered with the above-mentioned ten *mantras*.

Afterwards *Bali*, the propitiatory offerings be made with the following *Mantras*. The procedure here be followed in making these offerings in this way. With the mantras the offerings be put in the above mentioned directions on a *Pattal* (पत्तल) or *thali* (थाली) if at the time of offering any guest comes there these things be given to him or these be offered on the fire. These are the *mantras* of offering :—

ओं सानुगायेन्द्राय नमः । इससे पूर्व ।

with this in the east

ओं सानुगाय यमाय नमः । इससे दक्षिण ।

with this in the south

ओं सानुगाय वरुणाय नमः । इससे पश्चिम ।

with this in the west

ओं सानुगाय सोमाय नमः । इससे उत्तर ।

with this in the north

ओं मरुद्भ्यो नमः । इससे द्वार ।

with this on the gate

ओं अद्भ्यो नमः । इससे जल ।

in the water

ओं वनस्पतिभ्यो नमः ।

on Musal and Ukhal

ओं श्रियै नमः । इससे ईशान ।

in the corner of east and north

ओं भद्रकाल्यै नमः । इससे नैऋ त्य ।

in the corner of south east

ओं ब्रह्मपतये नमः । ओं वास्तुपतये नमः । इनसे मध्य ।

in the middle

ओं ब्रह्मपतये नमः । ओं दिवाचारिभ्यो भूतेभ्यो नमः । ओं नक्तंचारिभ्यो भूतेभ्यो नमः ।

above side

ओं सर्वात्मभूतये नमः ।

in the back

ओं पितृभ्यः स्वधायिभ्यः स्वधा नम । इससे दक्षिण ।

in the south

Om is the name of God, the protector of all.

Let us appreciate the property of *Indra* the air with its operative powers.[1]

Let us appreciate the property of solar heat with all its operative powers.[2]

Let us appreciate the property of *Varuna*, the water with all its operative powers.[3]

Let us appreciate the property of *Soma*, the electricity with all its operations and utility.[4]

Let us know the property of *Maruts*, the 49 varieties of airy substances with their respective operations in the firmanent.[5]

Let us appreciate the property of various kinds of waters with all their utilities.[6]

Let us appreciate the vegetative energy with its use and actions.[7]

Let us appreciate the plenty of prosperity.[8]

Let us appreciate the good qualities of night and its existing advantage in the world.[9]

Let us give respect to the person possessing all sorts of scientific knowledge.[10]

Let us appreciate the operations of all physical and non-physical forces of the universe.

Let us appreciate the qualities of the man who is the master of architecture.[1]

Let us distribute food to the creatures who wander and work out their acts in the day.

Let us give food to the creatures who play their parts in the night.

Let us provide with food to all the creatures.

Let us try for the betterment and progress of all the souls.

Let us give food and water to our living father and mother who expects their lively-hood from us. Thereafter taking the saltish food the house-holding men and women should distribute it to the following creatures :—

शुनां च पतितानां च श्वपचां पापरोगिणाम्
वायसानां कृमीणां च शनकैर्निर्वपेद भुवि ।

मनु० अ० ३ । श्लो० ९२ ।

Dogs, down trodden persons, worst men, persons having leprosy, Crows, worms, be given the six parts and these parts be put separately on the earth.

Now begins *Atithiyajna*, the respect and service for the guest.

The fifth is called the *Atithiyajna* in which the service of pious, altruistic, truth-preaching impartial, self-controlled, and all-serving enlightened persons is done with the provision of food etc. and the attainment of knowledge from them through answer and reply is involved. These *Panchamahayajnas* be performed by house-holding men and women daily.[4]

Hereafter comes the procedure of the *Pakshā yajna*, the yajna on the day of full-moon night and the day of full-dark night. After offering the oblation of doing *Agnihotra* the oblations of *Sthalipaka* prepared according to method mentioned previously in the *Samanya Prakarana*, should be offered with the following *Mantras* :—

ओं अग्नये स्वाहा । १ । ओं अग्नीषोमाभ्यां स्वाहा । २ ।
ओं विष्णवे स्वाहा । ३ ।

Let us know the property of *Agni*, the fire-whatever has been uttered herein is true.

Let us know the property of *Agnisoma*, The positive and negative electricity working in the world.

Let us know the property of *Vishnu*, The all-pervading force of the solar heat.

These are the oblations of the *Paurnamasi Paksha-yajna.* After offering these three oblations with the above-stated *mantra* the house-holder should offer the four *Vyahriti Ajyahuti* as have been described in the *Samanya Prakarana.* But here is a little difference from the above stated *Paurnamasi Paksha-yajna* in the *yajna* to be performed on the days of *Amavasya*, the full dark night. In Amavasya yajna the mantra 'ओम् इन्द्राग्नीभ्यां स्वाहा ।।' should be pronounced instead of ओम् अग्निषोमाभ्यां स्वाहा ।। The oblation of Sthalipaka be given with this *mantra.*

In this way the *Pakshayajna* be performed. But in whose house unfortunately the *Agnihatra* is not being performed, the procedure and preparations of *yajnakunda*, *yajnamaudapa*, *Agnyadhana*, *Samidadhana*, *Agharavajyahagahuti*, the sprinkling of water on the four sides of the *Vedi*, *Ishvaropasana*, *Svastivachana* and *Shahtikarana* also be accordingly accomplished on all occasions in the *Pakshayajna* etc.

When new crop of grain comes and when the new year begins respectively *Navashasyesti* and *Samatsaresti* be performed with the following Mantras : that is, at the arrival of new grain, the *navashasyesti* be performed first and thereafter the new grain be utilized in food etc. For performing the Navashasyesti and Navasamvatsaresti the day on which choice falls with pleasure be treated good and proper time. Preparing Mandapa for yajna in a clean field outside the village and city, performing the procedure prescribed for yajna in Samanyaprakarana, offering the oblations of Agharavajyabhagahuti, Vyahriti Ahuti and eight *Ajyahutis* the performer of *yajna* should offer five *Ajyahutis* of chief *homa* with the following Mantras :—

ओं पृथिवी द्यौः प्रदिशो दिशो यस्मै द्युभिरावृताः ।
तमिहेन्द्रमुपह्वये शिवा नः सन्तु हेतयः स्वाहा । १ ।
ओं यन्मे किञ्चिदुपेप्सितमस्मिन् कर्मणि वृत्रहन् ।
तन्मे सर्वं समृध्यतां जीवतः शरदः शतं स्वाहा । २ ।
ओं सम्पत्तिर्भूतिर्भूमिर्वृष्टिर्ज्यैष्ठ्यं श्रैष्ठ्यं श्रीः प्रजामिहावतु स्वाहा ।
इदमिन्द्राय—इदन्न मम । ३ ।

ओं यस्याभावे वैदिकलौकिकानां भूतिर्भवति कर्मणाम् । इन्द्रपत्नीमुपह्वये सीता सा मे त्वन्नपायिनी भुयात्कर्मणि कर्मणि स्वाहा । इदमिन्द्रपत्न्यै इदन्न मम । ४ ।

ओं अश्वावती गोमती सुनृतावती विभर्ति या प्राणभृतो अतन्द्रिता । खलमालिनीमुर्वरामस्मिन् कर्मण्युपह्वये ध्रुवां सा मे त्वनपायिनी भूयात् स्वाहा । इदं सीतायै-इदन्न मम । ५ ।

(पार० कां० २ कं० १७ । ६)

I adore the Almighty God named as *Indra* for whose manifestation and accomplishment of purpose the earth, heavenly region, directions and corners of directions are surrounded with lights and powers. May the phenomena of rainy season be for our prosperity, and happiness. Whatever has been uttered herein is true.[1]

O Lord Almighty ! May all that mine who is desirous to live hundred autumns, whatever I desire in this agricultural activity be accomplished and attained.[2] Whatever......

May prosperity and wealth, well-being and power, land for cultivation, rain, supremacy, excellence and good fortune guard the subject in this world and this action. Whatever has been uttered herein is true. The oblations offered is meant for Indra and it is not for me.[3]

I always praise the utility of *Sita* the line of the ploughshare which is protected by *Indra* the rain and air and in flourishing existence of which the Vedic acts and worldly acts are accomplished. May this line of plough share produce plenty of crop and grain for me in my activity of cultivation and other ventures. Whatever has been uttered herein is true. The oblation offered is meant for Indrapatni and it is not for me. [4]

Sita, the line of ploughshare which by its product becomes the give of horses, cows and good dealings and which without any inactivity protect the living creatures: I praise the utility of it which becomes adored with the series of the heap of crop heaped at a place to husk the grain and which is fertile. May it become the producing source of plenty of crop for me. Whatever has been uttered herein is true. The oblation offered is meant for *Sita* and it is not for me.[5]

These above mentioned oblations of ghee are the five oblation of the chief *homa* of *Navashayesti* and *Navaisamvatsaresṭi.* Thus they having been offered the four oblations be, thereafter, offered with the following *mantras*.

ओं सीतायै स्वाहा । १ । ओं प्रजायै स्याहा । २ ।
ओं शमायै स्वाहा । ३ । ओं भूत्यै स्वाहा । ४ ।
(तु०-पार० कां० २ । कं० १७, १०)

May there be good appreciation for *Sita*, the line of ploughshare. May there be prosperity of the Subject. May there reign prosperity and satisfaction. May there visit all fortunes. 4.

Thereafter one oblation of Svisiakrit, five oblations of Sthalipaka as has been given above beginning with the *Mantra* ओम् पृथिवी द्यौः O etc, eight *Ajyahuti* of *Samanyaprakarana* and four oblations of *Vyahriti-ahutis* be offered and thereafter *Vamadevyagana*, *Ishvaropasna*, *Svastivachana* and *Shantikarna* be performed to finish the *Yojna*.

SHALAKARMA

Now we will speak of the procedure of *Shalakarma*, the ceremony for house.

The house or the particular place built up by the people for accommodating men, keeping animal etc. and keeping safe the things and goods etc. is called *Shala*, It has two division of subjects—first the authority and second the procedure. Here we first quote authority and afterwards the procedure.

The authorities:—

उपमितां प्रतिमितामथों परिमितामुत ।
शालाया विश्र्ववाराया नद्धानि गि चृतामसि ॥ १ ॥

हविर्धानमग्निशालं पत्नीनां सदनं सदः ।
सदो देवानामसि देवि शाले ॥ २ ॥

It is proper for men when any one of them builds any house that the building be no nice and attractive that the learned persons seeing it praise, it must be well planned in order that the doors be in the right direction of doors, the cornors in the right direction of cornors, and the rooms be opposite rooms, it must be measured and square, it must be open for air with ventilations on all sides ; its bindings, and wall-making be strong and firm. O men, you build up the houses in the manner as the architects and mansions do build them 1.

In this house there be a fixed rooms for keeping safe the articles of *Homa*, the *Vedi* and place for *Agnihotra* be fixed, the rooms be marked and errected for accommodation of ladies there be separate rooms for men and learned persons, there be special rooms for living, sitting, meeting each other and conferring. In this way there be separate rooms for dinning, bathing, prayer and contemplation. The house built up in this way becomes accommodative and comfortable.[2]

ग्रन्तरा द्यां च पृथिवीं च यद्व्यचस्तेन शालां पति गृह्णामि त इमाम् ।
यदन्तरिक्षं रजसो विमानं तत्कृण्वेऽपमुदरं शेवधिभ्य तेन शालां प्रति गृह्णामि तस्मै ॥ ३ ॥

ऊर्जस्वती पृथिव्यां निर्मिता मिता ।
विश्वान्नं बिभ्रती शाले मा हिंसीः प्रतिगृहणतः ॥ ४ ॥
(ग्रथर्व० कां० ९ । सू० ३ । मं० १५, १६)

In the houses there be various grounds and places well neat and clean, there be arrangement for sun and light, this be made as firm as the earth. O house-holding lady ! I make the house for you quite symetrical with its space, you live in it and I will live in it. I decorate the spacious accommodation in the middle of the house and the roof specially measured in height etc. with the pleasant things for attaining pleasure and comfort. I accept such a house for the dealings of the house-hold life.[3]

The house should be wholesome, comfortable and able to encourage the spirit. It be full with plenty of wealth and fortunes. It must be full of juice, milk etc. and bullt up on the ground well measured up. It must be full of all sorts of cereals and be not anyhow uncomfortable and agonizing to the inmates.[4]

ब्रह्मणा शालां निमितां कविभिर्निमितां मिताम् ।
इन्द्राग्नी रक्षतां शालाममृतौ सौम्यं सदः ॥ ५ ॥

अथर्व० कां० ६ । सू० ६ मं १६ ।

May air and fire indestructible in their substance give protection and comfort to the inmates of the building errected in well measured and well-planned way by the expert engineers and architects and planned for comfort in all seasons by man who is the master of the four *Vedas.* That is, the fresh air entering the house remove off the bad air, the *homa* of odiferous ghee etc. be performed so that the fire be able to remove the air of bad smell and spread out the air of good smell. Such a house is wholesome and comfortable for always and the men should make and accept such houses for their living.[5]

या द्विपक्षा चतुष्पक्षा षट्पक्षा या निमीयते । अष्टापक्षां दशपक्षां शालां मानस्य पत्नींमग्निगर्भ इवाशये । ६ ।

अथर्व० का० ६ । सू० ३ । मं० २३ ।

O people ! the buildings which have two wings, which have four wings, which have six wings, which have eight or ten wings on their sides and all constructed in well-planned method stand straight like the *Agni,* the semen of man and woman known as firy substance which establishes it in the form of embryo in the womb. In the same way the doors of the building be directly straight on the equal measurement of one yard. The building of which the side wings are less in the area of three × three yards and the central portion be of six × six yards, and of which the side wings be of the area less than 4 × 4 yards and the central portion be of 8×8 yards or which the central portion be not more than 10 × 10 yards, should be constructed for the residence of house-holders. If any meeting place is to be made for the purpose, it have doors on all sides and round pillers in the middle and it be open so that the bad air go outside and fresh air enter into the building. There be ventilation, space, trees, flowers and the pond of lotus around the houses which accommodate house-holders.[6]

प्रतीचीं त्वा प्रतीचीनः शाले प्रं म्यहिंसतीम् ।
अग्निह्यं न्तरापश्र्वं ऋतस्य ऋतस्य प्रथमा द्वाः । ७ ।
अथर्व० कां० ६ । सू० ३ मं २२

I construct and accept the house which has its front in the east and door in the west and in which there is no danger and in which the door of west be just in the front of east, in which there be place for *Agni*, place for water and fixed place for the contemplation of God and His law and there be also a first gate.[7]

मा नः पाशं प्रति मुचो गुरु र्भारो लघुर्भव ।
वधूविम त्वा शाले यत्र कामं भरामसि । ८ ।
अथर्व० का० ६ । सू० ३ मं २४

O architects : you construct our building in such a way that it must not leave the bindings, the heavy weight be light and it be so that we could use it comfortably according to our desire like the married wife.[8]

When the building be completely finished whatever procedures be observed for entering into the building to live in it should be known as written below :

The Procedure :—When the construction of house is finished and house is ready it should be cleaned nicely, the four *Vedis* be prepared outside in four directions on the doors and one be made in the middle, or a *Kunda* of copper metal be made which could be taken everywhere and the performance of the procedure be accomplished on all the places in one *Kunda* only. All the articles of *Yajna* that is fuel wood, *ghee*, rice, sweet, odoriferous Vigour-giving things according to the prescription given in the *Samanyaprakarna* be cleaned, prepared and kept safe one day before the date of ceremony going to be held. On the auspicious day when the master of the house is in pleasant mood the ceremony be performed. The four priests of the *Yajna viz Hoter*, *Udgatar*, *Adhvaryu* and *Brahman* who are pious and learned be selected and appointed. The first sit in West until their places of sitting is not fixed according to their acts. The seat of *Hotar* amongst these priests be in the west and he should sit keeping his face eastward. The seat of *Adhvaryu* be fixed in the north and he should sit on his seat keeping his face southward. The seat of *Udgatar* be in the east and he should sit on his seat keeping his face westward. The *Brahman* be given seat in the south and he should take his seat keeping his face northward. Thus these four learned priest be given their respective seats and the master of the house take his seat in all such acts in the west keeping his face to the east. In the similar way the seats be arranged on the four sides of the central *Vedi* of the house.

Staying near the main door of in-coming and outgoing with the chief priest, the *Brahman*, offering one oblation with—ओम् अच्युताय भौमाय स्वाहा ॥ (पार०३।४।२) the master of the house raise the pole of the flag in which the flag is fixed. He should raise four flags on the four cornors of the building. The master of the house the performer of the ceremony raising the pole of flag should sprinkle water in the root-hole of the pole to make it firm. Again going out to the front of the door he should sprinkle water with the following mantras :

ओं इमामुच्छ्यामि भुवनस्य नाभिं वसोर्धारां प्रतरणीं वसूनाम् ।
इहेव ध्रुवां निमिनोमि शालां क्षेमे तिष्ठतु घृतमुक्षमाणा ॥ १ ॥

(पार० ३, ४, ४)

With this on the east door.

अश्वावती गोमती सूनृतावत्युच्छ्यस्व महते सौभगाय ।
आ त्वा शिशुराक्रन्दत्वा गावो धेनवो वाश्यमानाः ॥ २ ॥

(पार० ३, ४, ४)

With this on the south door.

आ त्वा कुकारस्तरुण आ वत्सो जगदैः सह ।
आ त्वा परिस्रुतः कुम्भ आदघ्नः कलशैरप ।
क्षेमस्य पत्नी बृहती सुवासा रयिं नो धेहि सुभगे सुवीर्यम् ॥ ३ ॥

(यार० ३, ४, ४)

With this on the west door.

आश्वावद्गोमदूर्जस्वत्पर्णं वनस्पतेरिव ।
अभि नः पूर्यतां रयिरिदमनुश्रेयो बसानः ॥ ४ ॥

(पार० ३, ४, ४)

With this on the front of north door.

I eraise this building which is like the centre of the globe and which is the spring of prosperity and river of wealth. I make this here firm and let it be for my well-being pouring light, butter etc.[1]

May this building by God's grace be full of horses, milching kines and good sentiment of inmates therein, and be for my great fortune. May there play children speaking and milch cows blowing[2]

Let the young children and small ones live in it with all the constructive movements and activities, let there be jug full of curd with other jars, let this grand and accommodating building known as tbs preserver of well-being and the store of fortunes give us the wealth endowed with quality of strength and vigour.[3]

As there flourish the leaves of a tree to it in the same manner let this building be full of horses, kines and grain and having good of ours pour out wealth to us.[4]

Afterwards, the master of the house decorating the gates of the building with flower, leaves of mango, the leave of plaintain to increase their beauties, says :

हे ब्रह्मन् ! प्रविशामीति । (पार० ३ । ४ । ५)

O Brahman ! may I enter this house ?

Brahman, the chief priest replies :—

वरंभवान् प्रविशतु i.e. Better you enter in. Thus taking the permission of *Brahman* he should enter into the house prononcing—ओम् ऋचं प्रपद्ये शिवं प्रपद्ये ॥ [पार० ३ । ४ । ६] i.e. may I attain the knowledge and may I attain all auspiciousness and prosperities. The master of the house should bring the ghee previously warmed, cleaned and mixed with odorifetous materials from the gate which he entered from. He should perform the

Agnayvdhana, Samidadhana, Jalàprokshana, Achamane according to the *Samauyaprakarna* and doing the acts of offering four ghee-oblations of *Agharavajyabhagahutis*, four of *Vyahriti*, and 9th oblation of *Svistakrit*, i.e. performing the acts of *Yajna* beginning from *Agnyahand* and ending at *Svistakrit* oblation in the *Vedis* of the doors at four directions should offer two oblations in the *Kunda* at the east door with the following two mantras :—

श्रों प्राच्या दिशः शालाय नमो महिम्ने स्वाहा ॥ १ ॥
श्रों देवेभ्यः स्वाह्येभ्यः स्वाहा ॥ २ ॥

In the same manner as mentioned above the two oblations of *Ghec* be offered one with each in the *Kunda* at the southern door with the following two mantras ;—

श्रों दक्षिणाया दिशः शालाया नमो महिम्ने स्वाहा ॥ १ ॥
ओं देवेभ्यः स्वाह्येभ्यः स्वाहा ॥ २ ॥

With the following mantras two oblations one by each be offered in the *Kunda* at the north door :—

ओं उदीच्या दिशः शालाया नमो महिम्ने स्वाहा ॥ १ ॥
ओं देवेंभ्यः स्वाह्येभ्य स्वाहा ॥ २ ॥

Two oblations with following mantras in the *Kunda* at the central *Vedi* be offered after the *Yajna* priests being seated in four directions properly :—

श्रों ध्रुवाया दिशःशालाया नमो महिम्ने स्वाहा ॥ १ ॥
श्रों देवेभ्यः स्वाह्येभ्यः स्वाहा । २ ।

Two oblations in the *Kunda* at central *Vedi* be offered again with the following mantras :—

श्रों ऊर्ध्वाया दिशः शालाया नमो महिम्ने स्वाहा ॥ १ ॥
ओं देवेम्यः स्वाह्येभ्यः स्वाहा । २ ।

The oblations of *ghee* again be offered in the Kunda of central *Vedi* with the following mantras :—

ओं दिशो दिशः शालाया नमो महिम्ने स्वाहा । १ ।
ओं देवेभ्यः स्वाह्येभ्यः स्वाहा । २ ।

Afterwards enkindling the fire in the *Vedi* of east door, arranging seats of *Brahman* and *hotar* etc. in the south of the *Vedi* and other sides properly, establishing one Jug full of water in the north of *Vedi*, having prepared the *shhalipaka* according to the method described in the *Samanyaprakarama* and going near and staying there at the door of entry and getting out the master of the house should enter into the middle room, seat the *Brahman* etc. priests on their respective peats and seat himself keeping his face eastward. He should, then, distribute the ghee warmed, prepared, cleaned and mixed with musk etc. odoriferous things in pots and keep these pots before all of them. Filling his spoon with ghee offer four oblations of ghee with the following *mantras* :—

ओं वास्तोष्पते प्रति जानीह्यस्मान्त्स्वावेशो अनमीवो भवा नः । यत्त्वेमहे प्रति तन्नो जुषस्व शन्नो भव द्विपदे शं चतुष्पदे स्वाहा । १ ।

वास्तोष्पते प्रतरणो न एधि गयस्फानो गोभिरश्वेभिरिन्वो ।
अजरास्ते सख्ये स्याम पितेव पुत्रान् प्रति नो जुषस्व स्वाहा । २ ।

वास्तोष्पते शग्मया संसदा ते सक्षीमहि रण्वया गातुमत्या ।
पाहि क्षेम उत योगे वरंनो यूयं पात स्वस्तिभिः सदा नः स्वाहा । ३ ।
ऋ० मं० ७ । सू० ५४ । (मं० १-३)

अमीवहा वास्तोष्पते विश्वा रूपाण्याविशन् ।
सखा सुशेव एधि नः स्वाहा । ४ ।
ऋ० मं० ७ । सू० ५५ । मं०

O master of the grand worldly structure ! grant your blessing to us. May our entrance in the house be wholesome for us. Whatever wealth we desire from you please give us. May you be gracious for our bipeds and quadrupeds. Whatever has been uttered therein is true.[1]

O master of the grand worldly structure ! Thou art the augmentator of our fortunes. O mighty power ! Come to us increasing our wealth with kines and horses. In your friendship we may not be overcome with old age before time. You shower your affection and grace upon us like a father to his sons.[2]

O master of the grand worldly structure by Thy grace we obtain the place auspicious, nice and full of wealth. Thou guard us properly in attaining whatever we have not attained and in preserving whatever we have attained. O Lord ! Thou protect us always with pleasure and plenty.[3]

O Master of grand worldly structure ! Thou art the dispeller of all calamities and disease. Thou pervadest all the forms and shapes of the world. Thou art our friend and be gracious upon us.[4]

Afterwards, the *sthalipaka* previously prepared be mixed with *ghee* keeping it in other pots of bronze and the pots be put before all the priests. Taking a small quantity of that the six oblations one by each, be offered with the following *mantras* :—

ओम् अग्निमिन्द्रं बृहस्पतिं विश्वांश्च देवानुह्वये ।
सरस्वतीञ्च बाजीञ्च वास्तु मे दत्तबाजिनः स्वाहा । १ ।

सर्पदेवजनान्त्सर्वान्हिमवन्तं सुदर्शनम् । वसूंश्च रूद्रानादित्यानीशाम जगदैः सह । एतान्त्सर्वान् प्रपद्येऽहं वास्तु मे दत्त वाजिनः स्वाहाः २ ।

ओं कर्त्तारञ्च विकर्त्तारं विश्वंकर्माणमोषधींश्च वनस्पतीन् । एतान्त्सर्वान् प्रपद्येऽहं वास्तु मे दत्त बाजिनः स्वासा । ४ ।

धातारं च विधातारं निधीनां च पतिं सह ।
एतान्त्सर्वान् प्रपद्येऽहं वास्तु मे दत्त बाजिनः स्वाहा । ५ ।
स्योनं शिवमिवं वास्तु दक्रं ब्रह्मपृजापती ।
सर्वाश्च देवतात्व स्वाहा । ६ ।   (पार ३, ६, ८

I describe the qualities operations etc. of *Agni*, *Indra*, *Brihaspati* and other physical and spiritual forces including *Saraswati* and *Vaji*. Let all of them being powerful give us homely comfort.[1]

I Know and describe the properties and actions of cloud, all the physical powers, beautiful mountain covered with the snow, *Vasus, Rudras, Adityas* and *Ishana* with all their powers. Let these powerful give us homely comfort.[2]

I also know and come into contact of morning part of the day, (anti-meridian) post-meridian with the occurance of meridian, dusk midnight, dawn which is grand in spread and full of lustre. Let these be the source of our homely comfort.[3]

I know *Kartar, Vikartar, Vishvakarma*, medicinal plants and trees. Let these powerful be source of our homely comfort.[4]

I came in contact of *Dhatar, Vidhatar,* with the master of treasures. Let all these powerful become the source of our homely comfort.[5]

Let all the forces like ***Brahman, Prajapati*** and all other mighty powers of the nature be source of making our entry and residence full of pleasure delight etc.

Afterwards the master of the house taking into a pot of bronze the leaves of उदुम्वर-गूलर (*Ficus Glomerate*), पलाश (*Butra Frondosa*), शाड्ल-दूर्वा cow-dung, curd, honey, *Ghee*, कुशा and barley and mixing them together should strew them at the doors with the following mantras and drop water also :

ओं श्रीश्व त्वा यशश्च पूर्वे सन्धौ गोपायेताम् ।

(पार० ३ । ४ । १०)

on the east door.

यज्ञश्च त्वा दक्षिणा च दक्षिणे सन्धौ गोपायेताम्

(पार० ३ । ४ । ११)

on the south door.

अन्नञ्च त्वा ब्राह्मणश्च पश्चिमे सन्धौ गोपायेताम्

(पार० ३ । ४ । १२)

on the west door.

ऊर्क च त्वा सूनृता चोत्तरे सन्धौ गोपायेताम् ॥

(पार० ३ । ४ । १३)

on the north door.

May fortune, fame guard this house on the east connecting entrance.

May the *Yajna* and gift of yajna protect this house on the south connecting entra nce.

May the grain and learnee *Brahmana* guard his house on the west connecting entrance.

May the power and good speech and act guard this house on the north connecting entrance.

Afterwards he remembering and praying God in the various directions, standing in the front of the doors according to the method and procedure laid down against the following mantras should pronounce them :—

केता च मा सुकेता च पुरस्ताद् गोपायेतामित्यग्निर्वै केताऽऽदित्यः सुकेता तौ प्रपद्ये ताभ्यां नमोऽस्तु तौ मा पुरस्ताद् गोपायेताम् ॥

with this in the east direction.

दक्षिणतो गोपायमानं च मा रक्षमाणा च दक्षिजतो गोपायेतामित्यहर्वं गोपायमानं रात्री रक्षमाणाते प्रपद्ये ताभ्यां नमोऽस्तु ते मा दक्षिणतो गोपायेताम् ॥ २ (पार० ३ । ४ । १५)

with this in the south direction.

दीदिविश्च मा जागृविश्च पश्चाद् गोपायेतामित्यन्नं वै दीदिविः प्राणो जागृविस्तौ प्रपद्ये ताभ्यां नमोऽस्तु तौ मा पश्चाद् गोपायेताम् ॥ ३ ॥ (पार० ३ । ४ । १६)

with this in the west direction.

Let *Keta* and *Suketa* become the source of our security in the front. Agni is *Keta* and the *Aditya* is *Suketa* and I know the operation of both. We take advantage from both of them. May by God's grace they protect us in the front.[1]

Let *Gopayamana* and *Rakshamana* guard us from the southern side. The day is *Gopayamana* and night *Rakshmana* and I know their utility. May they both by God's grace protect us in the south.[2]

Let *Didivi* and *Jagrivi* guard us from the West. The grain is *Didivi* and the Vital air *Jegrivi* and I realize the utility of both of them. May they both by God's grace protect us from the West.[3]

अस्वप्नश्च मानवद्राणश्चोत्तरतो गोपायेतामिति चन्द्रमा वा अस्वनो वायुर नवद्राणस्तौ प्रपद्ये ताभ्यां नमोऽस्तु तौ मौत्तरतो गोपायेतामिति ॥ ४ ॥

(पार० ३ । ४ । १७

with this in the north direction.

धर्मस्थूणाराजं श्रोस्तूपमहोरात्रे द्वारफलके । इन्द्रस्य गृहा वसुमन्तो वरूथिनस्तानहं प्रपद्ये सह प्रजया पशुभिस्सह । यन्मे किञ्चिद्स्त्यपहतः सर्वगणः सखायः साधुसम्मतः । तां त्वा शाले अरिस्टांवीरा गृहा नः सन्तु सर्वत ॥ ५ ॥

(पार० ३ । ४ । ८)

Let *Asvapna* and *Anavadrana* become the source of our seeurity from the north. This moon is *Asvapana* and *Vayu Anavadrana* and I know their operations. May they both protect us from the north.[4]

The two door-wings are like the piller of *Dharma* and *Lakshmi* and are like day and night. These houses (rooms) full of the herds of animal and wealth are like the house of king. I accept these rooms with progeny and wealth. Let us flourish in this house where have been invited relatives, well-wishers, intimate persons and the gathering of gents and ladies. May our houses be full of good children.[5]

Thus completing this procedure the master of the house should respect and entertain the *Hotar* etc. priests with their wives, friends and well-wishers and relatives. He should give *Dakshina* to deserving ones with full respect. The ladies see off ladies and gents see off gents in delight and pleasure. They taking leave to go to their houses give their blessings to the master and mistress of the house by the following sentence :

सर्वे भवन्तो ऽत्रानन्विताः सदा भूयासुः ॥

In this way there should be opening of the garden etc. There is only this variatlon that the *Homa* be performed in the side of air blowing to the garden, so that the flagrance of the *Homa* make the trees and plants flagrant. If there has been errected house this be also opened with the same procedure.

This is the end of the procedure of the ceremony concerned with the opening of house or entrance into the house etc.

Thus constructing houses etc. the house-holders should correctly discharge the duties assigned to them according to their *varnas*.

Now here is the definition of *Brahmana* and his assigned *duties*.

अध्यापनमध्ययनं यजनं याजनं तथा ।
दानं प्रतिग्रहश्चैव ब्राह्मणानामकल्पयत् ॥ १ ॥ मनु० (१ । ८८)
शमो दमस्तपः शौचं क्षान्तिरार्जवमेव च ।
ज्ञानं विज्ञानमास्तिक्यं ब्रह्मकर्म स्वभावजम् ॥ २ ॥
गीता० [१८ । ४२]

(1) Teaching ladies by ladies and men by men without deceit and with affection, (2) to learn all of the learnings completely, (3) performance of *Agnihotra* etc., (4) conducting of *yajna*, to give gift of gold etc. to the deserving persons, (5) to take gift from the house-holder who earn wealth with just, honest and pious methods. In these assigned duties learning, performming *yajna* and giving gift are three religious duties to be discharged by a *Brahman* while—teaching, conducting *yajna*, and take gift are three duties to be discharged to earn living.

---

* Dharma stands for just conduct. Nyaya means the dealings without partiality. To leave impartiality is the name of the freedom from violence, aversion, telling a lie etc. with abiding always by non-violence, non-aversion and truth, speaking. There is only one religion of all the men. But the **varnas** are known separately on the ground of the different duties assigned to them according to proper division and definition.

But the acceptance of gift is an inferior act. To earn living by teaching and conducting *yajna* is a superior act. Says *Manu* :—

प्रतिग्रहः प्रत्यवरः (मनु० १० । १०६

To allow not the mind in unrighteousness and check even the tendency of doing impiety; to keep the organs—ears etc. away from the unrighteousness and employ them in piety: to endure twain of cold, heat, blamishness, praise, hunger, thirst, respect and disrespect for the attainment of celibacy, learning and the accomplishment of *yoga*; to purify body etc, with water etc. and keep mind and spirit pure and free from attachment, aversion infatuation etc; to be not stimulant with anger, keeping the tendency of kindness even faced with the torture of blame and praise by others; to be not proud, to avoid pomposity and self-aggrandizement etc: to have the capacity of teaching all the scriptures with the distinctive knowledge of the co-relation of words and meanings; to know all the things from earth to God and take proper benefit of them with dexterity in arts and the practice of *yoga*, to be not against Divinity, *Vedas*, *Dharma*, unworldliness, the feeling of life after death and life before the birth, fructification of actions and the sense of emancipation, these nine acts and qualities be known as the *dharma* of the *Brahman Varna*. To abide with good qualities, acts and nature supreme to all. The men and women endowed with sueh deeds and qualities be known as *Brahmana* and *Brahmani*. Their marriage also be performed in conformisy to these virtues. They should be authorised as *Brahman* amongst all the men.

Now the definition and nature of Kshatriya

प्रजानां रक्षणं दानमिज्याध्ययनमेव च ।
विषयेष्वप्रसक्तिश्च क्षत्रियस्य समासतः ॥ १ । मनु० (१ । ८९)

शौर्यं तेजो धृतिर्दाक्ष्यं युद्धे चाप्यपलायनम् ।
दानमीश्वरभावश्च क्षात्रकर्म स्वभावजम् ॥ १ ॥ गीता० (१८ । ४३)

The systematic study of the *Ved* etc. scriptures with all the *angas* and *upangas* with observance of the discipline of continence, to perform the *Agnihotra* etc. *yajnas*, to impart knowledge and give gold etc. to the deserving ones and fearlessness to the subject; to protect always by all means to the subject—all these duties and conducts are included in the duties and definition of *Kshatriya.* To teach the science of armament, to administer justice and maintain the strength of army are the acts of living of the *Kshatriyas.*[1]

To remain ever unattached with the huntings of the organs, to be always self-controlled, to be always engaged in the acts of good actions, good conduct, and decency keeping away from the use of intoxicant drinks etc., covetousness and profligation, to be always fearless in the use of armery, in battle, even in the act causing death and the use of weapons on the enemies, to maintain bravery and becoming intrepid never yield to any one as timid and pauper; to be never confused and peturbed in the time of calamity, trouble and scarcity and be always unperturbed; to be capable and clever in the matter of battle, wordy fight, ambassadorial job, administration of justice etc., to be always ready in the warfares and never come into the grip of the enemy due to perturbation caused by the fear of war. to give gift; as God showing mercp on all like a father to his son gives the awards of pleasure and pain for the good and bad actions of the souls without any partiality and observes completely the good and bad acts of all as residing within all with his omniscience etc. so a *Kshatriya* should deal with his subjects and keep him aware of the good and bad activities of the subjects and officials of the state, to be always ready to administer justice and give happiness to subject, to be always ready in rewarding good persons and punishing offenders, and to make his spirit delighted and gratified by ploughing the soul into justice and piety keeping the body wholesome, strong, firm, vigorous and long-lived——these qualities and acts adopted and possessed by a man and a woman make them *Kshatriya* and *Kshatriya* respectively. The marriage of these should also be fixed in conformity to these qualities and acts. The *king* and the *queen* should administer justice to men and women and promote their good respectively as the *Brahmana* and *Brahmani* teach the men and women respectively. The *Kshatriyas* who are not crowned as *King* should join the services of proper designation in the state of the *King*.[2]

Now the definition and nature of Vaishya

पशूनां रक्षणं दानमिज्याध्ययनमेव च ।
वणिक्पथं कुसीदं च वैश्यस्य कृषिमेव च ॥ १ ॥ मनु [१० । ९०]

To study the true scriptures like *Veda* etc., to perform the *Agnihotra* etc. *yajna*, to give the gift of grain etc.——these three are the religious duties of the *Vaishyavarna* while to domesticate the animals like cows etc. and to sell the milk yielded by them, to know the languages of various countries, accounts, geology and the nature of soil, seed etc. to earn interest* to know the science of agriculture, preservation of grains and to know the method of testing mauure and soil, to know the method of ploughing and sowing of seeds etc. are the four acts of livelihood of a *Vaishya*. The man and woman who possess these qualities and acts are called *Vaishya* and *Valshya* respectively. Marriages in the couples of *Vaishya* should be settled in conformity to these qualities and acts.[1]

Now here comes the definition and nature of the Shudra Varna

एकमेव हि शूद्रस्य प्रभुः कर्म समादिशत् ।
एतेषामेव वर्णानां शुश्रूषामनसूयया ॥ १ ॥ मनु० (१ । ९१)

God has assigned only one act to *Shudra*, the individual who is uueducated, unable to grasp anything even being taught, strong in body and competent in serving others and that is, the service of the three *Varnas*—the *Brahmana*, *Kshatriya* and

---

* The interest should not more than 1-1/4 per cent and less than 1-1/4 per cent. If the return is twice of the invested money he should neither take a single pie nor give any thing on loan. Lesser interest he will take and greater wealth he would earn and neither there will be poverty nor the had progeny in his family.

Vaishya without grumbling and with pleasure. The man had woman possessing these qualitative defencies and the sense of service are known respectively *Shudra* and शूद्रा. The marriage settlement and the liberties to be given to them be considered in conforming to the scrutiny of their acts etc.

If the division and assignment of the four *Varna* be made according to these respective qualities and acts the society of men, family and country would attain all progrecs. If the men of the *Varna* possess the same qualities, acts and nature of the *Varnas* in which they are born it is a distinctive exception.

Now all the *Brahmana* etc. *Varna* should follow the following code of conduct and method in discharging their duties :—

वेदोदितं स्वकं कर्म नित्यं कुर्यादतन्द्रितः ।
तद्धि कुर्वन्यथाशक्ति प्राप्नोति परमां गतिम् ॥ १ ॥

नेहेतार्थान् प्रसंगेन न विरुद्धेन कर्मणा ।
न विद्यमानेष्वर्थेषु नार्त्यामपि यतस्ततः ॥ २ ॥

(मनु० अ० ४ । श्लो० १४: १५]

The *Varnas* like *Brahmana* etc., should daily discharge their duties assigned by the *Vedas* without any indolence and discharging these duties according to their capacity and powers attain the things aimed at upto the gain of salvation.[1]

A house-holder never should accumulate money and wealth with the help and cooperation of an evil man. He should neither acquire wealth ever through unrighteous deed nor concealing the thing present with him through deceiving others inspite of being faced by overwhelming calamities.[2]

इन्द्रियार्थेषु सर्वेषु न प्रसज्येत कामतः ।
अतिप्रसक्तिं चैतेषां मनसा सन्निवर्त्तयेत् ॥ ३ ॥

सर्वान् परित्यजेदर्थान् स्वाध्यायस्य विरोधिनः ।
यथा तथाऽध्यापयंस्तु सा ह्यस्य कृतकृत्यता ॥ ४ ॥

[मनु० अ० ४ । श्लो० १६, १७]

He should not be entangled in the sensual enjoyments with passion and should keep away entirely keen attachment of the sensual enjoyment i. e. the contact from the environment of mind. 3,

He should leave out all those things and acts which are anti to self study and righteousness. The successfulness of house-hold life lies in imparting knowledge in all the circumstances. 4.

बुद्धिवृद्धिकराण्याशु धन्यानि च हितानि च ।
नित्यं शास्त्राण्यवेक्षेत निगमांश्चैव वैदिकान् ॥ ५ ॥

यथा यथा हि पुरुषः शास्त्रं समधिगच्छति ।
तथा तथा विजानाति विज्ञानं चास्य रोचते ॥ ६ ॥

न संवसेच्च पतितैर्न चाण्डालैर्न पुवकशैः ।
न मूर्खैर्नावलिप्तैश्च नान्त्यैर्नान्त्यावसायिभिः ॥ ७ ॥

नात्मानमवमन्येत पूर्वाभिरसमृद्धिभिः ।
आमृत्योः श्रियमन्विच्छेन्नैनां मन्येत दुर्लभाम् ॥ ८ ॥

सत्यं ब्रूयात्प्रियं ब्रूयान्न ब्रूयात्सत्यमप्रियम् ।
प्रियं च नानृतं ब्रूयादेष धर्मः सनातनः ॥ ९ ॥

(मनु० अ० ४ । श्लो० १९, २०, ७९, १३७, १३८)

O women and men ! you always go through and see the beneficial scriptures which quickly increase genius etc. and *dharma* and wealth and the sciences laid down in the branches of the *Vedas*. 5.

As far as the man thinking over the scriptural dicta reaches their esoteric truth, knows more and more he becomes fond of the sciences. 6.

The house-holders of decency should not ever live with the men who are discarded, evil-doing, devoid of religious feelings wanderers. fool of false-arrogance, of bad nature and of mean intentions. 7

The house-holding people should not feel shy of their existence if they become poor after enjoying the life of plenty of wealth. They should not lament that they have gone poor. They should not even cry for this but should be engaged in perseverance for the increasement of riches and never think that riches are unattainable. 8.

Men should always speak truth and preach the people for their well-being. They should never use harsh words calling a fool, as fool, an one-eyed man as one-eyed before such persons. They should not tell a lie to appease others. This is the primeordial *dharma*. 9.

अभिवादयेद् वृद्धांश्च दद्याच्चैवासनं स्वकम् ।
कृताञ्जलिरुपासीत गच्छतः पृष्ठतोऽन्वियात् ॥ १० ॥

श्रुतिस्मृत्युदितं सम्यङ् निबद्धं स्वेषु कर्मसु ।
धर्ममूलं निषेवेत सदाचारमतन्द्रितः ॥ ११ ॥

आचाराल्लभते ह्यायुराचारादीप्सिताः प्रजाः ।
आचाराद्धनमक्षय्यमाचारो हन्त्यलक्षणम् ॥ १२ ॥

दुराचारो हि पुरुषो लोके भवति निन्दितः ।
दुःखभागी च सततं व्याधितोऽल्पायुरेव च ॥ १३ ॥

सर्वलक्षणहीनोऽपि यः सदाचारवान्नरः ।
श्रद्दधानोऽनसूयश्च शतं वर्षाणि जीवति ॥ १४ ॥

(मनु० ४ । १५४-१५८)

He should offer *Namaste* i. e. respect to men who are mature in experience and knowledge and mature in age. When such persons come near him he rising respectfully lead them to sit on his seat and sit near them with folded hand, answer their questions and when they are to go he should walk after them and going a little far send them off. The persons matured in experience and age should not of and on go everywhere without any aim and object. 10.

A house-holding man always leaving out the habit of indolence and being firm in his duties described in the *Vedas* and the duties given in the *Manusmriti* according to the *Vedas* should always follow the fundamental rule of conduct which is the original principle of religion—i.e., the turth and practice of the good persons and the persons of right thought, speech and deed. 11,

Long life, good progeny and in-exhaustible riches are attained by a man through practice of righteousness and this practice of righteousness abolishes all of the evil designs of irreligion. 12.

The man of bad conduct find him discarded everywhere, subjected to unhappiness and short-lived by the diseases. 13.

The person who is deprived of all other good qualities may attain the life of hundred years if he practises right conduct truthfulness, has fruitful sentiments of practising truth and is free from the tendencies of blaming others. 14

यद्यत्परवशं कर्म तत्तद्यत्नेन वर्जयेत् ।
यद्यदात्मवशं तु स्यात्तत्तत्सेवेत यत्नतः ॥ १५ ॥

सर्वं परवशं दुःखं सर्वमात्मवशं सुखम् ।
एतद्विद्यात्समासेन लक्षणं सुखः दुखयोः ॥ १६ ॥

अधार्मिको नरो यो हि यस्य चाप्यनृतं धनम् ।
हिंसारतश्च यो नित्यं नेहासौ सुखमेधते ॥ १७ ॥

(मनु० अ० ४। श्लो० १५९, १६०, १७०)

The man should always abondon with firm effort whatever is act of dependency and strictly adhere to whatever acts are independent. 15

The dependency to others is painful and independence is called happiness and this should be known the definition of happiness and unhappiness. 16.

The man who is irreligious and has acquired the wealth through irreligious or unrighteous means and methods and who is always indulgent in violence i. e. enmity does not ever attain happiness in this worldly and unworldly life i. e. after death.17

नाधर्मश्चरितो लोके सद्यः फलति गौरिव ।
शनैरावर्त्तमानस्तु कर्त्तुर्मूलानि कृन्तति ।।१८।।

यदि नात्मनि पुत्रेषु न चेत् पुत्रेषु नप्तृषु ।
न त्वेवन्तु कृतोऽधर्मः कर्त्तुर्भवति निष्फलः ।। १६ ।।

सत्यधर्मार्यवृत्तेषु शौचे चैवारमेत्सदा ।
शिष्यांश्च शिष्याद्धर्मेण वाग्बाहूदरसंयतः ।। २० ।।

(मनु० अ० ४ । श्लो० १७२, १७३, १७५)

Man should rest assure that the *Adharma* done in this world does not fructify soon like the cow whose service does not bring the result of milk rapidly. But the *Adharma* obstructing the happiness of its doer by and by cuts the root of the happiness and thus *Adharmi* man suffers from the sorrow and pain. 18.

If the consequences of *Adharma* do not come to doer in his own time they come to his sons, if not to them, also they come in the time of his grand-sons surely. But it is never possible that the act performed by a doer could not bring fruit and go fruitless. 19.

Therfore it is proper for all men to wander in the outside and internal purity performing the deeds of true religion and conduct of good men. They should always eacht and instrucht their disciples keeping them strict in the true *dharma*, putting their own voice, hands and abdomen in control.

परित्यजेदर्थकामौ यौ स्यातां धर्मवर्जितौ ।
धर्मं चाप्यसुखोदर्कं लोकविक्रुष्टमेव च ।।२१ ।।

धर्मं सनैस्संचिनुयाद्वल्मीकमिव पुत्तिकाः ।
परलोकसहायार्थं सर्वभूतान्यपीडयन् ।। २२ ।।

उत्तमैरुत्तमैर्नित्यं सम्बन्धानाचरेत्सह ।
निनीषुः कुलमुत्कर्षमधमानधर्मास्त्यजेत् ।। २३ ।।

वाच्यर्था नियताः सर्वे वाङ्मूला वाग्विनिःसृता ।
तान्तु यः स्तेनयेद्वाचं स सर्वस्तेयकृन्नरः ॥ २४ ॥
(मनु० अ० ४ । श्लो० १७६, २३८, २४५, २५६)

स्वाध्यायेन जपैर्होमैस्त्रैविद्येनेज्यया सुतैः ।
महायज्ञैश्च यज्ञैश्च ब्राह्मीयं क्रियते तनुः ॥ २५
(मनु० २ । २८)

One should renounce at once the ambitions, the wealth etc. which do not stand proper in conformity to the principles of *Dharma*. He should always keep him away from fallacious characterisitcs of *dharma*, that is, the actions bringing out pain afterwards and conducting the people towards the deeds of blamishness. 21.

A man without giving any pain to other creatures should accumulate options and opportunities of *dharma* slowly for the help of his life after death as the white ants pile up their citadel by and by. 22.

The man who wants to make his family excellent should leave out the company of mean persons and increase the contact and association with good persons. 23.

Take it for granted that the man who infringes the speech (i.e. tells a lie) in which all the worldly dealings are fixed, which is surely the origin and base of such dealings and through which all the worldly dealings are accomplished, comits the theft of all these things collectively. Therefore, he should always renounce telling a lie and speak truth.

It is obligatory to men that they read and teach the true scriptures like *Veda* etc; think over the meanings of *Gayatri*, *Om* etc; seriously; perform the acts of concentration, *Homa Agnihotra* etc., *Karmopasana*, knowledge, learning, *Istis* like *Paurnamasa etc.*, *Panchmahayajna*, *Agnistoma etc.*, administration of the country with justice, truth-speaking, proctice of *yoga* etc. and thereby make this body *Brahmi*, i.e. assigned with the purpose of attaining *Brahuman*. 25.

Now we take here scope and nature of *Sabha*, the parliament or assembly. The tasks which are of tremendous importance like the administration of the country should discharge after having been decided by the *Sabha*. Authorities on this subject :—

तं सभा च समितिश्च सेना च ॥ १ ॥

अथर्व० का १५ । सू० ६ । मं० २ ॥

सभ्य सभां मे पाहि ये च सभ्याः सभासदः ॥ २ ॥

अथर्व० का० १६ । सू० ५५ । मं० ६ ॥

त्रीणि राजाना विदथे पुरूणि परि विश्वानि भूषथः सदांसि ॥ ३ ॥

ऋ० मं० ३ । सू० ३८ । मं० ६ ॥

The Government of a country with honesty and righteousness etc., are the tasks and affairs which should be discharged and fulfilled by the parliament, war and army. 1.

O King ! (the presiding head of the parliament) you guard my parliament and promote its cause. Those learned righteous, adpet persons who are the members of the parliament should also do the planning and protection of the *Sabha* and thereby promote the good of all. 2.

They, the two groups of the ruler and the ruled formed from within the noble men of the subject should appoint three committees named as *Rajasabha*, *Dharmasabha* and *Vidyasabha* in achieving the aims of goods knowledge and beneficial deeds of this world and of the warfares and for the accomplishment of works of education etc. and promote the cause of all the affairs of the world. 3.

अनाम्नातेषु धर्मेषु कथं स्यादिति चेद्भवेत् ।
यं शिष्टा ब्राह्मणा ब्रूयुस्स धर्मः स्यादशङ्कितः ॥ १ ॥

धर्मेणाधिगतो यैस्तु वेदः सपरिबृंहणः ।
ते शिष्टा ब्राह्मणा ज्ञेयाः श्रुतिप्रत्यक्षहेतवः ॥ २ ॥

(मनु० अ० १२ । श्लो० १०८, १०९)

O men of house-hold life ! if you succept to any dubiousty in the tenets of religion which have not been referred to directly in the *Manusmriti* etc., you follow the practice of adepts without any doubt and take it granted as the tenet of *dharma*. 1.

All the persons cannot be adept but adepts are those who have studied the *Vedas* with their limbs with the discipline of *Brahmacharya*, who are competent to issue imparatives and injunctions through the vision of scriptural authority and authorities of validities like perception etc. and who are religious and altuistic. 2.

दशावरा वा परिषद् यं धर्मं परिकल्पयेत्।
त्र्यवरा वापि वृत्तस्था तं धर्मं न विचालयेत् ॥ ३ ॥

त्रैविद्यो हैतुकस्तर्की नैरुक्तो धर्मपाठकः।
त्रयश्चाश्रमिणः पूर्वे परिषत्स्याद्दशावरा ॥ ४ ॥

ऋग्वेदविद्यजुर्विच्च सामवेदविदेव च।
त्र्यवरा परिषज्ज्ञेया धर्मसंशयनिर्णये ॥ ५ ॥

एकोऽपि वेदविद्धर्मं यं व्यवस्येद् द्विजोत्तमः।
स विज्ञेयः परो धर्मो नाज्ञानामुदितोऽयुतैः ॥ ६ ॥

(मनु० अ० १२। श्लो० ११०-११३)

Let no man transgress that law which has been passed by an assembly of ten men learned and wise, or at the very least of three such men. 3.

This assembly must consist of members who are well-versed in the four *Vedas*, keen logician, masters of language and men conversant with the science of religion ; they must belong to the first three ordes—*Brahmacharya*, *Grihastha* and *Vanaprastha*. 4.

Also is competent in deciding the points of doubts raised in the matter of religious affairs is the assembly of three men which consists of the scholars of *Rigveda*, *Yajurveda* and *Samveda* respectively. More powerful and competent is the assembly if that consists of much more such persons.

Even the decision of one *Sanyasi* whs fo uill conversant with all the four *Vedas* is superior to all the tiwice-born (*Dvijas*) should be considered of the highest authority. 'But let no man abide by the decision of myriads of ignorant men. Only the decision of the learned *Sanyasi* and learned persons given with the authorities of the *Vedas* etc. should be strictly obeyed in the matter of religion. 6.

If there arises out any difference of opinion in the *Sabha*, the same should be decided by majority. If there is the equal number of opinions of both parties the opinion in this matter be sought of a *Sanyasi*. The opinion given by the *Sanyasis* who are well-wishers of all and devoid of all impartiality, should be taken as right and correct.

चतुर्भिरपि चैवैतैर्नित्यमाश्रमिभिर्द्विजैः ।
दशलक्षणको धर्मस्सेवितव्यः प्रयत्नतः ॥ ७ ॥
धृतिः क्षमा दमोऽस्तेयं शौचमिन्द्रियनिग्रहः ।
धीर्विद्या सत्यमक्रोधो दशकं धर्मलक्षणम् ॥८॥
(मनु० अ०६ । श्लो० ९१, ९२)

It is obligatory to the men of four *Ashramas* who are known as *Dvijas* that they strictly abide by the following *dharma* and keep them away from *adharma* with all their efforts. 7.

Dharma is the name of abiding by truth leaving partiality and renouncing untruth for always. There are eleven characteristics of *dharma* :—

Non-violence—Avoidence of doing unwell to any one with the intention of enmity.

Mental firmness—Remain always firm in *dharma* and never renounce it due to being perturbed with the matter of loss, profit and happiness and unhappiness.

Forgiveness—Obedience of the tenets of *dharma* with the sense of tolerance in the matter of blame, praise, respect and disrespect.

Control on mind and organs—Employment of mind in *dharma* removing it always from *adharma*.

Theft—To accept never the wealth of others in thought, action and deed with unjust and irreligious means.

Cleanliness—To keen clean and pure the mind and soul with the renouncement of attachment, aversion etc. and the body with utilization of water etc.

Control over organs—Engage the ear etc. external organs only in *dharma* keeping them away from *adharma*.

Intellect—To increase the power of intellect with true knowledge like *Veda* etc., the practice of *Brahmacharya* and the company of learned men leaving bad compaines, bad habits, drinking etc.

Experience—To attain the knowledge which consists of knowing the things from earth to God.

Truth—To accept truth, to speak truth and to obey truth.

Non-eneragement—To leave out anger etc. evils and to accept the qualities of peace. All these are called *Dharma* and the conduct of injustice, partiality is *adharma* which consists of :- violence, enmity, agileness and confusion of mind, to indulgence of mind in *adharma*, stealing, uncleanliness, uncontrolling of organs and their engagement in *adharma*, bad company, bad habits, to spoil the intellect by drinking intoxicant things, to be absolved in the ignorance which is a bad conduct conducive to the practice of *adharma*, to accept untruth and false-hood, to speak a lie, to *adharmi* and bad characteristic—are these eleven varieties of *adharma*. One should always be away from them.

न सा सभा यत्र न सन्ति वृद्धा वृद्धा ते ये न वदन्ति धर्मम् ।
नासौ धर्मो यत्र न सत्यमस्ति न तत्सत्यं यच्छलेनाभ्युपेतम् ॥ ९ ॥
महाभारते (उद्योग० अ० ३५ । श्लो० ५८)

सभां वा न प्रवेष्टव्यं वक्तव्यं वा समञ्जसम् ।
अब्रुवन् विब्रुवन्वापि नरो भवति किल्विषी ॥ १० ॥

धर्मो विद्धस्त्वधर्मेण सभां यत्रोपतिष्ठते ।
शल्यं चास्य न कृन्तन्ति विद्धास्तत्र सभासदः ॥ ११ ॥

(मनु० अ० ८ । श्लो० १३, १२)

विद्वद्भिः सेवितः सद्भिर्नित्यमद्वेषरागिभिः ।
हृदयेनाभ्यनुज्ञातो यो धर्मं स्तन्निबोधत ॥ १२ ॥

(मनु० अ० २ । श्लो० १)

Insolvent of the qualities of an assembly is that assembly where men of mature age, experience and practice are not the members, the persons are not the persons of mature qualities if they do not speak *dharma* when they are called for it, the *dharma* which is devoid of truth is not *dharma* and even the truth which embraces the sting of deception is not truth, 9.

Either a just and virtuous man should not enter an assembly or a court of justice, or when he does enter it, should invariably speak the truth. He, who looks on injustice perpetrated before his very eyes and still remains mute or says what is false or unjust, is the greatest sinner. 10.

Where, justice, having been wounded by injustice, approaches the court, and no one extracts the dart, shot by injustice from the wound, all the judges who constitute the bench would also be considered as wounded. 11.

O people ! you know it the *dharma* which is embraced and practised by learned men in conformity to dictates of their conscience. 12.

धर्म एव हतो हन्ति धर्मो रक्षति रक्षितः ।
तस्माद्धर्मो न हन्तव्यो मा नो धर्मो हतोऽवधीत् ॥ १३ ॥
वृषो हि भगवान्धर्मं स्तस्य यः कुरुते ह्यलम् ।
वृषलं तं विदुर्देवास्तस्माद्धर्मं न लोपयेत् ॥ १४ ॥

(मनु० अ० ८ । श्लो० १५, १६)

Where justice is destroyed by injustice and Truth by untruth under the very nose of the judges whilst they simply look on, all the judges in that court are as if dead, not one of them is alive. Justice being destroyed shall destroy the destroyer. Justice being protected shall protect the protector. Let no man, therefore, violate the laws of justice, lest justice, being destroyed destroy him.

He who violates the laws of justice—that gives power and prosperity, and showers happiness like rain from heaven—is considered as lowest of the low by the wise. Let no one, therefore, violate the laws of justice. 14.

न जातु कामान्न भयान्न लोभाद्धर्मं त्यजेज्जीवितस्यापि हेतोः ।
धर्मो नित्यः सुखदुःखे त्वनित्ये जीवो नित्यो हेतुरस्य त्वनित्यः ॥ १५ ॥
महाभारते (तु०-उद्योग० ४० । ११, १२)

यत्र धर्मो ह्यधर्मेण सत्यं यत्रानृतेन च ।
हन्यते प्रेक्षमाणानां हतास्तत्र सभासदः ॥ १६ ॥
मनु० (अ० ८। श्लो० १४)

निन्दन्तु नीतिनिपुणा यदि वा स्तुवन्तु,
लक्ष्मीस्समाविशतु गच्छतु व यथेष्टम्
अद्यैव वा मरणमस्तु युगान्तरे वा,
न्याय्यात्पथ प्रविचलन्ति पदं न धीरा ॥१७॥
भर्तृहरि (नीति शतक श्लो० ७४)

Righteousness should never be forsaken either through lust or fear or greed, even when there be chances of saving one's life by forsaking it. Righteousness is permanent; pain and pleasure are fleeting, The soul is immortal while means of living are changeful. 15.

Wherever the righteousness has been wounded with unrighteousness and truth with untruth in the presence of the members of the assembly the members should think them to be wounded 16.

Let diplomats condemn or praise: let prosperity come or go,

let death come this very moment or after ages the brave firm in intentions do not remove their steps from the path of justice and truth.

सं गच्छध्वं सं वदध्वं सं वो मनांसि जानताम् ।
देवा भागं यथा पूर्वे संजानाना उपासते ॥ १ ॥
ऋ० मं० १० । सू० १९१ । मं २ ॥

दृष्ट्वा रूपे व्याकरोत्सत्यानृते प्रजापतिः ।
अश्रद्धामनृतेऽदधाच्छ्रद्धाँसत्ये प्रजापतिः ॥ २ ॥
यजु० अ० १९ । मं० ७७ ॥

सह नाववतु सह नौ भुनक्तु सह वीर्यं करवावहै ।
तेजस्वि नावधीतमस्तु मा विद्विषावहै ।
ओं शान्तिश्शान्तिश्शान्तिः ॥ ३ ॥
तै० (आर०) अष्टमप्रपाठकः । प्रथमानुवाकः॥

O men of house-hold life ! I (God) gives you this command that as the learned persons knowing everything correctly and having studied and having attained knowledge, the accomplishment in *yoga*, distinguishing truth from untruth embrace truth so you attaining the correct knowledge of *dhrama* and *adhrama* benefit and disbenefit and becoming concordant in your minds follow the principles of *dharma* and you always following *dharma* and leaving out *adharma* converse with each others amicably and promote the cause of all. 1.

God, the omnipresent, omniscient, just, second to none, the master of all, the universal spirit aud creator and protector of the creation differentiates omnisciently between truth and untruth that is *dharma* and *adharma*. He commands you to confirm your faith in truth and disbelief in untruth and you follow His commandment.

We the couple of wife and husband, master and servant, friend and friend and son and father guard each other with love and affection and increase the power of each other with love. May our learning attained and taught be shining in brilliance, may we not be opponent of any one but to treat all with the sentiments of true friendliness. May we promoting the cause of all house-holders grow to strength in pleasure. May, by the grace of God whose name is *Om* and through our righteous perseverance the displasure of our body, mind and soul which is of three kind and caused by others be away from us and we showing love on each other, succeeding in attainment of *dharma artha*, *kama* and *moksha* remaining in happiness by ourselves increase the happiness of others.

Now here I would describe the procedure of the ceremony of *Vanaprastha*, the going to *jungle* rcnouncing the house-hold life.

Vanaprastha ceremony is that ceremony in which the man desiring to enter in, procreating children by marriage and on having got a grandson from his son through the procedure of his marriage after completing *Brahmacharya Ashram* i.e. on having got one of his son, enters the *Vanaprastha Ashram* and perform the following things after going to *jungle* :—

Authorities on the subject ;—

ब्रह्मचर्याश्रम समाप्य गृही भवेद गृही भूत्वा बनी भवेत् वनी भूत्वा प्रव्रजेत् ॥ १ । शतसथब्रह्मणे ।

ब्रतेन दीज्ञामाप्नोति दीक्षयाप्नोति दक्षिणाम् ।
दक्षिणा श्रद्धामाप्नोति श्रद्धया सत्यमाप्ते ॥ २ ॥

यजु० अ० १९ । मं० ३० ॥

It is proper for men that they completing *Brahmacharya Ashram* enter the house-hold life, and finishing the same enter the *Vanaprastha Ashram* and thereafter finally accept the discipline and duties of *Sanyasa Ashram*.

When a man accepts to observe the avowed disciplines of celibacy etc. and truth speaking etc. i.e. he accepts these things as code of conduct, he through this attains qualified admittance; through this he attains accomplishment in all the affairs, even through this accomplishment he attains love and aptitude for realizing truth and finally through this he attains truth or the knowledge of truth. Therefore, one should faithfully obey the discipline of *Bramacharya* and thereafter house-hold life and thence-forward the life of a *Vani*, the *Vanaprastha*. 2.

अभ्यादधामि समिधमग्ने व्रतपते त्वयि ।
व्रतञ्च श्रद्धां चोपैमीन्धे त्वा दीक्षितो ऽअहम् ॥ ३ ॥

यजु० अ० २० । म० २४ ॥

आ नयैतमा रभस्व सुकृतां लोकमपि गच्छतु प्रजानन्।
तीर्त्वा तमांसि बहुधा महान्त्यजो नाकमा क्रमतां तृतीयम् ॥ ४ ॥
अथर्व० कां० ९ । सू० ५ । मं० १ ॥

O self-refulgent God ! Thou art the master of all the vows and disciplines. May I having got qualified admittance in the affairs, observing the vows of *Brahmacharya* etc. *Ashramas* and being firm in thee, accept faith and attain the methods ways, for it. Therefore, as I offer this fuel into the fire of *yajna* so I make it ablaze by being firm on knowledge and vows. In the similar way I establish you in my heart and always get you refulgent in me. 3.

O house-holding man ! you knowing its aspects take initiative of this *Vanaprastha Ashrama*, you bring you mind to it from house-hold life, you attain the life *Vanaprastha Ashram* which is the state attained by the person of pious deeds. Men almost crossing over the great and deep darkness of ignorance and the pains etc. of the worldly attachments, i.e. keeping then away from and knowing the soul eternal and undecaying mount to the state of *Vnanprastha Ashram* which is free from worldly displeasures and anxieties.

भद्रमिकच्छन्त ऋषयस्स्वर्विदस्तपो दीक्षामुपनिषेदुरग्रे ।
ततो राष्ट्रं बलमोजश्च जातं तदस्मै देवा उपसंनमन्तु ॥ ५ ॥
अथर्व० कां १९ । सू० ४१ । मं० १ ।

मा नो मेधा मा नो दीक्षां मा नो हिंसिष्ट यत्तमः
शिवा नः सन्त्वायुषे शिवा भवन्तु मातरः ॥ ६ ॥
अथर्व० का० १९ । सू० ४१ । मं० ॥

O learned men ! as the seers who have attained happiness of house-hold life first entered into *Bramacharya Ashramas* and thereafter attain the good qualities of knowledge, control over organs etc. so you desiring your well-being enter into this *Vanaprastha Ashram* which is auspicious one. As a prince first observes the discipline of *Brahmacharya* and thereafter attains power, strength, fame and desires and protects the Kingdom, and all the learned, pious men respect him so all the people respect you when you have entered the *Vanaprastha Ashram.*

Let not our family men and relatives destroy my understanding entering into *Vanaprastha*, let not them destroy onr qualified admittance in this *ashrama*, let not them destroy our discipline of austerity like *pranayama* etc., let all the children be auspiciouse for us in my initiation of this *Ashrama* and for my life. Let our mothers, grand-mothers and the mothers of grand-mothers wish our well-beings. As they bless us for accepting this *Ashrama* so all the men allow me to accept this with pleasure. 6.

तपःश्रद्धे ये ह्युपवसन्त्यरण्ये शान्ता विद्वांसो भैक्षचर्यां चरन्तः ।
सूर्यद्वारेण ते विरजाः प्रयान्ति यत्रामृतः स पुरुषो ह्यव्ययात्मा ॥ ७ ॥
मुण्डकोपनि० मं० १ खं० २ । मं ११ ॥

O men ! those very learned men who live in the people of *jungle* peacefully and tranquibly practising *yoga* and centering faith in God, and depending for their living on the alms through sacred-begging live in the forest, become free from all sorts of evils, sins and attachments and through the vital air attain the state in which the unbegotten, immortal eternal God stands attained. Therefore the acceptance of *Vanaprastha* is an excellent thing and act. 7.

एवं गृहाश्रमे स्थित्वा विधिवत्स्नातको द्विजः ।
वने वसेत्तु नियतो यथावद्विजितेन्द्रियः ॥ १ ॥

गृहस्थस्तु यदा पश्येद् वलीपलितमात्मनः ।
अपत्यस्यैव चापत्यं तदारण्यं समाश्रयेत् ॥ २ ॥

सन्त्यज्य ग्राम्यमाहारं सर्वञ्चैव परिच्छदम् ।
पुत्रेषु भार्यां निक्षिप्य वनं गच्छेत्सहैव वा ॥ ३ ॥
(मनु० अ० ६ श्लो० १-३)

Dvija, the twice born persons like *Brahmana, Kshatriya* and *Vaishya* attaining complete knowledge through the prescribed procedure with *Brahmacharya,* taking both of the *Samavartan* ceremony, having full control over organs and spirit and finishing the tenure of house-hold life should enter into the life of forest-living. 1

The house-holders finding his skin loose, the hair totally grey and having got the sons of their sons should take shelter in the forest. 2.

When they are initiated to *Vanaprastha* they should eat only those things as food which are produced in villages, leave out the things of home-preparation and leave their wives amongst their sons or should take them with themselves to the forest. 3.

अग्निहोत्रं समादाय गृह्यं चाग्निपरिच्छदम् ।
ग्रामादरण्यं निःसृत्य निवसेन्नियतेन्द्रियः ।

(मनु० अ० ६ । श्लो० ४)

When a house-holder desires to become *Vanaprastha* he taking all the utensils of *Agnihotra* with him and leaving the village enter the forest and live therein having full control over organs 4.

स्वाध्याये नित्ययुक्तः स्याद्दान्तो मैत्रः समाहितः ।
दाता नित्यमनादाता सर्वभूतानुकम्पकः ॥ ५ ॥

तापसेष्वेव विप्रेषु याज्ञिकं भैक्ष्यमाहरेत् ।
गृहमेधिषु चान्येषु द्विजेषु वनवासिषु ॥ ६ ॥

एतान्श्चान्याश्च सेवेत दीक्षा विप्रो वने वसन् ।
विविधाश्चोपनिषदीरात्मसंसिद्धये श्रुतीः ॥ ७ ॥

मनु० अ० ६ । (श्लो० ७, २७, २९)

In the forest he should always engage him in the study and teaching of the scriptures like *Veda* etc., he having his mind and organs into cotrol keep him away from carnal lust. He should never indulge in objects and satisfaction of organs and even do not have co-habitation with his wife if she is living with him and should accept only service from her. He should treat all like friends, he ever alert in his duties, he ever a giver not taker and he always merciful onall the creatures. 5.

He should beg for his meals in only the houses of householders or *Vanaprastha* and learned pious men engaged in practising *yoga* and teaching and the people of the forests. 6.

Thus living in the forest he should follow the principles laid down for the *Vanaprastha* and should think over the meanings of the canons of the *Upanishads* to know correctly the nature of soul and God. In this way he should remain in this *Ashrama* until and unless he cultivates the desire of accepting the *Sanyasa Ashrama*. 7.

The procedure—The period of entering the *Vanaprastha Ashrama* has been fixed after 50 years of one's age. When one's son gets son one educating the affairs of house-holding life to his wife, son, brother, younger brother and daughter-in-law should make preparation to go to forest. If his wife desires to accompany him he can take her with him, otherwise he shuold make her arrangement with elder son with the advice that he would serve her entirely. He should also advise her wife that she would always educate and instruct her sons etc. to follow the path of righteousness and to deviate them from unrighteonsness.

Afterwards *yajnashala* and *Vedi* etc., be prepared according to the method described in *samanyaprakarana*. According to the *Samanyaprakarana* the utensils of *yajna* like ghee etc. be arranged. Thereafter performing the procedure of *Agnyadhana* by ओं भूर्भुवः स्वद्यौं०, and *Samidadhana* by अयन्त इध्म आत्मा० etc. *mantras* the man desiring to enter to *Vanaprastha* sprinkle water on the four sides of the *Vedi* beginning with the four *mantras*—ओम् अदितेऽनुमन्यस्व—etc. Then he should offer the four oblations of the *Agharavajyabhagahuti* and four *Vyahriti ahutis*. Thereafter he should recite the *mantras* of *Svastivachana* and *Shantikarana*. Afterwards preparing *Sthalipaka* and pouring *ghee* on it he should offer the oblations with the following *mantras* :—

ओं काय स्वाहा । कस्मै स्वाहा । कतमस्मै स्वाहा । स्वाहा । आधिमाधीताय स्वाहा । मनः प्रजापतये स्वाहा । चितंविज्ञातायादित्यै स्वाहा । अदित्यै मह्यै स्वाहा । अदित्यै सुमृडीकायै स्वाहा । सरस्वत्यै स्वाहा सरस्वत्यै पावकायै स्वाहा । सरस्वत्यै बृहत्यै स्वाहा । पूष्णे प्रपथ्याय स्वाहा । पूष्ण नरन्धिषाय स्वाहा । त्वष्ट्रे त्वष्ट्रे तुरीपाय स्वाहा । त्वष्ट्रे पुरुरूपाय स्वाहा ॥ यजु० अ० २२ । मं २० ॥

भुवनस्य पतये स्वाहा । अधिपतये स्वाहा । प्रजापतये स्वाहा ॥

यजु० अ० २२ । मं० ३२ ॥

ओम् आयुर्यज्ञेन कल्पताँ स्वाहा । प्राणो यज्ञेन कल्पताँ स्वाहा । अपानो यज्ञेन कल्पताँ स्वाहा । व्यानो यज्ञेन् कल्पताँ स्वाहा । उदानो यज्ञेन कल्पताँ स्वाहा । समानो यज्ञेन कल्पताँ स्वाहा । चक्षुर्यज्ञेन कल्पताँ स्वाहा । श्रोत्रं यज्ञेन कल्पताँ स्वाहा । वाग्यज्ञेन कल्पताँ स्वाहा मनो यज्ञेन कल्पताँ स्वाहा । आत्मा यज्ञेन कल्पताँ स्वाहा । ब्रह्मा यज्ञेन कल्पताँ स्वाहा । ज्योतिर्यज्ञेन कल्पताँ स्वाहा । स्वर्यज्ञेन कल्पताँ स्वाहा । पृष्ठंयज्ञेन कल्पताँ स्वाहा । यज्ञो यज्ञेन कल्पताँ स्वाहा ॥

यजु० अ० ३२ । मं० ३३

I prepare myself to know *Ka*, the all-blissful God, whatever has been uttered herein is true. 1

I prepare myself to know the *Ka*, the lord of the universe. Whatever...............true. 2

I prepare myself to know *Katama*, most blessed God. Whatever.....................true. 3

I prepare myself to know *adhi*, the sustainer of all and *Adhita*, whatever has been sustained i.e. the universe etc. Whatever...............true. 4

I prepare myself to control the mind which is the guarding factor of all creatures. Whatever...............true. 5

I prepare myself to know the faculty of mind, the intellect

and *aditi* the material cause of the universe. Whatever......... true. 6

I prepare myself to know the grand earth. Whatever......... true. 7

I prepare myself to know *Aditi,* God who is eternal and merciful. 8

I prepare myself to attain learning. Whatever.............. true. 9

I prepare myself to attain learning which purifies the conscience. Whatever...........true. 10

I prepare myself to attain learning and the speech which is grand and all-pervading. Whatever.............true. 11

I prepare myself to know *Pushana,* the air. Whatever......... true. 12

I prepare myself to know *Pushana,* the air which is pervading everywhere. Whatever..............true. 13

I prepare myself to know the air which gives protection to men. Whatever..............true. 14

I prepare myself to know *Tvaṣtar,* the shining sun. Whatever ....true. 15

I prepare myself to know *Tvastar,* which illumninate all. Whatever...........true. 16

I prepare myself to know *Tvastar,* who changes many forms or who has many colours. Whatever.............true. 17

I prepare myself to know the heat which pervades in the worlds. Whatever.............true. 18

I prepare myself to know the master of the universe. Whatever.............true. 19

I prepare myself to know the paramount lord of the universe Whatever...........true. 20

I prepare myself to attain the knowledge of *Prajapati*, the sou which is the guardian of all the organs. Whatever........ true. 21

May our life remain ever engaged in Performing self sacrificing acts. Whatever..................true. 22

May our vital energy succeed through self-sacrificing acts. Whatever..................true. 23

May our vital energy known as *apana* succeed through self-sacrificing acts. Whatever...............true. 24

May our vital energy known as *Vyana*, succeed through self-sacrificing acts. Whatever..............true. 25

May our vital energy known as *Udana*, succeed through self-sacrificing acts. Whatever...............true. 26

May our vital energy known as *Saman*, succeed through self-sacrificing acts. Whatever...............true. 27

May our eyes thrive through self-sacrificing acts. Whatever ....true. 28

May our ears flourish through self-sacrificing act. Whatever ....true. 29

May our mutual conversations succeed through self-sacrificing acts. Whatever..............true. 30

May our mind be ever engaged in self-sacrificing acts. Whatever..................true. 31

May our soul persevere in performing self-sacrificing acts. Whatever..............true. 32

May *Brahman*, the master of the four *Vedas* be ever engaged in performing self-secrificing acts. Whatever...........true. 33

May all enligtenments succeed through self-sacrificing acts. 34

May happiness come to me through self-sacrificing acts. Whatever.................true 35

May our questions and answers succeed through self-secrificing acts. Whatever..............true. 36

May our self-sacrificing acts prosper through self-sacrificing acts. Whatever...............true. 37

एकस्मै स्वाहा । द्वाभ्यां स्वाहा । शताय स्वाहा । एकशताय स्वाहा । व्युष्टयै स्वाहा । स्वर्गाय स्वाहा ॥

यजु० अ० २२ । मं० ३४ ॥

I prepare myself to know God who is one and second to none. Whatever............true. 38.

I prepare myself to know the relation of cause and effect. Whatever.........True 39.

I prepare myself to know hundred aspects of the worldly things. 40.

I prepare myself to know the things and operations prevailing in the world in the number of one hundred one. Whatever ....true. 41

I prepare myself to burn out whatever is distinctively attracting me towards the lustres of the world. Whatever............. true. 42.

I prepare myself to attain the happiness worldly and unworldly. Whatever...............true. 43.

Offering thus 43 oblations of *Sthalipaka* and *Ajya* with the above *mantras* one by each the four *Vyahriti Ahuti* be offered according to *Samanyaprakarana*. The *Sama Gana* according to the *Samanyaprakarana* be performed. Afterwards meeting the friends and well-wishers, putting the burden of house etc. on the sons, carrying the articles of *Agnihotra* he should go to forest and living in lovely place, practising *yoga*, thinking over scriptures, keeping the company of spiritual persons should engage him in seeing self and universal self. This is the end of the procedure of *Vanaprastha* sacrament.

Now we would describe the procedure of the sacrament of *anchorite*.

The ceremony of *Sanyasa,* the anchorite is that ceremony in which a man duly initiated]wonders on the earth with the motive of doing well-being to all renouncing all the cover of infatuation and partiality leading the life of resignation.

सम्यङ् न्यस्यन्त्यधर्मांचरणानि येन वा सम्यङ् नित्यं सत्कर्मस्वास्त उपवि शति येन स संन्यासः, सन्यासो विद्यते यस्य स संन्यासी ॥

The man who leaves out all the irreligious acts in entirely, takes active initiative in the acts of righteousness and becomes established and firm in the same is known as *Sanyasi* and the *Ashrama* he enters in with these initiatives is called *Sanyasa*.

The Period : Completing the discipline of continence and chastity, as has been described in the *Vanaprastha* ceremony one should enter the *Ashrama* of house-hold and finishing that should enter to the *Ashrama* of *Vanaprastha* and completing the same he should accept the life of a *Sanyasi,* the anchorite. This is the *Sanyasa* of order, i.e. the acceptance of *Sanyasa* after finishing the *Ashramas* according to their order. The second form of *Sanyasa* is as follows :—

यदहरेव विरजेत् तदहरेव प्रव्रजेद्वनाद्वा गृहाद्वा ॥

This is the sentence of *Shatapath Brahmana.*

On the day when a man has cultivated the firmness in mind for and has created a tendency of full resignation from worldly attachment, should accept the *Sanyasa* whether the time of *Vanaprastha* has been complete or not, or whether he has entered in the *Vanaprastha* or not. He can take *Sanyasa* even from the life of house-hold as main requirement of *Sanyasa* is the development of sense of non-attachment and true knowledge.

The third form of *Sanyasa*—

ब्रह्मचर्यादेव प्रव्रजेत् ॥

This is also the qvotation from *Brahmana*. A man, if attains the accomplishment in the discipline of celibacy and develop the tendency of resignation from all the attachments and infatuations with the attainment of true *Vairagya* and perfect knowledge, creates desire of doing good for all without any partiality and becomes decisive and firm that he would firmly follow the path of *Sanyasa* till the death, can accept *Sanyasa Ashrama* with the completion *Brahmacharya Ashrama* without entering household life and *Vanaprastha Ashrama*,

Authorities from the *Vedas* on the subject :

शर्यणावति सोममिन्द्रः पिबतु वृत्रहा :
बलं दधान आत्मनि करिष्यन् वीर्यं महदिन्द्रायेन्दो परिस्रव ॥ १ ॥
आ पवस्व दिशां पत आर्जीकात् सोम मीढ्वः ।
ऋतवाकेन सत्येन श्रद्धया तपसा सुत इन्द्रायेन्दो परिस्रव ॥ २ ॥
ऋ० मं० ९ । सू० ११३ । १-२ ॥

I God instruct to the man to be initiated to *Sanyasa* that as the Sun destroying clouds drinks the water from the earth which is full of many violent things so the man taking *Sanyasa* should drink the juice of fruits and cultivating the desire that he would attain a great power in his spirit, securing the mighty strength should accept *Sanyasa* and shower the knowledge of truc instructions for attaining higest power giving pleasures to all like moon. 1.

O *Sanyasin* ! you are celebrated with peace and tranquility, with the power of showering the conscience of all with truth, with the power of protection for all the people in all regions and with the qualities of mental and spiritual equilibrium. You becoming successful in your task through right speech, truthful voice, unbreakable aptitude, practice of *Pranayama* and *yoga* and geniality of temprament make pure your body, limbs, mind and intellect to attain God who is Almighty. 2.

ऋतं वदन्नृतद्युम्न सत्यं वदन्त्सत्यकर्मन् । श्रद्धां वदन्त्सोम राजन् धात्रा सोम परिष्कृत इन्द्रायेन्दो परि स्रव ॥ ३ ॥

ऋ० मं० ९ । सू० ११३ । मं० ४ ॥

O Anchorite ! you are enriched with the wealth of truth, and prominence of truth, you are the doer of truthful acts, you are balanced in life, you give pleasure to all as you are endowed with the power of *yoga* and you are pure with maintaining unity with God. You speaking right thing without partiality, speaking and expressing truth, speaking of the love in establishing truth, shining on all sides do all effort to attain the excellent power produced by *yoga*. 3.

यत्र ब्रह्मा पवमान छन्दस्यां३ वाचं वदन् । ग्राव्णा सोम महीयते सोमेनानन्दं जनयन्निन्द्रायेन्दो परि स्रव ॥ ४ ॥

ऋ० मं० ९ । सू० ११३ । मं० ६ ॥

O *Sanyasin* ! you are pious and impeller of pleasure in people. You preaching the voice of freedom, creating pleasure for all through knowledge, the practice of *yoga* and devotion of God, attain with all means God in whom the master of four *Vedas* secure greatness and through that respect, for getting the happiness of emancipation like cloud which prosper the world. 4.

यत्र ज्योतिरजस्रं यस्मिँल्लोके स्वर्हितम् । तस्मिन् मां धेहि पवमानामृते लोके अक्षित इन्द्रायेन्दो परि स्रव ॥ ५ ॥

ऋ० मं० ९ । सू० ११३ । मं० ६ ॥

O Almighty God ! Thou art the destroyer of the pains like ignorance etc. Thou art Pure by nature and the Guru of happiness that is a blessing for all. Thou establish me in Thy indestructible, immortal shelter wherein there remains always the inextinguishable light of the Thine with Thy eternal bliss and like parents shower on me thy happiness with Thine grace to make me attain great height of excellence. 5.

यत्र राजा वैवस्वतो यत्रावरोधनं दिवः ।
यत्रामूर्यह्वतीरापस्तत्र माममृतं कृधीन्द्रायेन्दो परि स्रव ॥ ६ ॥

ऋ० मं० ६ । सू० ११३ । मं० ८॥

O Happiness giving Divinity ! Thou make me establish myself in that Divine Powers of Thine in which the light of grand sun is shining with its lustre, in which there is obstecle of all-pervading electricity of the bad desire, in which the great causes like all-pervading space, airs invigorating vitality operate their functions and make me attain immortality, i.e. salvation and shower on me Thy mercy from all sides to attain the grandeur of life. 6.

यत्रानुकामं चरणं त्रिनाके त्रिदिवे दिवः । लोका यत्र ज्योतिष्मन्तस्तत्र माममृत कृधीन्द्रायेन्दो परि स्रव ॥ ७ ॥

ऋ० मं० ६ । सू० ११३ । मं० ६॥

O All-blessed God ! make me immortal in that realm wherein there is free movement according to one's own desire in the three spheres free from any kind of suffering and full of bliss and which is full of spiritual light. O Lord ! be gracious unto us for the attainment of that state of propriety. 7.

यत्र कामा निकामाश्च यत्र बध्नस्य विष्टपम् । स्वधा च यत्र तृप्तिश्च तत्र मामम् ते कृधीन्द्रायेन्दो परि स्रव ॥ ८ ॥

ऋ० मं० ६ । सू० ११३ । मं० १० ॥

O God ! make me immortal in that realm wherein all our desires and longings are fulfiled and which is the region of the supreme greatness and wherein are found all spiritual means of subsistence and self-fulfilment ; O lord be gracious into us for the attainment of that state of prosperity in order to cleave out the sufferings. 8.

यत्रानन्दाश्च मोदाश्च मुदः प्रमुदः आसते । कामस्य यत्राप्ताः कामास्तत्र मामामृतं कृधीन्द्रायेन्दो परि स्रव ॥ ६ ॥

ऋ० मं० ६ । सू० ११३ । मं० ११ ॥

O God ! make me immortal in that realm wherein happiness and bliss are in abundance. wherein felicity and cheerfulness are contained together and all the desires are fulfiled, O Lord ! be gracious to us for the attainment of that state of prosperity and in this way thou be attained by all the *Jivas* 9.

यद्देवा यतयो यथा भुवनान्यपिन्वत ।
अत्रा समुद्र आ गूळ्हमा सूर्य्यमजभर्त्तन ॥ १० ॥
ऋ० मं० १० । सू० ७२ । मं० ७ ॥

O perfectly accomplished anchorites ! As in this vast space is concealed God, the illuminator of all the shining bodies like sun etc., so you (attainig your self light) attain Him in your self and get happy with bliss and always make satisfied the householders of the globe with education and instruction. This is your paramount religious duty. 10.

भद्रमिच्छन्त ऋषयः स्वर्विदस्तपो दीक्षामुप नि षेदुरग्रे ।
ततो राष्ट्रं बलमोजश्च जातं तदस्मै देवा उप सं नमन्तु ॥ ११ ॥
अथर्व० कां० १९ । सू० ४१ । मं० १ ॥

O learned men ! all the learned persons pay their respects to the seers who are well-versed in the science of the *Vedas* have attained happiness and observing strictly the discepline of *Brahmacharya Ashram* with constancy and firmness, desiring the good of all secure the initiative of *Sanyasa*. Thereafter there may come to existence and maturity of the stately power, strength and vigour and thereby they obey the discipline of *Sanyasaram*.

Here are the Shlokas of Manusmriti

वनेषु तु विहृत्यैवं तृतीयं भागमायुषः ।
चतुर्थमायुषो भागं त्यक्त्वा संगान् परिव्रजेत ॥ १ ॥

अधीत्य विधिवद्वेदान् पुत्रांश्चोत्पाद्य धर्मतः ।
इष्ट्वा च शक्तितो यज्ञैर्मनो मोक्षे नियोजयेत् ॥ २ ॥

प्राजापत्यां निरूप्येष्टिं सर्ववेदसदक्षिणाम् ।
आत्मन्यग्नीन्समारोप्य ब्राह्मणः प्रव्रजेद् गृहात् ॥ ३ ॥

यो दत्त्वा सर्वभूतेभ्यः प्रव्रजत्यभयं गृहात् ।
तस्य तेजोमया लोका भवन्ति ब्रह्मवादिनः ॥ ४ ॥

आगारादभिनिष्क्रान्तः पवित्रोपचितो मुनिः ।
समुपोढेषु कामेषु निरपेक्षः परिव्रजेत् ॥ ५ ॥

अनग्निरनिकेतः स्याद् ग्राममन्नार्थमाश्रयेत् ।
उपेक्षकोऽसङ्कुसुको मुनिर्भावसमाहितः ॥ ४ ॥

नाभिनन्देत मरणं निभनन्देत जीवितम् ।
कालमेव प्रतीक्षेत निर्देशं भृतको यथा ॥ ७ ॥

दृष्टिपूतं न्यसेत्पादं वस्त्रपूतं जलम् पिबेत् ।
सत्यपूतां वदेद्वाचं मनःपूत समाचरेत् ॥ ८ ॥

अध्यात्मरति रासीनो निरपेक्षो निरामिषः ।
आत्मनैव सहायेन सुखार्थी विचरेदिह ॥ ९ ॥

क्लृप्तकेशनखश्मश्रुः पात्री दण्डी कुसुम्भवान् ।
विचरेन्नियतो नित्यं सर्वभूतान्यपीडयन् ॥ १० ॥

इन्द्रियाणां निरोधेन रागद्वेषक्षयेण च ।
अहिंसया च भूतानाममृतत्वाय कल्पते ॥ ११ ॥

दूषितोऽपि चरेद्धर्मं यत्र तत्राश्रम रतः ।
समः सर्वेषु भूतेषु न लिङ्गं धर्मकारणम् ॥ १२

फलं कतकवृक्षस्य यद्यप्यम्बुप्रसादकम् ।
न नामग्रहणादेव तस्य वारि प्रसीदति ॥ १३ ॥

प्राणायामा ब्राह्मणस्य त्रयोऽपि विधिवत्कृताः ।
व्याहृतिप्रणवैर्युक्ता विज्ञेयं परमं तपः ॥ १४ ॥

दह्यान्ते ध्मायमानानां धातूनां हि यथा मलाः ।
तथेन्द्रियाणां दह्यन्ते दोषा प्राणस्य निग्रहात् ॥ १५ ॥

प्राणायामैर्दहेद्दोषान् धारणाभिश्च किल्बिषम् ।
प्रत्याहारेण संसर्गान् ध्यानेनानीश्वरान् गुणान् ॥ १६ ॥

उच्चावचेषु भूतेषु दुर्ज्ञेयामकृतात्मभिः ।
ध्यानयोगेन संपश्येद् गतिमस्यान्तरात्मनः ॥ १७ ॥

सम्यग्दर्शनसंपन्नः कर्मभिर्न निबध्यते ।
दर्शनेन विहीनस्तु संसारं प्रतिपद्यते ॥ १८ ॥

अहिंसयेन्द्रियासङ्गैर्वैदिकैश्चैव कर्मभिः ।
तपसश्चरणैश्चोग्रैः साधयन्तीह तत्पदम् ॥ १९ ॥

यदा भावेन भवति सर्वभावेषु निःस्पृहः ।
तदा सुखमवाप्नोति प्रेत्य चेह च शाश्वतम् ॥ २० ॥

अनेन विधिना सर्वांस्त्यक्त्वा सङ्गाञ्छनैः शनैः ।
सर्वद्वन्द्वविनिर्मुक्तो ब्रह्मण्येवावतिष्ठते ॥ २१ ॥

इदं शरणमज्ञानामिदमेव विजानताम् ।
इदमन्विच्छतां स्वर्गमिदमानन्त्यमिच्छताम् ॥ २२ ॥

अनेन क्रमयोगेन परिव्रजति यो द्विजः ।
स विधूयेह पाप्मानं परं ब्रह्माधिगच्छति ॥ २३ ॥

मनु० अ ६ श्लो० ३३, ३६, ३८, ३९,४१, ४३, ४५, ४६, ४९, ५२, ६०
६६, ६७, ७०,-७५, ८०, ८१, ८४, ८५ ॥

In this way a mans pending the third part of life in the forests as a *Vanaprastha* i.e, 25 years in maximum and 12 years in minimum wandering the jungles should become anchorite in the fourth part of life i.e., after 70 years and renouncing all sorts of worldly lustres and attachments. 1,

According to the procedure of *Brahmcharyashram* studying all the four Vedas, entering into house-hold life and having procreated children, thereafter leading the life of *Vanaprasth* a in conformity to his power and performing *yajna*, one should enter into *Sanyashrama*-2,

The *Brahman* who is learned performing *Prajapatyesti* (in which the tuft and sacred thread are to be renounced), basing the *Agnis* named as *Ahavaniya*, *Garhapatya* and *Dakshinatya in* self should accept the life an anchorite even from the house-hold life. 3.

That Anchorite who speaks of the Great God, preaches the teaching of the *Veda* and have entered the *Sanyashram* from house-hold life giving all the creature, freedom from fear and preaching truth, gets his realm of emancipation and other realms full of resplendence. 4.

A person may take *Sanyasashram* from house-hold life or even from *Brahmacharyashrama* when he overcomes all the passions and desires and has nothing to do with them and has become pure in spirity, pure in conscience and considerate. 5.

An anchorite should be (Anagnih)* free from *Ahavaniya* etc. fire-kindling, should not anywhere make his permanent residence on his own accord, should take shelter of villages for his food and clothes, should never indulge with bad men and attaining firmness in intellect consideration in nature and seeking solution of his problems from God shoul do wander freely. 6.

He should never think of pleasure in his life and pain in his death. He like a servant waiting the arrival of his master, wait for time and his death. 7.

At the time of walking he keep his steps seeing his front, drink water after cleaning it through cloth-piece, use truth speaking to all i.e. express the righ thought to others and whatever he says and deals with should be done with the purity of mind. 8

He in this world making him constant in the spirituality, having no expectation from any one else, free from the habit using meat and intoxicant liquor, enjoying pleasure depending on his own self should walk from place to place and preach truth to people.

*Due to doubt caused by this word some ones do not burn the dead body of a **Sanyasi** and **Sanyasis** do not touch the fire. This is the sin which clings to sanyasis. Here the word **Anagni** stand to mean that **Ahavaniya** etc. fires should not be enkindled by a **Sanyasi** but it is here never meant that the touch of **Agni** and burning of dead body be abandoned.

He should have removed the hair of head, beard, moustaches and nails from time to time. He should have pot, stick and put on the clothes coloured in *Kusumbha**. Never inflicting pain on any creature he being firm in his spirit should always walk from place to place. 10.

That Anchorite who controlls his organs from being observed in bad things and habits destroys the evils of attachment and aversion, does the good of all the creatures without any feeling of enmity, attains emancipation. 11.

It is proper for an anchorite that he should always follow or translate into action the principle of Dharma in sprite of being blamed and dis-respected by foolish men. The same code of conduct should be adhered to by the persons of *Brahmacharya* etc. The procedure laid down for *Sanyasashram* is meant only for the purpose of doing good of all the living creatures developing and preserving a sence of equal understanding in all of them without any partiality. But it should be borne in mind that only having the signs like stick etc. is not *dharma*.

The seed *Nirmali* plant cleans the water but the craming of only its name is not sufficient to clean the water. To bring it, to powder it and to drop it into water is required to make the water clean. In the same manner the acceptance of *Ashramas* only by name does not serve any purpose. The success of accepting *Ashramas* lies in the translation of *dharma* into action and not otherwise. 13.

To make this sanctimonious *Ashrama* a success if a *Sanyasi* perform at least three *Pranayamas* according to the procedure of *yoga* adding seven *Pranavas* (ओम) prior to seven *Vyahritis*, as the *Pranayama mantra* has been mentioned in the *Grihastha Ashrama* and reciting the same, his performance should be taken as excellent austirity. 14.

Because as the dirty matter of metals is cast away from it

*Should wear clothes coloured in Gairik colour.

by heating the metal on fire so the dirty matters of the organs flee away from them through the control of vital breath. 15.

Therefore, it is proper for the *Sanyasis* that they restore in them the impartiality etc. qualities of Divine and burn out all the evils, leaving out the defects through *Pranayam*, the dirt of conscience through *Dharmas*, the defects caused by attachment and absorption in the enternal and external objects and the evils and infirmities caused by ignorance, partiality etc. and infidelity. 16.

Let an anchorite see through the *yoga* of thorough meditotion the movement i.e. the pervasiveness of God who is controlling everything from their within and without and who pervading small creatures, non-living creatures is not seen by the person who are impure in their spirt. 17.

An anchorite who has attained the ture knowledge or the philosophy of the six schools of philosophy never absorves in the evil avts. And the man who even being deprived of knowledge, education, practice of *yoga*, good company, the observance of religious rites and the knowledge of six schools of philosophy, does not attain the real denomination of a *Sanyasi* and emancipation, he comes to the world which is aimed at the birth and death. For such a foolish irreligious men the acceptance of *Sanyasa* is of no use and he deserves all sorts of discards. 18.

The *Sanyasis* who are free from enmity, the absorption in the objects of organs and are quite concerned with vedic piety, *Pranayama.* truth-speaking etc. good actions, may attain the realm of the attainment of God in this life and even in the present. The acceptance of *Sanyasa* by such persons is successful and they are worthy of all thanks. 19.

When a *Sanyasi* become free of this own greed for the worldly objects and thus becoming greedless, enjoys happiness till the

---

*Here the term 'निरन्तर' stands merely to devote that the unhappiness cannot interrupt the enjoyment of happiness in the fixed period of emancipation.

Here the term अनन्त stands to mean only this that the happiness to be enjoyed in emancipation has no end in the time of emancipation.

period* fixed for it in emancipation which is ultramundane attaining God therein and completing the string of this world, this birth and death. 20.

By this method the learned anchorite renouncing all the evils, of attachment by and by an specially becoming free from pleasure, sadness etc. duals of mental modifications makes him firm in *Brahman*. 21.

The man who only desiring to know reality behind the worldly scene and this *Ashram* accepts this *Sanyasashram* is secondary choice, should also practise to seek knowledge, good company of learned men, practice of yoga, recitation of Om syllabus and thorough consideration over its meaning. He is the only shelter of ignorant, i.e. of the *sanyasis* of secondary order, learned *Sanyasis* the seeker of pleasure and those desirous to attain endless happiness. 22.

Through this method of *Sanyasyoga* the *Dvija*, i.e. the *Brahman Kshatriya Vaishya*, who accepts the disciplines of *Sanyasa*, attains the Supreme God even in this world and in this life leaving out all the evils and absurdities. 23.

Procedure

The man who desires to be initiated to *Sanyasa* should, on the very day when he feels pleasure, after observing rules and vows i.e. three days fast with only drinking of milk, sleeping on the ground, *Pranayamo*, premeditation and recitation of syllabus Om in the lonely place, arrange one day before *Subha-mandapa Vedi, Samidha, Ghrita* etc. articles according to the procedure deseribed in the *Samanyaprakarana.* On the foruth day (i.e. the day of his pleasure and choice for taking *Sanyasa)* he should do *Pranayama*, meditation of God, recitation of Om rising two and half hours earlier before morning doing all the daily necessities and bath etc. At the time of sun-rising he should select and employ the righteous, learned men who are good house-holders as *yajna*-priests and thereafter the procedure of *Agnyadhane, Samidaohana*, heating of *ghee, Sthalipaka, Svastivachane, Shanti karan*, sprinkling of water around the *Vedi*, four *Agharavajya*-

bhagahuti and four *Vyahriti Ahuti* be performed. Thereafter the eleven oblations of *ghee* with the following *mantras* one with each be given :

ओं भुवनपतये स्वाहा ॥ १ ॥ ओं भूतानां पतये स्वाहा ॥ २ ॥

[यजु० अ० २ । मं०···२]

ओं प्रजापतये स्वाहा ॥ ३ ॥ [यजु० अ० १८ । मं० २८]

May I attain God who is the master of the worlds. Whatever has been uttered herein is true. 1.

May I attain God who is the master of all creatures. Whatever has been uttered herein is true. 2.

May I attain the Lord of all the worldly subjects. Whatever been uttered herein is true. 3.

The *yajmana*, who is going to take *Sanyasa* and two priests of the *yajna* should pour *ghee* on the boiled rice prepared previously and should offer the oblations of this boiled rice with the following *Mantras* adding *Svaha* in the end of them and the remaining two priests also offer the oblations with them :—

ओं ब्रह्म होता ब्रह्म यज्ञो ब्रह्मणा स्वरवो मिताः ।
अध्वर्युर्ब्रह्मणो जातो ब्रह्मणोऽन्तर्हितं हविः स्वाहा ॥ १ ॥

ब्रह्म स्रुचो घृतवतीर्ब्रह्मणा वेदिरुद्धिता । ब्रह्म यज्ञश्च सत्रं च ऋत्विजो ये हविष्कृतः । शमिताय स्वाहा ॥ २ ॥

अंहोमुच प्रभरे मनीषामा सुत्राव्णे सुमतिमावृणानः । इमामिन्द्र प्रति हव्यं गभाय सत्यास्सन्तु यजमानस्य कामाः स्वाहा ॥ ३ ॥

अंहोमुचे वृषभं यज्ञियानां विराजन्तं प्रथममध्वराणाम् । अपां नपातमश्विना हुवे धियेन्द्रेण म इन्द्रियं दत्तमोजः स्वाहा ॥ ४ ॥

यत्र ब्रह्मविदो यान्ति दीक्षया तपसा सह । अग्निर्मा तत्र नयत्वग्निर्मेधां दधातु मे । अग्नये स्वाहा ॥ इदमग्नये-इदन्न मम ॥ ५ ॥

यत्र० । वायुर्मा यत्र नयतु वायुः प्राणान् दधातु मे । वायवे स्वाहा ॥ इदं वायवे-इदन्न मम ॥ ६ ॥

यत्र० । सूर्यो मा तत्र नयतु चक्षुः सूर्यो दधातु मे । सूर्याय स्वाहा ॥ इदं सूर्याय-इदन्न मम ॥ ७ ॥

यत्र० । चन्द्रो मा तत्र नयतु मनश्चन्द्रो दधातु मे । चन्द्राय स्वाहा ॥ इदं चन्द्राय-इदन्न मम ॥ ८ ॥

यत्र० । सोमा मा तत्र नयतु पयः सोमो दधातु मे । सोमाय स्वाहा ॥ इदं सोमाय-इदन्न मम ॥ ९ ॥

यत्र० । इन्द्रो मा तत्र नयतु बलमिन्द्रो दधातु मे । इन्द्राय स्वाहा ॥ इद मिन्द्राय-इदन्न मम ॥ १० ॥

यत्र० । आपो मा तत्र नयन्त्वमृतं मोप तिष्ठतु । अद्भ्यः स्वाहा ॥ इद-मद्भ्यः-इदन्न मम ॥ ११ ॥

यत्र ब्रह्मविदो यान्ति दीक्षया तपसा सह । ब्रह्मा मा तत्र नयतु ब्रह्मा ब्रह्म दधातु मे । ब्रह्मणे स्वाहा । इदं ब्रह्मणे इदन्न मम ॥ १२ ॥

अथर्ववं कां० १९ । सू० ४२ । [तथा] सू० ४३ ॥

ओं प्राणापानव्यानोदानसमाना मे शुध्यन्ताम् ।

ज्योतिरहं विरजा विपाप्मा भूयासं स्वाहा ॥ १ ॥

वाङ् मनश्चक्षुः श्रोत्रजिह्वाघ्राणरेतोबुद्ध्याकूतिसंकल्पा मे शुध्यंताम्

ज्योतिरहं विरजा विपाप्मा भूयासं स्वाहा ॥ २ ॥

शिरः पाणिपादपार्श्वपृष्ठोरूदरजंघाशिश्नोपस्थपायवो मे शुध्यन्ताम् ।

ज्योति० ॥ ३ ॥

त्वक्चर्ममांससरुधिरमेदोमज्जास्नायवोऽस्थीनि मे शुध्यन्ताम् ।

ज्योति० ॥ ४ ॥

शब्दस्पर्शरूपरसगन्धा मे शुध्यन्ताम् । ज्योति० ॥ ५ ॥

पृथिव्यप्तेजोवायोराकाशा मे शुध्यन्ताम् । ज्योति० ॥ ६ ॥

अन्नमयप्राणमयमनोमयविज्ञानमयानन्दमया मे शुध्यन्ताम् ।

ज्योति० ॥ ७ ॥

विविस्ट्यै स्वाहा ॥ ८ ॥ कषोत्काय स्वाहा ॥ ९ ॥

उत्तष्ठि पुरुष हरित, लोहित पिङ्गलाक्षि वेहि देहि ददापयिता मे शुध्यन्ताम् ज्योति० ॥ १० ॥

ओं स्वाहा मनोवाक्कायकर्माणि मे शुध्यतान् । ज्योति० ॥ ११ ॥

अव्यक्तभावैरहङ्कारैंज्योति० ॥ १२ ॥

आत्मा मे शुध्यताम् ज्योति० ॥ १३ ॥

अन्तरात्मा मे शुध्यताम् । ज्योति० ॥ १४ ॥

परमात्मा मे शुध्यताम् । ज्योतिरहं विरजा विपाप्मा भूयासं स्वाहा* ॥ १५ ॥

By the *Veda* the nature of *Hotar* priest is defined, by the *Veda* the procedure of *yajna* is decided, by the *Veda* are described the method of *yajna*-poles, the *Adhvaiya* is appointed by the *Veda* the oblations etc. of *yajna* are described and prescribed in the *Vedas.* 1.

The *Veda* describes the method of spoon to drop *ghrita* oblations, the method of *Vedi* has been also described in the *Veda*, the big and small *yajnas* are described in the *Vedas*, the *yajna* priests have been also mentioned in the *Vedas.* and all this is meant for attaining peace. Whatever has been utterred herein is true. 2.

O almighty God ! in the performance of *yajnas* I fix and concentrate my intellect in Thee who is free from all defects and evils and protector of all. I chosing to have a good intellect obey

---

*This has been instructed to a **Sanyasi** in the **Mantras** beginning with **Pranapana** etc. and ending at **Parmatma** me **Shudhyatim** etc. that the men entering into **Sanyas** should strictly practice rules of **dharma**, true preaching, practice of **yoga** and possess the good qualties, acts and nature of satisfaction controll, peace. good characteristics etc. science and education, and meditate God knowing Him as his helper. They should with great effort control his mind, organs etc. from indulging in bad acts and employ them in good acts which are free from partiality, deception, cheating, irreligious dealings and should make others free from evils by giving proper education and instructions and should enjoy pleasure himself and extend it to others also.

the command to possess the spiritual wealth of this world and by *Thy* grace may all our desires be fulfiled. Whatever...true. 3

O teacher and preacher ! I pray with wisdom and action. God who is the giver of all the things of *yajna*, who is the main and first object of all the *yajnas* and is the protector of all the worldly objects. The almighty God has granted me vigour of organic quality. 4.

May self-refulgent God take me to that realm where go the knowers of Supreme Spirit with celebrated knowledge and austerity. May self-refulgent God grant me the wisdom. Whatever has been uttered herein is for obeying the command of *Agni*. The oblation offered is to obey the command of *Agni* and it is not for me. 5.

May the all-impelling God take me to the realm where go the knowers of supreme spirit with celebrated knowledge and austerity. May all-impelling God grant us vital energy. Whatever has been uttered herein is for obeying the command of All-impelling God. The oblation offered is meant to obey the command of *Vayu* and if is not for me. 6.

May the All-illuminating God take me to the realm where go the knowers of supreme spirit with celebrated knowledge and austerity. May all-illuminating God grant power of sight to my eyes. Whatever has been uttered herein is for obeying the command of all-illuminating God. The oblation offered herein is meant to obey the comment of all-illuminating God and it is not for me. 7.

May All-blissful Being, take me to the realm where go the knowers of supreme spirit with celebrated knowledge and austerity. May All-blissful Being make my mind hale and discriminate. Whatever has been uttered herein is for obeying the command of All-illuminating God. The oblation offered herein is meant to obey the command of All-illuminating God and it is not for me. 8.

May all-creating God take me to the realm where go the

knowers of supreme spirit with celebrated knowledge and austerity. May All-creating God keep watery substances of our body intact. Whatever has been uttered herein is for obeying the command of All-creating God. The oblation offered here are meant to obey the command of God and it is not for me. 9.

May the Almighty God take me to the realm where go knowers of supreme spirity. May Almighty God grant me strength. Whatever has been uttered herein is for obeying the command of Almighty God. The oblation offered is meant to obey the command of Almighty God and it is not for me. 10.

May the All-pervading God take me to the realm where go the knowers of supreme spirit with celebrated knowledge and austerity. May All pervading God make me immortal. Whatever has been uttered here is for obeying the command of All-pervading God. The oblation offered herein is meant to obey the command of All-pervading God and it is not for me. 11.

May the supernal being take me to the realm where go the knowers of Supreme Spirit with celebrated knowledge and austerity. May the Supernal Being grant me the knowledge of the *Veda*. Whatever has been uttered herein is for obeying the command of Supernal Being. The oblation offered is meant to obey the Command of Supernal Being and it is not for me. 12.

May my vital airs named as *Prana*, *apana*, *Samana*, *vyana* and *udana* be free from all sorts of impurities. May I attain highest light and become free from defects and free from sins and evils. Whatever has been uttered herein is true. 1.

May my organ of speech, mind, eyes, ears, tongue, nose, semen, intellect, resolution, become free from all sorts of impurities and be active. 2...........

May my head, hands, feet, sides, back, belt, abdomen, thighs falum, rectum be free all sorts of impurities......3.

May my skin, thick skin, flesh, blood, fat, marrow, nerves and bones become free from all sorts of impurities........4.

May my sound, touch, colour, taste and smell became free from all sorts of impurities.........5.

May the elements like earth, water, air, fire and ether forming my body become free from all sorts of impurities......6.

May the five sheaths of my body named as *annamaya, pranamaya*, *manomaya*, *Vijnanmaya* and *Anandmaya* become free from all sorts of impurities.........7.

May I know the nature of pervasiveness with which the pervading substances are endowed. 8.

May I know the name, from and action of the worldly and ultramundane objects.

O human spint ! you rtse above all this world obstacles as you are accompanied by *Sattva Rajas* and *tamas* elements of material cause. You give up all the things and resign. May the giver of knowledge become free from all the doubts...10.

May my mind, organ of speech, body and its activities be come free from all sorts of impurites......11.

May my intellect which is accompanied by unmahifesed resolution and egoestic tendencies become free from all sorts of impurities.........12.

May my soul be free from.........13.

May my conscience be free from all sorts of impurities......—14.

May God, the Super Soul within and without my self be distinct for me.........15.

Thereatter, the oblation of *ghee* be offered with the following *Mantras* :—

ओमग्नये स्वाहा ॥ १६ ॥ ओं विश्वेभ्यो देवेभ्य: स्वाहा ॥ १७ ॥

ओं ध्रुवाय भूमाय स्वाहा ॥ १८ ॥ ओं ध्रुवक्षितये स्वाहा ॥ १९ ॥

ओमच्युतक्षितये स्वाहा ॥ २० ॥

ओमग्नये स्विष्टकृते स्वाहा ॥ २१ ॥

ओं धर्माय स्वाहा ॥ २२ ॥ ओमधर्माय स्वाहा ॥ २३ ॥

श्रोमद्भ्यः स्वाहा ॥ २४ ॥ ओमोषधिवनस्पतिभ्यः स्वाहा ॥ २५ ॥
ओं रक्षोदेवजनेभ्यः स्वाहा ॥ २६ ॥ श्रों गृह्याभ्यः स्वाहा ॥ २७ ॥
श्रोमवसानेभ्यः स्वाहा ॥ २८ ॥ ओमवसानपतिभ्यः स्वाहा ॥ २९ ॥
ओं सर्वभूतेभ्यः स्वाहा ॥ ३० ॥ श्रों कामाय स्वाहा ॥ ३१ ॥
श्रोमन्तरिक्षाय स्वाहा ॥ ३२ ॥ श्रों पृथिव्यै स्वाहा ॥ ३३ ॥
श्रों दिवे स्वाहा ॥ ३४ ॥ ओं सूर्याय स्वाहा ॥ ३५ ॥
श्रों चन्द्रमसे स्वाहा ॥ ३६ ॥ श्रों नक्षत्रेभ्यः स्वाहा ॥ ३७ ॥
श्रोमिन्द्राय स्वाहा ॥ ३८ ॥ श्रों बृहस्पतये स्वाहा ॥ ३९ ॥
श्रों प्रजापतये स्वाहा ॥ ४० ॥ श्रों ब्रह्मणे स्वाहा ॥ ४१ ॥
ओं देवेभ्यः स्वाहा ॥ ४२ ॥ श्रों परमेष्ठिने स्वाहा ॥ ४३ ॥
श्रों तद्ब्रह्म ॥ ४४ ॥ श्रों तद्वायुः ॥ ४५ ॥
श्रों तदात्मा ॥ ४६ ॥ श्रों तत्सत्यम् ॥ ४७ ॥
ओं तत्सर्वम् ॥ ४७ ॥ तत्पुरोनमः ॥ ४९ ॥

अन्तश्चरति भूतेषु गुहायां विश्वमूर्तिषु । त्वं यज्ञस्त्वं वषट्कारस्त्वमिन्द्रस्त्वं रुद्रस्त्वं विष्णुस्त्वं ब्रह्म त्वं प्रजापतिः । त्वं तदाप श्रापो ज्योती रसोऽमृतं ब्रह्म भूर्भुवः स्वरों स्वाहा* ॥ ५० ॥

May I be able to attain the knowledge of fire, other, physical or spritual forces the region above. *Achyutkshiti*, *Dhruvakshiti*, *svistakrit Agni* etc. described in *mantras* from श्रोमग्नये स्वाहा to तत्पुरोनमः ।

O God ! thou art pervading all the sorms, all the creatures and in the recess of heart of all the men. Thou art known by the names of *Yajna*, *Vashatkara*, *India*, *Rudra*, *Vishnu*, *Brahman*: *Prajapati*, *Apah*, *Apojyotih*, *Rasa*, *Amrita*, *Brahma*, *Om*, *Bhuh*, *Bhuvah* and *Svah*.

After having offered the oblation of *ghee* with these fifty *mantras* mentioned above, the man going to accept *Sanyasa* get shaved the beard, moustache. hair i.e., performing complete shaving leaving only five or six small shoots without being shaved, should take bath.

Afterwards he should sprinkle and pour water on his head one hundred eight times with the *Mantras* of *Pursha Sukta*. Thereafter according to the procedure prescribed in *Grihastha ashrame*, he performing *Achamane* and *Pranayama*, keeping his eyes shut with folded hand, should offer four oblations, in mind, with the following four *Mantras* :—

ओं ब्रह्मणे नमः ॥ १ ॥ श्रोमिन्द्राय नमः ॥ २ ॥

ओं सूर्याय नमः ॥ ३ ॥ श्रों सोमाय नमः ॥ ४ ॥

श्रोमात्मने नमः ॥ ५ ॥ श्रोमन्तरात्मने नमः ॥ ६ ॥

इन छः मन्त्रों को जप के—

ओमात्मने स्वाहा ॥ १ ॥ श्रोमन्तरात्मने स्वाहा ॥ २ ॥

श्रों परमात्मने स्वाहा ॥ ३ ॥ श्रो प्रजापतये स्वाहा ॥ ४ ॥

All these are the names of God.

Afterwards the person going to take *Sanyasa* should perfrom the procedure of *Madhuparka* and thereafter doing *Pranayama* should recite the following *Mantras* in his mind:—

श्रों भूः सावित्रीं प्रविशामि तत्सवितुर्वरेण्यम् ॥ १ ॥

ओं भुवः सावित्रीं प्रविशामि भर्गो देवस्य धीमहि ॥ २ ॥

श्रों स्वः सावित्रीं प्रविशामि धियो यो नः प्रचोदयात् ॥ ३ ॥

श्रों भूर्भुवः स्वः सावित्रीं प्रविशामि तत्सवितुर्वरेण्यं भर्गो देवस्य धीमहि-धियो यो नः प्रचोदयात् ॥ ४ ॥

The oblations of *ghee* be offered in the *Vedi* with the following *Mantras* :—

श्रोमग्नये स्वाहा ॥ १ ॥ श्रों भूः प्रजापतये स्वाहा ॥ २ ॥

श्रोमिन्द्राय स्वाहा ॥ ३ ॥ श्रों प्रजापतये स्वाहा ॥ ४ ॥

श्रों विश्वेभ्यो देवेभ्यः स्वाहा—५—श्रों ब्रह्मण स्वाहा—६—

श्रों प्राणाय स्वाहा ॥ ७ ॥ श्रोमपानाय स्वाहा ॥ ८ ॥

श्रों व्यानाय स्वाहा ॥ ९ ॥ श्रोमुदानाय स्वाहा ॥ १० ॥

श्रों समानाय स्वाहा ॥ ११ ॥

These are the names of God as well as of the physical and spritual objects :—

He should offer the oblation of completion with the following *Mantras* :—

श्रों भूः स्वाहा—

Pronouncing the following sentences the man going to take *Sanyasa* should drop water on the ground before all present :—

पुत्रैषणायाश्च वित्तैषणायाश्च लोकैषणायाश्चोत्थायाथ भिक्षाचर्यं चरन्ति* ॥ श० कां० १४ [६-४१]

पुत्रैषणा वित्तैषणा लोकैषणा मया परित्यक्ता मत्तः सर्वभूतेभ्योऽभयमस्तु स्वाहा*—

Afterwards he standing in the naval-deep water, keeping his face eastward, meditating God and pronouncing the *Mantras*—पुत्रैषणायाश्च ० etc. should recite the following *Mantras* in his mind:—

ओं भूः सावित्रीं प्रविशामि तत्सवितुर्वरेण्यम् ॥

ओं भुवः सावित्रीं प्रविशामि भर्गो देवस्य धीमहि ॥

ओं स्वः सावित्रीं प्रविशामि धियो यो नः प्रचोदयात् ॥

ओं भूर्भुवः स्वः सावित्रीं प्रविशामि परो रजसे सावदोम् ॥

Thereafter he pronounce the following *Mantras* in mind:—

ओं भूः संन्यस्तं मया ॥ ओं भुवः संन्यस्तं मया ॥

ओं स्वः संन्यस्तं मया ॥

O All-protecting Self-existent God I have now renounced all the worldly attachments. O All-protecting most vitol power ! I have now renounced all the worldly attachments. O All-protecting, All-blissful God ! I have now renounced all the worldly attachments.

Afterwards the man being initated to *Sanyasa* filling his both hand-full with water, standing with his face kept eastward

---

*The **Sanyasis** who, rising above the desire of sons etc,. desire for wealth and desire for fame and withdrawing their minds from them and making their mind firm in God beg for living, give all the persons freedom from fear through their true preachings, i.e. He says "I, taking the water in my right hand palm have renounced the desire to sons etc., wealth etc., and fame from today. May all the creatures be fearless from me and this is my true word.

should drop the water in the east direction with the following *Mantra*—

ओं अभयं सर्वभूतेभ्यो मत्तः स्वाहा ॥

Let there be fearlessness for all from me.

Afterwards he should keep quiet and think the meaning of the follwing. *Mantra* as well as the meaning of *Shloka* from the *Manusmriti* :—

येना सहस्त्रं वहसि येनाग्ने सर्ववेदसम् ।
तेनेमं यज्ञं नो वह स्वर्देवेषु गन्तवे* ॥

अ० कां० ६ । सू० ५ । मं० १७ ।

This is the *Smriti* on the *Mantra.*

प्राजापत्यां निरूप्येष्टि सर्ववेदसदक्षिणाम् ।
आत्मन्यग्नीन् समारोप्य ब्राह्मणः प्रव्रजेद् गृहात् ॥

मनु० (अ० ६ । श्लो० ३८)

Its meaning has been given before.

O learned person ! as the fire holds all the objects of the world, as you accept the house-hold life, desire for worldly things, sacred thread, tuft etc. so you leave all this and may thereby I lead this *Sanyasashrama* with happiness to have and enjoy the company of the learned men and anchorites.

Thereafter he should take away one by one the five or seven shoots of the hair previously kept safe for the purpose of tuft, and taking the sacred thread in his hand from the body and filling the hands-full with water should throw out the hair, sacred thread with the water of *Ajali* in water with the following *Mantra.*

ओमापो वै सर्वा देवताः स्वाहा ॥ १ ॥ ओं भूः स्वाहा ॥ २ ॥

The waters are conducive to all physical elements. May I know the earth and God.

Thereafter the *Acharya* taking his disciple (the man accepting *Sanyasa*) out from the water, should give him the *Kaupin* (कौपीन) *Kativastra* (कटिवस्त्र) *Upavastra* (उपवस्त्र) and one *Angochha* (अंगोछा) with affection. The man taking *Sanyasa* should pronounce यो मे दन्ड:० etc., *Mantra* and take stick in his hand and then hold the idea of the *Ahavaniya* etc., fires of *yajnas* in his soul surrendering the materialization of their external and ritual performance i.e. he should spritualize them instead of their materialization. In spiritualizing fires to his inner-self he should think the meanings of these *mantras*:—

यो विद्याद् ब्रह्म प्रत्यक्षं परूंषि यस्य संभारा ऋचो यस्यानूक्यऽम् । १ ।

सामानि यस्य लोमानि यजुर्हृदयमुच्यते परिस्तरणमिद्धविः । २ ।

यद्वा अतिथिपतिरतिथीन् प्रतिपश्यति देवयजनं प्रेक्षते ॥ ३ ॥

यदभिवदति दीक्षामुपैति यदुदकं याचत्यपः प्रणयति ॥ ४ ॥

या एव यज्ञ आपः प्रणीयन्ते ता एव ताः ॥ ५ ॥

यदावसथान् कल्पयन्ति सदो हविर्धानान्येव तत्कल्पयन्ति ॥ ६ ॥

यदुपस्तृणन्ति बर्हिरेव तत् ॥ ७ ॥

तेषामासन्नानामतिथिरात्मन् जुहोति ॥ ८ ॥

स्रुचा हस्तेन प्राणे यूपे स्रुक्करेण वशट्करेण ॥ ९ ॥

एते वै प्रियाश्चाप्रियाश्चर्त्विजः स्वर्गं लोकं गनयन्ति यदतिथयः ॥ १० ॥

प्राजापत्यो वा एतस्य यज्ञो विततो य उपहरति ॥ ११ ॥

प्रजापतेर्वा एष विक्रमाननुविक्रमते य उपहरति ॥ १२ ॥

योऽतिथीनां स आहवनीयो यो वेश्मनि स गार्हपत्यो यस्मिन् पचन्ति स दक्षिणाग्निः ॥ १३ ॥

इष्टं च वा एष पूर्तं च गृहाणामश्नाति यः पूर्वोऽतिथेरश्नाति ॥ १४ ॥

अथर्व० कां० ९ । सू० ६ [(१) १—५, ७, ८, (२) ४—६, ११, १३ (३) १] ॥

The man who is able to know Supreme Being, whose strict nature etc., are to be treated as the utensils of *Homa*, whose truth-speaking and truth-preaching and *Rigveda* are to be treated as the words of him, should enter into the *Ashrama* of *Sanyasa*.

The man, the *samans* are treated to be whose hair, *yajur-veda* treated to be whose heart, and the seat, scriptures and other things are treated to be whose utensils of *Homa*, should take *Sanyasa*-2

Only the learned man, who serves the guests, and who sees guests with respectful eagerness, may enjoy the company of learned men as he is able to see them with respect-3.

When such a *Sanayasin* holds confabulation with others or pays his obeisance to other, he really accepts *Diksha*, the admittance, when he asks for water he, as if, drops water in the *Pranita* etc., *yajna* pots-4.

The waters which are used in the procedure of *yajna* are as if the performance of *Sanyasin* which takes place for such procedures. 5.

Whatever residential quarters a *Sanyasin* makes are choses for him are known as if the place of *yajna* and pots for keeping the *havis*. 6.

Whatever bidding etc., a *Sanyasi* makes for him is as if the shoot of *Kusha* in the *Yajna*. 7.

The guest who visits without fixed date when eats food and drinks juiceitic before the persons sitting there, as if offer oblations in the internal spiritual self in the form of offering oblation in the fire of the *Vedi*. 8.

Whatever oblations a *Sanaysin* offers with the spoon held in his hand are known as if the animals tied in the *yajana* posts and are treated to be binding of organs in and mind with vital air through the medium of spoon used for the performance of *Homa*, 9.

As these desired or not even desire *Sanyasins* come to a house-holders' house at various occasions like guest, so they increase the happiness of the house-holder. 10.

Real *Sanyasin* is exclusively he whose duties and effort to attain the Lord of the creatures are comprehensive like a *yajna* and who gives them to-most place. 11.

The *Sanyasin* who conveniently follows the duties of the *Sanyasashrama* which is the only *Ashrama* to attain God and Him, accepts all the good qualities. 12.

The good company of the pious *Sanyasin*, is the *Ahavaniya* for such a real *Sanyasi*, living in the house is *Garhapatya* and the digestion of food in the fire of digestion system is *Dakshinagni*. In this way he spiritualizes all these *Agnis*. 13.

The house-holder who takes his meal before giving it to a *Sanyasi* eats all his desired happiness and all his accomplishments attainable in the house-hold life. Therefore, it is obligatory for a house·holder that he take his food after serving food to guest. 14,

*तस्यैवं विदुषो यज्ञस्यात्मा यजमान., श्रद्धा पत्नी, शरीरमिध्ममुरो वेदिर्लोमानि बर्हिर्वेदः शिखा, हृदयं यूपः, काम आज्यं, मन्युः पशुस्तपोऽग्निर्दमः शमयिता, दक्षिणा वाग्घोता प्राण, उद्गाता चक्षुरध्वयुर्मनो, ब्रह्मा श्रोत्रमग्नीत्। यावद् ध्रियते सा दीक्षा, यदश्नाति तद्धविर्यत्पिबति तदस्य सोमपानं, यद्रमते तदुपसदो, यत्सञ्चरत्युपबिशत्युत्तिष्ठते च स प्रवर्ग्यो, यन्मुखं तदाहवनीयो, या व्याहृतिराहुतिर्यदस्य विज्ञानं तज्जुहोति, यत्सायं प्रातरत्ति तत्समिधं, यत्प्रातर्मध्यन्दिनं सायं च तानि सवनानि। ये अहोरात्रे ते दर्शपौर्णमासौ, येऽर्द्धमासाश्च ते चातुर्मास्यानि, य ऋतवस्ते पशुबन्धा, ये संवत्सराश्च परिवत्सराश्च तेऽह्र्गणाः, सर्ववेदसं वा एतत्सत्रं, यन्मरणं तदवभृथः, एतद्वै जरामर्यमग्निहोत्रं सत्रं, य एवं विद्वानुदगयने प्रमीयते देवानामेव महिमानं गत्वाऽऽदित्यस्य सायुज्यं गच्छत्यथ यो दक्षिणे प्रमीयते पितृणामेव महिमानं गत्वा चन्द्रमसः सायुज्यं सलोकतामाप्नोत्येतौ वै सूर्योचन्द्रमसोर्महिमानौ ब्राह्मणो विद्वानभिजयति, तस्माद् ब्रह्मणो महिमानमाप्नोतिः तस्माद् ब्रह्मणो महिमानमित्युपनिषत्॥ तैत्ति० प्रपा० १०। अनु० ६४॥

Hence forward we give the meaning of *Taittriya Aranyaka*—

The spirit of the learned man who has thus accepted

Sanyasa is attributed to be as the *yajmana*, his falth that is the iove for establishing truth, right piety and altruistic attitude is attributed to be as *Patni* the wife; his body as fuel; breast as *Vedi*, hair as *kushas*; his knowledge of the *vedas* and the practice of the tenets tuft; his heard *yajna* post; his desire as *ghee*; his anger as animal his austerity including the practice of real codes of religion. *Pranayama*, *yoga* as *Agni* the fire; his restraint over his organs from evil conduct and employment of them in good conduct with constancy as *Shamayita*, who gives punishment to wicked, his speech as the gift of fearlessness to others; his vital air as *hotar*; his eys as *udgatar*, his mind as *Adhvaryu*; his ear as *Brahman* and *Agnidhra*; who fetches fire; whatever he accept is attributed to be as the acceptance of *Diksha*; whatever he eats as *Havi* the ghee etc; whatever water, milk etc. he drinks as drinking of *Soma*-juice; whatever he walks here and there as *upasad*; whatever he does as walking, sitting and standing as *Pravargya* his mouth as *Ahavaniya*; his pronouncement of *Vyahritis* or his grasping of science of offering oblation as performance of *Homa*; whatever he eats in morning and evening is attributed to be as the fuels of the fire of *yajna*; his morning, meridian and evening work as three *savanas* of *yajna*; his night and days are trated as *Darsha* and *Purnamasa*, his half months and months as *Chaturmasya*; his seasons as *Pashubandha*, *samvatsar* and *Parivatsara* as his *Ahargana*, that is the *Vrata* of night of three night: *serva vedas*, i.e. the renouncement of tuft, sacred thread and previous *ashramas* as *satra*; his death as *Avabhritha*; for a *sanyasin*. This is the *yajna* which has its extension till old age and death in the form of preaching of truth and practice of *yoga* which he has to continue till throughout his life. The learned who accepting *sanyasa* leaves his body after having attained the knowledge and practiee of *yoga* securing the greatness of learned men, attains God who is self-refulgent. The person who is deprived of the science of *yoga* dies in *Dakshnianyana* sphere of worldly nature. He, always attain rise and fading like the phases of moon, securing the father and mother again and again. The learned *sanyasi* who over-come these two kinds greatness, having attained the contact of God enjoys the happiness of salvation till the period fixed for it,

Further authorities on the subject

*न्यास इत्याहुर्मुनीषिणो ब्रह्माणम् । ब्रह्मा विश्वः कतमः स्वयम्भूः प्रजापतिः संवत्सर इति । संवत्सरोऽसावादित्यो य एष आदित्ये पुरुषः स परमेष्ठी ब्रह्मात्मा । याभिरादित्यस्तपति रश्मिभिस्ताभिः पर्जन्यो वर्षति, पर्जन्येनौषधिवनस्पयः प्रजायन्त ओषधिवनस्पतिभिरन्नं भवत्यन्नेन प्राणाः प्राणैर्बलं बलेन तपस्तपसा श्रद्धा श्रद्धाया मेधा मेधाया मनीषा मनीषाया मनो मनसा शान्तिः शान्त्या चित्तं चित्तेन स्मृतिं स्मृत्या स्मारं स्मारेण विज्ञानं विज्ञानेनात्मानं वेदयति, तस्मादन्नं ददन्त्सर्वाण्येतानि ददात्यन्नात् प्राणा भवन्ति भूतानां प्राणैर्मनो मनसश्च विज्ञानं विज्ञानादानन्दो ब्रह्मयोनिः । स वा एष पुरुषः पञ्चधा पञ्चात्मा येन सर्वमिदं प्रोतं पृथिवी चान्तरिक्षं च द्यौश्च दिशश्चावान्तरदिशश्च स वै सर्वमिदं जगत् स भूतं स भव्यं जिज्ञासक्लृप्त ऋतजा रयिष्ठाः श्रद्धा सत्यो महस्वांस्तमसो वरिष्ठात् । ज्ञात्वा तमेवं मनसा हृदा च भूयो न मृत्युमुपयाहि विद्वान् । तस्मान् न्यासमेषां तपसामतिरिक्तमाहुः । वसुरण्वो विभूरसि प्राणे त्वमसि सन्धाता ब्रह्मंस्त्वमसि विश्वसृत्तेजोदास्त्वमस्यग्नेरसि वर्चोदास्त्वमसि सूर्यस्य द्युम्नोदास्त्वमसि चन्द्रमस उपयामगृहीतोऽसि ब्रह्मणे त्वा महसे । ओमित्यात्मानं युञ्जीत । एतद्वै महोपनिषदं देवानां गुह्यम् । य एवं वेद ब्रह्मणो महिमानमाप्नोति तस्माद् ब्रह्मणो महिमानमित्युपनिषत् ॥ तैत्ति० प्रपा १० अनु० ६३ ॥

Since the meaning of this *Anuvak* is easy, therefore, here we give the purport of the piece only. The anchorite who accepts *sanyasa* with the method of true meaning of the *sanyasa* described by us previously becomes the devotee of God.

God is infinite and pervading the sun etc., worlds and by His grandeur and grace the sun shines. By this shining comes rain, from rain grow luxuriantly the herbs and trees, therefrom product of grain, from grain or food are produced vitality, from vitality the strength and vigour, thereform comes into existence the austerity, i.e., *Pranayama*, practice of *yoga* and from, them in their turn come out faith, the desire of embracing truth, thence come out intellect, descrimination comes out therefrom, then comes knowledge, from it rises up the tendency of knowledge, from it comes out peace, from peace come out consciousness, from consciouness rises rememberance, from rememberance grows up the knowledge of priority and posterity and even from it rises the tendency of science of God and through it the anchorite knows his spirit and also make others know it. Therefore, giving of cerials is excellent as vitality, strength and science of spirituality come out from it. God is the vital force of all from whom all this universe has been pervaded. He is the creater of all the worlds and he created the world in previous cycle and would create it afterwards also. O anchorite ! you developing acute desire to know Him attain His knowledge and do not die and take birth again and again but attain great happiness having freed yourself from the bondage, Therefore the *Sanyasa* has been celled the austerity of all austerities and excellent among all of them. O God ! Thou art omnipresent as thou pervadest all. Thou art the vitality of all, the creater of all, the sustainer of all, and the illuminator of the resplendent bodies like sun etc. Thou art more refulgent than fire, Thou art giver of knowledge, Thou art the maker of sun as well as illumintor of the light of the moon. Thou art the greatest worshipable Lord. Pronouncing the syllable Om in mind the anchorite should place his soul into God. He who in prescribed manner knows this excellent system of knowledge grasped by the learned ones rising to status of attaining God enjoys the happiness.

Whatever a Sanyasi should do and whatever he should not,

दृते दृंह मा मित्रस्य मा चक्षुषा सर्वाणि भूतानि समीक्षन्ताम् । मित्रस्याहं चक्षुषा सर्वाणि भूतानि समीक्षे । मित्रस्य चक्षुषा समीक्षामहे ॥ १ ॥ यजु० अ० ३६ । मं० १८ ॥

अग्ने नय सुपथा रायेऽअस्मान् विश्वानि देव वयुनानि विद्वान्
युयोध्यस्मज्जुहुराणमेनो भूयिष्ठान्ते नमऽउक्तिं विधेम ॥२ ॥

यस्तु सर्वाणि भूतान्यात्मन्नेवानुपश्यति ।
सर्वभूतेषु चात्मानं ततो न वि चिकित्सति ॥ ३ ॥

यस्मिन्त्सर्वाणि भूतान्यात्मैवाभूद्विजानतः ।
तत्र को मोहः कः शोक एकत्वमनुपश्यतः ॥ ४ ॥
यजु० अ० ४० । मं० १६, ६, ७ ॥

परीत्य भूतानि परीत्य लोकान् परीत्य सर्बा प्रदिशो दिशश्च ।
उपस्थाय प्रथमजामृतस्यात्मनात्मानमभि सं विवेश ॥ ५ ॥
यजु० अ० ३२ । मं० ११ ॥

ऋचो अक्षरे परमे व्योमन् यस्मिन् देवा अधि विश्वे निषेदुः ।
यस्तन्न वेद किमृचा करिष्यति य इत्तद्विदुस्त इमे समासते ॥ ६ ॥
ऋ० मं १ । सू० १६४ । मं० ३९ ॥

समाधिनिर्धूतमलस्य चेतसो निवेषितस्यात्मनि यत्सुखं भवेत ।
न शक्यते वर्णयितुं गिरा तदा स्वयं तदन्तः करणेन गृह्यते ॥ ७ ॥
[मैत्रायणी उपनिषद् ४ । ९]

O Lord ! the dispeller of the darkness of ignorance and all sorts of pains, please make me firm in the conviction of and lead me forward on the path of *Sanyasa* so that all the living beings may look towards me with the eye of a friend. May I also look towards all living beings with the eye of friend. May we look toward one another ever with the eye of a friend. 1.

O Divine *Agni* (self-refulgent and Pain-dispelling God) please lead us on the path of virtue for the acquirement of physical as well as spiritual wealth as thou knowest all the procedure of works and wisdom underlying therein. Please remove the sinful acts from us which make us stray so that we may remain ever engaged in uttering Thy praise in various ways.

The anchorite who sees all beings in the Supreme Being and his own spirit and Supreme Spirit pervading all beings does not remain in suspense. That he is the real *Sanyasi* is he who realizing. God Om in present, controlling all from within and the observer of all sees the benefit and loss of pain and pleasure of all like his own. 3.

For such a learned *Sanyasi* who knows that all the living creatures dwelling in Him are sentient of pleasure and pain like his own self what grief and sorrow then remain, for he sees the one alone. 4.

The wise *Sanyasi* knowing fully all the creatures, all the words, all the quarters and having access to first product of the law eternal enters directly and fully into the Divine Self by his self. 5.

O ye anchorites ! what benefit and happiness would gain from the study of *Vada* etc. scriptures the man who does not know Indestructible God in whom are residing the *Vedas*, all the worlds like earth etc., and all the learned men. That is the knowledge of God can never be attained without learned and he who gaining knowledge does not know God and does not follow His commands, has lost his great purpose of assuming human body. The learned men who know God make them firm in the grandeur and grace of God through Concentration. 6.

Whatever pleasure of happiness visits to the man who has dispelled the dirt of conscience through concentration and has made firm place for his soul in God, can never be described or explained through the organ of speech and it can only be realized by the conscience which has attained it. That is this happiness can never come into description completely. Therefore, *Sanyasins* should establish them in God and obeying his command i.e. engaged in the impartial, correct, righteousness should make the men happy by preaching truth and disseminating true knowledge. 7.

संमानाद् ब्राह्मणो नित्यमुद्विजेत विषादिव ।
अमृतस्येव चाकाङ्क्षेदवमानस्य सर्वदा ॥ १ ॥ [मनु० २ । १६२]

यमान् सेवेत सततं न नियमान् केवलान् बुधः ।
यमान् पतत्यकुर्वाणो नियमान् केवलान् भजन् ॥ २ ॥
[मनु० ४ । २०४]

A *Sanyasi* should be afraid of the worldly respect treating it like poision and be desirous of the disrespect like nectar as the man who fears from disrespect and desire respect becoming the fond of praise falls from his position becoming deceptive and lier. Therefore, be there disrespect or respect, be there aggrandizement or insult, be there life or death, be there profit or loss, may be, one love or he create enimity, may be, food, water, cloth, good residence available or not, whether be badly cold or hot weather etc. he should forbear them and should always be firm in refuting *Adharma* proving *Dharma*. He should never accept any thing as excellent *dharma* but these duties.

Neither he should worship any thing but God, nor he should obey any thing against the tenets of the *Vedas*. He should never treat rare or gross and inert matter and even the soul as the substitute of God. He should always accept God as his master and him as his servant and should preach the same idea to others also, He should preach the principles which are conducive to the progress of house-holders, conducive to the augmentation of love free from enemity in father, mother children, wife, husband, brother, sister, friend, neighbours, attendents, elders and youngers.

He should warn people against the study the books like Bible, *Quran*, *Pnrana*, false-pleading and *Kavyalankara* the study and bearing of which make a man passionate and be fallen. He should not ever accept any one as diety of worship except one God, any thing as तीर्थ except education, practice of *yoga*, good company, truth-speaking and should not ever accept and make one accept the idols of stone etc. except the living idols like learned persons. He should not ever preach to house-holders of any other worshippable idol except the living parents, teachers, guest wife for husband and husband for wife. *Sanyasa* should aways be ready to spread the teachings of the Vedic religion and to refute false religions which do not stand in conformity to the *Vedas*.

He should himself have and make others to have faith in true scriptures like the *Vedas* etc. and should himself discard and make others discard the religions and books which are against the *Vedas*. Possessing good characteristics, actions and nature in him should try to make every one alike and should strictly observe the rules and disciplines of *Sanyasa* which have been previously mentioned. He should never renounce the act of refuting whatever is to be refutable. He should ever be used of refuting the preaching and teachings of *Asuras* i.e. the persons who treat *Brahman*, the Supreme Spirit. He should sprerad the idea of the qualities, action and nature of Paramount God. Doing such deeds he be pleased and happy and make others happy.

He should alwayas exercise into practice non-violence. speaking of truth, embracing of truth end acting according to truth. He should neither take ever any thing of others through injustice in thought, speech and action nor preach any one to do so. Keeping him always continental and keeping him away from eight kinds of sexual inter-courses preserving semen fluid promoting to gain long life should do the good of all. He should be free from the evils of pride etc. and should never entangle himself in the lustre of the worldly wealths etc. He should always observe the five *yamas* and with them the five *Niyamas* which are described here. The internal and external cleanliness, the perseverance free from the pleasure and displeasure caused by benefit and loss respectively, acceptance of impartial justice as *dharma* and practice of *pranayama yoga* etc. recitation of syllable Om, its meditation in mind and thinking of its meaning———the lord of the universe, and surrender of self to the command of Supreme Lord described in the *Vedas*, enjoyment of blessedness graced by God in life time and attainment of salvation full of blessedness after death———are the chief codes of conduct fixed for a *Sanyasin*.

O Paramount God ! O Lord of the universe ! O omniscient one ! O controller of all from within ! O merciful one ! O just, all-blissfull and infinite Lord ! O Eternal, Pure, Intelligent, ever free from bondage ! O Ever mature one ! O Immortal and undecaying ever-pure Supreme Power ! Please by Thy grace making these anchorites engaged in their duties prescribed previously lead them to attain the happiness of absolute salvation.

Here ended the procedure of *Sanyasa* sacrement.

———

Now here we would describe the last rites of the dead

The last rites of the dead body is called the *Antyesti Sanskara.* There is no other *Sanskar,* thereafter for this body. This is also called by the names of *Naramedha, Purushmedha, Narayaga* and *Purusheayaga.*

भस्मान्तं शरीरम् ॥ यजु० अ० ४० । मं १५ ॥
निषेकादिश्मशानान्तो मन्त्रैर्यस्योदितो विधि ॥ मनु० [२ । १६]

The sacrement or rite prescribed for the body implies upto the time of reducing it to ashes.

The beginning of the body implies the ceremony of impregnation and end of it implies the cremation i.e., the consignment of body to fire to reduce it to ashes.

Question, Are the rites like *Dashogatra Ekadashah, Dvadashah, Sapindkarma,* monthly or annual *Gaya shraddha* mentioned in the *Gurudapurana* etc, are false ?

Answer. Yes, surely false as there is no injunction for such things in the *vedas* and therefore they should not be done. The soul departing from the body has neither any connection or relation at all with the previous reletives nor these living relatives have any connection with it. The soul has to take birth according its own desert.

Q. Where does this soul go after death ?

A. To the realm of *yama.*

Q. What is to be called the realm of *yama* ?

A. The realm of *vayu,* the air.

Q. What is this realm of *vayu* ?

A. The space or the void.

Q. Is the *yamaloka* mentioned in the *Gurudapurana* etc. false ?

A. Certainly it is false.

Q. Why then people of the world believe therein ?

A. Due to the absence of knowledge and teaching of the *vedas*. The story concocted and incorporated with *yama* is entirely false as the term *yama* stands to mean the names of following things :—

पलिद्यमा ऋषयो देवजा इति ॥ १ ॥ ऋ० नं० १ । सू० १६४ ।
मं० १५ ॥

शकेन वाजिनो यमम् ॥ २ ॥ ऋ० म० २ । सू० ५ । मं १ ॥
यमाय जुहुता हविः । यमं ह यज्ञो गच्छत्यग्निदूतो अवंकृतः ॥ ३ ॥
ऋ० म० १० । सू० १४ । मं० १३ ॥

यमः सूयमानो विष्णु सम्भियमाणो वायु पूयमानः ॥ ४ ॥
यजु० अ० ८ । मं ५७ ॥

वाजिनं यमम् ॥ ५ ॥ ऋ० मं० ८ । सू० २४ । मं० २२ ॥
यमं मातरिश्वानमाहुः ॥ ६ ॥ ऋ० मं० १ । सू० १६४ । मं ४६ ॥

Here the *yamas* are the names of seasons. 1.

Here *yama* is the name of God. 2.

Here *yama* is the name of *Agni*, the fire. 3.

Here *yamas* are the names of air, electricty and the sun. 4.

Here also the *yama* is the name of *vayu* as it has swiftness. 5.

Here *yama* is the name of God.

All these things are called *yama* and therefore, all the fables and fancies of the *Purana* etc. are false.

Procedure (as well as requirements in serial numbers)

विधि—संस्थिते भूमिभागं खानयेद्दक्षिणपूर्वस्यां दिशि दक्षिणापरस्यां वा ॥ १ ॥ दक्षिणाप्रवणं प्राग्दक्षिणाप्रवण वा प्रत्यग्दक्षिणाप्रवणमित्येके ॥ २ ॥ यावानुद्बाहुकः पुरुषस्तावदायामम् ॥ ३ ॥ [व्याममात्रं तिर्यक् ॥ ४ ॥] वितस्त्यर्वाक् ॥ ५ ॥ केशश्मश्रु लोमनखानीत्युक्तं पुरुस्तात् ॥ ६ ॥ द्विगुल्फं बर्हिराज्यं च ॥ ७ ॥ दधन्यत्र सर्पिरानयन्त्येतत् पित्र्यं पृषदाज्यम् ॥ ८ ॥ अथैतां

दिशमग्नीन्नयन्ति यज्ञपात्राणि च ॥ ६ ॥ आश्वलायन गृ० अ० ४ । कण्डि १ ।
सू० ६-१०, १५-१७ । तथा कण्डि० २ । सू० १ ॥

1. The dead, if male, should be given bath by men and if female should be given bath by woman. Paste of the rubbed sandal-wood should be applied on the body and it should be dressed with new clothes.

2. Ghee should be in equal proportion to the weight of the dead. Well-to-do persons can use more *ghee* but if in the case of the poor the *ghee* should not be less than 1/2 maund in weight and it should be arranged by a moneyed man or head of the *Panchayata* or by the contribution from the people. Well-to-do persons should mix in ghee the following things in the proportion described against each :

Kesar, saffron—One *masha* in each one *seer* of *ghee*

Kasturi, Musk—One *ratti* „ „ „

Agar Acquilaria Malaccensis—One *seer* in each one maund.

Tagar Veleriana Walichli — „ „ „

Sandal-wood powder — „ „ „

Comphor—as the circumstances permit.

3. Well-to-do persons should arrange for one maund sandal-wood, Twelve maunds fuel wood and *samagri* two times of the weight of the dead body.

4. All these things should be carried to the cremation ground.

5. If there is permanent *Kunda* in the cremation ground for the purpose of cremation, it should be used, if not, the new one should be dug out. The dimension of *kunda* should be as per the following measurements :

i Length should be equal to the length of a man standing with his hands raising up.

ii Breadth should be equal to the breadth of a person sleeping with his two hands stretched, i.e., it should be broader than 1 1/2 yards.

iii Depth should be equal to the height of a standing man's chest.

iv The bottom should be of a yard in breadth.

6. *Kunda* should be made clean and if cow-dung, is available, it should be purified by applying that.

7. Fuel wood should be arranged in the *kunda* just as the bricks are arranged in the wall.

8. *Ghee* should be molten.

9. Big spoons should be fixed or tied firmly in long sticks for offering oblations in the fire of the *kunda*. They should be four. Four persons should offer *ahutis* at a time. Spoons should have such capacities that each of them could contain *ghee* in the quantity not more than one *chhatak* and not less than half of a *chhatak*.

10. Cremation ground should be situated in the south direction.

11. Dead body should be laid on the fuel-pyre arranged in the *kunda* and be totally covered with fuel wood. The head of the dead should be placed in north direction.

12. Hair of the dead should be removed before giving bath to it.

13. Lamp of *ghee* should be lighted. A man should enkindle a piece of camphor from the lamp and should light the pyre. In lighting the pyre he should first begin from the head and end at the feet. Thus whole pyre should be lighted.

Afterwards the oblations should be offered in the blazing fire of the *kunda* with the following *mantras*.

ओमग्ने स्वाहा ॥

ओ सोमाय स्वाहा ॥

ओ लोकाय स्वाहा ॥

ओमनुमतये स्वाहा ॥

ओ स्वर्गाय लोकाय स्वाहा ॥

It is for *Agni*. Whatever is uttered herein is right.

It is for *Soma*. ,, ,, ,,

It is for *Loka* ,, ,, ,,
(this world)

It is for *Anumati* ,, ,, ,,
(Earth)

It is for *Svarga* ,, ,, ,,
(other world)

Offering the oblations with these five *mantras* fire should be got ablaze and afterwards four persons standing separately should use to offer oblations with the *vedic mantras* and they should drop the oblation in the fire at the sound of *Svaha*.

Ved mantras

सूर्यं चक्षुर्गच्छतु वतिमात्मा द्यां च गच्छ पृथिवीं च धर्मणा ।
अपो व गच्छ यदि तत्र ते हितमोषधीषु प्रतितिष्ठा शरीरैः स्वाहा ।१।

O man ! after thy death may the power of thy sight be absorbed in the sun and may thy soul go to the atmosphere and may thou go to the luminous region or the earth in accordance with the meritorious deeds thou hast performed here, go to the waters, if it be thy lot and go to the plants assuming different bodies.

अजो भागस्तपसा तं तपस्व तं ते शोचिस्तपतु तं ते अर्चि ।
यास्ते शिवास्तन्वो जातवेदस्ताभिर्वहैनं सुकृतामु लोकं स्वाहा ॥ २ ॥

अवसृज पुनरग्ने पितृभ्यो यस्त आहुतश्चरति स्वधाभिं ।
आयुर्वसान उप वेतु शेषः संगच्छतां तन्वा जातवेदः स्वाहा ॥ ३ ॥

अग्नेर्वर्म परिगोभिर्व्ययस्व सम्प्रोर्णुष्व पीवसा मेदसा च ।
नेत्त्वा धृष्णुर्हरसा जर्हृषाणो वधृग्विधक्ष्यन्पर्यङ्खयाते स्वाहा ॥ ४ ॥

यं त्वमग्ने समदहस्तमु खिर्वापया पुनः ।
कियाम्ब्वत्ररोहतु पाकदूर्वा व्यल्कशा स्वाहा ॥ ५ ॥

ऋ० मं० १० । सू १३ मं० ३, ४, ५, ७ १३ ॥

परेयिवांसं प्रवतो महीरनु बहुभ्यः पन्थामनुपस्पशानम् ।
वैवस्वतं संङ्गमनं जनानां यमं राजानं हविषा दुवस्य स्वाहा ॥ ६ ॥

यमो नो गातुं प्रथमो विवेद नैषा गव्यूतिरपभर्तवा उ ।
यत्रा नः पूर्वे पितरः परेयुरेना जज्ञानाः पथ्या३ अनुस्वा स्वाहा ॥ ७ ॥

मातली कव्यैर्यमो अङ्गिरोभिर्बृहस्पतिर्ऋक्वभिर्वावृधानः ।
यांश्च देवा वावृधुर्ये च देवान्त्स्वाहान्ये स्वधयान्ये मदन्ति स्वाहा ॥ ८ ॥

इमं यम प्रस्तरमा हि सीदाङ्गिरोभिः पितृभिः संविदानः ।
आत्वा मन्त्राः कविशस्ता वहन्त्वेना राजन्हविषा मादयस्व स्वाहा । ९ ।

अङ्गिरोभिरागहि यज्ञियेभिर्यम वैरूपैरिह मादस्व ।
विवस्वन्तं हुवेयः पिता तेऽस्मिन्यज्ञे बर्हिष्या निषद्य स्वाहा ॥ १० ॥

प्रेहि प्रेहि पथिभिः पूर्व्येभिर्यत्रा नः पूर्वे पितरः परेयुः ।
उभा राजानास्वधया मदन्ता यमं पश्यासि वरुणं च देवं स्वाहा ॥११॥

सं गच्छस्व पितृभिः सं यमेनेष्टापूर्तेन परमे व्योमन् ।
हित्वायावद्यं पुनरस्तमेहि सं गच्छस्व तन्वा सुवर्चाः स्वाहा ॥ १२ ॥

अपेत वीत वि च सर्पतातोऽस्मा एतं पितरो लोकमक्रन् ।
अहोभिरम्दिरक्तुभिर्व्यक्तं यमो ददात्यवसानमस्मै स्वाहा ॥ १३ ॥

यमाय सोमं सुनुत यमाय जुहुता हविः ।
यमं घ यज्ञो गच्छत्यग्निदूतो अरङ्कृतः स्वाहा ॥ १४ ॥

यमाय घृतवद्धविर्जुहोत प्र च तिष्ठत ।
स नो देवेष्वा यमद्दीर्घमायुः प्र जीवसे स्वाहा ॥ १५ ॥

यमाय मधुमत्तमं राज्ञे हव्यं जुहोतन ।
इदं नम ऋषिभ्यः पूर्वजेभ्यः पूर्वेभ्य पथिकृद्भ्यः स्वाहा ॥१६ ॥

ऋ० मं० १० । सू० १४ ॥ [मं० १-५, ७-९, १३-१५]

कृष्णः श्वेतोऽरुषो यामो अस्य ब्रध्न ऋज्र उत शोणो यशस्वान् ।
हिरण्यरूपं जनिता जजान स्वाहा ॥ १७ ॥

ऋ० मं १० । सू० २० । मं ९ ॥

Here the instruction has been given to soul which is eternal, O jiva ! (Soul) your that part, i.e. the soul is separate from body etc. and is unborn and eternal by nature. You make it pure through the practice of austerity. Whatever part, i.e. body, the mortal one be burnt by fire. God, who is self-refulgent grant light to soul. May God who is the all-pervading power grant the soul those good bodies (at the time of rebirth to the soul and may He send the soul to the realm of where the men of good acts go. 2

This dead body has been consigned to flame, O Lord of the universe ! and has been surrounded with *ghee* etc. on all the sides. God gives protection to soul and sends this to see the parent again. In the period of rebirth *jiva* again assuming the body again endowed with length of life and God, who is all-pervading power grants him new strong body. 3

This *jiva* gets its dead body burnt in fire with *ghee* etc. This *jiva* gets it united with the body which possesses sufficient flesh, fat etc. in the series of rebirth. Let he should acquire such a proof that the overpowering fire could not burn his body with *ghee* etc. again and again the cycle of the births and death This fire many times burn the body in various deaths after briths. Therefore, the salvation which is a sound proof be attained by *jivas*.

When this fire burns the body completely and become calm (at some time past) the grass etc. grow on this place and water waters down them. 5

O *jiva* ! you always serve with the oblations of *ghee* etc, in the fire *yama*, the air which is powerful, which is also the cause of death, which gives the way to other *jivas* which is the master of living creatures and which is the source of moving sun etc. heavenly bodies in their respective and joint course. 6

The paramount *yama* (God) knows the good and bad acts of all the *jivas*. Never can be violated and removed by anyone the Divine way of discriminating good and evil deserts in which the fore-fathers have traversed and all other creatures having birth knowing this way tread it in confirmity to their deserts and destined consequnces. 7

As grow and please the man of riches with poets, the man controlling him with the scientists of vitality, and the master of vedic speech with verses of the *vedas* so every one should enjoy with them. Amongst such persons are some ones who give pleasure to learned persons, some enjoy with the performance of *yajnas* and others are served to please with food etc. 8

O *yama* (self-controlled *jiva*) if you have to enjoy the fruit of you some previous actions you will have to come in this world again by birth, you will have to enjoy in the company of the learned men and parent etc. you will have to come across the *mantras* pronounced by learned men and you would have to enjoy with the things which are meant for porforming *yajnas.* 9

O *jiva* ! you according to your previous acts, have to come to this world with vitalities and various forms and have to make lighted yourself and others. You have to participate in the affairs of the world. I, the devotee of God will try to attain Him who is as bright as sun and who is your protection. 10

O *jivas* ! you should tread the path which our fore-fathers have trodden since eternity. O *jiva* ! you try your best to see both the shining and playing in the matter, God almighty and your soul. 11

O *jiva* ! you leaving out the sins come again to this and have the company of father and mother and establish yourself in the all-pervading God with control of organs and good philanthropic acts. You shine in the world again with body full of strength and transparency. 12

The men, who come to cremation ground move from it, go here and there and leave it. The learned men has made this place for the dead. God has provided this with days, nights and dew for cremating the dead. 13

O *Jivas* ! You crush Soma plant to obey the command of God and you offer oblations in the fire for obeying the command of God. The *yajna* accomplished and performed in *Agni* goes to firmament. 14.

O *Jivas* ! You always perform *yajnas* with oblation of *ghee* etc. for purifying air and for attaining God and have communion with God, God is amongst all the powerful forces who gives us long life to enjoy a good longevity. 15.

O *Jivas* ! You offer the sweet oblations in the fire for purification of the air which rules over the firmament. Let this our obeisance be due to seers, living fore-fathers who have made the path for us.

O *Jivas* ! This world is a chariot which is black, white, bright red and tremendous in length and breadth and it moves very slowly. It has many things which give name and fame. This world full of wealth like gold etc., has been created only by God.

The four persons offering oblations after giving seventeen oblations of *ghee* with these above mentioned *mantras* should thereafter offer oblations in the same manner with the following *mantras* :—

प्राणेभ्यः साधिपतिकेभ्यः स्वाहा ॥ १ ॥

पृथिव्यै स्वाहा ॥ २ ॥ अग्नये स्वाहा ॥ ३ ॥

अन्तरिक्षाय स्वाहा ॥ ४ ॥ वायवे स्वाहा ॥ ५ ॥

दिवे स्वाहा ॥ ६ ॥ सूर्याय स्वाहा ॥ ७ ॥

दिग्भ्यः स्वाहा ॥ ८ ॥ चन्द्राय स्वाहा ॥ ९ ॥

नक्षत्रेभ्यः ॥ १० ॥ अद्भ्यः स्वाहा ॥ ११ ॥

वरुणाय स्वाहा ॥ १२ ॥ नाभ्यै स्वाहा ॥ १३ ॥

पूताय स्वाहा ॥ १४ ॥ वाचे स्वाहा ॥ १५ ॥

प्राणाय स्वाहा ॥ १६ ॥ प्राणाय स्वाहा ॥ १७ ॥

चक्षुषे स्वाहा ॥ १८ ॥ चक्षुषे स्वाहा ॥ १९ ॥

श्रोत्राय स्वाहा ॥ २० ॥ श्रोत्राय स्वाहा ॥ २१ ॥

लोमभ्य स्वाहा ॥ २२ ॥ लोमभ्य स्वाहा ॥ २३ ॥

त्वचे स्वाहा ॥ २४ ॥ त्वचे स्वाहा ॥ २५ ॥

लोहिताय स्वाहा ॥ २६ ॥ लोहिताय स्वाहा । २७ ॥
मेदोभ्यः स्वाहा ॥ २८ ॥ मेदोभ्य स्वाहा ॥ २९ ॥
माँसेभ्यः स्वाहा ॥ ३० ॥ माँसेभ्या स्वाहा ॥ ३१ ॥
स्नावभ्यः स्वाहा ॥ ३२ ॥ स्नावभ्य स्वाहा ॥ ३३ ॥
अस्थय्यः स्वाहा ॥ ३४ ॥ अस्थभ्यः स्वाहा ॥ ३५ ॥
मज्जभ्यः स्वाहा ३६ ॥ मज्जभ्यः स्वाहा ॥ ३७ ॥
रेतसे स्वाहा ॥ ३८ ॥ पायवे स्वाहा ॥ ३९ ॥
आयासाय स्वाहा ॥ ४० ॥ प्रायसाय स्वाहा ॥ ४१ ॥
संयासाय स्वाहा ॥ ४२ ॥ वियासाय स्वाहा ॥ ४३ ॥
उद्यसाय स्वाहा ॥ ४४ ॥ शुचे स्वाहा ॥ ४५ ॥
शोचते स्वाहा ॥ ४६ ॥ शोचमानाय स्वाहा ॥ ४७ ॥
शोकाय स्वाहा ॥ ४८ ॥ तपसे स्वाहा ॥ ४९ ॥
तप्यते स्वाहा ॥ ५० ॥ तप्यामानाय स्वाहा ॥ ५१ ॥
तप्ताय स्वाहा ॥ ५२ ॥ धर्माय स्वाहा ॥ ५३ ॥
निष्कृत्यै स्वाहा ॥ ५४ ॥ प्रायश्चित्यै स्वाहा ॥ ५५ ॥
भेषजाय स्वाहा ॥ ५६ ॥ यमाय स्वाहा ॥ ५७ ॥
अन्तकाय स्वाहा ॥ ५८ ॥ मृत्यवे स्वाहा ॥ ५९ ॥
ब्रह्मणे स्वाहा ॥ ६० ॥ ब्रह्महत्यायै स्वाहा ॥ ६१ ॥
विश्वेभ्यो देवेभ्यः स्वाहा ॥ ६२ ॥ द्यावापृथिवीभ्यःँस्वाहा ॥ ६३ ॥

यजु० अ० ३९ [म० १-३ १०-१३]

O *Jivas*! Know all these things described in the *Mantras* and they are as under :—

Airs of vitality with their strengh, the earth, the fermament, the heavenly region, direction, fire, air, the sun, the moon, the stars, air, purity, eye, ear, hair, skin, blood, fat, flesh, sinews, bones, marrows, semen, rebirth, perserverance, good effort, various activities, uplift, waters, naval, tongue, cleanliness, purifying, enlightenment, sadness, austerity, various activities and agencies of austerity, day, vengeance, repentence, medicine, air, time, death, Supreme Spirit, disobedience of *Vedic* commands, all the physical and spiritual forces and the twain of earth and heaven.

After offering the separate oblations with these above-mentioned sixty three *mantras* the oblations further be offered with the following *mantras* :—

सूर्यं चक्षुषा गच्छ वातमात्मना दिवं च गच्छ पृथिवीं च धर्मभिः ।
अपो वागच्छ यदि तत्र ते हितमोषधीषु प्रतितिष्ठा शरीरैः स्वाहा ।१।

सोम एकेभ्यः पवते घृतमेक उपासते ।
येभ्यो मधु प्रधावति तांश्चिदेवापि गच्छतात् स्वाहा ॥ २ ॥

ये चित्पूर्व ऋतसाता ऋतजाता ऋतावृधः ।
ऋषीन् तपस्वतो यम तपोजां अपि गच्छतात् स्वाहा ॥ ३ ॥

तपसा ये अनाधृष्यास्तपसा ये स्वर्ययुः ।
तपो ये चक्रिरे महस्तांश्चिदेवापि गच्छतात् स्वाहा ॥ ४ ॥

ये युद्धयन्ते प्रधनेषु शूरासो ये तनूत्यजः ।
ये वा सहस्रदक्षिणास्तांश्चिदेवापि गच्छतात् स्वाहा ॥ ५ ॥

स्योनास्मै भव पृथिव्यनृक्षरा निवेशनी ।
यच्छास्मै शर्म सप्रथाः स्वाहा ॥ ६ ॥

अपेमं जीवा अरुधन् गृहेभ्यस्तन्निर्वहत परि ग्रामादित ।
मृत्युर्यमस्यासीद् दूतः प्रचेता असून् पितृभ्यो गमयांचकार स्वाहा ॥ ७ ॥

यमः परोऽवरो विवस्वान् ततः परं नाति पश्यामि किञ्चन ।
यमे अध्वरो अधि मे निविष्टो भुवो विवस्वानन्वाततान स्वाहा ॥ ८ ।

अपागूहन्नमृतां मर्त्येभ्यः कृत्वा सवर्णामदधुर्विवस्ते ।
उताश्विनावभरद् यत्तदासीदजहादु द्वा मिथुना सरण्यूः स्वाहा ॥ ९ ॥

इमौ युनज्मि ते वह्नी असुनीताय वोढवे ।
ताभ्यां यमस्य सादनं समितीश्चाव गच्छात् स्वाहा ॥ १० ॥

अथर्व० का० १८ । सू० २ (मं० ७, १४-१७, १९, २७, ३२, ३३, ५६)

O *Jiva* ! You go to the sun through eye, you go to air through vital air, you go to space and earth with your *dharmas*, and go to water and plants if your previous actions are to bear fruit there under God's dispensation of justice.

There are persons who use only juice etc. of plants, there are others who use *ghee* etc, there are also others who use honey may God make the *Jivas* able to get amongst such ones.

O *yama* ! (self-controlled *jiva*) you attain the status of seers observing all austerities and the men who raised their positions from strict observances of austerity and also the status of the men, who are elders and are engaged performing *yajnas*, speaking and dealing in with truth and are dissiminator of truth. 3.

O *Jiva* ! you attain the status of even those persons, who have been unsurmountable in austerity and have gained the state of happiness through hardship and who have observed strict disciplines of hardship. 4.

O *Jiva* ! you attain the status of those persons who are brave and fight in the tremendous battles, who leaves there body in such undertakings, who give the gift of thousands of rupees etc. in *yajnas*. 5.

May this earth be free from thorny difficulties for this departing soul (if it takes rebirth), may it give him accommodation and may it give him ample happiness. 6.

O *Jiva* ! leave this dead whom you have surrounded upto this time under affection and love, you live with others in group and lead the life in this world. You know and realize that the death is, the messenger of God and it has made the vital airs of the living body leave and go to the rays of moon. Do not suffer from the sadness caused by the bereavement. 7.

O *Jivas* ! you realize that the Ordainer of the universe who is the paramount amongst all the powers and there I do not see anyone more supreme to Him. All our *yajnas* are aimed at the attainment of All controlling God. It is sustainer who has spread out this earth. 8.

The forces working out in the night conceal *Saranya*, the light of the Sun in them for the sake of mortal beings, and return it to the Sun making it full of many colours. This light of Sun gives food to the vital airs called *Prana* and *apana*. This creates the twain of night and day. 9.

O *Jivas* ! I, God, unite two kinds of heat (gross and rare) to make your body endowed with vital airs in the time of rebirth, able for doing its work. Through these two you enjoy in the realm of air and in the assemblies of men. 10

After offering ten oblations with these above mentioned ten *mantras* the further oblations be offered with the following *mantras* :—

अग्नये रयिमते स्वाहा । १ ।

पुरुषस्य सयावर्यपेदघानि मृज्महे ।
यथा नो अत्र नापरः पुरा जरस आयति स्वाहा । २ ।

[तै० आ० प्र० ६ । अ० १]

य एतस्य पथो गोप्तारस्तेभ्यः स्वाहा । ३ ।
य एतस्य पथो रक्षितारस्तेभ्यः स्वाहा । ४ ।
य एतस्य पथोऽभिरक्षितारस्तेभ्यः स्वाहा । ५ । रव्यात्रे स्वाहा । ६ ।
अपाख्यात्रे स्वाहा । ७ । अभिलालपते स्वाहा । ८ ।
अपलालपते स्वाहा । ९ । अग्नेय कर्मकृते स्वाहा । १० ।
यमत्र नाधीमस्ततस्मै स्वाहा । ११ । [तै० आ० प्र० ६ । अ० २]
अग्नये वैश्वानराय सुवर्गाय लोकाय स्वाहा । १२ ।

[तै० आ० प्र० ६ । अ० ३]

आयातु देवः सुमनाभिरुतिभिर्यमो ह वेद प्रयताभिरक्ता ।
आसीदताꣳसुरुप्रयते ह बर्हिष्यूर्जाय जात्यै मम शत्रुहत्यै स्वाहा । १३ ।
योऽस्य कौष्ठय जगतः पार्थिवस्यैक इद्वशी ।
यमं भङ्ग्यश्रवो गाय यो राजाऽनपरोध्यः । स्वाहा । १४ ।
यमं गाय भङ्ग्यश्रवो यो राजाऽनपरोध्यः ।
येनाऽऽपो नद्यो धन्वानि येन द्यौः पृथिवी दृढा स्वाहा । १५ ।
हिरण्यकक्ष्यान्त्सुधुरान् हिरण्याक्षानयःशफान् ।
अश्वाननश्शतो दानं यमो राजाभितिष्ठति स्वाहा । १६ ।
यमो दाधार पृथिवीं यमो विश्वमिदं जगत् ।
यमाय सर्वमित्तस्थे यत् प्राणद्वायुरक्षितं स्वाहा । १७ ।

यथा पञ्च यथा षड् यथा पञ्चदर्षय: ।
यमं यो विद्यात् स ब्रूयाद्यथैंक ॠर्षिविजानते स्वाहा । १८ ।

त्रिकद्रुकेभि: पतति षड्‌र्वीरेकमिद् बृहत् ।
गायत्रीत्रिष्टुप्छन्दाँसि सर्वाता यम आहिता स्वाहा । १६ ।

अहरहर्नयमानो गामश्वं पुरुषं जगत् ।
वैवस्वतो न तृप्यति पञ्चभिर्मानवैर्यम: स्वाहा । २० ।

वैवस्वतो विवच्यन्ते यमे राजनि ते जना: ।
ये चेह सत्येनेच्छन्ते य उ चानृतवादिन: स्वाहा । २१ ।

ते राजन्निह विविच्यन्तेऽथा यन्ति त्वामुप ।
देवांश्च ये नमस्यन्ति ब्राह्मणांश्चपचित्यति स्वाहा । २२ ।

यस्मिन्वृक्षे सुपलाशे देवै: संपिबते यम: ।
अत्रा नो बिश्पति: पिता पुराणो अनुवेनति स्वाहा । २३ ।

उत्ते तभ्नोमि पृथिवीं त्वत्परीमं लोकं निदधन्मो अहँरिषम । एतां
स्थूणां पितरो धारयन्तु तेऽत्रा यम: सादनात्ते मिनोतु स्वाहा । २४ ।
[तैं० आ० प्र० ६ । अ० ७]

यथाऽहान्यनुपूर्वं भवन्ति यथर्त्तव ऋतुभिर्यन्ति क्लृप्ता: ।
यथा न: पूर्बमपरो जहात्येबा धातरायूंषि कल्पयैषां स्वाहा । २४ ।
नहि ते अग्ने तनुवै क्रूरं चकार मर्त्य: । कपिर्बभस्ति तेजनं पुनर्जरायुर्गौरिव ।
अप न: शोशुचदघमग्ने शुशुग्ध्य रयिम् । अप न शोशुचदघं मृत्यवे
स्वाहा । २६ । तैत्ति० प्र पा० ६ । अनु० । १०॥

One should know the property of *Agni* which is the producer of all the metalurgical wealth. 1

The man departing has three bodies-gross, rate and causal. All of us should clean us removing dirt of sin. We should lead life in such a way that in this world no disease or cause of death could come to us before the old age. 2

The rays of the moon etc. which are the protecting forces of the path by which the *jiva* departing from body having are body does go. 3

We should know the preserving forces like medicine etc. which protect the body. 4

Also know of the preserver of these paths. 5

We should always take notice of act which spreads out our fame. 6

Also we should know of the act which defame us. 7

Also we should know the acts and qualities which tell the story of the good acts of the *jivas*. 8

Also we know those things which do not tell the qualities of good acts of the *jivas*. 9

We should know the properties of fire which becomes the means of the grand acts like *Agnihotra* etc. 10

We should try to grasp in mind whatsoever we are not remembering at this juncture. 11

To attain the realm of happiness and light we should know the fire named as *Vaishvanara* which remains in the body of all. 12

May *yama*, God the ordainer of the universe come into our knowledge with His powers of protection and preservation. May our time of prayer be connected with the adorations given in the *vedas*. Let the men and women participate and take seat in our vast *yajnas* performed for the purpose of attaining grains, good birth and dispelling of the internal enemies like, covetousness, passion, aversion etc. 13

O *jivas* ! you sing with the artistic method the prayer of all-ordaining God who is pervading all the nook and corner of this world, who is the ordainer of all this earthly world and is the unobstructed king of all this. 14

O *jivas* ! Sing with artistic methods the prayer of ordainer God who is the unobstructed King of all and who has held firm the waters, rivers, deserts, heaven, and earth. 15

Divinity, the imperial majesty is controlling all the world like earth etc. which have gold light in their minds which have their axis, which have resplendent things in them, which are as strong and as steel and He is the master of all and He gives the gift of various worldly things to us. 16

The ordainer of the universe is upholding this earth and He is governing and upholding whole universe. Everything living which has been preserved and maintained by air is under His control. 17

He who knows *yama*, the All-controlling Divinity and His laws can know whatever are the five gross elements, six seasons, fifteen lunar dates and seven stars called seven *Rishis.* In reality only All knowing God can declare that He knows everything. 18

Through His three powers, integration, disintegration, and regulation God produces or gets produced six grand things—— the firmament, earth, water, plants, strength and true *vedic* speech. The grand Lord is only one. The metres like *Gayatri Tristup* etc. are contained in All-controlling God. 19

God, the controller and ordainer of the planets and bodies like sun etc. Every day changing to various phenomena the world having the form of cow, horse, man etc. never ends His task. 20

Only on the acceptance of the principle that there exists one all ordaining God the rational discrimination can be made between the men who desire the dealings with honesty and justice and those who are dishonest and unjust in their dealings. 21

O refulgent God ! in this world at the time of death are discriminated the men who serve and respect learned men and who serve the masters of the *vedic* speech. These are the men who attain you. 22

Our father who is the master of all the worldly subjects

launches His activities continuously from eternity on the same nice world-tree on which the *jiva* with other *jivas* enjoys the benefit thereof. 23

O *jivas* ! I, God, uphold this earth for you, I have created the creatures on this earth, I never give pain to anyone. Let the men of wisdom amongst you maintain this world-pillar. Let the King of the land give you all the residence and accommodation to abide. 24

As the days pass one after another, as the seasons united with each other come and go, as the latter does not leave former in the same way manage the lives of the men, my Lord ! 25

O self-refulgent God ! no man, in your cosmos perform any thing or act which is cruel and fatal to his body, like a monkey, this soul dominated by *Rajas* influlences ever encourage and invigorate its enthusiasm. Let it guard itself like the cow which protects her embryo skin-cover. O Self refulgent God ! please make us able to burn our sins and purify my wealth, i.e. make us earn the wealth through right means. Please purify ourselves from sins to face the death. 26

The 26 oblations with these above *mantras* be offered, Thus there are one hundred twenty one oblations, in all, from 'अग्नये स्वाहा' to 'मृत्यवे स्वाहा' ।

If four persons are engaged in offering oblations the number of oblation thus becomes four hundred eighty four and only two persons give oblations then they bocome two hundred forty two oblations. If there is more *ghee* the oblations be offered again with these one hundred twenty one *mantras*. These be repeated as long as the body is completely burnt.

When the dead body is burnt all the persons washing their clothes, taking bath, perform the procedure of *Swastivachan, Shantikarana* and prayer as described in the *Samanyaprakarana* at the home of the man in whose house the death has occured, the after having cleaned smeared with smearing things and washed house. They should then offer the oblations of *ghee* mixed with odoriferous substances pronouncing the *mantras* of *Swastivachna* and *Shantikarana* adding the word स्वाहा where the *mantras* ends. So that the air of the dead go out from the house, fresh air enter it and all remain healthy in their mind. If on the day there comes night : Some oblations be offered and on the following day the oblations with the *mantras Swastivachana* and *Shantikarana* be offered.

Thereafter, when there comes the third day from the date of the death, any relative of the dead man go to the cremation ground, picking the burnt bones from the pyre put it at any separate place in the cremation ground. Besides this there remains nothing to be done for the dead as it has been previously proved by the *mantras* of *Yajurveda* भस्मान्तॅशरीरम् that there is no rite to be done for the dead except consigning the mortals to the flame and picking the burnt bones (from the ashes and throw it somewhere in the cremation ground). Yes ! if he happens to be a well-to-do man he himself in his life time or his relatives after his death in whatever quantity the money or wealth they like, give for or use in the activities of propagating the *dharma* inculcated in the *Vedas*, spreading the teachings and preachings of the *Vedas*, and supporting and protecting orphans ——is an excellent thing.

Here ends the procedure of the rite of the dead.

Appendix

The equivalent English word for the articles herbs etc, used in sacrament of Sanskarvidhi—

पलाश	Butra Frondosa
शमी	Mimosa Suma
पीपल	Ficus Religiosa
बड़	Banyan
गूलर या उदुम्बर	Ficus Glomerata
अम्ब आम्र	Mangotree
बिल्व	Aegle Marmelos
कस्तूरी	Musk
केशर	Rotileria Tinetoria, safron
अगर	Aquilaria Agellocha
तगर	Tabernamutana Caronaria
श्वेतचन्दन	White Sandal wood
इलायची	Feronia Elephantom
जायफल	Nutmeg
जावित्री	Mace
उड़द	Phaseolus Radiatus
सोमलता गिलोय	Cocculus Cordi Colius
आंबा हल्दी हल्दी	Turmeric
कुष्ठ	Costus Speciosus Aralucus
जटामांसी	Asparagus Racemsus
शिलाजीत	Rock-Exudation
मुस्ता	Cyperus Rotumdus
भद्रमोथ	A kind of Cyperus
हरीतकी	Terminailia Chebula
अश्वत्थ	Ficus Religiosa
सूंठ	Dry Ginger
शाही पशु का कांटा	The Quill of Porcupine
तिल	Sesumum
मूग	Phaseolus Mungo
जमालगोटा	Clerodendum Phlo Moides
कण्टकारी	Solanum